LINCOLN BIBLE INSTITUTE

P9-DFN-101

THE WORLD'S GREAT SCRIPTURES

Books by Lewis Browne

HISTORIES, ETC.

Stranger Than Fiction: a short history of the Jews.
This Believing World: the great religions of mankind.
The Graphic Bible: Genesis to Revelation in maps & charts.
Since Calvary: an interpretation of Christian history.
How Odd of God: an introduction to the Jews.
Something Went Wrong: a summary of modern history.

BIOGRAPHIES

That Man Heine
Blesséd Spinoza

NOVELS

All Things Are Possible
Oh, Say, Can You See!
See What I Mean?

ANTHOLOGIES

The Wisdom of Israel
The World's Great Scriptures

THE WORLD'S GREAT SCRIPTURES

AN ANTHOLOGY OF THE SACRED BOOKS OF THE TEN PRINCIPAL RELIGIONS

Compiled and annotated with historical
introductions and interpretive comments

by LEWIS BROWNE

Author of "This Believing World" etc.

with decorations and maps by the editor

NEW YORK   1946

THE MACMILLAN COMPANY

COPYRIGHT, 1946, BY LEWIS BROWNE

All rights reserved—no part of this book may be reproduced in any form without permission in writing from the publisher, except by a reviewer who wishes to quote brief passages in connection with a review written for inclusion in magazine or newspaper.

PRINTED IN THE UNITED STATES OF AMERICA

First Printing

290.82
B88

Jan. 2-50 - $3.69 - Baker's Book Store

5690

To a Deeply Religious Man
and a Very Dear Friend:

UPTON SINCLAIR

CONTENTS

THE RELIGIONS OF THE WORLD

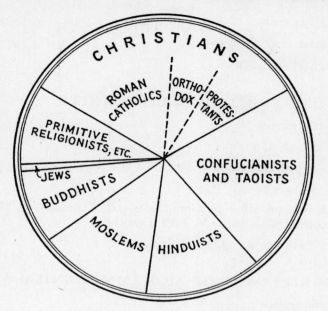

ROMAN CATHOLICS 329,775,663	ORTHODOX CATHOLICS 127,629,986	PROTESTANTS 137,945,530

CONFUCIANISTS
350,600,000
TAOISTS

HINDUISTS
230,150,000

MOSLEMS
220,000,000

BUDDHISTS
150,000,000

JEWS
10,000,000

PRIMITIVE
RELIGIONISTS, ETC.
200,000,000

NOTE:
*These figures are necessarily
uncertain. They are taken from
the World Almanac 1940, 1946*

PREFACE

There is increasing wonder nowadays about religions other than our own, and that is a good thing. It is good because such wonder is imperative if we are to begin fitting ourselves for this world we live in. Bigotry was endurable in earlier times, for the planet was roomier then, and peoples could keep somewhat apart. But today our world is so shrunken that bigotry has become like cholera in a crowded camp.

Our first need, therefore, is sanitation. Our minds must be opened up, swept clean, thoroughly aired. Bigotry is not born of ignorance, which is simply *non*-knowledge. It is a product of stupidity, which is *wrong* knowledge. The minds of bigots are worse than bare of truth; they are full of falsehood. And that is why they are so grave a menace: being polluted, they cannot help but spread disease. "The trouble with the world," said old Artemus Ward, "ain't that people don't know, but that they know what ain't so." And unless that trouble is swiftly remedied, the world seems doomed.

So one has a right to rejoice in the growing wonder concerning mankind's religions. It shows we are tiring of stupidity in this field and striving to acquire at least ignorance. That is very good.

But only as a first step, for ignorance is at best a negative gain. Wonder must give way to questioning, uncertainty to research. We must *know* what our neighbors believe—and to do that, obviously, we must go to their scriptures.

Once that was impossible, for most of those scriptures were closed to us. They were sealed in strange languages—Sanskrit, Pali, Chinese, and the like—languages often meaningless even to the believers themselves. But that is no longer the case. Thanks to the great philologists of recent generations, all the seals are broken now, and translations exist of virtually every important holy book. The sacred literature of the entire world can be read today in English.

And it needs to be read. Not all of it, of course, for that would take too long, and prove too tedious. (One English translation of the *Sacred Books of the East* alone fills forty-nine volumes!) But the crucial portions, the truly basic scriptures, these certainly should be read, for without a knowledge of their contents there can be no understanding our fellowmen.

Therefore this anthology. In it I have tried to gather up all that seems to me most vital in the world's holy books, all that is most enlightening in them, and therefore most worth reading. The selection follows a bias, of course, but one which is, I trust, defensible. (Seeing that I concede its presence, perhaps it should not be called a bias at all, but rather a principle.) It operates on two levels: first, among the various religions, and second, within each canon.

Let me explain how and why.

It will be observed—and no doubt complained—that whole sections are devoted to two dead religions, yet not a page to a number that are very much alive. I have given no space to Jainism, for example, or to Sikhism, Shintoism, Mormonism, Bahaism, or Christian Science. This, however, was not due to caprice on my part. Space could not possibly be given to *all* the religions, so I favored those which seemed historically the most important. I wanted to be objective, and therefore had to consider not the quality of each creed, but the extent of its influence in the world. By that standard, the dead religions of old Babylon and Egypt, which produced the earliest of all scriptures, most certainly outrank any minor living cult.

Again it will be observed—and perhaps even more sharply complained—that when I do give space to a religion, I lay almost all the stress on just one of its aspects. But this, too, is done on principle. There are, I realize, at least three aspects to every great religion: faith, hope, and charity. Faith is the theology, hope is the ritual, and charity is the ethics. In choosing my selections, however, I have deliberately concentrated on the third, quoting few passages of a strictly theological nature, and almost none that deal with ritual. The Creation stories in the different scriptural canons, the myths and miracles, the theogonies and the ophanies—all these are omitted. So are the liturgical regulations, the sacrificial cults, the spells, thaumaturgies, and ceremonial systems. The entire emphasis is on the ethical element in each religion, on the moral laws and social preachments.

Here is the reason. What we need is a keener awareness of the kinship between all religions, and nowhere is this kinship so marked as on the ethical level. Men may differ grossly in what and how they worship, but not in why and how they believe they should behave. They may be divided by that which their priests assert to be divine, but not by what their prophets prescribe as humane. See, for example, how common is the Golden Rule. You find it in one form or another in the scriptures of *all* the major religions. Witness—

BRAHMANISM: "This is the sum of duty: Do naught unto others which would cause you pain if done to you." *Mahabharata, 5, 1517*

BUDDHISM: "Hurt not others in ways that you yourself would find hurtful." *Udana-Varga 5, 18*

CONFUCIANISM: "Is there one maxim which ought to be acted upon throughout one's whole life? Surely it is the maxim of loving-kindness: Do not unto others what you would not have them do unto you." *Analects 15, 23*

TAOISM: "Regard your neighbor's gain as your own gain, and your neighbor's loss as your own loss." *T'ai Shang Kan Ying P'ien.*

ZOROASTRIANISM: "That nature alone is good which refrains from doing unto another whatsoever is not good for itself." *Dadistan-i-dinik, 94, 5*

JUDAISM: "What is hateful to you, do not to your fellowman. That is the entire Law; all the rest is commentary." *Talmud, Shabbat 31a*

CHRISTIANITY: "All things whatsoever ye would that men should do to you, do ye even so to them: for this is the Law and the Prophets. *Matthew 7, 12*

ISLAM: "No one of you is a believer until he desires for his brother that which he desires for himself." *Sunnah.*

There are distinctions of phrasing in those eight quotations, but no difference in meaning. Though diverse, they are not at all divergent, and in this they typify the various ethical systems. Consequently it is only right that those systems receive most attention. "Charity" is not the whole of any religion; each has also its "faith" and "hope."

But "charity" is the greatest of the three elements because it is the common denominator among all religions. In that sense, if no other, it is truly basic, and properly dominates this collection of the World's Great Scriptures.

LEWIS BROWNE

Santa Monica,
California.

THE SCRIPTURES OF BABYLONIA

AN ETHICAL FRAGMENT
TO THE GOD OF RIGHTEOUSNESS
A CATALOGUE OF SINS
VANITY OF VANITIES
THE BABYLONIAN JOB
THE CODE OF HAMMURAPI

INTRODUCTION

The most ancient of all sacred writings come from Mesopotamia, the "Land between the Rivers," where man is said to have first learnt to till the soil and trade its produce. There the first cities arose, and the chief of them, Babylon, became the seat of what may have been the first great civilization. The basis of all civilization is writing, and in Babylon this art was already well developed nearly five thousand years ago.

Eventually that civilization disappeared, and its very memory was blotted out. Only within the last century have we begun to rediscover it in the ruins dotting the land now called Iraq. Luckily for us, an Assyrian King who lived about 650 B.C. caused records to be made of what documents and traditions had survived from the great old days. Luckily, too, these records were inscribed on clay tablets, so they in turn were able to survive down to our own time. Now that our archeologists have dug up and deciphered that library, and many additional writings on clay and stone, we can form a fairly clear idea of the glory that once was Babylonia. It was a land where people developed high industry, carried on wide commerce, cultivated many arts, and even evolved certain sciences. Above all, it was a forcing-house for religion, producing the most elaborate cults, and raising not alone priestcraft but also ethicism to unprecedented levels.

In the beginning the Babylonian religion seems to have been a crude demon-worship imported from the desert, but eventually it tended to become an almost monotheistic faith. Though many gods continued to be recognized, there was increasing reverence for only one, most notably Shamash, the spirit of the sun. Hymns were offered to Shamash, as well as sacrifices; and they were noble hymns, some *of them. Their language shows them to have been more than mere incantations, more than just magic phrases strung together to work a spell. Their dominant note is awe rather than fear; they seem to reflect soul-searching humility rather than terror-born superstition.*

In addition to such hymns there are poems of a strikingly ethical nature, troubled ponderings on the nature of life, the wages of sin, and the causes of evil. Finally there is the great Code of Hammurapi, the oldest collection of laws known to man. All in all, these various scriptures must be rated high, even when judged solely for their intrinsic worth.

But they have also an extrinsic value, since it seems evident that they profoundly influenced the scriptures of the Jews—which in turn molded the scriptures of the Christians and the Mohammedans. There are innumerable analogies and homologies between the Old Testament and the far older Babylonian writings, and these are most plausibly explained by the known fact that the Jews were exiles in Babylon—from 586 to 536 B.C.—when they gave final form to their "Mosaic" books.

The Biblical stories of the Creation, the Flood, the Confusion of Tongues, and the like, seem unmistakably derived from Babylonian sources. The same appears to be true of many of the Pentateuchal social laws, and perhaps most of the sacerdotal regulations. True, the Jews amended all that they borrowed, turning coarse myths into moral preachments, and magic rites into pious symbols. (To cite a single example, the Babylonian shabatum, which was a day of bad luck, was metamorphosed into the Hebrew Sabbath, a day of holy rest.) The fact remains, however, that the Jews did apparently borrow, and this in itself ought to prove how rich was Babylonia's lore.

Here are a few selections illustrative of the more or less ethical side of that lore.

AN ETHICAL FRAGMENT

The clay tablets containing the literature of ancient Babylonia are replete with such fragments as the one quoted below. They are hortatory texts, revealing a stout if not exalted morality, a prudent, earthy, honesty-pays attitude, not unlike that expounded in Old Testament writings such as the BOOK OF PROVERBS. *It is striking to see how Shamash, who in the more primitive documents is merely a sun-deity demanding nothing but ritual sacrifices, is here described as a Heavenly Power deeply concerned about justice and social decency.*[1]

Slander not, but speak kindness;
Speak not evil, but show good will;
Whoso slanders and speaks evil—
Unto him will Shamash requite it
    by . . . his head.
Open not wide thy mouth, guard
    thy lips;
If thou art provoked, speak not at
    once;
If thou speakest hastily, thou shalt
afterwards have to atone therefor;
Soothe (rather) thy spirit with silence.
Offer daily unto thy god
Sacrifice, prayer, the incense most meet (for the Deity):
Before thy god shalt thou have a heart of purity.
It is that which is due to the deity.
Prayer, supplication, and casting down of the face
Shalt thou render to him early in the morning, then he shall send
    plenty.
In thy learning look at the tablet:
Fear of God brings forth grace;
Sacrifice gives increase of life;

[1] Translation by A. Jeremias in Hastings' *Encyclopedia of Religion and Ethics,* (Scribner, New York, 1928; T. & T. Clark, London), vol. iii., p. 747.

And prayer cancels sin.
He who fears the gods will not call in vain;
He who fears Anunnaki prolongs his life.
With friend and companion thou shalt not speak (evil);
Base things shalt thou not utter, . . .
If thou dost promise, give. . .
Thou shalt not rule tyrannically;
He who does so: his god is offended with him.
He is not acceptable to Shamash: he (Shamash will recompense him
    with evil.
Offer food, give wine to drink;
Seek truth, provide, and . . .
One who does this: his god has delight in him.
He is acceptable to Shamash: he (Shamash) will recompense him
    with good.

TO THE GOD OF RIGHTEOUSNESS

Here is another text revealing how Shamash, the primitive sun-deity, had become invested with moral attributes and metamorphosed into the Divine Judge. The poem, some 200 lines in length, represents the sun's activity as a mysterious force by means of which all wickedness is frustrated and all wrong-doers are brought to book.[2]

At thy rising the gods of the land assemble;
Thy terrible radiance overwhelms the land.
From all lands together resound as many tongues:
Thou dost know their designs; thou dost behold their footsteps,
Unto thee do all men look up together.
Thou causest the evil-doer . . . to tremble;
Out of the depths thou bringest those who perverted justice.

O Shamash, by the just judgment which thou dost speak
Thy name is glorious,
Thou standest beside the traveller whose way is toilsome;
To the voyager who fears the flood thou givest (courage).
On paths that were never explored thou (guidest) the hunter;
O Shamash. . .
Whoso devises wickedness, his horn thou destroyest.
Whoso meditates oppression, his dwelling is overturned.
The wicked judge thou causest to see bonds;

[2] Translated by A. Jeremias, in Hastings' *Encyclopedia of Religion and Ethics*, vol. v., pp. 445-446.

Whoso takes a bribe, and does not judge righteously, on him thou
　　inflictest punishment.
Whoso takes no bribe, but makes intercession for the weak,
Well-pleasing is this to Shamash, he increaseth his life.
An upright judge, who renders righteous judgment,
Prepares for himself a palace: a prince's house is his abode.
Whoso gives money for excessive interest, what does he increase?
He overreaches himself for gain, empties his own purse.
Whoso gives money for just interest . . .
Well-pleasing is this to Shamash: he increaseth his own life. . . .
He overreaches himself for gain, empties (his purse). . . .
He who keeps . . . who lets too much be paid,
The curse of the people shall seize him. . . .
He who oppresses his inferiors, he is noted down with the pen.
Those who work evil, their seed has not continuance;
Whose mouth, full of lying, avails not before thee.
Thou burnest their utterance, rendest it asunder, yea, thou. . .
Thou hearest the down-trodden, as thou movest over them; thou
　　discoverest their right;
Each one, every one, is entrusted into thy hand.
Thou rulest over their judgments; what is bound, thou dost loose.
Thou hearest, O Shamash, prayer, supplication, and homage,
Submission, kneeling, whispered prayer, and prostration.
From his deepest breast the needy crieth unto thee,
The feeble, the weak, the afflicted, the poor—
With a lament, a petition, he ever appeals to thee,
He whose family is far away, whose city is a great way off.
The shepherd, with the fruits of the field, appeals to thee. . . .
The travelling merchant, the trader who carries the bag,
Appeals to thee; the fisher of the deep,
The hunter, the slaughterer, the keeper of cattle,
The fowler . . . appeals to thee.
The house-breaker, the thief—though an enemy of Shamash—
The vagrant upon the way of the desert, appeals to thee.
The wandering dead one, the fleeting shadow,
O Shamash, appealed to thee.
Thou hast not rejected those who appealed (to thee);
Those who thus kneel, for them thou, loosing (them from evil),
　　restorest their purity.

Those who thus render homage, their homage dost thou receive.
But they fear thee; they reverence thy name;
Before thy greatness men continually bow down.

A CATALOGUE OF SINS

Here is another cuneiform text deserving to rank, if only for historical reasons, with the world's ethical scriptures. It may have been recited originally as an incantation, listing all the various transgressions which might account for a sickness. The ancient Babylonians appear to have been certain that the wages of sin are invariably disease.[3]

Has he estranged father and son?

Has he estranged mother and daughter?

Has he estranged mother-in-law and daughter-in-law?

Has he estranged brother and brother?

Has he estranged friend and friend?

Has he failed to set a prisoner free,

Or not loosed one who was bound?

Is it outrage against his superior, hatred of his elder brother?

Has he despised father and mother, insulted his elder sister

By giving to the younger, and withholding from the elder?

To Nay has he said Yea?

To Yea has he said Nay?

Has he spoken impurity,

Spoken wickedness,

Used an unjust balance,

Taken base money?

[3] Translation by A. Jeremias in Hastings' *Encyclopedia of Religion and Ethics,* vol. v., p. 446.

Has he disinherited a legitimate son, installed an illegitimate?
Has he drawn false boundaries,
Deranged boundary, march, and precinct?
Has he intruded upon his neighbor's house,
Approached his neighbor's wife,
Shed his neighbor's blood,
Stolen his neighbor's garment?
Has he refused to let a man escape his power,
Driven an honest man from his family,
Broken up a well-cemented clan,
Revolted against a chief?
Was he honest with his mouth, while false in heart?
With his mouth was he full of Yea, in his heart full of Nay?
Is it because of the injustice that he meditated
In order to disperse the righteous, to destroy (them),
To wrong, to rob, to cause to be robbed,
To have dealings with evil?
Is his mouth unclean?
Are his lips froward?
Has he taught impurity, instilled unseemly things?
Has he concerned himself with sorcery and witchcraft?
Has he promised with heart and mouth, but not kept faith;
Dishonored the name of his god by (withholding) a gift,
Dedicated something, but kept it back,
Given something (flesh for sacrifice) . . . but eaten it?
By whatsoever thing he is bewitched: let it be revealed!
(Be it revealed) whether he has eaten anything that made an abomi-
    nation for his city;
Whether he has spread a calumny through his city;
Whether he has brought his city into evil repute. . . .

VANITY OF VANITIES

If the Hebrew BOOK OF ECCLESIASTES *is considered a scriptural document, surely the following fragment should be accounted no less. It is taken from the great* Gilgamesh Epic, *the most notable literary production of the ancient Babylonians. Though probably a late insertion—the bulk of the Epic consists of quite primitive myths and fabulous tales—it is still certainly well over three thousand years old.*[4]

Gilgamesh, why dost thou wander about?
The life that thou seekest, thou shalt not find.
When the gods created men,
Upon men did they also impose death,
And retained life in their own hands.
Thou, O Gilgamesh, gratify thy flesh;
Enjoy thyself by day and night;
Make a feast of joy every day;
Day and night be wanton and happy.
Let thy garments be unsoiled;
Let thy head be clean, and wash thyself with water.
Look upon the little ones whom thy hand holds;
Let thy wife rejoice upon thy bosom.

[4] Translation by A. Jeremias, *ibid.*, vol. v., p. 447.

THE BABYLONIAN JOB

The following document may be of Assyrian rather than Babylonian origin, but in either case it certainly antedates the Hebrew BOOK OF JOB *by many centuries. Though incomparably less wondrous in language and profundity, it is nevertheless sufficiently reminiscent of the Biblical poem to deserve the title modern scholars have given it.*

The first tablet—here omitted—describes the afflictions which have befallen Tabi-utul-Enlil. The second opens with a reflection on the sadness of life experiences and the difficulty of penetrating the ways of the gods to ascertain how to please them; and, as in the case of Job, the reflections are interspersed with laments about the author's own forlorn condition.[5]

I had reached and passed the allotted time of life;
Whithersoever I turned—evil upon evil.
Misery had increased, justice was gone,
I cried to my god, but he did not show me his countenance;
I prayed to my goddess, but she did not raise her head.
The diviner-priest could not determine the future by an inspection,
The necromancer did not through an offering justify my suit,
The oracle-priest I appealed to, but he revealed nothing,
The chief exorcizer did not by his rites release me from the ban.
The like of this had never been seen;
Whithersoever I turned, trouble was in pursuit.

[5] From *The Civilization of Babylonia and Assyria*, translation and comments by M. Jastrow, Jr., by permission of J. B. Lippincott Company.

Despite all his piety, the author was smitten with disease and he therefore indulges in the gloomy thought that the ways of the gods are mysterious. One can never be certain of pleasing them. The fate of man is uncertain. Joy changes to grief suddenly, and apparently without rhyme or reason.

As though I had not always set aside the portion for the god,
And had not invoked the goddess at the meal,
Had not bowed my face, and brought my tribute,
Not taught his people fear and reverence,
Not invoked his god, eaten of his (the god's) food;
Neglected his goddess, and did not offer to her a libation.
With the oppressor who has forgotten his lord,
Who has profaned the sacred name of his god, am I rated.
Royal prayer—that was my joy;
Its celebration—my delight.
I taught my country to guard the name of the god,
To honor the name of the goddess I accustomed my people.
The glorification of the king I made like unto that of a god,
And in the fear of the palace I instructed the people.
I thought that such things were pleasing to a god.
What, however, seems good to oneself, to a god is displeasing,
What is spurned by oneself finds favor with a god;
Who is there that can grasp the will of the gods in heaven?
The plan of a god full of mystery—who can understand it?
How can mortals learn the way of a god?
He who was alive yesterday is dead to-day;
In an instant he is cast into grief, of a sudden he is crushed;
For a moment he sings and plays,
In a twinkling he wails like a mourner. . . .
Like a plant of the marsh, I was uprooted, thrown on my back.
Food became bitter and putrid,
The malady dragged on its course.
Though without food, hunger diminished;
The sap of my blood he drained.
Nourishment was withheld. . .
My flesh was wasted, my body grew wan.
I took to my bed, unable to leave the couch.
The house became my prison;

As fetters for my body, my hands were powerless,
As pinions for my person, my feet were stretched out,
My discomfiture was painful, the pain severe.
A strap of many twists has struck me,
A sharply-pointed spear pierced me.
All day the pursuer followed me,
At night he granted me no respite whatever,
As though wrenched, my joints were torn apart,
My limbs were shattered and rendered helpless.
In my stall I passed the night like an ox,
I was saturated like a sheep in my excrements;
The disease of my joints baffled the chief exorcizer,
And my omens were obscure to the diviner,
The exorcizer could not interpret the character of my disease,
No god came to my aid, taking me by the hand.
No goddess had compassion for me, coming to my side.

*The third tablet evidently continued the plaint, but soon passed
on to an account of a dream sent to the sufferer which gives him a
reassuring message from Marduk that he will be. released from his
sufferings. It is to be regretted that this portion of the composition
is so poorly preserved, for it must have contained the reason why
Marduk decided to come to the relief of the pious sufferer. We are
left to conjecture why, but it is plausible to assume that Marduk is
seized with pity and recognizes that Tabi-utul-Enlil did not merit the
punishment sent to him. Perhaps it was even suggested that the sufferings were sent as a trial of his piety, though this in default of direct
evidence must not be regarded as more than a conjecture. At all
events, Tabi-utul-Enlil is healed, and we are given a vivid picture of
how, as a result of his final appeal to Marduk, the demons of disease
are driven away by a mighty storm.*

The nightmare, disturbing my rest, filled and darkening the heavens
    as with smoke.
The aches and groans like those of a lion,
He stirred up as in a storm and filled the earth,
The violent headache, which overthrows the strong,
He tore out . . . and bathed me with the dew of the night.
My eyeballs, which were covered with a veil of night (cataract),

Through a mighty wind he drove away the veil and made them shine
    brilliantly.
My ears, which had been closed and bolted as those of a deaf person,
He removed their deafness and opened their hearing.
My nose, which through the force of the fever was choked up,
He healed the hurt so that I could breathe again.
My lips, which had been closed through exhausted strength,
He reduced their swelling and loosened their bonds.
My mouth, which had been covered, so that with difficulty I uttered
    sounds,
He purified, like copper he made it shine.
My teeth, which had been seized so that they were pressed together,
He opened a space between them and strengthened their base.
The tongue, which was swollen so that I could not move it,
He took away its coating so that speech returned.
The throat, which was compressed, closed up like that of a corpse,
He healed so that my breast resounded like a flute.
My spittle, which had been shut off so that it could not come forth,
He loosened the bonds, opening them like a door.

In this strain, no doubt, the poem continued to the close—in illustration of the lesson to be derived from Tabi-utul-Enlil's terrible yet marvelous experience. Like the Biblical poem detailing Job's sufferings and the discourse of the problem involved, our composition ends in a kind of non sequitur. The problem is not solved, at least not to our satisfaction, for the just and innocent continue to suffer.

The consolation, however, remains that the mercy of the gods in the end never fails. Even though one may be already in the jaws of death, a god can still save one. Though diviners and exorcizers fail, Marduk can intervene directly and restore the wasted body to perfect vigor. So all ends happily—at least for Tabi-utul-Enlil.

THE CODE OF HAMMURAPI

It was under King Hammurapi (2123–2081 B.C.) that the city of Babylon attained its earliest glory. Being ambitious to "enlighten the land and advance the welfare of the people," this monarch prepared and published the first comprehensive law-code of which we have any knowledge. Carved on a huge stone monument, the 282 ordinances of the Code continued to be observed throughout the Empire for many centuries. Reading it now—the monument was unearthed in 1901—we can see where the Hebrews may have learnt their law of "an eye for an eye," and many another enactment which they came to attribute to Moses. Though exceedingly harsh—all the heavier crimes are made punishable by death—the Code is nevertheless enormously impressive because of the ardor with which it seeks to prevent capricious injustices and casual oppressions.[6]

LAWS OF JUSTICE WHICH HAMMURAPI, THE WISE KING, ESTABLISHED. A righteous law, and pious statute did he teach the land.

Hammurapi, the protecting king am I. I have not withdrawn myself from the men, whom Bel gave to me, the rule over whom Marduk gave to me, I was not negligent, but I made them a peaceful abiding-place. I expounded all great difficulties, I made the light shine upon them. With the mighty weapons which Zamama and Ishtar entrusted to me, with the keen vision with which Ea endowed me, with the wisdom that Marduk gave me, I have uprooted the enemy above and below (in north and south), subdued the earth, brought prosperity to the land, guaranteed security to the inhabitants in their homes; a disturber was not permitted. The great gods have called me, I am the salvation-bearing shepherd, whose staff is straight, the good shadow that is spread over my city; on my breast I cherish the inhabitants of the land of Sumer and Akkad; in my shelter I have let them repose in peace; in my deep wisdom have I enclosed them. That the strong might not injure the weak, in order to protect the widows and orphans . . . in order to bespeak justice in the land, to settle

[6] Translated by L. W. King in *The Letters and Inscriptions of Hammurapi* (Luzac, London, 1900).

all disputes . . . I have set up these my precious words, written upon
my memorial stone, before the image of me, as king of righteousness. . . .

By the command of Shamash, the great judge of heaven and earth,
let righteousness go forth in the land by the order of Marduk, my
lord, let no destruction befall my monument. In E-Sagil, which I love,
let my name be ever repeated; let the oppressed, who has a case at
law, come and stand before this my image as king of righteousness;
let him read the inscription, and understand my precious words: the
inscription will explain his case to him; he will find out what is just,
and his heart will be glad, so
that he will say:

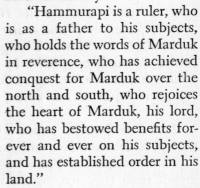

"Hammurapi is a ruler, who
is as a father to his subjects,
who holds the words of Marduk
in reverence, who has achieved
conquest for Marduk over the
north and south, who rejoices
the heart of Marduk, his lord,
who has bestowed benefits forever and ever on his subjects,
and has established order in his
land."

When he reads the record,
let him pray with full heart to
Marduk, my lord, and Zarpanit,
my lady; and then shall the protecting deities and the gods,
who frequent E-Sagil, graciously grant the desires daily presented
before Marduk, my lord, and Zarpanit, my lady.

In future time, through all coming generations, let the king, who
may be in the land, observe the words of righteousness which I have
written on my monument; let him not alter the law of the land which
I have given, the edicts which I have enacted; my monument let him
not mar. If such a ruler have wisdom, and be able to keep his land
in order, he shall observe the words which I have written in this inscription; the rule, statute, and law of the land which I have given;
the decisions which I have made will this inscription show him; let
him rule his subjects accordingly, speak justice to them, give right deci-

sions, root out the miscreants and criminals from this land, and grant prosperity to his subjects.

Hammurapi, the king of righteousness, on whom Shamash has conferred right (or law) am I. My words are well considered; my deeds are not equaled; to bring low those that were high; to humble the proud, to expel insolence. If a succeeding ruler considers my words, which I have written in this my inscription, if he do not annul my law, nor corrupt my words, nor change my monument, then may Shamash lengthen that king's reign, as he has that of me, the king of righteousness, that he may reign in righteousness over his subjects. If this ruler do not esteem my words, which I have written in my inscription, if he despise my curses, and fear not the curse of God, if he destroy the law which I have given, corrupt my words, change my monument, efface my name, write his name there, or on account of the curses commission another so to do, that man, whether king or ruler or commoner, no matter what he be, may the great God (Anu), the Father of the gods, who has ordered my rule, withdraw from him the glory of royalty, break his scepter, curse his destiny. May Bel, the lord, who fixeth destiny, whose command can not be altered, who has made my kingdom great, order a rebellion which his hand can not control; may he let the wind of the overthrow of his habitation blow, may he ordain the years of his rule in groaning, years of scarcity, years of famine, darkness without light, death with seeing eyes be fated to him; may he (Bel) order with his potent mouth the destruction of his city, the dispersion of his subjects, the cutting off of his rule, the removal of his name and memory from the land. . . .

May Ishtar, the goddess of fighting and war, who unfetters my weapons, my gracious protecting spirit, who loveth my dominion, curse his kingdom in her angry heart; in her great wrath, change his grace into evil, and shatter his weapons on the place of fighting and war. May she create disorder and sedition for him, strike down his warriors, that the earth may drink their blood, and throw down the piles of corpses of his warriors on the field; may she not grant him a life of mercy, deliver him into the hands of his enemies, and imprison him in the land of his enemies. . . .

May he lament the loss of his life-power, and may the great gods of heaven and earth, the Anunaki, altogether inflict a curse and evil upon the confines of the temple, the walls of this E-barra (the Sun temple of Sippara), upon his dominion, his land, his warriors, his subjects, and his troops. May Bel curse him with the potent curses of his mouth that can not be altered, and may they come upon him forthwith. . . .

SUNDRY ENACTMENTS

If a son strike his father, his hands shall be hewn off.

If a man put out the eye of another man, his eye shall be put out.

If he break another man's bone, his bone shall be broken.

If he put out the eye of a freed man, or break the bone of a freed man, he shall pay one gold mina.

If he put out the eye of a man's slave, or break the bone of a man's slave, he shall pay one-half of its value.

If a man knock out the teeth of his equal, his teeth shall be knocked out.

If he knock out the teeth of a freed man, he shall pay one-third of a gold mina.

If any one strike the body of a man higher in rank than he, he shall receive sixty blows with an ox-whip in public.

If a free-born man strike the body of another free-born man of equal rank, he shall pay one gold mina. . . .

If during a quarrel one man strike another and wound him, then he shall swear, "I did not injure him wittingly," and pay the physicians. . . .

If a physician make a large incision with an operating knife and cure it, or if he open a tumor (over the eye) with an operating knife, and saves the eye, he shall receive ten shekels in money.

If the patient be a freed man, he receives five shekels.

If he be the slave of some one, his owner shall give the physician two shekels.

If a physician make a large incision with the operating knife, and kill him, or open a tumor with the operating knife, and cut out the eye, his hands shall be cut off.

If a physician make a large incision in the slave of a freed man, and kill him, he shall replace the slave with another slave. . . .

If a builder build a house for some one, and does not construct it properly, and the house which he built fall in and kill its owner, then that builder shall be put to death.

If it kill the son of the owner, the son of that builder shall be put to death.

If it kill a slave of the owner, then he shall pay slave for slave to the owner of the house.

If it ruin goods, he shall make compensation for all that has been ruined, and inasmuch as he did not construct properly this house which he built and it fell, he shall re-erect the house from his own means.

If a builder build a house for some one, even though he has not yet completed it; if then the walls seem toppling, the builder must make the walls solid from his own means. . . .

If a shipbuilder build a boat for some one, and do not make it tight, if during that same year that boat is sent away and suffers injury, the shipbuilder shall take the boat apart and put it together tight at his own expense. The tight boat he shall give to the boat owner. . . .

If any one hire an ox or an ass, and a lion kill it in the field, the loss is upon its owner.

If any one hire oxen, and kill them by bad treatment or blows, he shall compensate the owner, oxen for oxen. . . .

If any one be too lazy to keep his dam in proper condition, and does not so keep it; if then the dam break and all the fields be flooded, then shall he in whose dam the break occurred be sold for money, and the money shall replace the corn which he has caused to be ruined.

If he be not able to replace the corn, then he and his possessions shall be divided among the farmers whose corn he has flooded.

If any one open his ditches to water his crop, but is careless, and the water flood the field of his neighbor, then he shall pay his neighbor corn for his loss.

If a man let in the water, and the water overflow the plantation of his neighbor, he shall pay ten *gur* of corn for every ten *gan* of land.

If a shepherd, without the permission of the owner of the field, and without the knowledge of the owner of the sheep, lets the sheep into a field to graze, then the owner of the field shall harvest his crop, and the shepherd, who had pastured his flock there without permission of the owner of the field, shall pay to the owner twenty *gur* of corn for every ten *gan*. . . .

If any one have a claim for corn or money upon another and imprison him; if the prisoner die in prison a natural death, the case shall go no further.

If the prisoner die in prison from blows or maltreatment, the master of the prisoner shall convict the merchant before the judge. If he was a free-born man, the son of the merchant shall be put to death; if it was a slave, he shall pay one-third of a mina of gold, and all that the master of the prisoner gave he shall forfeit.

If any one fail to meet a claim for debt, and sell himself, his wife, his son, and daughter for money or give them away to forced labor: they shall work for three years in the house of the man who bought them, or the proprietor, and in the fourth year they shall be set free. . . .

If any one "point the finger" (slander) at a sister of a god or the wife of any one, and can not prove it, this man shall be taken before the judges and his brow shall be marked.

If a man take a woman to wife, but have no intercourse with her, this woman is no wife to him.

If a man's wife be surprised with another man, both shall be tied and thrown into the water, but the husband may pardon his wife and the king his slaves.

If a man violate the wife (betrothed or child-wife) of another man, who has never known a man, and still lives in her father's house, and sleep with her and be surprised, this man shall be put to death, but the wife is blameless. . . .

If a man is taken prisoner in war, and there is a sustenance in his house, but his wife leave house and court, and go to another house: because this wife did not keep her court, and went to another house, she shall be judicially condemned and thrown into the water.

If any one be captured in war and there is no sustenance in his house, if then his wife go to another house this woman shall be held blameless.

If a man be taken prisoner in war and there be no sustenance in his house and his wife go to another house and bear children; and if later her husband return and come to his home: then this wife shall return to her husband, but the children follow their father.

If any one leave his house, run away, and then his wife go to another house, if then he return, and wishes to take his wife back: because he fled from his home and ran away, the wife of this runaway shall not return to her husband.

If a man wish to separate from a woman who has borne him children, or from his wife who has borne him children: then he shall give that wife her dowry, and a part of the usufruct of field, garden, and property, so that she can rear her children. When she has brought up her children, a portion of all that is given to the children, equal as that of one son, shall be given to her. She may then marry the man of her heart.

If a man wishes to separate from his wife who has borne him no children, he shall give her the amount of her purchase money and the dowry which she brought from her father's house, and let her go. . . .

If a man's wife, who lives in his house, wishes to leave it, plunges into debt, tries to ruin her house, neglects her husband, and is judicially convicted: if her husband offer her release, she may go on her way, and he gives her nothing as a gift of release. If her husband does not wish to release her, and if he take another wife, she shall remain as servant in her husband's house.

If a woman quarrel with her husband, and say: "You are not congenial to me," the reasons for her prejudice must be presented. If she is guiltless, and there is no fault on her part, but he leaves and neglects her, then no guilt attaches to this woman, she shall take her dowry and go back to her father's house.

THE SCRIPTURES OF EGYPT

THE BOOK OF PTAH-HOTEP
HYMNS TO THE ONE GOD
THE LAMENT OF A WEARY SOUL
THE BOOK OF THE DEAD

INTRODUCTION

There is considerable dispute as to whether civilization dawned first in Mesopotamia or Egypt, but none as to where it rose higher. If we compare merely the religious developments in the two regions, we can see how much greater was the progress made in Egypt.

For one thing, the trend toward monotheism was carried much farther there. During one reign, indeed, it was carried—or rather pushed—to the limit. That was the reign of the great Amenhotep IV (1375–1350 B.C.), when the people were ordered to abjure all their old gods and worship only Aton. Amenhotep's purpose may have been in part political—the swollen power of the priests serving the old gods had begun to menace the authority of the throne—but his language, at least, was indisputably spiritual. Aton, to this Egyptian, was more than just another deity. He was the One God in the universe, the Lord of Heaven, the Master of Life, the Father and Mother of all mankind. That anyone in Egypt so long ago—generations before the appearance of Moses—should have been capable of voicing such a conception, gives proof of the phenomenal progress attained there in religious thought.

It is not the only proof. The revolution attempted by Amenhotep came merely as a climax to centuries of evolution, and there are much older scriptures than his which are in their own way no less impressive. They reveal that throughout Egypt's history there was a persistent groping away from terror and necromancy toward enlightenment and ethics. The evidence can be seen not alone in the writings of and for the learned, but even in the liturgies cherished by the populace.

From first to last the basic religion of Egypt was a harrowing con-

cern about the Hereafter. That was why the dead were embalmed, swaddled in spells, buried beneath pyramids. But even this concern took on in time an ethical overtone. For their own worth, therefore, as well as their antiquity, the scriptures of ancient Egypt deserve more than just passing attention. Read with care, they can be richly rewarding.

THE BOOK OF PTAH-HOTEP

Ptah-hotep, who lived around 2600 B.C., is the most ancient author known to us by name, and this document has therefore been called the "oldest book in the world." It is probably of somewhat later origin, and may have been ascribed to Ptah-hotep only because of his traditional fame as one of Egypt's earliest sages. Even if that be the case, it is still an exceedingly ancient work, for it appears to have been widely taught in the Egyptian schools fully four thousand years ago.

The book aims to be a guide to the Good Life, and is replete with the shrewdest sort of earthly wisdom. Whoever composed it deserves to rank with the greatest sages of all time.[1]

Beginning of the arrangement of the good sayings, spoken by the noble lord, the divine father, beloved of God, the son of the king, the first-born of his race, the prefect and feudal lord Ptah-hotep, so as to instruct the ignorant in the knowledge of the arguments of the good sayings. It is profitable for him who hears them, it is a loss to him who shall transgress them.

He says to his son: Be not arrogant because of that which thou knowest; deal with the ignorant as with the learned; for the barriers of art are not closed, no artist being in possession of the perfection to which he should aspire. But good words are more difficult to find than the emerald, for it is by slaves that that is discovered among the rocks of pegmatite.[2] . . .

[1] Translated in *The Sacred Books and Early Literature of the East* (Park, Austin and Lipscomb, London, 1917), vol. 2, pp. 63–78.

[2] Literally, "being found by female slaves." The emerald is usually found in pegmatite, a compound of feldspath and quartz, out of which it was picked. The "Papyrus Ebers" inform us that the powder of pegmatite was used in the composition of a dentifrice.

If thou findest a disputant while he is hot,[3] and if he is superior to thee in ability, lower the hands, bend the back, do not get into a passion with him. As he will not let thee destroy his words, it is utterly wrong to interrupt him; that proclaims that thou art incapable of keeping thyself calm, when thou art contradicted.

If then thou hast to do with a disputant while he is hot, imitate one who does not stir. Thou hast the advantage over him if thou keepest silence when he is uttering evil words. "The better of the two is he who is impassive," say the bystanders, and thou art right in the opinion of the great.

If thou hast, as leader, to decide on the conduct of a great number of men, seek the most perfect manner of doing so that thy own conduct may be without reproach. Justice is great, invariable, and assured; it has not been disturbed since the age of Osiris. To throw obstacles in the way of the laws is to open the way before violence. Shall that which is below gain the upper hand, if the unjust does not attain to the place of justice? even he who says: I take for myself, of my own free-will; but says not: I take by virtue of my authority. The limitations of justice are invariable; such is the instruction which every man receives from his father.

Inspire not men with fear, else God will fight against thee in the same manner. If any one asserts that he lives by such means, God will take away the bread from his mouth; if any one asserts that he enriches himself thereby, God says: I may take these riches to myself. If any one asserts that he beats others, God will end by reducing him to impotence. Let no one inspire men with fear; this is the will of God. Let one provide sustenance for them in the lap of peace; it will then be that they will freely give what has been torn from them by terror.

If thou art among the persons seated at meat in the house of a greater man than thyself, take that which he gives thee, bowing to the ground. Regard that which is placed before thee, but point not at it; regard it not frequently; he is a blameworthy person who departs from this rule. Speak not to the great man more than he requires, for one knows not what may be displeasing to him. Speak when he invites thee and thy word will be pleasing.

If thou art one of those who bring the messages of one great man to another, conform thyself exactly to that wherewith he has charged

---

[3] Literally, "in his hour." A god is said to be "in his hour" when he is warlike.

thee; perform for him the commission as he hath enjoined thee. Beware of altering in speaking the offensive words which one great person addresses to another; he who perverts the truthfulness of his way, in order to repeat only what produces pleasure in the words of every man, great or small, is a detestable person.

If thou art an agriculturist, gather the crops in the field which the great God has given thee, fill not thy mouth in the house of thy neighbors; it is better to make oneself dreaded by the possessor. As for him who, master of his own way of acting, being all-powerful, seizes the goods of others like a crocodile in the midst even of watchmen, his children are an object of malediction, of scorn, and of hatred on account of it, while his father is grievously distressed, and as for the mother who has borne him, happy is another rather than herself. But a man becomes a god when he is chief of a tribe which has confidence in following him.

Be active during the time of thy existence, doing more than is commanded. Do not spoil the time of thy activity; he is a blameworthy person who makes a bad use of his moments. Do not lose the daily opportunity of increasing that which thy house possesses. Activity produces riches, and riches do not endure when it slackens.

If thou art a wise man, bring up a son who shall be pleasing to God. If he conforms his conduct to thy way and occupies himself with thy affairs as is right, do to him all the good thou canst; he is thy son, a person attached to thee whom thine own self hath begotten. Separate not thy heart from him. . . . But if he conducts himself ill and transgresses thy wish, if he rejects all counsel, if his mouth goes according to the evil word, strike him on the mouth in return. Give orders without hesitation to those who do wrong, to him whose temper is turbulent; and he will not deviate from the straight path, and there will be no obstacle to interrupt the way.

If thou art a leader, setting forward thy plans according to that which thou decidest, perform perfect actions which posterity may remember, without letting the words prevail with thee which multiply flattery, which excite pride and produce vanity.

If thou art a leader of peace, listen to the discourse of the petitioner. Be not abrupt with him; that would trouble him. Say not to him, "Thou hast already recounted this." Indulgence will encourage him to accomplish the object of his coming. . . . The way to obtain

a clear explanation is to listen with kindness.

If thou desirest to excite respect within the house thou enterest, for example the house of a superior, a friend, or any person of consideration, in short everywhere where thou enterest, keep thyself from making advances to a woman, for there is nothing good in so doing. There is no prudence in taking part in it, and thousands of men destroy themselves in order to enjoy a moment, brief as a dream, while they gain death, so as to know it. It is a villainous intention, that of a man who thus excites himself; if he goes on to carry it out, his mind abandons him. For as for him who is without repugnance for such an act, there is no good sense at all in him.

If thou desirest that thy conduct should be good and preserved from all evil, keep thyself from every attack of bad humor. It is a fatal malady which leads to discord, and there is no longer any existence for him who gives way to it. For it introduces discord between fathers and mothers, as well as between brothers and sisters; it causes the wife and the husband to hate each other; it contains all kinds of wickedness, it embodies all kinds of wrong. When a man has established his just equilibrium and walks in this path, there where he makes his dwelling, there is no room for bad humor.

Be not of an irritable temper as regards that which happens beside thee; grumble not over thy own affairs. Be not of an irritable temper in regard to thy neighbors; better is a compliment to that which displeases than rudeness. It is wrong to get into a passion with one's neighbors, to be no longer master of one's words. When there is only a little irritation, one creates for oneself an affliction for the time when one will again be cool.

If thou art wise, look after thy house; love thy wife without alloy. Fill her stomach, clothe her back; these are the cares to be bestowed on her person. Caress her, fulfil her desires during the time of her existence; it is a kindness which does honor to its possessor. Be not brutal; tact will influence her better than violence. . . . Open thy arms for her, resplendent to her arms; call her, display to her thy love.

Do not repeat any extravagance of language; do not listen to it; it is a thing which has escaped from a hasty mouth. If it is repeated, look, without hearing it, toward the earth; say nothing in regard to it. Cause him who speaks to thee to know what is just, even him who provokes to injustice; cause that which is just to be done, cause it to triumph. As for that which is hateful according to the law, condemn it by unveiling it.

If thou art a wise man, sitting in the council of thy lord, direct thy thought toward that which is wise. Be silent rather than scatter

thy words. When thou speakest, know that which can be brought against thee. To speak in the council is an art, and speech is criticized more than any other labor; it is a contradiction which puts it to the proof.

If thou art powerful, respect knowledge and calmness of language. Command only to direct; to be absolute is to run into evil. Let not thy heart be haughty, neither let it be mean. Do not let thy orders remain unsaid and cause thy answers to penetrate; but speak without heat, assume a serious countenance. As for the vivacity of an ardent heart, temper it; the gentle man penetrates all obstacles. He who agitates himself all the day long has not a good moment; and he who amuses himself all the day long keeps not his fortune. Aim at fulness like pilots; once one is seated another works, and seeks to obey one's orders.

Disturb not a great man; weaken not the attention of him who is occupied. His care is to embrace his task, and he strips his person through the love which he puts into it. That transports men to God, even the love for the work which they accomplish. Compose then thy face even in trouble, that peace may be with thee.

Teach others to render homage to a great man. If thou gatherest the crop for him among men, cause it to return fully to its owner, at whose hands is thy subsistence. But the gift of affection is worth more than the provisions with which thy back is covered. For that which the great man receives from thee will enable thy house to live, without speaking of the maintenance thou enjoyest, which thou desirest to preserve; it is thereby that he extends a beneficent hand, and that in thy home good things are added to good things. Let thy love pass into the heart of those who love thee; cause those about thee to be loving and obedient.

If thou art annoyed at a thing, if thou art tormented by some one who is acting within his rights, get out of his sight, and remember him no more when he has ceased to address thee.

If thou hast become great after having been little, if thou hast become rich after having been poor, when thou art at the head of the city, know how not to take advantage of the fact that thou hast reached the first rank, harden not thy heart because of thy elevation; thou art become only the steward of the good things of God. Put not behind thee the neighbor who is like unto thee; be unto him as a companion.

If thou aimest at polished manners, call not him who thou accostest. Converse with him especially in such a way as not to annoy him. Enter on a discussion with him only after having left him time to saturate his mind with the subject of the conversation. If he lets his ignorance display itself, and if he gives thee an opportunity to disgrace him, treat him with courtesy rather; proceed not to drive him into a corner; crush him not; worry him not; in order that in his turn he may not return to the subject, but depart to the profit of thy conversation.

Let thy countenance be cheerful during the time of thy existence. When we see one departing from the storehouse who has entered in order to bring his share of provision, with his face contracted, it shows

that his stomach is empty and that authority is offensive to him.
Let not that happen to thee.

If thou takest a wife . . . let her be more contented than any
of her fellow-citizens. She will be attached to thee doubly, if her chain
is pleasant. Do not repel her; grant that which pleases her; it is to
her contentment that she appreciates thy direction.

If thou hearest those things which I have said to thee, thy wisdom
will be fully advanced. After having listened to them the pupil will
become a master, even he who shall have properly listened to the
sayings because he shall have heard them. Let him win success by
placing himself in the first rank; that is for him a position perfect

and durable, and he has nothing further to desire forever. By knowledge his path is assured, and he is made happy by it on the earth.
The wise man is satiated by knowledge; he is a great man through
his own merits. His tongue is in accord with his mind; just are his lips
when he speaks, his eyes when he gazes, his ears when he hears. The
advantage of his son is to do that which is just without deceiving
himself.

When a son receives the instruction of his father, there is no error
in all his plans. Train thy son to be a teachable man whose wisdom
is agreeable to the great. Let him direct his mouth according to that
which has been said to him; in the docility of a son is discovered his
wisdom. His conduct is perfect, while error carries away the unteach-

able. To-morrow knowledge will support him, while the ignorant will be destroyed.

As for the man without experience who listens not, he effects nothing whatsoever. He sees knowledge in ignorance, profit in loss; he commits all kinds of error, always accordingly choosing the contrary of what is praiseworthy. He lives on that which is mortal, in this fashion. His food is evil words, whereat he is filled with astonishment. That which the great know to be mortal he lives upon every day, flying from that which would be profitable to him, because of the multitude of errors which present themselves before him every day.

A son who attends is like a follower of Horus; he is happy after having attended. He becomes great, he arrives at dignity, he gives the same lesson to his children. Let none innovate upon the precepts of his father; let the same precepts form his lessons to his children. "Verily," will his children say to him, "to accomplish what thou sayest works marvels."

Cause therefore that to flourish which is just, in order to nourish thy children with it. If the teachers allow themselves to be led toward evil principles, verily the people who understand them not will speak accordingly. Then all the world considers them as masters and they inspire confidence in the public; but their glory endures not so long as would please them. Take not away then a word from the ancient teaching, and add not one; put not one thing in place of another; beware of uncovering the rebellious ideas which arise in thee; but teach according to the words of the wise.

Let thy thoughts be abundant, but let thy mouth be under restraint, and thou shalt argue with the great. Put thyself in unison with the ways of thy master; cause him to say: "He is my son," so that those who shall hear it shall say: "Praise be to her who has borne him to him!" Apply thyself while thou speakest; speak only of perfect things; and let the great who shall hear thee say: "Twice good is that which issues from his mouth!"

Do that which thy master bids thee. Twice good is the precept of our father, from whom we have issued, from his flesh. What he tells us, let it be fixed in our heart; to satisfy him greatly let us do for him more than he has prescribed. Verily a good son is one of the gifts of God, a son who does even better than he has been told to do. For his master he does what is satisfactory, putting himself with all his heart on the part of right.

So I shall bring it about that thy body shall be healthful, that the King shall be satisfied with thee in all circumstances, and that thou shalt obtain years of life without default.

It has caused me on earth to obtain one hundred and ten years of life, along with the gift of the favor of the King among the first of those whom their works have ennobled, satisfying the King in a place of dignity.

It is finished, from its beginning to its end, according to that which is found in writing.

HYMNS TO THE ONE GOD

The growth of religious thought in Egypt reached its climax during the reign of the great Amenhotep IV, in the fourteenth century B.C. *He sought to break completely with the old polytheism and force his people to worship but one god, Aton. He changed his own name to Ikhn-aton ("Worshipper of Aton") and wrote—or at least inspired— a number of hymns to the glory of this deity. The two examples quoted below are typical, and show the heights of religious exaltation attained by this earliest of all monotheisms.*[4]

I

HYMN TO ATON, THE CREATOR

Splendor and Power of Aton

Thy dawning is beautiful in the horizon of the sky,
O living Aton, Beginning of life!
When thou risest in the eastern horizon
Thou fillest every land with thy beauty.
Thou art beautiful, great, glittering, high above every land,
Thy rays, they encompass the lands, even all that thou hast made.
Thou art Re, and thou carriest them all away captive [5]
Thou bindest them by thy love.
Though thou art far away, thy rays are upon earth;
Though thou art on high, thy footprints are the day.

NIGHT

When thou settest in the western horizon of the sky,
The earth is in darkness like the dead;
They sleep in their chambers,
Their heads are wrapped up,

[4] Translated by J. H. Breasted, *Development of Religion and Thought in Ancient Egypt* (Scribner, New York, 1912. Hodder and Stoughton, London). The division into stanzas, and the subtitles, are the translator's.

[5] There is a pun here on the word Re, which is the same as the word used for "all."

Their nostrils are stopped,
And none seeth the other,
While all their things are stolen
Which are under their heads,
And they know it not.
Every lion cometh forth from his den,
All serpents, they sting.
Darkness . . .
The world is in silence,
He that made them resteth in his horizon.

DAY AND MAN

Bright is the earth when thou
    risest in the horizon.
When thou shinest at Aton
    by day
Thou drivest away the dark-
    ness.
When thou sendest forth thy
    rays,
The Two Lands (Egypt) are
    in daily festivity,
Awake and standing upon
    their feet

When thou hast raised them up.
Their limbs bathed, they take their clothing,
Their arms uplifted in adoration to thy dawning.
Then in all the world they do their work.

DAY AND THE ANIMALS AND PLANTS

All cattle rest upon their pasturage,
The trees and the plants flourish,
The birds flutter in their marshes,
Their wings uplifted in adoration to thee.
All the sheep dance upon their feet,
All winged things fly,
They live when thou hast shone upon them.

DAY AND THE WATERS

The barks sail up-stream and down-stream alike.
Every highway is open because thou dawnest.
The fish in the river leap up before thee.
Thy rays are in the midst of the great green sea.

CREATION OF MAN

Creator of the germ in woman,
Maker of seed in man,
Giving life to the son in the body of his mother,
Soothing him that he may not weep,
Nurse even in the womb,
Giver of breath to animate every one that he maketh!
When he cometh forth from the body . . . on the day of his birth,
Thou openest his mouth in speech,
Thou suppliest his necessities.

CREATION OF ANIMALS

When the fledgling in the egg chirps in the shell,
Thou givest him breath therein to preserve him alive.
When thou hast brought him together,
To the point of bursting it in the egg,
He cometh forth from the egg
To chirp with all his might.
He goeth about upon his two feet
When he hath come forth therefrom.

THE WHOLE CREATION

How manifold are thy works!
They are hidden from before us,
O sole God, whose powers no other possesseth.[6]
Thou didst create the earth according to thy heart
While thou wast alone:
Men, all cattle large and small,
All that are upon the earth,

---

[6] The shorter hymns follow the phrase "sole God," with the addition, "beside
whom there is no other."

That go about upon their feet;
All that are on high,
That fly with their wings.
The foreign countries, Syria and Kush,
The land of Egypt;
Thou settest every man into his place,
Thou suppliest his necessities.
Every one has his possessions,
And his days are reckoned.
The tongues are divers in speech,
Their forms likewise and their skins are distinguished.
For thou makest different the strangers.

WATERING THE EARTH IN EGYPT AND ABROAD

Thou makest the Nile in the Netherworld,
Thou bringest it as thou desirest,
To preserve alive the people.
For thou hast made them for thyself,
The lord of them all, resting among them;
Thou lord of every land, who risest for them.
Thou Sun of day, great in majesty.
All the distant countries,
Thou makest also their life,
Thou hast set a Nile in the sky;
When it falleth for them,
It maketh waves upon the mountains,
Like the great green sea,
Watering their fields in their town.
How excellent are thy designs, O lord of eternity!
There is a Nile in the sky for the strangers
And for the cattle of every country that go upon their feet.
But the Nile, it cometh from the Netherworld for Egypt.

THE SEASONS

Thy rays nourish every garden;
When thou risest they live,
They grow by thee.
Thou makest the seasons

In order to create all thy work:
Winter to bring them coolness,
And heat that they may taste thee.
Thou didst make the distant sky to rise therein,
In order to behold all that thou hast made,
Thou alone, shining in thy form as living Aton,
Dawning, glittering, going afar and returning.
Thou makest millions of forms
Through thyself alone;
Cities, towns, and tribes, highways and rivers.
All eyes see thee before them,
For thou art Aton of the day over the earth. . . .

REVELATIONS TO THE KING

Thou art in my heart,
There is no other that knoweth thee
Save thy son Ikhn-aton.
Thou hast made him wise
In thy designs and in thy might.
The world is in thy hand,
Even as thou hast made them.
When thou hast risen they live,
When thou settest they die;
For thou art length of life of thyself,
Men live through thee,
While their eyes are upon thy beauty
Until thou settest.
All labor is put away
When thou settest in the west . . .
Thou didst establish the world,
And raise them up for thy son,
Who came forth from thy limbs,
The King of Upper and Lower Egypt,
Living in Truth, Lord of the Two Lands,
Nefer-khepru-Re, Wan-Re (Ikhn-aton),
Son of Re, living in Truth, lord of diadems,
Ikhn-aton, whose life is long;
And for the chief royal wife, his beloved,

Mistress of the Two Lands, Nefer-nefru-Aton, Nofretete,
Living and flourishing forever and ever.

II

THE KING'S OWN HYMN

Thy rising is beautiful, O living Aton, lord of Eternity;
Thou art shining, beautiful, strong;
Thy love is great and mighty,
Thy rays are cast into every face.
Thy glowing hue brings life to hearts,
When thou hast filled the Two
    Lands with thy love.
O God who himself fashioned
    himself,
Maker of every land,
Creator of that which is upon
    it:
Men, all cattle large and small,
All trees that grow in the
    soil,
They live when thou dawnest
    for them.
Thou art the mother and the
    father of all that thou hast
    made.

As for their eyes, when thou dawnest,
They see by means of thee.
Thy rays illuminate the whole earth,
And every heart rejoices because of seeing thee,
When thou dawnest as their lord.

When thou settest in the western horizon of the sky,
They sleep after the manner of the dead,
Their heads are wrapped up,
Their nostrils are stopped,
Until thy rising comes in the morning,
In the eastern horizon of the sky.

Their arms are uplifted in adoration of thee,
Thou makest hearts to live by thy beauty,
And men live when thou sendest forth thy rays,
Every land is in festivity:
Singing, music, and shoutings of joy
Are in the hall of the Benben-house,
Thy temple in Akhet-Aton, the seat of Truth,
Wherewith thou art satisfied.
Food and provision are offered therein;
Thy pure son performs thy pleasing ceremonies,
O living Aton, at his festal processions.
All that thou hast made dances before thee,
Thy august son rejoices, his heart is joyous,
O living Aton, born in the sky every day.
He begets his august son Wanre (Ikhn-aton)
Like himself without ceasing. . . .
Even me, thy son, in whom thou art satisfied,
Who bears thy name.
Thy strength and thy might abide in my heart,
Thou art Aton, living forever. . . .
Thou hast made the distant sky to rise therein,
In order to behold all that thou hast made,
While thou wast alone.
Millions of life are in thee to make them live,
It is the breath of life in the nostrils to behold their rays.
All flowers live and what grows in the soil
Is made to grow because thou dawnest.
They are drunken before thee.
All cattle skip upon their feet;
The birds in the marsh fly with joy,
Their wings that were folded are spread,
Uplifted in adoration to the living Aton,
The maker. . . .

THE LAMENT OF A WEARY SOUL

The great passion of the early Egyptians was to insure immortality by embalming the dead and sealing them in monstrous tombs. As the centuries passed, however, and men began to see the pyramids crumble despite all the care that had gone into their building, a spirit of doubt began to enter many minds. By the time of the Middle Empire (2500 B.C.–1600 B.C.) there seems to have been a good deal of skepticism not alone as to the certainty but even the desirability of life after death. This led to the writing of bitter laments which were apparently chanted by mourners as part of the funeral ritual.

The following is such a lament, and consists of four parts. In the first the dead man describes the abhorrence in which his name is held by the world, and in the second the injustice of it, seeing how iniquitous is that world. (The refrain, "To whom do I speak today," evidently means, "What sort are these who dare to despise me?") In the third part he rejoices in the thought of death, and only in the fourth does he make any concessions to the orthodox creed. There he proclaims his confidence that he will yet be justified by the great god, Re, to whom he will speak up yonder.[7]

I

Lo, my name is abhorred,
Lo, more than the odor of birds
On summer days when the sky is hot.
Lo, my name is abhorred,
Lo, more than a fish-receiver
On the day of the catch when the sky is hot.
Lo, my name is abhorred,
Lo, more than the odor of fowl
On the willow-hill full of geese.
Lo, my name is abhorred,
Lo, more than the odor of fishermen

[7] Translated in *The Sacred Books and Early Literature of the East*, vol. 2, pp. 92–95.

By the shores of the marshes
    when they have fished.
Lo, my name is abhorred,
Lo, more than the odor of croc-
    odiles,
More than sitting under the
    bank full of crocodiles.
Lo, my name is abhorred,
Lo, more than a woman,
Against whom a lie is told her
    husband.

II

To whom do I speak to-day?
Brothers are evil,
Friends of to-day are not of love.
To whom do I speak to-day?
Hearts are thievish,
Every man seizes his neighbor's goods.
To whom do I speak to-day?
The gentle man perishes,
The bold-faced goes everywhere.
To whom do I speak to-day?
He of the peaceful face is wretched,
The good is disregarded in every place.
To whom do I speak to-day?
When a man arouses wrath by his evil conduct,
He stirs all men to mirth, although his iniquity is wicked.
To whom do I speak to-day?
Robbery is practised,
Every man seizes his neighbor's goods.
To whom do I speak to-day?
The pest is faithful,
But the brother who comes with it becomes an enemy.
To whom do I speak to-day?
Yesterday is not remembered,
Nor is . . . in this hour.
To whom do I speak to-day?

Brothers are evil . . .
To whom do I speak to-day?
Faces pass away,
Every man with face lower than those of his brothers.
To whom do I speak to-day?
Hearts are thievish,
The man upon whom one leans has no understanding.
To whom do I speak to-day?
There are no righteous,
The land is left to those who do iniquity.
To whom do I speak to-day?
There is dearth of the faithful . . .
To whom do I speak to-day?
There is none here of contented heart;
Go with him (the apparently contented) and he is not here.
To whom do I speak to-day?
I am laden with wretchedness,
Without a faithful one.
To whom do I speak to-day?
Evil smites the land,
It hath no end.

III

Death is before me to-day
Like the recovery of a sick man,
Like going forth into a garden after sickness.
Death is before me to-day
Like the odor of myrrh,
Like sitting under the sail on a windy day.
Death is before me to-day
Like the odor of lotus-flowers,
Like sitting on the shore of drunkenness.
Death is before me to-day
Like the course of the freshet,
Like the return of a man from the war-galley to his house.
Death is before me to-day
Like the clearing of the sky,
Like a man fowling therein toward that which he knew not.

Death is before me to-day
As a man longs to see his house
When he has spent years in captivity.

IV

He who is yonder
Shall seize the culprit as a living god,
Inflicting punishment of wickedness on the doer of it.
He who is yonder
Shall stand in the celestial bark,
Causing that the choicest of the offerings there be given
    to the temples.
He who is yonder
Shall be a wise man who has not been repelled,
Praying to Re when he speaks.

THE BOOK OF THE DEAD

This, the most important of the ancient Egyptian scriptures, was really a book for the dead. It is in the main a collection of hymns and magic spells guaranteed to transport the soul of the deceased through the darkness of the underworld to the blessed "Field of Reeds" where dwelt the great god Osiris. Though parts of it belong to the remotest period, the document as a whole was probably not compiled until around 1400 B.C. It was then declared that "he who knows this book on earth, or on whose coffin it has been written . . . shall find bread, beer, and much meat (awaiting him) on the altar-table of Re; he shall receive a portion of land in the garden of Aalu . . . and shall flourish again even as he did on earth."

Three brief excerpts are given below: the first a typical hymn, the second a typical spell, and the third a formal assertion of innocence which seems to have been the high point in the ritual. It is hardly plausible that this assertion was intended to be taken as literally true. More probably it was offered as an earnest of the dead soul's wish that it were true. In any case, it is impressive as testimony to the high moral aspirations which had already been attained in ancient Egypt.[8]

I

A Hymn of Praise to Re-Heru-Khuti (Re-Harmakhis) when he setteth in the western part of Heaven. He (i.e., the deceased) saith:

"Homage to thee, O Re who in thy sitting art Tem-Heru-khuti (Tem-Harmakhis), thou divine god, thou self-created being, thou primeval matter from which all things were made. When thou appearest in the bows of thy bark men shout for joy at thee, O maker of the gods! Thou didst stretch out the heavens wherein thy two eyes might travel, thou didst make the earth to be a vast chamber for thy *Khus*, so that every man might know his fellow. The *Sektet* boat is glad, and the *Matet* boat rejoiceth; and they greet thee with exaltation as thou journeyest along. The god Nu is content, and thy mariners

---

[8] The translations are by E. A. W. Budge, in his "The Papyrus of Ani." in *The Book of the Dead* (Medici Society, London, 1913).

are satisfied; the uraeus-goddess hath overthrown thine enemies, and thou hast carried off the legs of Apep. Thou art beautiful, O Re, each day, and thy mother Nut embraceth thee; thou settest in beauty, and thy heart is glad in the horizon of Manu, and the holy beings therein rejoice. Thou shinest there with thy beams, O thou great god, Osiris, the everlasting Prince. The lords of the zones of the Tuat in their caverns stretch out their hands in adoration before thy *Ka* (double), and they cry out to thee, and they all come forth in the train of thy form shining brilliantly. The hearts of the lords of the Tuat (underworld) are glad when thou sendest forth thy glorious light in Amentet; their two eyes are directed toward thee, and they press forward to see thee, and their hearts rejoice when they do see thee. Thou harkenest

unto the acclamations of those that are in the funeral chest, thou doest away with their helplessness and drivest away the evils which are about them. Thou givest breath to their nostrils and they take hold of the bows of thy bark in the horizon of Manu. Thou art beautiful each day, O Re, and may thy mother Nut embrace Osiris . . . , victorious."

II

The Chapter of giving a heart to Osiris Ani in the Underworld. He saith:

"May my heart be with me in the House of Hearts! May my heart be with me, and may it rest there, or I shall not eat of the cakes of Osiris on the eastern side of the Lake of Flowers, neither shall I have a boat wherein to go down the Nile, nor another wherein to go up, nor shall I be able to sail down the Nile with thee. May my mouth be given to me that I may speak therewith, and my two legs to walk therewith, and my two hands and arms to overthrow my foe. May the doors of heaven be opened unto me; may Seb, the Prince of the gods, open wide his two jaws unto me; may he open my two eyes which are blindfolded; may he cause me to stretch apart my two legs which are bound together; and may Anpu (Anubis) make my thighs firm so that I may stand upon them. May the goddess Sekhet make me to rise so that I may ascend unto heaven, and may that be done which I command in the House of the *ka* (double) of Ptah (i.e., Memphis). I understand with my heart. I have gained the mastery over my heart, I have gained the mastery over my two hands, I have gained the mastery over my legs, I have gained the power to do whatsoever my *ka* (double) pleaseth. My soul shall not be fettered to my body at the gates of the underworld; but I shall enter in peace and I shall come forth in peace."

III

Hail, thou whose strides are long, who comest forth from Annu (Heliopolis), I have not done iniquity.

Hail, thou who art embraced by flame, who comest forth from Kher-aba, I have not robbed with violence.

Hail, thou divine Nose (Fenti), who comest forth from Khe-mennu (Hermopolis), I have not done violence to any man.

Hail, thou who eatest shades, who comest forth from the place where the Nile riseth, I have not committed theft.

Hail, Neha-hau, who comest forth from Re-stau, I have not slain man or woman.

Hail, thou double Lion-god, who comest forth from heaven, I have not made light the bushel.

Hail, thou whose two eyes are like flint, who comest forth from Sekhem (Letopolis), I have not acted deceitfully.

Hail, thou Flame, who comest forth as thou goest back, I have not purloined the things which belong unto God.

Hail, thou Crusher of bones, who comest forth from Suten-henen (Heracleopolis), I have not uttered falsehood.

Hail, thou who makest the flame to wax strong, who comest forth from Het-ka-Ptah (Memphis), I have not carried away food.

Hail, Qerti (i.e., the two sources of the Nile), who come forth from Amentet, I have not uttered evil words.

Hail, thou whose teeth shine, who comest forth from Ta-she (i.e., the Fayyum), I have attacked no man.

Hail, thou who dost consume blood, who comest forth from the house of slaughter, I have not killed the beasts, which are the property of God.

Hail, thou who dost consume the entrails, who comest forth from the *mabet* chamber, I have not acted deceitfully.

Hail, thou god of Right and Truth, who comest forth from the city of double Maati, I have not laid waste the lands which have been plowed.

Hail, thou who goest backward, who comest forth from the city of Bast (Bubastis), I have never pried into matters to make mischief.

Hail, Aati, who comest forth from Annu (Heliopolis), I have not set my mouth in motion against any man.

Hail, thou who art double evil, who comest forth from the nome of Ati, I have not given way to wrath concerning myself without a cause.

Hail, thou serpent Uamemti, who comest forth from the house of slaughter, I have not defiled the wife of a man.

Hail, thou who lookest upon what is brought to him, who comest forth from the Temple of Amsu, I have not committed any sin against purity.

Hail, Chief of the divine Princes, who comest forth from the city of Nehatu, I have not struck fear into any man.

Hail, Khemiu (i.e., Destroyer), who comest forth from the Lake of Kaui, I have not encroached upon sacred times and seasons.

Hail, thou who orderest speech, who comest forth from Urit, I have not been a man of anger.

Hail, thou Child, who comest forth from the Lake of Heq-at, I have not made myself deaf to the words of right and truth.

Hail, thou disposer of speech, who comest forth from the city of Unes, I have not stirred up strife.

Hail, Basti, who comest forth from the Secret city, I have made no man to weep.

Hail, thou whose face is turned backward, who comest forth from the Dwelling, I have not committed acts of impurity. . . .

Hail, Leg of fire, who comest forth from Akhekhu, I have not eaten my heart.

Hail, Kenemti, who comest forth from the city of Kenemet, I have abused no man.

Hail, thou who bringest thine offering, who comest forth from the city of Sau (Sais) I have not acted with violence.

Hail, thou god of faces, who comest forth from the city of Tchefet, I have not judged hastily.

Hail, thou who givest knowledge, who comest forth from Unth, I have not . . . and I have not taken vengeance upon the god.

Hail, thou lord of two horns, who comest forth from Satiu, I have not multiplied my speech overmuch.

Hail, Nefer-Tem, who comest forth from Het-ka-Ptah (Memphis), I have not acted with deceit, and I have not worked wickedness.

Hail, Tem-Sep, who comest forth from Tattu, I have not uttered curses on the King.

Hail, thou whose heart doth labor, who comest forth from the city of Tebti, I have not fouled water.

Hail, Ahi of the water, who comest forth from Nu, I have not made haughty my voice.

Hail, thou who givest commands to mankind, who comest forth from Sau, I have not cursed the god.

Hail, Neheb-kau, who comest forth from thy city, I have not sought for distinctions.

Hail, thou whose head is holy, who comest forth from thy habitations, I have not increased my wealth, except with such things as are justly mine own possessions.

Hail, thou who bringest thine own arm, who comest forth from Aukert (underworld), I have not thought scorn of the god who is in my city.

THE SCRIPTURES OF HINDUISM

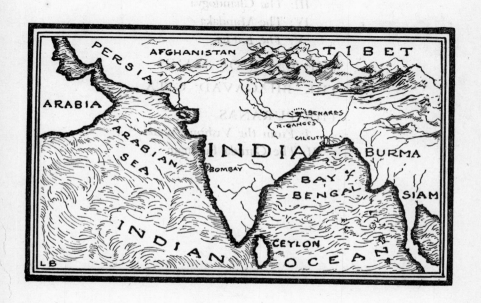

INTRODUCTION

Hinduism is the oldest of all living religions, and one of the most popular. Its adherents—some two hundred and thirty million—outnumber, for example, all the Protestant Christians on earth. In fairness, however, it must be conceded that Hinduism is really a multitude of religions which are united almost solely by geography and a common sacred lore.

The scriptures comprising that lore belong roughly to three different periods. First there is the RIG VEDA, a collection of hymns chanted by the Aryan tribesmen who settled in the Punjab around 1500 B.C. The faith reflected in those hymns is entirely animistic, the gods being personifications of natural phenomena like fire, thunder, fermented juice, and so forth. The ritual is equally primitive, consisting solely of sacrifices, flatteries, and spells. There is no inkling in the RIG VEDA of doctrines like transmigration, institutions like caste, tendencies like asceticism, or almost anything else that came to characterize Hinduism later on. Those ancient Aryans appear to have been a rough, tough, lusty lot, simple barbarians full of earthy wants and childlike imaginings.

Eventually, however, this stock moved from the arid Punjab to the lush valley of the Ganges—perhaps around 1000 B.C.—and the new conditions of life profoundly modified the pristine religion. The hymns of the RIG VEDA continued to be revered, but they had to be interpreted now, for their language had become archaic and their significance altogether mysterious. This fostered the growth of a learned class which became in time a priestly caste, and of a learned literature which became in turn a mysterious lore.

The literature was of two kinds: ritual books called Brahmanas,

and philosophical commentaries called UPANISHADS. *In both the theology centered around one god named Brahman, who was described
as the impalpable essence of the infinite universe, the indefinable
vital stuff underlying all of Nature. Salvation could be obtained solely
through union with this Brahman, and the main problem was how
such a union could best be effected. The ritual books maintained that
the priests held the key, and therefore urged slavish observance of
all priestly ordinances and exactions. The philosophical texts, on the
other hand, insisted that each individual held the key, and that it
could be turned only by those who devoted themselves to asceticism
and contemplation. These two prescriptions were expounded at endless length and between them they all but buried the earlier faith.
For some eight hundred years—approximately* 1000 *to* 200 B.C.—*the
prevailing religion was no longer Vedaism but Brahmanism.*

*Finally this in turn became supplanted by the jungle-growth of
sects, cults, and philosophies which is modern Hinduism. Its most
venerated scriptures are two enormous epics, the* Ramayana *and the*
Mahabharata, *the latter of which contains the great* BHAGAVAD GITA.
In addition there are eighteen popular texts called PURANAS, *a number
of esoteric documents called* Tantras, *and a mass of sacred liturgies,
books of magic, and collections of myths. Though never formally
canonized, these scriptures acquired abiding sanctity, being likened
to a divine ocean from which the devout could distil the nectar of
sublime and absolute Truth.*

*Hinduism differs from Brahmanism most of all in that it is less
abstract, less inhibited, less refined, and more human. Its gods are
many and very personal, and they are worshipped intimately and with
passion. Brahman, the ultimate Cosmic Force, is to most of the
populace a mere shadow in the pantheon. They prefer to pray to
deities more easily comprehended, especially Vishnu, the savior-god
who often walks the earth as a man, and Shiva, the "Lord of Demons,"
who holds wild court on the mountain-tops. They believe they can
be saved neither by regimented ritualism nor abstruse meditation,
but rather by* bhakti, *wild and clamorous devotion. On its lowest level,
Hinduism is very like a jungle, hot, steamy, and crawling with terror.*

*But it has also its higher levels, and on these the religion is
superlatively advanced. True, the ethical doctrine may seem to us
distorted, for the emphasis is on denial of carnal wants rather than
their progressive adaptation, and on despairing flight from Nature*

rather than determined effort to master it. But the basic philosophy, on the other hand, has deep appeal, for it is closely reasoned, and in a mystical way completely valid. It insists that all sensory life is transitory and therefore meaningless, and that the individual can really live only if, like a spark, he loses himself in the fire which is Life in the universal sense.

Ever since the scriptures of Hinduism were first made known to the Western World—and that happened barely a century ago—they have attracted increasing admiration. One who reads the following passages with sufficient patience and understanding can hardly fail to find the reason.

THE RIG VEDA

The most ancient Hindu scriptures are certain documents called the VEDAS—at least a hundred are in existence—of which the RIG VEDA is the oldest and most important. The Sanskrit word veda is the remote ancestor of the English "wit" and the German "wissen," and can be freely translated "knowledge." Specifically it means the sort of knowledge which will help a man win the favor of the gods. The word rig means "song of praise," and the RIG VEDA is a collection of over a thousand such songs arranged in ten cycles or books.

According to tradition, these psalms are as old as creation, and were miraculously revealed to various families of priests. Modern scholars believe they were composed between three and four thousand years ago. They reflect the beliefs of the tough Aryan tribesmen who had beaten their way down from Central Asia and overrun the plains of northern India. When first discovered by the western world, early in the nineteenth century, the Vedas were hailed as expressions of the noblest religious fervor, wondrous poems full of the mystic insight and pure spirituality. Soberer study, however, has revealed them to be little more than priestly runes, grandly phrased incantations calculated to secure health, wealth and children in this life, and happiness in the life to come. They contain little of ethical import, and therefore hardly belong in this Anthology. Nevertheless, five of the psalms are quoted below—there are more than a thousand in the RIG VEDA alone—in order to acquaint the reader with the nature of this literature. The first, addressed to Agni, the god of fire, is the hymn which opens the RIG VEDA. The second is noteworthy because it purports to be the utterance of a female divinity, and is strikingly pantheistic in tone. The third presents a peculiarly advanced conception of Creation, and the fourth an equally advanced idea of God. The fifth is, from our particular point of view, most impressive of all, for it is altogether ethical in content.[1]

[1] The translations are taken from Ralph T. H. Griffith's Hymns of the Rig-Veda, 2 vols. (Benares, E. J. Lazarus & Co., 1896).

I

I worship by hymns Agni, the high-priest of the sacrifice, the deity, the sacrificial priest who presents oblations to the deities and is the possessor of great riches.

May Agni, lauded by the ancient and modern Rishis, conduct the deities hither (*i.e.*, in this sacrifice).

Through Agni, the worshiper comes by wealth which multiplies daily, which is the source of fame and which secures heroes.

O Agni, the sacrifice, around which thou residest, is unimpeded and reaches the celestials in heaven.

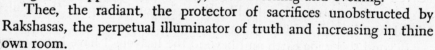

May Agni, the presenter of oblations, the attainer of success in works, ever truthful, highly illustrious for many noble deeds, divine, come hither with the celestials.

Whatever good, O Agni, thou mayest confer upon the giver of oblations, that, indeed, O Angiras, belongs to thee.

Bowing unto thee mentally, O Agni, we approach thee daily, both morning and evening.

Thee, the radiant, the protector of sacrifices unobstructed by Rakshasas, the perpetual illuminator of truth and increasing in thine own room.

Like unto a father to his son, O Agni, be easily accessible unto us; be ever present with us for our well-being.[2]

Book i, 1

II

I travel with the Rudras and the Vasus, with the Adityas and All-Gods I wander.

I hold aloft both Varuna and Mitra, Indra, and Agni, and the pair of Asvins.

[2] This translation is by the modern Hindu poet, Manmutha Dutt.

I cherish and sustain high-swelling Soma, and Tvashtar I support, Pushan and Bhaga.

I load with wealth the zealous sacrificer who pours the juice and offers the oblation.

I am the Queen, the gatherer-up of treasures, most thoughtful, first of those who merit worship.

Thus Gods have established me in many places with many homes to enter and abide in.

Through me alone all eat the food that feeds them—each man who sees, breathes, hears the word outspoken.

They know it not, but yet they dwell beside me. Hear, one and all, the truth as I declare it.

I, verily, myself announce and utter the word that Gods and men alike shall welcome.

I make the man I love exceedingly mighty, make him a sage, a Rishi, and a brahmin.

I bend the bow for Rudra that his arrow may strike and slay the hater of devotion.

I rouse and order battle for the people, and I have penetrated earth and heaven.

On the world's summit I bring forth the Father: my home is in the waters, in the ocean.

Thence I extend o'er all existing creatures, and touch even yonder heaven with my forehead.

I breathe a strong breath like the wind and tempest, the while I hold together all existence.

Beyond this wide earth and beyond the heavens I have become so mighty in my grandeur.

Book x, 125

III

Then was not non-existent nor existent: there was no realm of air, no sky beyond it.

What covered in, and where and what gave shelter? Was water there, unfathomed depth of water?

Death was not then, nor was there aught immortal: no sign was there, the day's and night's divider.

That One Thing, breathless, breathed by its own nature: apart from it was nothing whatsoever.

Darkness there was: at first concealed in darkness this All was indiscriminated chaos.

All that existed then was void and formless: by the great power of Warmth was born that Unit.

Thereafter rose Desire in the beginning—Desire, the primal seed and germ of Spirit.

Sages who searched with their heart's thought discovered the existent's kinship in the non-existent.

Transversely was their severing line extended: what was above it then, and what below it?

There were begetters, there were mighty forces, free action here and energy up yonder.

Who verily knows and who can here declare it, whence it was born and whence comes this creation?

The Gods are later than this world's production. Who knows then whence it first came into being?

He, the first origin of this creation, whether he formed it all or did not form it,

Whose eye controls this world in highest heaven, he verily knows it, or perhaps he knows not.

Book x, 129

IV

He established the earth and this heaven:
Who is the God to whom we shall offer sacrifice?

He who gives breath, he who gives strength, whose command all the bright gods revere, whose shadow is immortality, whose shadow is death: Who is the God to whom we shall offer sacrifice?

He who through his might became the sole king of the breathing and twinkling world, who governs all this, man and beast: Who is the God to whom we shall offer sacrifice?

He through whose might these snowy mountains are, and the sea, they say, with the distant river (the Rasa), he of whom these regions are indeed the two arms: Who is the God to whom we shall offer sacrifice?

He through whom the awful heaven and the earth were made fast, he through whom the ether was established, and the firmament; he who measured the air in the sky: Who is the God to whom we shall offer sacrifice?

He to whom heaven and earth, standing firm by his will, look up, trembling in their mind; he over whom the risen sun shines forth: Who is the God to whom we shall offer sacrifice?

When the great waters went everywhere, holding the germ (Hiranya-garbha), and generating light, then there arose from them the sole breath of the gods: Who is the God to whom we shall offer sacrifice?

He who by his might looked even over the waters which held power (the germ) and generated the sacrifice (light), he who alone is God above all gods: Who is the God to whom we shall offer sacrifice?

May he not hurt us, he who is the begetter of the earth, or he, the righteous, who begat the heaven; he who also begat the bright and mighty waters: Who is the God to whom we shall offer sacrifice?

Pragapati, no other than thou embraces all these created things. May that be ours which we desire when sacrificing to thee: may we be lords of wealth! [3]

Book x, 121

V

The gods have not ordained hunger to be our death: even to the well-fed man comes death in varied shape.

The riches of the generous man never waste away, while he who will not give finds none to comfort him.

The man with food in store who, when the needy comes in miserable case begging for bread to eat,

Hardens his heart against him—even when of old he did him service—finds not one to comfort him.

Bounteous is he who gives unto the beggar who comes to him in want of food and feeble.

Success attends him in the shout of battle. He makes a friend of him in future troubles.

No friend is he who will offer nothing to his friend and comrade who comes imploring food.

[3] This last verse, identifying the "Unknown God" with Pragapati, is generally regarded as a later addition.

Let him depart—no home is that to rest in—and rather seek a stranger to support him.

Let the rich satisfy the poor implorer, and bend his eye upon a longer pathway.

Riches come now to one, now to another. and like the wheels of cars are ever rolling.

The hands are both alike: their labour differs. The yield of sister milchkine is unequal.

Twins even differ in their strength and vigour: two, even kinsmen, differ in their bounty.

Book x, 117

THE UPANISHADS

As time passed, new meanings had to be read into the old VEDAS, *for life kept advancing and the religion had to follow suit. As a result there arose vast bodies of sacred commentary, first priestly, and later philosophical. The priestly commentaries, called the* Brahmanas, *are unquoted in this Anthology because they deal almost entirely with ritual matters. But the philosophical commentaries, known as the* UPANISHADS, *have a decided place here. They contain much of mankind's profoundest speculations on the mysteries of Existence, and have influenced, either directly or indirectly, much of the world's highest thought.*

The Sanskrit root shad *means "to be seated," and the classic* UPANISHADS *report the secret teachings which were imparted to those who sat at the feet of India's sages from about the eighth to the sixth century* B.C. *There are said to be over two hundred of these documents in existence, but most of them have never yet been even seen by Western scholars. The following excerpts* [4] *are taken from the five* UPANISHADS *which have won the widest renown—in part because they are among the least difficult to comprehend. Seeking as they do to penetrate. the most inscrutable of all problems, even these, however, do not make easy reading. They cannot be understood at all unless one masters the meaning of certain terms which have perforce been left untranslated. These are:*

BRAHMAN: *the Supreme Essence, the Soul of the Universe, the invisible, uncreated Infinite which is manifest in all visible and created things. To know and become part of the Brahman is the highest goal of Hindu religious meditations.*

HARI: *one of the names of the god Vishnu, but here used usually as a pious ejaculation.*

OM (A-U-M): *the mystic symbol for the Brahmanic trinity. To meditate on OM means to make the mind blank to all sensory impressions and to concentrate on abstract thought alone. This is*

[4] Translated by F. Max Müller in *Sacred Books of the East* (Clarendon Press, Oxford).

imperative—even if impossible—for it is considered the first step towards the attainment of true knowledge. The formula Hari! Om! is sometimes translated "Let us meditate profoundly and in peace." Or, when expressed as a prayer: "God give us peace and the wisdom born of meditation." This is the thought pervading all the Upanishads.

I

This excerpt, from the Aitareya Upanishad, gives one of the earliest Hindu accounts of the origin, development, and destiny of the individual soul.

Verily, from the beginning he (the Self) is in man as a germ, which is called seed.

This seed, which is strength gathered from all the limbs of the body, he (the man) bears as self in his self (body). When he commits the seed to the woman, then he (the father) causes it to be born. That is his first birth.

That seed becomes the self of the woman, as if one of her own limbs. Therefore it does not injure her.

She nourishes his (her husband's) self (the son) within her. She who nourishes is to be nourished.

The woman bears the germ. He (the father) elevates the child even before the birth, and immediately after.

When he thus elevates the child both before and after his birth, he really elevates his own self,

For the continuation of these worlds (men). For thus are these worlds continued.

This is his second birth.

He (the son), being his self, is then placed in his stead for the performance of all good works.

But his other self (the father), having done all he has to do, and having reached the full measure of his life, departs.

And departing from hence he is born again. That is his third birth. . . .

Who is he whom we meditate on as the Self? Which is the Self?

That by which we see form, that by which we hear sound, that by which we perceive smells, that by which we utter speech, that by which we distinguish sweet and not sweet, and what comes from the heart and the mind, namely, perception, command, understanding, knowledge, wisdom, seeing, holding, thinking, considering, readiness (or suffering), remembering, conceiving, willing, breathing, loving, desiring?

No, all these are various names only of knowledge (the true Self).

And that Self, consisting of knowledge, is Brahman. . . . All the five great elements, earth, air, ether, water, fire—these and those which are, as it were, small and mixed, and seeds of this kind and that kind, born from eggs, born from the womb, born from heat, born from germs, horses, cows, men, elephants, and whatsoever breathes, whether walking or flying, and what is immovable—all that is produced by knowledge (the Self).

It rests on knowledge (the Self). The world is produced by knowledge (the Self). Knowledge is its cause.

Knowledge is Brahman.

II

The following passages are from the Brihadaranyaka, *perhaps the most coherent and illuminating of all the* UPANISHADS. *It expounds— especially in the third and fourth chapters—the gist of Upanishadic doctrine concerning the Oversoul. If Yajnavalkya, whose responses carry the burden of the teaching, was a real person—and not, as many scholars suspect, a fictional composite—he certainly ranks with the profoundest sages of all time.*

When Yajnavalkya was about to enter upon another stage of life (*i.e., become a hermit*), he said (*to his wife*): Maitreyi, I am about to wander forth from this my house. Behold! let me make a final settlement between thee and Katyayani (*his second wife*).

Then said Maitreyi: My Lord, if this whole earth, full of wealth, were mine, should I be immortal thereby?

Nay, said Yajnavalkya: As the life of the rich even so would thy life be. But there is no hope of immortality by reason of wealth.

Then said Maitreyi: That by which I cannot become immortal, what can I do with that? But what my Lord knoweth, tell that to me.

Then said Yajnavalkya: Thou who wast dear to me, hast by this become increasingly so. Come, I will expound it to thee.

Verily, a husband is not dear, for love of the husband; but for love of the Atman is a husband dear. A wife is not dear for love of the wife, nor are sons, nor the worlds, nor all creatures. All is not dear for love of all, but for love of the Atman is all dear.

Verily, it is the Atman that should be seen, hearkened to, pondered on, O Maitreyi! When we have seen and heard and understood the Atman, then the universe is known.

Just as when a lute is being played, one cannot seize the sound; but by grasping the lute itself, the sound is also seized, so from the Atman are all these things breathed forth.

As all waters find their centre in the sea; all sounds in the ear; all precepts in the mind; all knowledge in the heart; as a lump of salt, cast into the water doth dissolve so thou canst not seize it again, but wherever thou tastest it is salty, thus verily this Great Being, infinite, limitless, is compact of knowledge.

II. iv. 1–12

He who dwelleth in the earth, yet is other than the earth, whom the earth knoweth not, who directeth the earth from within, He is thy Soul, the Ruler within, the Immortal.

He who dwelleth in the waters, in the fire, in the air; He who dwelleth in the sun, moon, and stars, who dwelleth in space, in darkness and light; who dwelleth in all beings; in the breath, in the eye, in the ear, in the mind; in all things, yet is other than all things, whom all things do not know;

The unseen Seer, the unheard Hearer, the unthought Thinker, the unknown Knower; He is thy Soul, the Ruler within, the Immortal. There is no other seer, no other hearer, no other discerner, no other knower than He.

III. vii. 3–23

Yajnavalkya came to Janaka, King of Videha. So now the King asked him: What is the light of man?

Yajnavalkya answered him: The sun, O King! For with the sun indeed as his light, man moveth around, goeth about his labour, and returneth.

But when the sun hath set, Yajnavalkya, what then is the light of man?

The moon, indeed, is his light; for with the moon as his light, man moveth about and performeth his labour.

When the moon hath set, Yajnavalkya, what is the light of man?

Fire, indeed, is his light, by the fire he performeth his labour.

When the sun hath set, and the moon hath set, and the fire is gone out, what then is the light of man?

The soul, indeed, is his light; for with the soul as his light, man moveth about, performeth his labour and returneth.

And there are for the soul two states, one here in this world and one in the other world; and betwixt them the state of sleep when it seeth both those states together.

Having subdued by sleep all that belongeth to the body, sleepless itself, it looketh down upon the sleeping senses.

Leaving its lower nest in breath's protection, and upward from that nest immortal soaring, wherever it listeth it doth roam about immortal, the golden-pinioned only swan of spirit. It moveth in a dream-state up and downward, divinely assuming many shapes and forms.

Then, as a falcon, or an eagle, having flown about in space, exhausted foldeth its wings, and is borne to its nest; so doth the spirit haste to that state in which, asleep, it feeleth no desire and dreameth no more dreams.

This, indeed, is its true form, free from desire, free from fear. For as one embraced by a beloved woman knoweth not of anything without or within, so also the soul in the embrace of the Self knoweth naught without or within.

Then is a father not a father, a mother not a mother, the worlds not worlds, the gods not gods. He is not followed by good, not followed by evil, for then he hath passed beyond all the sorrows of the heart.

Verily, while he doth not there see with the eyes, yet he is seeing. For sight is inseparable from the seer, because it cannot perish.

Verily, while he doth not taste, speak, hear, think, touch, know, yet he is tasting, speaking, hearing, thinking, touching, knowing. For taste, speech, hearing, thought, touch, knowing, are inseparable from the seer; for they cannot perish.

An ocean is that one seer without any duality; this is the Brahma world, O King! (Thus did Yajnavalkya instruct him). This is his highest goal, this is his highest success, his highest world; this is his highest bliss. All other creatures live on a small portion of that bliss.

IV. iii. 1–32

As a goldsmith, taking a piece of gold, reduceth it to a new and more beautiful form, just so this soul, striking down this body and dispelling its ignorance, maketh unto itself a new and beautiful form like that of Brahma.

According as one acteth, according as one conducteth himself, so doth he become. The man of good deeds becometh good. The man of evil deeds becometh evil. One becometh pure by virtuous action, bad by bad action.

They who know the breathing of the breath, the seeing of the eye, the hearing of the ear, the thinking of the mind, they have comprehended the ancient, primeval Brahma.

IV. iv. 4, 5, 18

III

The following excerpts are from the Chandogya, *which shares importance with the* Brihadaranyaka *as the most ancient of the* UPANISHADS.

All this is Brahman. Let a man meditate on that visible world as beginning, ending and breathing in it (the Brahma).

Now man is a creature of will. According to what his will is in this world, so will he be when he has departed this life. Let him therefore have this will and belief.

The intelligent, whose body is spirit, whose form is light, whose thoughts are true, whose nature is like ether (omnipresent and invisible), from whom all works, all desires, all sweet odors and tastes proceed; he who embraces all this, who never speaks, and is never surprised,

He is myself within the heart, smaller than a corn of rice, smaller than a corn of barley, smaller than a mustard-seed, smaller than a

canary-seed or the kernel of a canary-seed. He also is my self within the heart, greater than the earth, greater than the sky, greater than heaven, greater than all these worlds.

He from whom all works, all desires, all sweet odors and tastes proceed, who embraces all this, who never speaks and who is never surprised, he, my self within the heart, is that Brahma. When I shall have departed from hence, I shall obtain him (that Self). He who has this faith has no doubt; thus said Sandilya, yea, thus he said.

The Sage said to his son: "Learn from me the true nature of sleep. When a man sleeps here, then, my dear son, he becomes united with the True, he is gone to his own Self.

"As a bird when tied by a string flies first in every direction, and finding no rest anywhere, settles down at last on the very place where it is fastened, exactly in the same manner, my son, that living Self in the mind, after flying in every direction, and finding no rest anywhere, settles down on breath; for indeed, my son, mind is fastened to breath. . . .

"As the bees make honey by collecting the juices of distant trees, and reduce the juice into one form,

"And as these juices have no discrimination, so that they might say, I am the juice of this tree or that, in the same manner, my son, all these creatures, when they have become merged in the True, either in deep sleep or in death, know not that they are merged in the True.

"Whatever these creatures are here, whether a lion, or a wolf, or a boar, or a worm, or a midge, or a gnat, or a mosquito, that they become again and again.

"Now that which is that subtile essence, in it all that exists has its self. It is the True. It is the Self, and thou, O Svetaketu, art it."

"Please, Sir, inform me still more," said the son.

"Be it so, my child," the father replied.

"If some one were to strike at the root of this large tree here, it would bleed, but live. If he were to strike at its stem, it would bleed, but live. If he were to strike at its top, it would bleed, but live. Pervaded by the living Self that tree stands firm, drinking in its nourishment and rejoicing. But if the live, the living Self, leaves one of its branches, that branch withers; if it leaves a second, that branch withers; if it leaves a third, that branch withers. If it leaves the whole tree, the whole tree withers. Thus the human body indeed withers and dies when the living Self has left it; the living Self dies out. That which is that subtile essence, in it all that exists has its self. It is the True. It is the Self, and thou, Svetaketu, art it."

"Please, Sir, inform me still more," said the son.

"Be it so, my child," the father replied. "Fetch me from thence a fruit of the Nyagrodha tree."

"Here is one, Sir."

"Break it."

"It is broken, Sir."

"What do you see there?"

"These seeds, almost infinitesimal."

"Break one of them. What do you see there?"

"Not anything, Sir."

The father said: "My son, that subtile essence which you do not perceive there, of that very essence this great Nyagrodha tree exists. That which is the subtile essence, in it all that exists has its self. It is the True. It is the Self, and thou, O Svetaketu, art it. Place this salt in water, and then wait on me in the morning."

The son did as he was commanded.

The father said to him: "Bring me the salt, which you placed in the water last night."

The son having looked for it, found it not, for, of course, it was melted.

The father said: "Taste it from the surface of the water. How is it?"

The son replied: "It is salt."

"Taste it from the middle. How is it?"

The son replied: "It is salt."

"Taste it from the bottom. How is it?"

The son replied: "It is salt."

Then the father said: "Here also, in this body, forsooth, you do not perceive the True, my son; but there indeed it is. That which is the subtle essence, in it all that exists has its self. It is the True. It is the Self, and thou, O Svetaketu, art it."

Said a venerable sage to his pupil:

"He who meditates on memory as God, is, as it were, lord and master as far as memory reaches—he who meditates on memory as God."

"Sir, is there something better than memory?"

"Yes, there is something better than memory."

"Sir, tell it me."

"Hope is better than memory. Fired by hope does memory read the sacred hymns, perform sacrifices, desire sons and cattle, desire this world and the other. Meditate on hope. He who meditates on hope as God, all his desires are fulfilled by hope, his prayers are not in vain; he is, as it were, lord and master as far as hope reaches—he who meditates on hope as God."

"Tell me, Sir, is there something better than hope?"

"Yes, spirit is better than hope. As the spokes of a wheel hold to the nave, so does all this, beginning with names and ending in hope, hold to spirit. Father means spirit, mother is spirit, brother is spirit, sister is spirit. When one understands the True, then one declares the True. One who does not understand it, does not declare the True. This understanding, however, we must desire to understand. When one perceives, then one understands. One who does not perceive, does not understand. Only he who perceives, understands. This perception, however, we must desire to understand."

"Sir, I desire to understand it."

"When one believes, then one perceives. One who does not believe, does not perceive. Only he who believes, perceives. The Infinite is bliss. There is no bliss in anything finite. Infinity only is bliss. This Infinity, however, we must desire to understand."

"Sir, I desire to understand it."

"Where one sees nothing else, hears nothing else, understands nothing else, that is the Infinite. Where one sees something else, hears something else, understands something else, that is the finite. The Infinite is immortal, the finite is mortal. . . . The Infinite indeed is below, above, behind, before, right and left—it is indeed all this. Now follows the explanation of the Infinite as the I; I am below, I am above, I am behind, before, right and left—I am all this.

"Next follows the explanation of the Infinite as the Self; Self is below, above, behind, before, right and left—Self is all this. He who sees, perceives, and understands this, loves the Self, delights in the Self, revels in the Self, rejoices in the Self—he becomes a master of himself."

As large as all space is, so large is that spiritual essence within the heart. Both heaven and earth are contained within it, both fire and air, both sun and moon, both lightning and stars; and whatever there is of him, the Self, here in the world, and whatever is not, namely, whatever has been or will be, all that is contained within it.

By the old age of the body this spiritual essence does not age; by the death of the body, it is not killed. This inner essence, not the body itself, is the true mansion of God. In it all desires are contained. It is the Self, free from sin, free from old age, from death and grief, from hunger and thirst, which desires nothing but what it ought to desire, and imagines nothing but what it ought to imagine. Now as here on earth people follow as they are commanded, and depend on the object which they are attached to, be it a country or a piece of land.

And as here on earth, whatever has been acquired by exertion, perishes, so perishes whatever is acquired for the next world by sacrifices and other good actions performed on earth. Those who depart from hence without having discovered the Self and those true desires, for them there is no freedom in all the worlds. But those who depart from hence, after having discovered the Self and those true desires, for them there is freedom in all the worlds.

This body is mortal and always held by death. It is the abode of that Self which is immortal and without body. When in the body, by thinking this body is I and I am this body, the Self is held by pleasure and pain. So long as he is in the body, he cannot get free from pleasure and pain. But when he is free of the body, when he knows himself different from the body, then neither pleasure nor pain touches him.

The wind is without body, the cloud, lightning, and thunder are without body, without hands, feet, etc. Now as these, arising from this heavenly ether, appear in their own form, as soon as they have approached the highest light

Thus does that serene being, arising from this body, appear in its own form, as soon as it has approached the highest light, the knowledge of Self. He in that state is the highest person. He moves about there laughing or eating, playing and rejoicing in his mind, be it with women, carriages, or relatives, never minding that body into which he was born.

IV

The following passages are from the Mundaka, *one of the few Upanishads written, like the archaic* VEDAS, *in verse, not prose. It shows the shift from belief in sacrifices to insistence on meditation as the highest religious activity. Ironically, at one time the* Mundaka *appears to have been regularly chanted during the course of the sacrificial ceremonies.*

FIRST MUNDAKA

. . . Saunaka, the great householder, approached Angiras respectfully and asked: "Sir, what is that through which, if it is known, everything else becomes known?"

He said to him: "Two kinds of knowledge must be known, this is what all who know Brahman tell us, the higher and the lower knowledge.

"The lower knowledge is the Rig-Veda, Yagur-Veda, Sâma-Veda, Atharva-Veda, Sikshâ (phonetics), Kalpa (ceremonial), Vyâkarana (grammar), Nirukta (etymology), Khandas (meter), Gyotisha (astronomy); but the higher knowledge is that by which the Indestructible (Brahman) is apprehended.

"That which can not be seen, nor seized, which has no family and no caste, no eyes nor ears, no hands nor feet, the eternal, the omnipresent (all-pervading), infinitesimal, that which is imperishable, that it is which the wise regard as the source of all beings.

"As the spider sends forth and draws in its thread, as plants grow on the earth, as from every man hairs spring forth on the head and the body, thus does everything arise here from the Indestructible.

"The Brahman swells by means of brooding (penance); hence is produced matter (food); from matter breath, mind, the true, the worlds (seven), and from the works performed by men in the worlds, the immortal (the eternal effects, rewards, and punishments of works).

"From him who perceives all and who knows all, whose brooding (penance) consists of knowledge from him (the highest Brahman) is born that Brahman, name, form, and matter (food)."

This is the truth; the sacrificial works which they (the poets) saw in the hymns of the Veda have been performed in many ways. Practise them diligently, ye lovers of truth, this is your path that leads to the world of good works!

When the fire is lighted and the flame flickers, let a man offer his oblations between the two portions of melted butter, as an offering with faith. . . .

But frail, in truth, are those boats, the sacrifices, the eighteen, in which this lower ceremonial has been told. Fools who praise the sacrifices as the highest good, are subject again and again to old age and death.

Fools dwelling in darkness, wise in their own conceit, and puffed up with vain knowledge, go round and round staggering to and fro, like blind men led by the blind.

Children, when they have long lived in ignorance, consider themselves happy. Because those who depend on their good works are, owing to their passions, improvident, they fall and become miserable when their life in the world which they had gained by their good works is finished.

Considering sacrifice and good works as the best, these fools know no higher good, and having enjoyed their reward on the height of heaven, gained by good works, they enter again this world or a lower one.

But those who practice penance and faith in the forest, tranquil, wise, and living on alms, depart free from passion through the sun to where that immortal Person dwells whose nature is imperishable.

Let a Brâhmana, after he has examined all these worlds which are gained by works, acquire freedom from all desires. Nothing that is eternal (not made) can be gained by what is not eternal (made). Let him, in order to understand this, take fuel in his hand and approach a Guru who is learned and dwells entirely in Brahman.

To that pupil who has approached him respectfully, whose thoughts are not troubled by any desires, and who has obtained perfect peace, the wise teacher truly told that knowledge of Brahman through which he knows the eternal and true Person.

SECOND MUNDAKA

This is the truth. As from a blazing fire sparks, being like unto fire, fly forth a thousandfold, thus are various beings brought forth from the Imperishable, my friend, and return thither also.

That heavenly Person is without body, he is both without and within, not produced, without breath and without mind, pure, higher than the high Imperishable.

From him when entering on creation are born breath, mind, and all organs of sense, ether, air, light, water, and the earth, the support of all.

Fire (the sky) is his head, his eyes the sun and the moon, the quarters his ears, his speech the Vedas disclosed, the wind his breath, his heart the universe; from his feet came the earth; he is indeed the inner Self of all things.

From him comes Agni (fire), the sun being the fuel; from the moon (Soma) comes rain (Parganya); from the earth herbs; and man gives seed unto the woman. Thus many beings are begotten from the Person (purusha).

From him come the Rig, the Sâman, the Yagush, the Dîkshâ (initiatory rites), all sacrifices and offerings of animals, and the fees bestowed on priests, the year too, the sacrificer, and the worlds, in which the moon shines brightly and the sun.

From him the many Devas too are begotten, the Sâdhyas (genii), men, cattle, birds, the up and down breathings, rice and corn for sacrifices, penance, faith, truth, abstinence, and law.

Manifest, near, moving in the cave of the heart is the great Being. In it everything is centered which ye know as moving, breathing, and blinking, as being and not-being, as adorable, as the best, that is beyond the understanding of creatures.

That which is brilliant, smaller than small, that on which the worlds are founded and their inhabitants, that is the indestructible Brahman, that is the breath, speech, mind; that is the true, that is the immortal. That is to be hit. Hit it, O friend!

Having taken the Upanishad as the bow, as the great weapon, let him place on it the arrow, sharpened by devotion! Then having drawn it with a thought directed to that which is, hit the mark, O friend, viz., that which is the Indestructible!

Om is the bow, the Self is the arrow, Brahman is called its aim. It is to be hit by a man who is not thoughtless; and then, as the arrow becomes one with the target, he will become one with Brahman.

In him the heaven, the earth, and the sky are woven, the mind also with all the senses. Know him alone as the Self, and leave off other words! He is the bridge of the Immortal.

He moves about, becoming manifold within the heart where the arteries meet, like spokes fastened to the nave. Meditate on the Self as Om! Hail to you that you may cross beyond the sea of darkness!

He who understands all and who knows all, he to whom all this glory in the world belongs, the Self, is placed in the ether, in the heavenly city of Brahman (the heart). He assumes the nature of mind, and becomes the guide of the body of the senses. He subsists in food, in close proximity to the heart. The wise who understand this, behold the Immortal which shines forth full of bliss.

The fetter of the heart is broken, all doubts are solved, all his works and their effects perish when he has been beheld who is high and low (cause and effect).

In the highest golden sheath there is the Brahman without passions and without parts. That is pure, that is the light of lights, that is it which they know who knows the Self.

The sun does not shine there, nor the moon and the stars, nor these lightnings, and much less this fire. When he shines, everything shines after him; by his light all this is lighted.

That immortal Brahman is before, that Brahman is behind, that Brahman is right and left. It has gone forth below and above; Brahman alone is all this; it is the best.

THIRD MUNDAKA

Two birds, inseparable friends, cling to the same tree. One of them eats the sweet fruit, the other looks on without eating.

On the same tree man sits grieving, immersed, bewildered by his own impotence (an-îsa). But when he sees the other lord (îsa) contented and knows his glory, then his grief passes away.

When the seer sees the brilliant maker and lord of the world as the Person who has his source in Brahman, then he is wise, and shaking off good and evil, he reaches the highest oneness, free from passions;

For he is the Breath shining forth in all beings, and he who understands this becomes truly wise, not a talker only. He revels in the Self, he delights in the Self, and having performed his works (truthfulness, penance, meditation, etc.) he rests, firmly established in Brahman, the best of those who know Brahman.

By truthfulness, indeed, by penance, right knowledge, and abstinence must that Self be gained; the Self whom spotless anchorites gain is pure, and like a light within the body.

The true prevails, not the untrue; by the true the path is laid out, the way of the gods (devayânah), on which the old sages, satisfied in their desires, proceed to where there is that highest place of the True One.

That (true Brahman) shines forth grand, divine, inconceivable, smaller than small; it is far beyond what is far and yet near here, it is hidden in the cave of the heart among those who see it even here.

He is not apprehended by the eye, nor by speech, nor by the other senses, not by penance or good works. When a man's nature has become purified by the serene light of knowledge, then he sees him, meditating on him as without parts.

That subtle Self is to be known by thought (ketas) there where breath has entered fivefold; for every thought of men is interwoven with the senses, and when thought is purified, then the Self arises.

Whatever state a man whose nature is purified imagines, and whatever desires he desires for himself or for others, that state he conquers and those desires he obtains. Therefore let every man who desires happiness worship the man who knows the Self.

He (the knower of the Self) knows that highest home of Brahman, in which all is contained and shines brightly. The wise who, without desiring happiness, worship that Person, transcend this seed; they are not born again.

He who forms desires in his mind is born again through his desires here and there. But to him whose desires are fulfilled, and who is conscious of the true Self within himself, all desires vanish, even here on earth.

That Self can not be gained by the Veda, nor by understanding, nor by much learning. He whom the Self chooses, by him the Self can be gained. The Self chooses him (his body) as his own.

Nor is that Self to be gained by one who is destitute of strength, or without earnestness, or without right meditation. But if a wise man strives after it by those means (by strength, earnestness, and right meditation), then his Self enters the home of Brahman.

When they have reached him (the Self), the sages become satisfied through knowledge, they are conscious of their Self, their passions have passed away, and they are tranquil. The wise, having reached him who is omnipresent everywhere, devoted to the Self, enter into him wholly.

Having well ascertained the object of the knowledge of the Vedanta, and having purified their nature by the Yoga of renunciation, all anchorites, enjoying the highest immortality, become free at the time of the great end (death) in the worlds of Bráhmâ.

Their fifteen parts enter into their elements, their Devas (the senses) into their corresponding Devas. Their deeds and their Self with all his knowledge become all one in the highest Imperishable.

As the flowing rivers disappear in the sea, losing their name and their form, thus a wise man, freed from name and form, goes to the divine Person, who is greater than the great.

He who knows that highest Brahman becomes even Brahman. In his race no one is born ignorant of Brahman. He overcomes grief, he overcomes evil; free from the fetters of the heart, he becomes immortal.

And this is declared by the following Rig-verse: "Let a man tell this science of Brahman to those only who have performed all necessary acts, who are versed in the Vedas, and firmly established in the lower Brahman, who themselves offer an oblation to the one Rishi (Agni), full of faith, and by whom the rite of carrying fire on the head has been performed, according to the rule of the Atharvanas."

The Rishi Angiras formerly told this true science; a man who has not performed the proper rites does not read it. Adoration to the highest Rishis! Adoration to the highest Rishis!

V

This, the Kat'ha Upanishad, is perhaps the most familiar of all to the Western world. It tells how Yama, the god of death, was persuaded to impart his knowledge to man. The point is stressed, however, that this knowledge is limited, since even Yama is ignorant of the certain ultimate truths.

The narrative recounts that a certain Vajasravara, being eager for heavenly rewards, decided to sacrifice all his possessions, including even his young son, Nachiketas. As the offerings are being handed to the priests, this boy's heart fills with faith, and he thinks to himself:

Unblessed, surely, are the worlds to which a man goes by giving as his promised present at a sacrifice cows which have drunk water, eaten hay, given their milk, and are barren.

Then, addressing his father, Nachiketas says: Dear father, to whom wilt thou give me?

(*His father does not answer.*)

Nachiketas (*again*): Dear father, to whom wilt thou give me?

(*Still his father does not answer.*)

Nachiketas (*for the third time*): Dear father, to whom wilt thou give me?

Vajasravara (*angrily*): I shall give thee unto Death!

Nachiketas (*to himself*): I go as the first, at the head of many who have still to die; I go in the midst of many who are now dying. What will be the work of Yama, the ruler of the departed, which today he has to do unto me? Look back how it was with those who came before, look forward how it will be with those who come hereafter. A mortal ripens like corn, like corn he springs up again.

Nachiketas enters into the abode of Yama (Death), and there is no one to receive him. Thereupon one of the attendants of Yama speaks.

Attendant: Fire enters into the houses, when one of the Brahmin caste enters as a guest. That fire is quenched by this peace-offering —bring water, O Yama! A Brahmana that dwells in the house of a foolish man without receiving food to eat destroys his hopes and expectations, his possessions, his righteousness, his sacred and his good deeds, and all his sons and cattle.

Yama, returning to his house after an absence of three nights, during which time Nachiketas has received no hospitality from him, speaks in apology.

Death: O Brahmana, as thou, a venerable guest, hast dwelt in my house three nights without eating, therefore choose now three boons. Hail to thee! and welfare to me!

Nachiketas: O Death, as the first of the three boons I choose that my father be pacified, kind, and free from anger towards me; and that he may know me and greet me, when I shall have been dismissed by thee.

Death: Through my favour thy father will know thee, and be again towards thee as he was before. He shall sleep peacefully through the night, and free from anger, after having seen thee freed from the mouth of death.

Nachiketas: In the heaven-world there is no fear; thou art not there, O Death, and no one is afraid on account of old age. Leaving behind both hunger and thirst, and out of the reach of sorrow, all rejoice in the world of heaven. Thou knowest, O Death, the fire-sacrifice which leads us to heaven; tell it to me, for I am full of faith. Those who live in the heaven-world reach immortality—this I ask as my second boon.

Death: I tell it thee, learn it from me, and when thou understand-est that fire-sacrifice which leads to heaven, know, O Nachiketas, that it is the attainment of the endless worlds, and their firm support, hidden in darkness.

Death then tells him of that fire-sacrifice, the beginning of all the worlds, and what bricks are required for the altar, and how many, and how they are to be placed. And Nachiketas repeats all as it has been told to him.

Death: I give thee now another boon; that fire-sacrifice shall be named after thee, take also this many-coloured chain. He who has three times performed this Nachiketa rite, and has been united with the three (father, mother, and teacher), and has performed the three duties (study, sacrifice, almsgiving), overcomes birth and death. When he has learnt and understood this fire, which knows (or makes us know) all that is born of Brahman, which is venerable and divine, then he obtains everlasting peace. He who knows the three Nachiketa fires, and knowing the three piles up the Nachiketa sacrifice, he, having first thrown off the chains of death, rejoices in the world of heaven, beyond the reach of grief. This, O Nachiketas, is thy fire which leads to heaven, and which thou hast chosen as thy second boon. That fire all men will proclaim. Choose now, O Nachiketas, thy third boon.

Nachiketas: There is that doubt, when a man is dead—some say-ing, he is; others, he is not. This I should like to know, taught by thee; this is the third of my boons.

Death: On this point even the gods have doubted formerly; it is not easy to understand. That subject is subtle. Choose another boon, O Nachiketas, do not press me, and let me off that boon.

Nachiketas: On this point even the gods have doubted indeed, and thou, Death, hast declared it to be not easy to understand, and another teacher like thee is not to be found—surely no other boon is like unto this.

Death: Choose sons and grandsons who shall live a hundred years, herds of cattle, elephants, gold, and horses. Choose the wide abode of earth, and live thyself as many harvests as thou desirest. If thou canst think of any boon equal to that, choose wealth, and long life. Be king, Nachiketas, on the wide earth. I make thee the enjoyer of all desires. Whatever desires are difficult to attain among mortals, ask for them according to thy wish; these fair maidens with their chariots and musical instruments—such are indeed not to be obtained by men—be waited on by them whom I give to thee, but do not ask me about dying.

Nachiketas: These things last till to-morrow, O Death, for they wear out this vigour of all the senses. Even the whole of life is short. Keep thou thy horses, keep dance and song for thyself. No man can be made happy by wealth. Shall we possess wealth, when we see thee? Shall we live, as long as thou rulest? Only that boon which I have chosen is to be chosen by me. What mortal, slowly decaying here below, and knowing, after having approached them, the freedom from decay enjoyed by the immortals, would delight in a long life, after he has pondered on the pleasures which arise from beauty and love? No, that on which there is this doubt, O Death, tell us what there is in that great hereafter. Nachiketas does not choose another boon but that which enters into the hidden world.

Death: The good is one thing, the pleasant another; these two, having different objects, chain a man. It is well with him who clings to the good; he who chooses the pleasant, misses his end. The good and pleasant approach man: the wise goes round about them and distinguishes them. Yea, the wise prefers the good to the pleasant, but the fool chooses the pleasant through greed and avarice.

Thou, O Nachiketas, after pondering all pleasures that are or seem delightful, hast dismissed them all. Thou hast not gone into the road that leadeth to wealth, in which many men perish.

Wide apart and leading to different points are these two, ignorance, and what is known as wisdom. I believe Nachiketas to be one who desires knowledge, for even many pleasures did not tear thee away. Fools dwelling in darkness, wise in their own conceit, and puffed up with vain knowledge, go round and round, staggering to and fro, like blind men led by the blind. The hereafter never rises before the eyes of the careless child, deluded by the delusion of wealth. "This is the world," he thinks, "there is no other"—thus he falls again and again under my sway.

He (the Self) of whom many are not even able to hear, whom many, even when they hear of him, do not comprehend; wonderful is a man, when found, who is able to teach him (the Self); wonderful is he who comprehends him, when taught by an able teacher. That (Self), when taught by an inferior man, is not easy to be known, even though often thought upon; unless it be taught by another, there is no way to it, for it is inconceivably smaller than what is small. That doctrine is not to be obtained by argument, but when it is declared by another, then, O dearest, it is easy to understand. Thou hast obtained it now; thou art truly a man of true resolve. May we have always an inquirer like thee!

Nachiketas: I know that what is called a treasure is transient, for that eternal is not obtained by things which are not eternal. Hence the Nachiketa fire-sacrifice has been laid by me first; then, by means of transient things, I have obtained what is not transient, the teaching of Yama.

Death: Though thou hadst seen the fulfilment of all desires, the foundation of the world, the endless rewards of good deeds, the shore where there is no fear, that which is magnified by praise, the wide abode, the rest, yet being wise thou hast with firm resolve dismissed it all. The wise who, by means of meditation on his Self, recognizes the Ancient, who is difficult to be seen, who has entered into the dark, who is hidden in the cave, who dwells in the abyss, as God, he indeed leaves joy and sorrow far behind.

A mortal who has heard this and embraced it, who has separated from it all qualities, and has thus reached the subtle Being, rejoices, because he has obtained what is a cause for rejoicing. The house of Brahman is open, I believe, O Nachiketas.

Nachiketas: That which thou seest as neither this nor that, as neither effect nor cause, as neither past nor future, tell me that.

Death: That word or place which all the Vedas record, which all penances proclaim, which men desire when they live as religious students, that word I tell thee briefly, it is Om. That imperishable syllable means Brahman, that syllable means the highest Brahman;

he who knows that syllable, whatever he desires, is his. This is the best support, this is the highest support; he who knows that support is magnified in the world of Brahma.

The knowing Self is not born, it dies not; it sprang from nothing, nothing sprang from it. The Ancient is unborn, eternal, everlasting; he is not killed, though the body is killed. If the killer thinks that he kills, if the killed think that he is killed, they do not understand; for this one does not kill, nor is that one killed.

The Self, smaller than small, greater than great, is hidden in the heart of that creature. A man who is free from desires and free from grief sees the majesty of the Self by the grace of the Creator.

Though sitting still, he walks far; though lying down, he goes everywhere. Who, save myself, is able to know that God who rejoices and rejoices not?

The wise who knows the Self as bodiless within the bodies, as unchanging among changing things, as great and omnipresent, does never grieve. That Self cannot be gained by the Veda, nor by understanding, nor by much learning. He whom the Self chooses, by him the Self can be gained. The Self chooses him (his body) as his own.

But he who has not first turned away from his sickness, who is not tranquil, and subdued, or whose mind is not at rest, he can never obtain the Self (even) by knowledge.

Who then knows where he is, he to whom the Brahmanas and Kshatriyas are (as it were) but food, and death itself a condiment? There are the two, drinking their reward in the world of their own works, entered into the cave of the heart, dwelling on the highest summit. Those who know Brahman call them shade and light; likewise, those householders who perform the Trinachiketa sacrifice. May we be able to master that Nachiketa rite which is a bridge for sacrificers; also that which is the highest, imperishable Brahman for those who wish to cross over to the fearless shore.

Know the Self to be sitting in the chariot, the body to be the chariot, the intellect (buddhi) the charioteer, and the mind the reins. The senses they call the horses, the objects of the senses their roads. When he (the highest Self) is in union with the body, the senses, and the mind, then wise people call him the Enjoyer.

He who has no understanding and whose mind (the reins) is never firmly held, his senses (horses) are unmanageable, like vicious horses of a charioteer. But he who has understanding and whose mind is always firmly held, his senses are under control, like good horses of a charioteer.

He who has no understanding, who is unmindful and always impure, never reaches that place, but enters into the round of births. But he who has understanding, who is mindful and always pure, reaches indeed that place, whence he is not born again. But he who has understanding for his charioteer, and who holds the reins of the mind, he reaches the end of his journey, and that is the highest place of Vishnu.

Beyond the senses there are the objects, beyond the objects there is the mind, beyond the mind there is the intellect, the Great Self is beyond the intellect. Beyond the Great there is the Undeveloped, beyond the Undeveloped there is the Person (purusha). Beyond the Person there is nothing—this is the goal, the highest road. That Self is hidden in all beings and does not shine forth, but it is seen by subtle seers through their sharp and subtle intellect.

A wise man should keep down speech and mind; he should keep them within the Self which is knowledge; he should keep knowledge within the Self which is the Great; and he should keep that (the Great) within the Self which is the Quiet.

Rise, awake! having obtained your boons, understand them! The sharp edge of a razor is difficult to pass over; thus the wise say the path to the Self is hard.

He who has perceived that which is without sound, without touch, without form, without decay, without taste, eternal, without smell, without beginning, without end, beyond the Great, and unchangeable, is freed from the jaws of death.

The Self-existent pierced the opening of the senses so that they turn forward: therefore man looks forward, not backward into himself. Some wise man, however, with his eyes closed and wishing for immortality, saw the Self behind.

Children follow after outward pleasures, and fall into the snare of widespread death. Wise men only, knowing the nature of what is immortal, do not look for anything stable here among things unstable. That by which we know form, taste, smell, sounds, and loving touches, by that also we know what exists besides. This is that which thou hast asked for. The wise, when he knows that by which he perceives all objects in sleep or in waking is the great omnipresent Self, grieves no more. He who knows this living soul which eats honey (perceives objects) as being the Self, always near, the lord of the past and the future, henceforward fears no more.

There is that ancient tree, whose roots grow upward and whose branches grow downward—that indeed is called the Bright, that is called Brahman, that alone is called the Immortal. All worlds are contained in it, and no one goes beyond.

Whatever there is, the whole world, when gone forth from the Brahman, trembles in its breath. That Brahman is a great terror, like a drawn sword. Those who know it become immortal. From terror of Brahman fire burns, from terror the sun burns, from terror Indra and Vayu, and Death, as the fifth run away.

If a man could not understand it before the falling asunder of his body, then he has to take body again in the worlds of creation.

As in a mirror, so Brahman may be seen clearly here in this body; as in a dream, in the world of the fathers; as in the water, he is seen about in the world of the Gandharvas; as in light and shade, in the world of Brahma.

Having understood that the senses are distinct from the Atman, and that their rising and setting, their waking and sleeping, belong to them in their distinct existence and not to the Atman, a wise man grieves no more.

Beyond the senses is the mind, beyond the mind is the highest created Being, higher than that Being is the Great Self, higher than the Great, the highest Undeveloped. Beyond the Undeveloped is the Person, the all-pervading and entirely imperceptible. Every creature that knows him is liberated, and obtains immortality. His form is not to be seen, no one beholds him with the eye. He is imagined by the heart, by wisdom, by the mind. Those who know this, are immortal.

When the five instruments of knowledge stand still together with the mind, and when the intellect does not move, that is called the highest state. This, the firm holding back of the senses, is what is called Yoga. He must be free from thoughtlessness then, for Yoga comes and goes.

He, the Self, cannot be reached by speech, by mind, or by the eye. How can it be apprehended except by him who says: "He is"? By the words "He is," is he to be apprehended, and by admitting the reality of both the invisible Brahman and the visible world, as coming from

Brahman. When he has been apprehended by the words "He is," then his reality reveals itself.

When all desires that dwell in his heart cease, then the mortal becomes immortal, and obtains Brahman. When all the ties of the heart are severed here on earth, then the mortal becomes immortal—here ends the teaching.

There are a hundred and one arteries of the heart, one of them penetrates the crown of the head. Moving upwards by it, a man at his death reaches the Immortal; the other arteries serve for departing in different directions.

The Person not larger than a thumb, the inner Self, is always settled in the heart of men. Let a man draw that Self forth from his body with steadiness, as one draws the pith from a reed. Let him know that Self as the Bright, as the Immortal; yes, as the Bright, as the Immortal.

Having received this knowledge taught by Death and the whole rule of Yoga [meditation], Nachiketas became free from passion and death, and obtained Brahman. Thus it will be with another also who knows what relates to the Self.

THE LAWS OF MANU

Though not included in their canon, the CODE OF MANU *has been so profoundly revered by the devotees of Brahmanism that it certainly deserves to be counted one of their scriptures. The work appears to be the product of numerous authors, some of whom may have lived as early as the fifth century* B.C. *In its present form, however, it probably does not date back further than the second century* B.C. *Manu is the Noah of Hindu tradition, the semi-divine hero who survived a primeval Deluge and founded a new race of men. The ascription to him is therefore quite unhistorical, and scholars are inclined to trace the origin of the Code to certain ordinances first published by a family of priests known as the Manavas.*

The work, which consists of twelve books, is only partially concerned with law in the strict sense of the word. Mostly it recounts legends, prescribes sacrificial and ceremonial rites, and discusses abstruse theological problems. From beginning to end, however, its spirit is distinctly ethical—and often quite nobly so, as many of the following selections will show.[5]

Wound not others, do no one injury by thought or deed, utter no word to pain thy fellow creatures.

He who habitually salutes and constantly pays reverence to the aged obtains an increase of four things: length of life, knowledge, fame, and strength.

A believer may receive pure knowledge even from a Sudra (Untouchable), and a lesson in the highest virtue even from a loose woman.

Book ii

Where women are honored, there the gods are pleased; but where women are not honored, there no sacred rite yields good reward.

Book iii

Depend not on another, but lean instead on thyself. . . . True happiness is born of self-reliance. . . .

[5] These selections are culled from *The Ordinances of Manu,* translated from the Sanskrit by A. C. Burnell (London, Kegan Paul, Trench, Trubner & Co., 1891).

By falsehood a sacrifice becomes vain; by self-complacency the reward for austerities is lost; by boasting the goodness of an offering is brought to naught. . . .

8:90

A Brahmana (*member of the priestly caste*) having lived the first quarter of his life with a Guru, should live, having taken a wife, the second quarter of his life in his own house. A Brahmana should live, except in distress, following the calling which is his, without doing any injury to beings, or with little injury. . . .

According to his ability, a householder must give to beggars, and a portion is to be made for beings as well as he can without inconvenience to his family.

Although wild with passion, he must not approach his wife on the appearance of her courses; nor must he even sleep with her on a common bed. For a man who approaches a woman when menstruating, the learning, glory, strength, sight, and also longevity, are destroyed.

One should not eat with his wife, nor look at her eating, sneezing, yawning, or sitting at her ease. A good Brahmana desirous of glory may not see her adorning her eyes (with collyrium), smeared with oil, naked, or bringing forth a child. . . .

One should speak truth, and speak what is pleasant; one should not speak unpleasant truth: one should not speak pleasant falsehood. This is fixed law.

Book iv

Having considered the source of flesh, and the slaughter and confinement of animals, one should cease from eating all flesh. There is no fault in eating flesh, nor in drinking intoxicating liquor, nor in copulation, for that is the occupation of beings, but cessation from them produces great fruit.

The learned become pure by tranquillity; those doing what is not to be done, by gifts; those with concealed sin, by muttering sacred texts; the most learned in the Vedas, by austerity. By earth and water what is to be purified is made pure; a river becomes pure by its velocity; a woman defiled by her mind becomes pure by her courses; a Brahmana, by renunciation of the world. The limbs become pure by water; the mind becomes pure by truth; the self of beings by knowledge and austerity; the intellect becomes pure by knowledge. . . .

No act is to be done according to her own will by a young girl, a young woman, or even by an old woman, though in their own houses. In her childhood a girl should be under the will of her father; in her youth, of her husband; her husband being dead, of her sons; a woman should never enjoy her own will. She must never wish separation of her self from her father, husband, or sons, for by separation from them a woman would make both families contemptible. She must always be cheerful and clever in household business, with the furniture well cleaned, and with not a free hand in expenditure.

The good wife of a husband, be he living or dead, if she desire the world where her husband is, must never do anything disagreeable to him. But she may at will when he is dead emaciate her body by living on pure flowers, fruits, and roots. She may not, however, when her husband is dead, mention even the name of another man. She must be till death subdued, intent, chaste, following that best law which is the rule of wives of a single husband. But the woman who, from desire of offspring, is unfaithful to her dead husband, meets with blame here, and is deprived of her husband's place in the next world.

She who, restrained in mind, speech, and body, is not unfaithful to her husband, attains the abode of her husband, and is called virtuous by the good. A twice-born man must burn a wife of such behaviour and of the same caste, if dying before him, by means of the sacred fire and sacrificial vessels, according to rule.

Having used the fires for the last rites to his wife dying before him, he may marry again, and again establish the sacred fires also.

Book v

Now a king, desirous to inspect suits, should, subdued, enter the assembly with Brahmanas and ministers who know mantras. There, seated or standing, having stretched forth his right hand, with humble vesture and ornaments, he should inspect the affairs of the parties. Day by day he should judge separately cases under the eighteen titles by reasons drawn from local usage and the treatises.

Of these titles, the first is non-payment of debt; next pledges; sale without ownership; partnership and non-delivery of what has been given; also non-payment of wages; breach of contract; revocation of sale and purchase; disputes between master and servant; also the law of disputes about boundaries; assault and slander; theft; violence; also adultery; the law between man and woman; partition; dicing; and games with animals. These eighteen topics occur in the settlements of suits here.

One should not enter the court or what is correct must be spoken; a man who speaks not, or speaks perversely, is sinful.

The king should cause a Brahmana to swear by truth; a Kshatrıya by his steed and his weapons; a Vaisya by his cows, his seed, and his gold; but a Sudra by all wicked deeds[6] Or he may cause him to hold fire, or cause him to dive into the water, or even let him touch the heads of his wife and son one after the other. He whom the lighted fire does not burn, he whom the water does not cause to rise to the surface, and he who within a short time meets with no misfortune,—these must be recognized as pure in respect to their oath. . . .

A business transaction is not legal when it has been performed by a drunken person, a crazy person, a person in distress, a slave, a child an old man, or one not duly authorized. . . .

What is given by force, used by force, and also what is written by force—in short all things done by force, Manu said, are as if not done. . . .

A decision in regard to the boundary-lines of a field, spring, pond, garden, or house, shall be established by an appeal to the neighbours. If the neighbours lie concerning the boundary over which men are disputing, each one of them shall be fined the medium fine by the king. If it is impossible to settle the boundary-line, a king who knows the right should himself, and alone, in order to do them a kindness, point out the ground: so stands the law.

A thief must, with loosened hair and a firm bearing, approach the king and proclaim his theft, saying: "Thus have I done; punish me"; while he bears to the king upon his shoulder a club, or a staff of acacia

---

[6] These are the four main castes: priest, warrior, merchant, laborer.

wood, a spear sharp at both ends, or an iron rod. By being punished or by being released the thief is freed from the crime of theft; but if the king does not punish him, he himself receives the crime of the thief. . . .

He who takes from a spring either the rope or the bucket, and he who breaks open a water-tank, should receive a fine of one masa, and replace it in this place.

Death is the penalty if one steals more than ten measures of grain; where the amount is less he must pay a fine eleven times the value of the grain, and in either case be made to return the property to that owner. But cutting off the hand is enjoined for stealing less than one hundred but more than fifty palas; where the amount is less, however, one should ordain a fine eleven times as great as the worth of the things stolen. . . .

Wherever right is oppressed, there may the twice-born take arms; also where, brought on by some unlucky time, calamity has come upon the twice-born castes. And in self-defence, in a struggle for gifts, and when peril threatens a woman or a Brahmana, he who thus kills a man in a just cause does no wrong. Thus let him, without hesitating, kill any one attacking him with a weapon in his hand, even if it be a Guru, a child, an old man, or a Brahmana who is very learned. No sin comes at any time upon the slayer for causing, whether openly or in secret, the death of one who attacks him with a weapon in his hand, for thus anger meets anger.

He who addressed the wife of another at a watering-place, in a forest or wood, or at the union of rivers, would incur the sin of adultery. Attendance upon her, sporting with her, touching her ornaments or clothes, sitting upon a bed with her, all this is called adultery. If any man touches a woman upon an improper part of her body, or being thus touched by her submits to it with patience, this is all called adultery, if done by mutual consent. One who is not a Brahmana deserves capital punishment for committing adultery. The wives of all the four castes must always be most carefully guarded.

The king should not cause a girl who tries to seduce a man of high caste to pay any fine at all; but he ought to compel a girl to live confined at home if she make love to a man of low caste.

A Brahmana should support both a Kshatriya and Vaisya whose means of livelihood have been diminished, making them attend each to his respective duties, but without causing them any cruelty. But if a

Brahmana through avarice, and because he possesses the power, compel twice-born men who have received the initiation into the caste order to do the work of a slave when they do not wish it, he shall be fined six hundred panas by the king. But a Sudra, whether bought or not bought, the Brahmana may compel to practise servitude; for that Sudra was created by the Self-existent merely for the service of the Brahmana.

Wife, son, and slave, these three are said to be without property: whatever property they acquire is his to whom they belong.

Book viii

One should give a girl in marriage according to rule to that suitor who is of high family, handsome, and of like caste, even though she has not reached the age of puberty. Better that the girl, even if she has arrived at the age of puberty, should remain at home till her death than that one should ever give her to a suitor lacking in good qualities.

At thirty years of age a man may marry a beloved girl of twelve years, or, if he is thrice eight years, he may marry a girl of eight years; if his religious duties would otherwise be unfulfilled he may marry at once.

Let there be mutual fidelity ending in death alone; this, in short, should be acknowledged as the highest law of duty for man or wife.

Book ix

THE BHAGAVAD GITA

This "Song of God" has been called the Gospel of Hinduism, for it is at once the most exalted and popular of all Hindu religious writings. Its authorship is unknown, and scholars say it may have been composed at any time between the fifth and second centuries B.C. *Some insist that it is of composite origin, reflecting the opinions of many generations of Hindu writers. Even if that be the case, the document is so integrated that it has the effect of a homogeneous work, and it has long served the Hindu believers as the classic compendium of their crucial religious doctrines.*

The GITA *forms one small section of the Mahabharata, an enormous epic consisting of some hundred thousand verses recounting the legendary feud between two branches of a royal family. It is obviously an insertion there, like the jewel in a turban, and all that holds it in place is one tenuous thread basted into the narrative. The Mahabharata relates how the long feud ended in a climacteric battle, and the* GITA *is the dialogue which is supposed to have taken place on the eve of that bloody event. The chief participants are two: the virtuous prince, Arjuna, and his mysterious charioteer, who is none other than the Blessed Lord Krishna in disguise. Arjuna, a redoubtable champion in many an earlier battle, is suddenly overcome by qualms when he realizes he is about to slay his own flesh and blood. "What can we hope for from this killing of kinsmen?" he cries. "Rather than that . . . . let them kill me. That will be better."*

There follow eighteen chapters of counsel, admonition, enlightenment and exhortation in the course of which Krishna covers the whole field of religious and ethical quandaries. Prompted by Arjuna's doubts, the All-Knowing One waxes now philosophical, now declamatory, now pedantic, now mystical. In the end, however, he becomes in the purest sense religious, simply declaring:

> *"Lay down all duties*
> *In me, your refuge.*
> *Fear no longer,*
> *For I will save you.*
> *From sin." . . .*

Briefly here are some of the basic ideas expounded in the GITA. *The beginning and end of all that exists is One who is without beginning, the "great Lord of the Universe." Though distinct from material things—and even from men's immaterial souls—He yet works in and acts through them constantly. In a sense He, the Oversoul, is the father of all creatures, having planted the seed in Nature, which is their mother. It is He, therefore, that determines their final fate, intervening when they do evil, and periodically becoming even as one of them in order to establish that which is good. He is not merely just but also merciful, showing love to all who strive to become at one with Him.*

How can such striving be accomplished? In three ways. First by inaction: by deliberately fleeing the world, renouncing the flesh, and devoting oneself exclusively to meditation. But better by far—and here lies the great contrast between the GITA *and earlier Hindu writings—altogether better is the way of action. A man should not seek to avoid material duties and obligations. On the contrary, performing them is the surer path to spiritual grace—so long as the performance is unmarred by selfishness. If one does what is commanded without thought of reward, leaving to God the outcome and to other men the gain, then one is certain to be saved. Best of all the ways, however, is that of simple faith. This is the way open to all men regardless of station. Even sinners can use it, even Untouchables, even women. Let a person only love God and he will know God—and through knowing God become one with God. Says Krishna:*

> "Give me your whole heart,
> Love and adore me,
> Worship me always. . . .
> And you shall find me.
> This is my promise." . . .

It is easy to understand why the GITA *has been more widely translated than any other Asiatic document. In English alone there are scores of versions, most of them either too pedantic to be comprehensible, or too casual to be trustworthy. A most happy exception is the very recent version by Swami Prabhavananda and Christopher Isherwood, published by The Marcel Rodd Co., Hollywood, Calif. (1946). In a noteworthy introduction to this version, Aldous Huxley writes:*

"The Bhagavad Gita is perhaps the most systematic scriptural statement of the Perennial Philosophy. To a world at war, a world that, because it lacks the intellectual and spiritual prerequisites to peace, can only hope to patch up some kind of precarious armed truce, it stands pointing, clearly and unmistakably, to the only road of escape from the self-imposed necessity of self-destruction. For this reason we should be grateful to Swami Prabhavananda and Mr. Isherwood for having given us this new version of the book—a version which can be read, not merely without that dull aesthetic pain inflicted by all too many English translations from the Sanskrit, but positively with enjoyment."

It is from this version that the following excerpts have been taken with the kind permission of the translators and publisher.

1: ARJUNA'S DILEMMA

Then the prince looked on the array, and in both armies, he recognised fathers and grandfathers, teachers, uncles, sons, brothers, grandsons, fathers-in-law, dear friends, and many other familiar faces.

When he saw all those ranks of kinsmen, he was filled with deep compassion, and he spoke despairingly, as follows:

Krishna, Krishna,
Now as I look on
These my kinsmen
Arrayed for battle,
My limbs are weakened,
My mouth is parching,
My body trembles,
My hair stands upright,
My skin seems burning,
My brain is whirling
Round and round,

I can stand no longer:
Krishna, I see such
Omens of evil!

What can we hope from
This killing of kinsmen?
What do I want with
Victory, empire,
Or their enjoyment?
O Giver of Enlightenment,
How can I care for
Power or pleasure,
My own life, even,
When all these others. . . .
Stand here ready
To risk blood and wealth
In war against us?

Knower of all things,
Though they should slay me
How could I harm them?
I cannot wish it:
Never, never,
Not though it won me
The throne of the three worlds;
How much the less for
Earthly lordship! . . .

What is this crime
I am planning, O Krishna?
Murder most hateful,
Murder of brothers!
Am I indeed
So greedy for greatness?

Rather than this
Let those evil [men]
Come with their weapons
Against me in battle:

5690

I shall not struggle,
I shall not strike them.
Now let them kill me,
That will be better.

*Having spoken thus, Arjuna threw aside his arrows and his bow
in the midst of the battle-field. He sat down on the seat of the chariot,
and his heart was overcome with sorrow.*

2: THE YOGA OF KNOWLEDGE

*Then Krishna spoke to him,
saying:*
O Arjuna, is this hour of
battle the time for scruples and
fancies? Are they worthy of
you, who seek enlightenment?
Any brave man who merely
hopes for fame or heaven
would despise them.

What is this weakness? It
is beneath you. Is it for nothing
men call you the foe-consumer?
Shake off this cowardice, Arjuna. Stand up.

And Arjuna answered:
Bhisma and Drona [*leaders
on the other side*] are noble
and ancient, worthy of the
deepest reverence. How can I greet them with arrows, in battle? If I
kill them, how can I ever enjoy my wealth, or any other pleasure? It
will all be cursed with blood guilt. I would much rather spare them,
and eat the bread of a beggar.

Which will be worse, to win this war, or to lose it? I scarcely know.
Good men stand in the enemy ranks. If we kill them, none of us will
wish to live.

Is this real pity that I feel, or only a delusion? My mind gropes
about in darkness. I cannot see where my duty lies. Krishna, I beg

LINCOLN BIBLE INSTITUTE

you, tell me frankly and clearly what I ought to do. I am your disciple. I put myself into your hands. Show me the way.

> Not this world's kingdom,
> Supreme, unchallenged,
> No, nor the throne
> Of the gods in heaven,
> Could ease this sorrow
> That numbs my senses!

When Arjuna, the foe-consuming, the never-slothful, had spoken thus, he added: "I will not fight," and was silent.

Then to him who thus sorrowed between the two armies, Krishna spoke, smiling:

Your words are wise, Arjuna, but your sorrow is for nothing. The truly wise mourn neither for the living nor for the dead.

There was never a time when I did not exist, nor you, nor any of these kings. Nor is there any future in which we shall cease to be.

Just as the dweller in this body passes through childhood, youth and old age, so at death he merely passes into another kind of body. The wise are not deceived by that.

Feelings of heat and cold, pleasure and pain, are caused by the contact of the senses with their objects. They come and they go, never lasting long. You must accept them.

A serene spirit accepts pleasure and pain with an even mind, and is unmoved by either. He alone is worthy of immortality.

That which is non-existent can never come into being, and that which is can never cease to be. Those who have known the inmost Reality know also the nature of *is* and *is not*.

That Reality which pervades the universe is indestructible. No one has power to change the Changeless.

Bodies are said to die, but That which possesses the body is eternal. It cannot be limited, or destroyed. Therefore you must fight. . . .

He Who dwells within all living bodies remains forever indestructible. Therefore, you should never mourn for anyone. . . .

Realize that pleasure and pain, gain and loss, victory and defeat, are all one and the same: then go into battle. Do this and you cannot commit any sin.

Poise your mind in tranquillity. Take care neither to acquire nor to hoard. Be established in the consciousness of the Atman, always.

When the whole country is flooded, the reservoir becomes superfluous. So, to the illumined seer, the Vedas are all superfluous.

You have the right to work, but for the work's sake only. You have no right to the fruits of work. Desire for the fruits of work must never be your motive in working. Never give way to laziness, either.

Perform every action with your heart fixed on the Supreme Lord. Renounce attachment to the fruits. Be even-tempered in success and failure; for it is this evenness of temper which is meant by yoga.

Work done with anxiety about results is far inferior to work done without such anxiety, in the calm of self-surrender. Seek refuge in the knowledge of Brahman. They who work selfishly for results are miserable. . . .

Hearing this, Arjuna spoke up:
Krishna, how can one identify a man who is firmly established and absorbed in Brahman? In what manner does an illumined soul speak? How does he sit? How does he walk?
Krishna replied:

> He knows bliss in the Atman
> And wants nothing else.
> Cravings torment the heart:
> He renounces cravings.
> I call him illumined.

> Not shaken by adversity,
> Not hankering after happiness:
> Free from fear, free from anger,
> Free from the things of desire.
> I call him a seer, and illumined. . . .

> Water flows continually into the ocean
> But the ocean is never disturbed:
> Desire flows into the mind of the seer
> But he is never disturbed.
> The seer knows peace:
> The man who stirs up his own lusts
> Can never know peace.

He knows peace who has forgotten desire.
He lives without craving:
Free from ego, free from pride.
This is the state of enlightenment in Brahman:
A man does not fall back from it
Into delusion.
Even at the moment of death
He is alive in that enlightenment:
Brahman and he are one.

3: KARMA YOGA

And Arjuna said:
But, Krishna, if you consider knowledge of Brahman superior to any sort of action, why are you telling me to do these terrible deeds?

Your statements seem to contradict each other. They confuse my mind. Tell me one definite way of reaching the highest good.

So Krishna declared:
I have already told you that, in this world, aspirants may find enlightenment by two different paths. For the contemplative is the path of knowledge: for the active is the path of selfless action.

Freedom from activity is never achieved by abstaining from action. Nobody can become perfect by merely ceasing to act. In fact, nobody can ever rest from his activity [7] even for a moment. All are helplessly forced to act, by the gunas.

A man who renounces certain physical actions but still lets his mind dwell on the objects of his sensual desire, is deceiving himself. He can only be called a hypocrite. The truly admirable man controls his senses by the power of his will. All his actions are disinterested. All are directed along the path to union with Brahman.

[7] Here "activity" includes mental action, conscious and subconscious.

Activity is better than inertia. Act, but with self-control. If you are lazy, you cannot even sustain your own body.

The world is imprisoned in its own activity, except when actions are performed as worship of God. Therefore you must perform every action sacramentally, and be free from all attachment to results.

But when a man has found delight and satisfaction and peace in the Atman, then he is no longer obliged to perform any kind of action. He has nothing to gain in this world by action, and nothing to lose by refraining from action. He is independent of everybody and everything. Do your duty, always; but without attachment. That is how a man reaches the ultimate truth; by working without anxiety about results. In fact, Janaka [8] and many others reached enlightenment, simply because they did their duty in this spirit. Your motive in working should be to set others, by your example, on the path of duty.

Whatever a great man does, ordinary people will imitate; they follow his example. Consider me: I am not bound by any sort of duty. There is nothing, in all the three worlds, which I do not already possess; nothing I have yet to acquire. But I go on working, nevertheless. If I did not continue to work untiringly as I do, mankind would still follow me, no matter where I led them. Suppose I were to stop? They would all be lost. . . .

At this Arjuna asked:

Krishna, what is it that makes a man do evil, even against his own will; under compulsion, as it were?

And Krishna answered:

Rage and lust; the ravenous, the deadly:
Recognize these: they are your enemies.

Smoke hides fire,
Dust hides a mirror,
The womb hides the embryo:
By lust the Atman is hidden.

[8] A royal saint mentioned in the *Upanishads*.

Lust hides the Atman in its hungry flames,
The wise man's faithful foe.

Intellect, senses and mind
Are fuel to its fire:
Thus it deludes
The dweller in the body,
Bewildering his judgment.

Therefore, Arjuna, you must first control your senses, then kill this evil thing which obstructs discriminative knowledge and realization of the Atman.

The senses are said to be higher than the sense-objects. The mind is higher than the senses. The intelligent will is higher than the mind. What is higher than the intelligent will? The Atman Itself.

You must know Him who is above the intelligent will. Get control of the mind through spiritual discrimination. Then destroy your elusive enemy, who wears the form of lust.

4: RENUNCIATION THROUGH KNOWLEDGE

And Krishna continued:

What is action? What is inaction? Even the wise are puzzled by this question. Therefore, I will tell you what action is. When you know that, you will be free from all impurity. You must learn what kind of work to do, what kind of work to avoid, and how to reach a state of calm detachment from your work. The real nature of action is hard to understand.

He who sees the inaction that is in action, and the action that is in inaction, is wise indeed. Even when he is

engaged in action he remains poised in the tranquillity of the
Atman.

> The seers say truly
> That he is wise
> Who acts without lust or scheming
> For the fruit of the act:
> His act falls from him,
> Its chain is broken,
> Melted in the flame of my knowledge.
> Turning his face from the fruit,
> He needs nothing:
> The Atman is enough.
> He acts, and is beyond action.
>
> Not hoping, not lusting,
> Bridling body and mind,
> He calls nothing his own:
> He acts, and earns no evil.
>
> What God's Will gives
> He takes, and is contented.
> Pain follows pleasure,
> He is not troubled:
> Gain follows loss,
> He is indifferent:
> Of whom should he be jealous?
> He acts, and is not bound by his action.

5: THE YOGA OF RENUNCIATION

Now Arjuna said:
You speak so highly of the renunciation of action; yet you ask me
to follow the yoga of action. Now tell me definitely: which of these is
better?

And Krishna answered:
> Action rightly renounced brings freedom:
> Action rightly performed brings freedom:

Both are better
Than mere shunning of action.

When a man lacks lust and hatred,
His renunciation does not waver.
He neither longs for one thing
Nor loathes its opposite:
The chains of his delusion
Are soon cast off.

The yoga of action, say the ignorant,
Is different from the yoga of the knowledge of
        Brahman.

The wise see knowledge and action as one:
They see truly.
Take either path
And thread it to the end:
The end is the same.
There the followers of action
Meet the seekers after knowledge
In equal freedom.

It is hard to renounce action
Without following the yoga of action.
This yoga purifies
The man of meditation,
Bringing him soon to Brahman. . . .

6: THE YOGA OF MEDITATION

And Krishna continued:

He who does the task
Dictated by duty,
Caring nothing
For fruit of the action,
He is a yogi,
A true monk.

But he who follows
His vow to the letter
By mere refraining:
Lighting no fire
At the ritual offering,
Making excuse
For avoidance of labor,
He is no yogi,
No true monk.

For you must understand that what has been called yoga is really renunciation; since nobody can practice the yoga of action who is anxious about his future, or the results of his actions. . . .

The Yogi should retire into a solitary place, and live alone. He must exercise control over his mind and body. He must free himself from the hopes and possessions of this world. He should meditate on the Atman unceasingly.

The place where he sits should be firm, neither too high nor too low, and situated in a clean spot. He should first cover it with sacred grass, then with a deer skin; then lay

a cloth over these.[9] As he sits there, he is to hold the senses and imagination in check, and keep the mind concentrated upon its object. If he practices meditation in this manner, his heart will become pure.

[9] The choice of materials is traditional, but not important for the spiritual aspirant of today. Any convenient seat will do.

His posture must be motionless, with the body, head and neck held erect, and the vision indrawn, as if gazing at the tip of the nose. He must not look about him.

> So, with his heart serene and fearless,
> Firm in the vow of renunciation,
> Holding the mind from its restless roaming,
> Now let him struggle to reach my oneness,
> Ever-absorbed, his eyes on me always,
> His prize, his purpose.

If a yogi has perfect control over his mind, and struggles continually in this way to unite himself with Brahman, he will come at last to the crowning peace of Nirvana, the peace that is in me.

Yoga is not for the man who overeats, or for him who fasts excessively. It is not for him who sleeps too much, or for the keeper of exaggerated vigils. Let a man be moderate in his eating and his recreation, moderately active, moderate in sleep and in wakefulness. He will find that yoga takes away all his unhappiness.

When can a man be said to have achieved union with Brahman? When his mind is under perfect control and freed from all desires, so that he becomes absorbed in the Atman, and nothing else. "The light of a lamp does not flicker in a windless place": that is the simile which describes a yogi of one-pointed mind, who meditates upon the Atman. When, through the practice of yoga, the mind ceases its restless movements, and becomes still, he realizes the Atman. . . .

Then Arjuna said:

Krishna, you describe this yoga as a life of union with Brahman. But I do not see how this can be permanent. The mind is so very restless. . . .

And Krishna answered:

Yes, Arjuna, the mind is restless, no doubt, and hard to subdue. But it can be brought under control by constant practice, and by the exercise of dispassion. Certainly, if a man has no control over his ego, he will find this yoga difficult to master. But a self-controlled man can master it, if he struggles hard, and uses the right means.

Then Arjuna said:

Suppose a man has faith, but does not struggle hard enough? His mind wanders away from the practice of yoga and he fails to reach perfection. What will become of him then?

When a man goes astray from the path to Brahman, he has missed both lives, the worldly and the spiritual. He has no support anywhere. Is he not lost, as a broken cloud is lost in the sky?

This is the doubt that troubles me, Krishna; and only you can altogether remove it from my mind. Let me hear your answer.

And Krishna answered:

No, my son. That man is not lost, either in this world or the next. No one who seeks Brahman ever comes to an evil end.

Even if a man falls away from the practice of yoga, he will still win the heaven of the doers of good deeds, and dwell there many long years. After that, he will be reborn into the home of pure and prosperous parents. He may even be born into a family of illumined yogis. But such a birth in this world is more difficult to obtain.

He will then regain that spiritual discernment which he acquired in his former body; and so he will strive harder than ever for perfection. Because of his practices in the previous life, he will be driven on toward union with Brahman, even in spite of himself. For the man who has once asked the way to Brahman goes further than any mere fulfiller of the Vedic rituals. By struggling hard, and cleansing himself of all impurities, that yogi will move gradually toward perfection through many births, and reach the highest goal at last.

7: KNOWLEDGE AND EXPERIENCE

And Krishna continued:

Devote your whole mind to me, and practice yoga. Take me for your only refuge. I will tell you how, by doing this, you can know me in my total reality, without any shadow of doubt. I will give you all this knowledge, and direct spiritual experience, besides. When a man has that, nothing else in this world remains to be known.

> Who cares to seek
> For that perfect freedom?
> One man, perhaps,

In many thousands.
Then tell me how many
Of those who find freedom
Shall know the total
Truth of my being?
Perhaps one only. . . .

8: THE WAY TO ETERNAL BRAHMAN

Then Arjuna asked:
Tell me, Krishna, what Brahman is. What is the Atman, and what is the creative energy of Brahman? Explain the nature of this relative world, and of the individual man.

Who is God who presides over action in this body, and how does He dwell here? How are you revealed at the hour of death to those whose consciousness is united with you?

And Krishna answered:
Brahman is that which is immutable, and independent of any cause but Itself. When we consider Brahman as lodged within the individual being, we call Him the Atman. The creative energy of Brahman is that which causes all existences to come into being.

The nature of the relative world is mutability. The nature of the individual man is his consciousness of ego. I alone am God who presides over action, here in this body.

At the hour of death, when a man leaves his body, he must depart with his consciousness absorbed in me. Then he will be united with me. Be certain of that. Whatever a man remembers at the last, when he is leaving the body, will be realized by him in the hereafter; because that will be what his mind has most constantly dwelt on, during this life.

Therefore you must remember me at all times, and do your duty. If your mind and heart are set upon me constantly, you will come to me. Never doubt this.

Make a habit of practicing meditation, and do not let your mind be distracted. In this way you will come finally to the Lord, who is the light-giver, the highest of the high.

> He is all-knowing God, lord of the emperors,
> Ageless, subtler far than mind's inmost subtlety,
> Universal sustainer,
> Shining sunlike, self-luminous.

> What fashion His form has, who shall conceive of it?
> He dwells beyond delusion, the dark of Maya.
> On Him let man meditate
> Always, for then at the last hour . . .

Great souls who find me have found the highest perfection. They are no longer reborn into this condition of transience and pain. . . .

The scriptures declare that merit can be acquired by studying the Vedas, performing ritualistic sacrifices, practicing austerities and giving alms. But the yogi who has understood this teaching of mine will gain more than any who do these things. He will reach that universal source, which is the uttermost abode of God.

9: THE YOGA OF MYSTICISM

And Krishna continued:

> Since you accept me
> And do not question,
> Now I shall tell you
> That innermost secret:
> Knowledge of God
> Which is nearer than knowing,
> Open vision
> Direct and instant.

Understand this
And be free forever
From birth and dying
With all their evil.

This is the knowledge
Above all other:
Purifier
And king of secrets,
Only made plain
To the eye of the mystic. . . .

This entire universe is pervaded by me, in that eternal form of mine which is not manifest to the senses. Although I am not within any creature, all creatures exist within me. I do not mean that they exist within me physically. That is my divine mystery. You must try to understand its nature. My Being sustains all creatures and brings them to birth, but has no physical contact with them.

For, as the vast air, wandering worldwide,
Remains within the ether always,
So these, my wandering creatures,
Are always within me. . . .

Fools pass blindly by the place of my dwelling
Here in the human form, and of my majesty
They know nothing at all,
Who am the Lord, their soul.

Vain is their hope, and in vain their labor, their
    knowledge:
All their understanding is but bewilderment;
Their nature has fallen into the madness
Of the fiends and monsters. . . .

10: DIVINE GLORY

And after Krishna spoke further in this manner, Arjuna declared:
You are Brahman, the highest abode, the utterly holy. . . .

Therefore teach me now, and hold back no word in the telling,
All the sum of your shapes by which the three worlds are pervaded;
Tell me how you will make yourself known to my meditation;
Show me beneath what form and disguise I must learn to behold you;
Number them all, your heavenly powers, your manifestations:
Speak, for each word is immortal nectar; I never grow weary.

And Krishna answered:
O Arjuna, I will indeed make known to you my divine manifestations: but I shall name the chief of these, only. For, of the lesser variations in all their details, there is no end.

I am the Atman that dwells in the heart of every mortal creature: I am the beginning, the life-span, and the end of all. . . .

Whatever in this world is powerful, beautiful or glorious, that you may know to have come forth from a fraction of my power and glory.
But what need have you, Arjuna, to know this huge variety? Know only that I exist, and that one atom of myself sustains the universe.

11: THE VISION OF GOD

And when he had spoken these words, Sri Krishna, Master of all yogis, revealed to Arjuna his transcendent, divine Form, speaking from innumerable mouths, seeing with a myriad eyes, of many marvelous aspects, adorned with countless divine ornaments, brandishing all kinds of heavenly weapons, wearing celestial garlands and the raiment of paradise, anointed with perfumes of heavenly fragrance, full of revelations, resplendent, boundless, of ubiquitous regard.

Suppose a thousand suns should rise together into the sky: such is the glory of the Shape of Infinite God.

Then was Arjuna, that lord of mighty riches, overcome with wonder. His hair stood erect. He bowed low before God in adoration, and clasped his hands, and spoke:

Ah, my God, I see all gods within your body;
Each in his degree, the multitude of creatures;
See Lord Brahma throned upon the lotus;
See all the sages, and the holy serpents.

Universal Form, I see you without limit,
Infinite of arms, eyes, mouths and bellies—
See, and find no end, midst, or beginning.

Crowned with diadems, you wield the mace and discus,
Shining every way—the eyes shrink from your splendor
Brilliant like the sun; like fire, blazing, boundless.

You are all we know, supreme, beyond man's measure,
This world's sure-set plinth and refuge never shaken,
Guardian of eternal law, life's Soul undying.

Birthless, deathless; yours the strength titanic,
Million-armed, the sun and moon your eyeballs,
Fiery-faced, you blast the world to ashes,

Fill the sky's four corners, span the chasm
Sundering heaven from earth. Superb and awful
Is your Form that makes the three worlds tremble. . . .

When I see you, Vishnu, omnipresent,
Shouldering the sky, in hues of rainbow,
With your mouths agape and flame-eyes staring—
All my peace is gone; my heart is troubled.

Now with frightful tusks your mouths are gnashing,
Flaring like the fires of Doomsday morning—
North, south, east and west seem all confounded—
Lord of devas, world's abode, have mercy! . . .

12: THE YOGA OF DEVOTION

And Arjuna continued:
Some worship you with steadfast love. Others worship God the unmanifest and changeless.. Which kind of devotee has the greater understanding of yoga?

Whereupon Krishna answered:
Those whose minds are fixed on me in steadfast love, worshipping me with absolute faith. I consider them to have the greater understanding of yoga. . . .

Quickly I come
To those who offer me
Every action,
Worship me only,
Their dearest delight,
With devotion undaunted.

Because they love me
These are my bondsmen
And I shall save them
From mortal sorrow
And all the waves
Of Life's deathly ocean. . . .

A man should not hate any living creature. Let him be friendly and compassionate to all. He must free himself from the delusion of "I" and "mine." He must accept pleasure and pain with an equal tranquillity. He must be forgiving, ever-contented, self-controlled, united constantly with me in his meditation. His resolve must be unshakable. He must be dedicated to me in intellect and in mind. Such a devotee is dear to me.

He neither molests his fellow men, nor allows himself to become disturbed by the world. He is no longer swayed by joy and envy, anxiety and fear. Therefore he is dear to me.

He is pure, and independent of the body's desire. He is able to deal with the unexpected: prepared for everything, unperturbed by anything. He is neither vain nor anxious about the results of his actions. Such a devotee is dear to me.

He does not desire or rejoice in what is pleasant. He does not dread what is unpleasant, or grieve over it. He remains unmoved by good or evil fortune. Such a devotee is dear to me.

His attitude is the same toward friend and foe. He is indifferent to honor and insult, heat and cold, pleasure and pain. He is free from attachment. He values praise and blame equally. He can control his speech. He is content with whatever he gets. His home is everywhere and nowhere. His mind is fixed upon me, and his heart is full of devotion. He is dear to me.

This true wisdom I have taught will lead you to immortality. The faithful practice it with devotion, taking me for their highest aim. To me they surrender heart and mind. They are exceedingly dear to me. . . .

Thus did Krishna continue, seeking to make clear the most veiled of mysteries. And finally he said:

Now I have taught you that wisdom which is the secret of secrets. Ponder it carefully. Then act as you think best. These are the last words that I shall say to you, the deepest of all truths. I speak for your own good. You are the friend I chose and love.

> Give me your whole heart,
> Love and adore me,
> Worship me always,
> Bow to me only,
> And you shall find me:
> This is my promise
> Who love you dearly.

Lay down all duties
In me, your refuge.
Fear no longer,
For I will save you
From sin and from bondage.

You must never tell this holy truth to anyone who lacks self-control and devotion, or who despises his teacher and mocks at me. But the man who loves me, and teaches my devotees this supreme truth of the Gita, will certainly come to me. No one can do me a higher service than this. No one on earth can be dearer to me.

And if any man meditates upon this sacred discourse of ours, I shall consider that he has worshipped me in spirit. Even if a man simply listens to these words with faith, and does not doubt them, he will be freed from his sins and reach the heaven of the righteous.

Have you listened carefully, Arjuna, to everything I have told you? Have I dispelled the delusions of your ignorance?

Whereupon Arjuna answered:
Yea, by your grace, O Lord, my delusions have been dispelled. My mind stands firm. Its doubts are ended. I will do your bidding.
Om! Peace! Peace! Peace!

THE PURANAS

The PURANAS ("Ancient Lore") are a collection of eighteen books which form a sort of popular encyclopedia of Hindu religion and practice. Their date is uncertain, but they could hardly have been composed before the fourth century A.D. at the very earliest. Everything is to be found in them—theology, history, mythology, ethics, old songs, old wives' tales, crude superstition and high idealism. Their appeal is obviously to the common people, to those unable to comprehend—let alone accept—the philosophical teachings expounded in the classic Vedic documents. Many gods are extolled, especially Brahma, Vishnu, and Siva, and great value is attached to the offering of sacrifices and the making of pilgrimages. The basic aim appears to be to smooth the path of religion for the ordinary man and woman, to make mere rites the price of salvation. At the same time, however, these writings do not ignore the importance of common righteousness and decency. Good deeds, they insist, will raise a soul to heaven as surely as wicked ones will plunge it into a variety of hells. Though hardly among the most exalted of the world's sacred writings, the PURANAS rank well enough among those that have attained the widest devotion.

The following passages are typical of the ethical elements in two of the best-known PURANAS.[10]

I

WHAT DOTH THE LORD REQUIRE?

He who does not vilify another either in his presence, or in his absence, who does not speak untruth, does not injure others, pleases Vishnu the best. He is best pleased with him who does not covet another's wife, wealth, and who does not bear ill feeling towards any. Vishnu is pleased with him who neither beats nor slays any animate or inanimate thing. . . . He is always satisfied with him who is ever

[10] These excerpts are from *The Vishnu Purana*, as translated by H. H. Wilson and edited by M. N. Dutt (Calcutta, 1894).

anxious for the welfare of all creatures, his children and his own soul. Vishnu is always pleased with that pure-minded man whose mind is not sullied with anger and other passions. He best worships Vishnu who observes the duties laid down by scripture for every caste and condition of life; there is no other mode. . . .

THE DUTIES OF THE CASTES

The Brahmana *(member of priestly caste)* must advance the well-being of all and do injury to none—for the greatest wealth of a Brahmana consists in cherishing kind feelings towards all. He must consider with an equal eye the jewel and stone belonging to another. He should at proper seasons beget offspring with his wife.

The duties of the Kshatriya *(member of warrior caste)* consist in making gifts to the Brahmanas at pleasure, in worshipping Vishnu with various sacrifices and receiving instructions from the preceptor. His principal sources of maintenance are arms and protection of the earth. But his greatest duty consists in guarding the earth. By protecting the earth a king attains his objects, for he gets a share of the merit of all sacrifices. If a king, by maintaining the order of caste, represses the wicked, supports the pious, he proceeds to whatever region he desires.

The Father of Creation has assigned to the Vaisyas *(members of the merchant caste)*, for their maintenance, the feeding of the cattle, commerce, and agriculture. Study, sacrifice, and gift are also within the duties of the Vaisyas: besides these, they may also observe the other fixed and occasional rites.

The Sudra (*member of servant caste*) must maintain himself by attending upon the three higher castes, or by the profits of trade, or the earnings of mechanical labour. He may also make gifts, offer the sacrifices in which food is presented, and he may also make obsequial offerings.

Besides these, the four castes have their other duties, namely—the acquisition of wealth for the support of servants, cohabitation with their wives for the sake of children, kindness towards all creatures, patience, humility, truth, purity, contentment, decorum of manners, gentleness of speech, friendliness, freedom from envy or avarice and the habit of vilifying. These also constitute the duties of every condition of life.

In cases of emergency a Brahmana may follow the occupations of a Kshatriya or Vaisya; the Kshatriya may adopt those of Vaisya and Vaisya those of Kshatriya: but the last two should never adopt the functions of the Sudra if they can avoid them.

THE DUTIES OF ALL HOUSEHOLDERS

As soon as a son is born his father should perform the ceremonies consequent upon the birth of a child and all other initiatory ceremonies. . . .

Upon the tenth day after birth the father should give a name to the child, the first term of which shall be the name of a god and the second of a man. . . . A name should not be devoid of any meaning, should not be indecent, absurd, inauspicious, or dreadful. It should contain an even number of syllables; it should not be too long nor too short, nor too full of long vowels, but contain a due proportion of short vowels and be easily articulated.

After going through these initiatory ceremonies and being purified the youth should acquire knowledge from his preceptor. And having acquired knowledge from the preceptor and given him presents, he should, desirous of entering the order of householders, marry. . . .

He must not marry a girl who is vicious or unhealthy, born of a low family, or suffering from any disease; one who may have been badly trained, one who talks improperly, one who has inherited some disease from father or mother; one who has a beard and has got a masculine appearance. . . . one who has dimples in her cheeks when laughing. The learned should not marry a girl who has not got a tender countenance. . . . The wise and prudent should not marry one whose hands and legs are heavy, who is a dwarf or who is very tall. . . .

Having bathed and . . . having recited introductory prayers, offered oblations with fire, food to guests, to Brahmanas, to his elders and to his family, the householder should take his meal, wearing unsullied cloth, excellent garlands, and sprinkled with perfumes. He must not eat with a single garment on, nor with wet hands and feet. . . .

With a smiling countenance, happy and attentive, let him take good and wholesome food boiled with clean water, procured from no mean person, nor by improper means, nor improperly cooked. Having given a part to his hungry companions he should take food without reproach from a clean, handsome vessel which must not be placed upon a low stool or bed.

He must not take his food in an unbecoming place or out of season or in an unsuitable mood, giving the first morsel to fire. . . .

After he has taken his food, he should, facing the east or the north, rinse his mouth, and having washed his hands up to the wrist, he should again sip water. . . .

He who but for illness lies in bed at the hours of sunrise and sunset is guilty of iniquity. Therefore a man should rise before the sun in the morning and sleep not until after it has set. . . .

The householder, as his means allow, should show hospitality to any guest who may come, receiving him with the salutation of evening, and offering him water to wash his feet, a seat, a supper and a bed. The sin consequent upon not receiving hospitably a guest who comes after sunset is eight times greater than that of turning away one who comes during the day. A person should therefore particularly show respect to him who seeks refuge after sunset, for the respect, given to his satisfaction, will afford pleasure to all the celestials. The householder should, therefore, as his means permit him, give a guest food, potherbs, water, a bed, a mat, or if he cannot give anything more, ground only on which to lie.

Having taken his evening meal and washed his feet, a householder should take rest. His bed must be complete and made of wood, it must have ample space, must not be cracked nor uneven, nor dirty nor infested by insects, and must have a bedding. The householder must sleep with his head either to the east or to the south; any other position is unhealthy.

In proper time, under the influence of an auspicious planet and in an auspicious moment, he should go to his wife if she is not unbathed, sick, unwell, unwilling, angry, pregnant, hungry or over-fed. He should also be free from all these imperfections and should be neatly dressed and adorned and excited by tenderness and affection. Having bathed, wearing garlands, using perfumes, delighted and animated by desire, he should go to his wife—not being hungry and excited with anxiety. There are certain days on which the use of unguents, flesh and women is prohibited, as the eighth and fourteenth lunar days, new-moon and full-moon and the entrance of the sun into a new sign. On these occasions the wise should control their appetites and engage in the worship of the celestials as laid down in scripture, in meditation and prayer. And he who acts otherwise will be doomed to a hell where he will be constrained to live upon ordure. A man should not excite his desires by medicines nor satisfy them with unnatural objects or in public or holy places. A man should not go to a woman under a huge tree, in the courtyard, in a place of pilgrimage, in pasturage, where four streets meet, in a cremation ground, in a garden or in the waters. On all these occasions mentioned before, in the morning or in the evening, or being unclean, the wise should not cohabit with women. . . . A man should not think voluptuously of another's wife, nor should he speak to her for that purpose; for such a wight will be born in his next life as a creeping insect. The cohabitation with another's wife is a source of fear to him both in this life and in the next—for in this he loses his longevity and in the next he is doomed to hell. Considering all these things a man should approach his own wife in proper season or even at other times.

The householder should . . . not misappropriate another's property nor should he treat him unkindly. He should always speak amiably and the truth, and should not speak out publicly another's faults.

A man should not . . . (when in the company of others) clean his teeth, nor blow his nose nor gape without covering his mouth, nor clear his throat, nor cough, nor laugh loudly, nor emit wind with noise, nor bite his nail . . . nor put his beard into his mouth, nor crumble a clod of clay, nor look upon the planets when he is unclean.

He should not see another's wife when she is naked nor see the sun at the time of its rising or setting. He should not express disgust at a dead body, for the odour of it is the produce of the moon. . . .

He who, having controlled himself, puts a stop to the sources of all these imperfections, meets with no obstacle in the acquisition of piety, wealth and desire. Final emancipation is in his grasp who is sinless towards them who commit mischief by him, who speaks amicably to them who use harsh words and whose soul melts with benevolence. The earth is upheld by the truthfulness of those who have controlled their passions, and who, always following pious observances, are not sullied by desire, covetousness and anger. A prudent man should always cultivate that in act, thought and speech, which conduces to the well-being of all living creatures both in this world and the next.

PREPARE TO MEET THY MAKER

Death sooner or later is inevitable. As long as man lives he is immersed in manifold afflictions, like the seed of the cotton amidst the down that is to be spun into thread. In acquiring, losing, and preserving wealth there are many griefs; and so there are in the misfortunes of our friends. Whatever is produced that is most acceptable to man; that, Maitreya, becomes a seed whence springs the tree of sorrow. Wife, children, servants, houses, lands, riches, contribute much more to the misery than to the happiness of mankind. Where could man, scorched by fires of the sun of this world, look for felicity, were it not for the shade afforded by the tree of emancipation? Attainment of the divine being is considered by the wise as the remedy of the threefold class of ills that beset the different stages of life, conception, birth and decay, as characterized by that only happiness which effaces all other kinds of felicity however abundant, and as being absolute and final.

It should therefore be the assiduous endeavour of wise men to attain unto God. He dwelleth eternally in all beings and all things dwell in him; and thence the Lord Vasudeva is the creator and preserver of the world. He, though identical with all beings, is beyond and separate from material nature, from its products, from properties and from imperfections; he is beyond all investing substance; he is universal soul; all the interstices of the universe are filled up by him; he is one with all good qualities; and all created beings are endowed with but a small portion of his individuality. Assuming various shapes, he bestows benefits on the whole world, which was his work. Glory, might, dominion, wisdom, energy, power and other attributes are collected in him. Supreme of the supreme, in whom no imperfections abide, lord over finite and infinite, god in individuals and universals, visible and invisible, omnipotent, omnipresent, omniscient, almighty. The wisdom, perfect, pure, supreme, undefiled and one only by which he is conceived, contemplated and known, that is wisdom; all else is ignorance.

II [11]

WISE COUNSEL

Double-tongued are the snakes and the malicious; their cruel mouths are the source of many an evil to man. Avoid the company of an erudite miscreant: is not the serpent that bears a gem on its hood doubly dangerous for the stone? Who is he that dreadeth not the malicious who work mischief without any provocation and who are but the serpents in human form? Words of spite drop down from the mouths of the malicious; the fangs of serpents secrete deadly venom.

Sit in the assembly of the honest; combine with those that are good and virtuous; nay, seek out a noble enemy where enmity cannot be helped and have nothing to do with the wicked and the unrighteous. Even in bondage thou shalt live with the virtuous, the erudite and the truthful; but not for a kingdom shalt thou stay with the wicked and the malicious.

The vile are ever prone to detect the faults of others, though they be as small as mustard seeds, and persistently shut their eyes against their own, though they be as large as Vilva fruits. I come to the conclusion, after much deliberation, that pleasure exists not where desire or affection has room to be. True happiness lies in the extinction of all emotions. Apprehension is where affection is. Where there is affection there is misery. Pain has its root in love or affection. Renounce affection and you shall be happy. This human body is a theatre of pleasure and pain, and they come into being with the self of a man.

[11] These excerpts are from *The Garuda Puranam*, ed. by M. N. Dutt (Calcutta, 1908).

Dependence or bondage is misery. Liberty or emancipation is the only happiness vouchsafed to man.

Nobody is any one's friend. Nobody is any one's enemy. Friendship and enmity are bound to each other by a distinct chain of cause and effect (self-interest). A source of solace in grief, a succour in distress, and a repository of happiness and confidence: O who has created the two letters "Mitram" (friend), which are more precious than a mine of gems! By the single utterance of the two letters "Hari" a fettered self makes a step towards emancipation. A man does not repose so much confidence in his sons, wives and brothers as he implicitly places in his own natural friend. Gamble not and make no pecuniary transactions with a man, nor see his wife in his absence; these three being the essentials of a permanent amity.

Never stay in a lonely place with your own daughters, sisters or stepmothers. The field of lust takes advantage of solitude and pleads evil counsel to the heart to which the learned have been known to yield. How absurd is the love god in his frolics! A man naturally shuns a woman who loves him and is easily available to him, and covets one whose touch is the forfeit of life. Easier it is to determine the velocity of a horse or of a storm, or even the depth of an unfathomable ocean; but how puerile is the attempt at sounding a heart that loves not. It is the absence of a nook of vantage, or the want of leisure or of a person making love-overtures to her, that mainly accounts for the chastity of a woman. It is only rarely when a couple is fondly attached to each other that the wife is true at heart. A son should not think, out of a sense of decorum, what is done by his mother in a passion of love.

A courtesan is a dependant even in respect of her sleep, the sole aim of her life being to regale the hearts of her visitors as long as they can decently bear their wine. She is a sort of perpetual smiling machine, being obliged to hammer out a horse-laugh, even with the weight of a life-long grief, misery and futility lying heavy on her heart. Her person is sold to others for money, while she often meets a violent death. Fire, water, a king, a woman, a fool, or a serpent used or provoked by another, should be regarded as fatal. What wonder is it that a man well-versed in letters will pass as an erudite one? What is surprising in the fact that a king who is learned in the science of politics will rule justly as a virtuous prince? What is there to wonder, if a young and beautiful woman, proud and conscious of her charms, leads a gay and fast life? What is there to surprise, if an indigent person commits a crime? Let not your neighbour know of your weakness, but rather observe his weak points unseen, like a turtle, from your own housetop. Amorous fancies spontaneously occur even in the mind of a girl who has been incarcerated from her infancy in a moated castle in the nether worlds. Who can pretend to conquer a woman?

How can I believe a rich man to be an anchorite, and a drunken woman chaste? Trust not the untrustworthy nor confide any secret in your friend, lest he might betray you in a fit of anger. A vast, deep and childlike faith in all, a universal clemency, and a close and watchful veiling of his own god-like inherent virtues, are the traits which mark a noble soul.

What wise man will believe in a woman, in a serpent, in a king, in the services done by his own enemy, in the infallible nature of his own knowledge and memory and in the enjoyment of the worldly pleasures, even for once in life? Trust not those who are unworthy of credence. Do not repose unbounded faith even in the trustworthy, lest they might bring about your ruin and overthrow by betraying it.

He who rests confident after having made a reconciliation with his enemy, is sure to a fall one day like a man who peacefully reposes on a tree-top. Be not too mild nor too fierce, but subdue a mild enemy with a mild means and a fierce one with fierce measures. Be not too straight nor too crooked. Crooked trees are left standing while the straight ones are felled by a forester. Trees that are laden with fruits are bent under their burden, a heavy rain-cloud seems to touch the ground with the weight of its charge; but a fool and a dry wood break under pressure but know no bending. Pleasure and pain come and go without asking. Men, like cats, are ever ready to pounce upon happiness. Many a happiness walks before and after a virtuous man, the contrary being the case with the iniquitous. A counsel heard by six ears (discussed among three men) is soon divulged; heard by four it is kept secret for a while. He who keeps his own counsel baffles the scrutiny of the god Brahma.

IN PRAISE OF LEARNING

The parents of a child are but his enemies when they fail to educate him properly in his boyhood. An illiterate boy, like a heron amidst swans, cannot shine in the assembly of the learned. Learning imparts a heightened charm to a homely face. Knowledge is the best treasure that a man can secretly hoard up in life. Learning is the revered of the revered. Knowledge makes a man honest, virtuous and endearing to the society. It is learning alone that enables a man to better the condition of his friends and relations. Knowledge is the holiest of the holies, the god of the gods, and commands the respect of crowned heads; shorn of it a man is but an animal. The fixtures and furniture of one's house may be stolen by thieves; but knowledge, the highest treasure, is above all stealing.

THE SCRIPTURES OF BUDDHISM

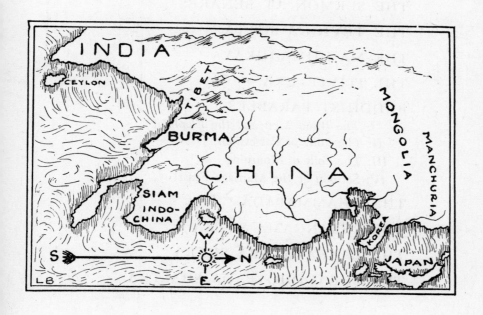

INTRODUCTION

Of the eight major living religions, four—Buddhism, Confucianism, Taoism, and Zoroastrianism—originated during the same century, the sixth B.C. Of these, Buddhism remains to this day the most virile and most widespread. It can claim about a hundred and fifty million adherents massed in the Far East, and numerous converts scattered everywhere else—notably in California.

Buddhism began as a Hindu sect founded by a certain Siddharta Gotama (born circa *560 B.C.) who became known as the Buddha, "Enlightened One." He is said to have been the son of a petty ruler in the Himalayan foothills, a rich and spoiled young man who suddenly abandoned wife and child and all the luxuries of his estate in order to become a* bhikku, *a "wanderer." There were many such "wanderers" in India at the time, sensitive creatures revolted by the vanities of the world who sought peace for their souls in mortification of the flesh. Gotama consorted with them for several years, drifting from one hermit haunt to another, but finally became convinced their life was no less vain than that of ordinary men. Whereupon, going off all alone, he meditated hard and daringly, until all at once a light dawned on him, and he saw a way to be truly saved. Thenceforth for forty-five years he went up and down the land telling about this Way, and urging his fellowmen to pursue it.*

His teaching, in essence, was as follows. To be saved, he said, one must neither afflict nor indulge the flesh, for both these extremes were "low, vulgar, ignoble, and profitless." Life for the ascetic was no less wretched than for the libertine because in either case there was subservience to emotions and bondage to passions. But all emotions and passions were inherently fraudulent, since their source was earthly existence, and that itself was a sheer delusion. The really real existence was on another plane altogether, that of Nirvana, where there was no sensory feeling whatsoever, no pain, no fear, no love, no hate, no anything save the peace of wantlessness and the bliss of utter rest. Nirvana was not a heaven to be entered after death through the intervention of priests and the generosity of gods. It could be attained even while one was still alive, and solely through one's own efforts. All one had to do was practice kindness, fortitude, and selflessness, put away impatience, wrath, and avarice, concentrate on the lasting values, cleave to the eternal truths. In short, one needed merely to follow the Noble Eightfold Path of the Right Views, Right Aspirations, Right Speech, Right Conduct, Right Occupation, Right Effort, Right Thought and Right Contemplation. This, however, was far from easy, and Buddha therefore insisted that whoever would enter Nirvana ought first to withdraw from the world and become a monk. He organized a brotherhood of such monks, and it was through them that his sayings were preserved, and eventually spread all over the world.

Buddhism remained one of many dissident sects in India until the third century B.C., when an energetic monarch named Asoka saw its worth and made it the state religion. By that time, however, it had already acquired two distinct forms, and though Asoka adopted the more primitive of them, the one called Hinayana, it was the other, the Mahayana, which eventually made the greater stir in the world. Each produced its own scriptures, and these have come down to us in three languages: Pali, Sanskrit, and Chinese.

The books written in Pali, which was Buddha's mother-tongue, are clearly the oldest and presumably the most authentic. Buddha himself, of course, did not write them—like so many ancient Masters, he taught solely by word of mouth—and they present at most a record of what later generations believed he did and said. In spite of this, however, they probably contain much that is historically valid.

The Pali books were formally canonized at the behest of King Asoka, and they are the only ones accepted by the Buddhists of Ceylon, Burma, and Siam, where the religion survives in the Hinayana form. This canon consists of three collections of texts and is therefore called the TI-PITAKA, "Three Baskets." (In a crude way the division is comparable to that of the Jewish canon into the "Law," the "Prophets," and the "Writings.") The first, the "Basket of Discipline," deals mostly with the duties incumbent on the Buddhist monks and nuns. The second, the "Basket of Doctrine," contains the sermons, proverbs, parables, and poems expounding Buddha's beliefs. The third, the "Basket of Higher Learning," delves into the abstruse philosophy which rapidly grew up around the whole religion.

Less ancient than the Pali scriptures, and also more variegated, are the books written originally in Sanskrit or Chinese. These reflect the many new influences exerted on the religion in the course of its spread across the face of the Far East and form what might inexactly be termed the Mahayana canon.

In the Pali scriptures, Buddha is still altogether human, and his gospel is primarily ethical. It teaches a way of salvation which is as severe as it is cogent: a man must flee the world, forswear the flesh, and devote himself solely to contemplation of that which is eternal. He must become an arhat, a saint, allowing the machinery of life to wear itself out in him, so that finally he can sigh, "I have nothing more to do, and nevermore need I be reborn." Thus alone can he attain the final Nirvana, that supernal blessedness which is Infinite Nothingness.

But in the Sanskrit scriptures, Buddha is already divine, and his gospel is primarily a way of worship. They insist that one need not become a monk in order to be saved. Even a layman, if he will but pray long and ardently enough, can enter Nirvana, for prayer is pleasing to Buddha, and Nirvana is the heavenly realm to which he gathers all who have properly pleased him. Here, therefore, is a real theology rather than an ethical system, and its emergence explains why Buddhism, in the Mahayana form, was able to sweep most of the Far East. All the old gods could be taken over by this new religion—they were merely called earlier manifestations of Buddha—and all the old myths, superstitions, spells, and rites.

It would be a gross error, however, to consider Mahayana Buddhism nothing but a crude, polytheistic, ritualized perversion of the more primitive faith. In certain respects it was actually an improvement over the Hinayana form, for it was less nihilistic, less misanthropic, more worldly, practicable, and humane.

Both canons are represented in the following selections.

THE LAKHANA SUTTANTA

Here is a typical sutta, *"saying," which may well have been uttered by Buddha himself. Like all teachers in a day when writing materials were exceedingly scarce, and knowledge had to be imparted orally, he must have made constant use of formulae which could be readily memorized by his disciples. This passage is to be found in the* Lakhana Suttanta, *one of the longer lectures in the "Basket of Doctrine."* [1]

The brother . . . in whom the intoxicants are destroyed, who has lived the life, who has done his task, who has laid low his burden, who has attained salvation, who has utterly destroyed the fetter of rebirth, who is emancipated by the true gnosis, he is incapable of perpetrating nine things:

1. He is incapable of deliberately depriving a living creature of life.

2. He is incapable of taking what is not given so that it constitutes theft.

3. He is incapable of sexual impurity.

4. He is incapable of deliberately telling lies.

5. He is incapable of laying up treasure for indulgence in worldly pleasure as he used to do in the life of the house.

6. He is incapable of taking a wrong course through partiality.

7. He is incapable of taking a wrong course through hate.

8. He is incapable of taking a wrong course through stupidity.

9. He is incapable of taking a wrong course through fear.

[1] Translated by T. W. and C. A. F. Rhys Davids in *The Sacred Books of the Buddhists*, vol. iv (Oxford University Press, 1921).

These nine things the arahant in whom the mental intoxicants are destroyed, who has lived the life, whose task is done, whose burden is laid low, who has attained salvation, who has utterly destroyed the fetter of becoming, who is emancipated by the true gnosis, is incapable of perpetrating.

THE SUTRA OF FORTY-TWO SECTIONS

There are many passages in the Buddhist scriptures which might be described as "Christian"—except that they were written centuries before Jesus was born. Here is one taken from the Sutra of Forty-two Sections, *a work held in such high esteem that it was among the first to be translated by the Buddhist missionaries in foreign lands. It is known to have been translated into Chinese as early as 67 A.D.*[2]

And the Blessed One observed the ways of society and noticed how much misery came from malignity and foolish offences done only to gratify vanity and self-seeking pride.

And the Buddha said: "If a man foolishly does me wrong, I will return to him the protection of my ungrudging love; the more evil comes from him, the more good shall go from me; the fragrance of goodness always comes to me, and the harmful air of evil goes to him."

A foolish man, learning that the Buddha observed the principle of great love which commends the return of good for evil, came and abused him. The Buddha was silent, pitying his folly.

When the man had finished his abuse, the Buddha asked him, saying: "Son, if a man declined to accept a present made to him, to whom would it belong?" And he answered: "In that case it would belong to the man who offered it."

"My son," said the Buddha, "thou hast railed at me, but I decline

[2] Translation by Paul Carus in his *Gospel of Buddha* (Open Court, La Salle, Ill., 1917).

to accept thy abuse, and request thee to keep it thyself. Will it not be a source of misery to thee? As the echo belongs to the sound, and the shadow to the substance, so misery will overtake the evil-doer without fail."

The abuser made no reply, and Buddha continued:

"A wicked man who reproaches a virtuous one is like one who looks up and spits at heaven; the spittle soils not the heaven, but comes back and defiles his own person.

"The slanderer is like one who flings dust at another when the wind is contrary; the dust does but return on him who threw it. The virtuous man cannot be hurt and the misery that the other would inflict comes back on himself."

The abuser went away ashamed, but he came again and took refuge in the Buddha, the Dharma, and the Sangha.

THE KHAGGAVISANA SUTTA

Here is another sutta *which may date from Buddha's time. According to tradition, it was delivered at the request of his dearest disciple, Ananda, and contains the doctrines taught by some of the lesser "buddhas" who preceded the great Gotama. The document is usually referred to as* Khaggavisana Sutta, *"The Rhinoceros Discourse."* [3]

1. Having abandoned the practising of violence toward all objects, not doing violence to any one of them, let one wish not for children. Why wish for a friend? Let one walk alone like a rhinoceros.

2. There are friendships to one who lives in society; this our present grief arises from having friendships; observing the evils resulting from friendship, let one walk alone like a rhinoceros.

3. He who is kind toward much-beloved friends loses his own good from his mind becoming partial; observing such danger in friendship, let one walk alone like a rhinoceros.

4. As a spreading bush of bamboo is entangled in various ways, so is the longing for children and wives: not clinging to these, even like a bamboo just sprouting forth, let one walk alone like a rhinoceros.

5. As a beast of the forest prowls, free, withersoever he will for pasture, even so let a wise man, observing solitude, walk alone like a rhinoceros.

[3] Reprinted from *The Sacred Books and Early Literature of the East*, vol. x., edited by Prof. Charles F. Horne, Ph.D. (Parke, Austin, and Lipscomb, New York and London, 1917).

6. Whilst resting, standing, going, traveling, leave must be obtained by one living in the midst of friends; let one, observing solitude which is not pleasing to others, walk alone like a rhinoceros.

7. If one lives in the midst of company, love of amusement and desire arise; strong attachment for children arises; let therefore one who dislikes separation, which must happen sooner or later from those beloved, walk alone like a rhinoceros.

8. Whoever is possessed of the four Appamannas,[4] and is not opposed to any person, is contented with whatever he gets, endures sufferings and is fearless, let him walk alone like a rhinoceros.

9. Some there are, also difficult to please, even though they be ascetics; on the other hand, there are also some laymen difficult to propitiate; therefore let one, not minding other men's children, walk alone like a rhinoceros.

10. Let a hero abandoning the ways of the world, and also flinging off the bonds of the household, like a Kovilara-tree, which has cast off its leaves, walk alone like a rhinoceros.

11. If a wise man secures a wise friend who will act in concert with him, being firmly established in good principles, he will live happily with him, overcoming all afflictions.

12. If a wise man secures not a wise friend who will act in concert with him, being firmly established in good principles, let him, like a king who has abandoned the country conquered by him, walk alone like a rhinoceros.

13. Certainly we praise the acquisition of friendship; but good friends should be admitted into one's company; not obtaining such friends, let one, subsisting on pure food, walk alone like a rhinoceros.

14. Noticing how even two glittering armlets of gold, though well made by a goldsmith, strike against each other, let one walk alone like a rhinoceros.

15. Thus, being with a second beside myself, I must either speak too much and be angry with him; observing this danger, for the future, let a man walk alone like a rhinoceros.

16. Desires are indeed various, sweet and pleasing to the mind; they churn the mind in different ways; observing the distress resulting from desires, let one walk alone like a rhinoceros.

17. This body is a calamity, an excrescence, a danger, a disease, a

[4] Friendliness, compassion, good-will, and equanimity.

dart of sorrow, a fear to me; observing this danger resulting from desires, let one walk alone like a rhinoceros.

18. There are cold, heat, hunger, thirst, wind, sun, gadflies, snakes; having overcome all these various things, let a man walk alone like a rhinoceros.

19. As the huge-bodied, white-spotted, noble elephant wanders in the forest, whithersoever he will, deserting his herd, so also let one walk alone like a rhinoceros.

20. The attaining of even temporary Samadhi (meditation) by any one who is attached to society is impossible; such is the teaching of the kinsman of the Sun; let one, having heard this, walk alone like a rhinoceros.

21. Thus overcoming those things which injure faith, having attained firmness of mind, and reached the right path, I have indeed arrived at complete knowledge and have nothing left to be known. Let one walk alone like a rhinoceros.

22. Divested of greediness, deceit, longings, not disparaging others unjustly, in the whole world; released from evil affections and ignorance; desireless, let one walk alone like a rhinoceros.

23. Let one cast away a sinful friend who looks to wicked things, or is established in wicked actions: let the same person associate not with one fond of pleasure, and procrastinating in doing good things. Let him walk alone like a rhinoceros.

24. Let him serve a friend who is very learned, versed in morals, great, and possessed of a quick understanding; having known the real meaning of things, let him remove his doubts and walk alone like a rhinoceros.

25. Indifferent to amusements, lust, and the pleasures of the world; not beautifying oneself, despising ornaments, and speaking the truth, let one walk alone like a rhinoceros.

26. Having abandoned the different kinds of desire, founded on child, wife, father, mother, wealth, corn, relations, let one walk alone like a rhinoceros.

27. Let a wise man, having discovered that such is attachment, that there is in it but little happiness, that it is but insipid, that there is more affliction in it than comfort, that it is a fish-hook, walk alone like a rhinoceros.

28. Having cast off the bonds, like a fish which breaks the net in

the water, like a fire that returns not to the spot already burned up, let one walk alone like a rhinoceros.

29. With his eyes looking downward, not moving quickly, with his senses guarded, his mind restrained, not burdened with lust, not burning with desire, let one walk alone like a rhinoceros.

30. Having abandoned the ways of the householder, clothed in yellow robes, like a Parichhatta-tree, which is densely covered with leaves, having given up laymanship, let one walk alone like a rhinoceros.

31. Not being greedy of savory things, not being unsteady, nor maintained by others, begging from house to house without any distinction, not having a mind attached to this or that family, let one walk alone like a rhinoceros.

32. Having cast off the five Nivaranas (evil tendencies) of the mind, having cleared away all the obscurities of the mind, having extinguished the folly of friendship, not allied to anything, let one walk alone like a rhinoceros.

33. Having thrown behind him pleasure and pain, and first doing away with good and bad intentions, having then secured the middle state, which is pacific and pure, let one walk alone like a rhinoceros.

34. Possessed of courage, persevering in the attainment of Param-attha [5] with a mind not inactive, without living in idleness, resolute in perseverance, endowed with a strong and powerful mind, let one walk alone like a rhinoceros.

35. Looking forward to the extinction of desires, being diligent, not foolish, becoming a good ascetic, endowed with presence of mind, acquainted with justice, observing the rules of the hermits, energetic, let one walk alone like a rhinoceros.

36. Not abandoning the Patisallana meditations, practicing the Law daily, remembering the evil consequences of repeated births, let one walk alone like a rhinoceros.

37. Like a lion which fears not noises, unobstructed like the wind whistling through a net, not touching anything like the lotus-leaf untouched by water, let one walk alone like a rhinoceros.

38. As the lion, the king of beasts, powerful from his teeth, lives committing violence and overcoming all, even so let one dwell in hermitages in far-away deserts.

[5] The supreme good.

39. In fit time, observe kindness, impartiality, mercy, freedom from sin, and delight at the prosperity of others: unopposed to the whole world, let one walk alone like a rhinoceros.

40. Having abandoned lust, malice, ignorance, having broken the bonds of transmigration, entertaining no fears for the loss of life, let one walk alone like a rhinoceros.

41. Men associate with and serve others for the sake of an object; friends who have no object in view are difficult to obtain. They are wise enough to gain some object for themselves. Men are not pure. Let one walk alone like a rhinoceros.

THE SERMON AT BENARES

Here is one of the most renowned of all the suttas, the "Discourse on the Foundation of the Kingdom of Righteousness," often called the "Benares Sermon." It is supposed to have been Gotama's first discourse after he became "enlightened," and probably does summarize the faith he sought to promulgate. Tradition has woven a gorgeous tapestry of miracles around the delivery of the sermon. One pious chronicler declares: "So many angels thronged to listen that the heavens were emptied, and the sound of their approach was like the hailing of a storm. . . . The assembled multitude was infinite in number, and each of the countless listeners thought the Blessed One was addressing him alone, and in his own tongue, although the language used was actually Magadhi."

Such tales, however, are almost less astounding than the sermon itself. Here is a scheme of salvation completely devoid of superhuman elements, saying nothing about the soul, or the gods, or the World to Come. It pleads solely for an inward change of heart, and urges nothing but conscientious self-culture and self-discipline. The translator, Professor T. W. Rhys Davids, indulges in no exaggeration when he describes the delivery of this discourse as "a turning-point in the religious history of man."

The text from which the present translation was made is now preserved in the British Museum. It is actually engraved on plates of silver, and each sentence is given twice to prevent the misreading of a single word.[6]

There are two extremes, O brethren,[7] which a holy man should avoid—the habitual practice of . . . self-indulgence, which is vulgar and profitless . . . and the habitual practice of self-mortification, which is painful and equally profitless.

[6] The translation (with slight alterations) is reprinted from *The Sacred Books and Early Literature of the East*, edited by Horne, vol. x (Parke, Austin, and Lipscomb, New York and London, 1917).

[7] The word in the original is *bhikkus*, literally "beggars." It is sometimes translated as "priests" or "monks" or "mendicants," but Buddha's disciples had no sacerdotal powers, took no vows of obedience, and were not in any sense mere vagrants.

There is a middle path, O brethren, discovered by the Tathagata (Buddha)—a path which opens the eyes, and bestows understanding, which leads to peace of mind, to the higher wisdom, to full enlightenment, to Nirvana. Verily! it is this noble eightfold path; that is to say:

> Right views;
> Right aspirations;
> Right speech;
> Right conduct;
> Right livelihood;
> Right effort;
> Right mindfulness; and
> Right contemplation.[8]

This, O brethren, is that middle path, avoiding these two extremes, discovered by the Tathagata—that path which opens the eyes, and bestows understanding, which leads to peace of mind, to the higher wisdom, to full enlightenment, to Nirvana!

Now this, O brethren, is the noble truth concerning suffering.

Birth is attended with pain, decay is painful, disease is painful, death is painful. Union with the unpleasant is painful, painful is separation from the pleasant; and any craving that is unsatisfied, that too is painful. In brief, the five aggregates which spring from attachment (the conditions of individuality and their cause)[9] are painful.

This then, O brethren, is the noble truth concerning suffering.

Now this, O brethren, is the noble truth concerning the origin of suffering.

Verily, it is that thirst (or craving), causing the renewal of existence, accompanied by sensual delight, seeking satisfaction now here,

[8] Professor Davids thus expands the meaning of this Buddhist teaching of the "Noble Path":
1. Right Views; free from superstition or delusion.
2. Right Aims; high, and worthy of the intelligent, earnest man.
3. Right Speech; kindly, open, truthful.
4. Right Conduct; peaceful, honest, pure.
5. Right Livelihood; bringing hurt or danger to no living thing.
6. Right Effort; in self-training, and in self-control.
7. Right Mindfulness; the active, watchful mind.
8. Right Contemplation; earnest thought on the deep mysteries of life.

[9] One might express the central thought of this First Noble Truth in the language of the nineteenth century by saying that pain results from existence as an individual. It is the struggle to maintain one's individuality which produces pain—a most pregnant and far-reaching suggestion.

now there—that is to say, the craving for the gratification of the passions, or the craving for a future life, or the craving for success in this present life.

This then, O brethren, is the noble truth concerning the origin of suffering.

Now this, O brethren, is the noble truth concerning the destruction of suffering.

Verily, it is the destruction, in which no passion remains, of this very thirst; the laying aside of, the getting rid of, the being free from, the harboring no longer of this thirst.

This then, O brethren, is the noble truth concerning the destruction of suffering.

Now this, O brethren, is the noble truth concerning the way which leads to the destruction of sorrow. Verily! it is this noble eightfold path; that is to say:

Right views;
Right aspirations;
Right speech;
Right conduct;
Right livelihood;
Right effort;
Right mindfulness; and
Right contemplation.

This then, O brethren, is the noble truth concerning the destruction of sorrow.

That this was the noble truth concerning sorrow, was not, O brethren, among the doctrines handed down, but there arose within me the eye to perceive it, there arose the knowledge of its nature, there arose the understanding of its cause, there arose the wisdom to guide in the path of tranquillity, there arose the light to dispel darkness from it.

And again, O brethren, that I should comprehend that this was the noble truth concerning sorrow, though it was not among the doctrines handed down, there arose within me the eye, there arose the knowledge, there arose the understanding, there arose the wisdom, there arose the light.

And again, O brethren, that I had comprehended that this was the noble truth concerning sorrow, though it was not among the doctrines handed down, there arose within me the eye, there arose the knowledge, there arose the understanding, there arose the wisdom, there arose the light.

That this was the noble truth concerning the origin of sorrow, though it was not among the doctrines handed down, there arose within me the eye; but there arose within me the knowledge, there arose the understanding, there arose the light.

And again, O brethren, that I should put away the origin of sorrow, though the noble truth concerning it was not among the doctrines handed down, there arose within me the eye, there arose the knowledge, there arose the understanding, there arose the wisdom, there arose the light.

And again, O brethren, that I had fully put away the origin of sorrow, though the noble truth concerning it was not among the doctrines handed down, there arose within me the eye, there arose the knowledge, there arose the understanding, there arose the wisdom, there arose the light.

And again, O brethren, that I should fully realize the destruction of sorrow, though the noble truth concerning it was not among the doctrines handed down, there arose within me the eye, there arose the knowledge, there arose the understanding, there arose the wisdom, there arose the light.

And again, O brethren, that I had fully realized the destruction of sorrow, though the noble truth concerning it was not among the doctrines handed down, there arose within me the eye, there arose the knowledge, there arose the understanding, there arose the wisdom, there arose the light.

That this was the noble truth concerning the way which leads to the destruction of sorrow, was not, O brethren, among the doctrines handed down; but there arose within me the eye, there arose the knowledge, there arose the understanding, there arose the wisdom, there arose the light.

And again, O brethren, that I should become versed in the way which leads to the destruction of sorrow, though the noble truth concerning it was not among the doctrines handed down, there arose within me the eye, there arose the knowledge, there arose the understanding, there arose the wisdom, there arose the light.

And again, O brethren, that I had become versed in the way which leads to the destruction of sorrow, though the noble truth concerning it was not among the doctrines handed down, there arose within me the eye, there arose the knowledge, there arose the understanding, there arose the wisdom, there arose the light.

So long, O brethren, as my knowledge and insight were not quite clear, regarding each of these four noble truths in this triple order, in this twelvefold manner—so long was I uncertain whether I had attained to the full insight of that wisdom which is unsurpassed in the heavens or on earth, among the whole race of Samanas and brahmins, or of gods or men.

But as soon, O brethren, as my knowledge and insight were quite clear regarding each of these four noble truths, in this triple order, in this twelvefold manner—then did I become certain that I had attained to the full insight of that wisdom which is unsurpassed in the heavens or on earth, among the whole race of Samanas and brahmins, or of gods or men.

And now this knowledge and this insight has arisen within me. Immovable is the emancipation of my heart. This is my last existence. There will now be no rebirth for me!

THE TEVIGGA SUTTA

The following, from the Tevigga Sutta, is part of a long dialogue giving Buddha's arguments against the way of salvation taught by the religion he sought to overthrow. In it he explains why the priests of Brahminism can have no real knowledge of the God they worship, and therefore cannot possibly guide men to a union with Him. Buddha maintains that a union with the Infinite can indeed be achieved, but solely through the discipline he calls "Right Conduct." [10]

Then the young brahman, Vasettha, said to the young brahman, Bharadvaga: There is a holy man named Gotama . . . staying in the Mango grove nearby . . . who is of high renown and is even said to be "a fully enlightened One," blessed and worthy, abounding in wisdom and goodness, happy, with knowledge of the world, unsurpassed as a guide to erring mortals, a teacher of gods and men, a blessed Buddha. Come, Bharadvaga, let us go to the place where this Samana Gotama is staying, let us ask him and what he declares let us bear in mind. Very well, assented Bharadvaga.

So these two young brahmans went on to the place where the Blessed One was staying. When they had come there they exchanged with the Blessed One greetings and compliments of friendship and

[10] Translated by T. W. Rhys Davids in *Sacred Books of the East*, vol. xi (Clarendon Press, Oxford, 1900).

civility and sat down beside him. When they were thus seated, one spoke up and said to the Blessed One:

"As we were taking exercise, walking up and down, there sprang up a conversation between us as to which was the true path to union with Brahma. . . . Not being able to agree, we decided to refer the dispute to you. . . . Various Brahmans, Gotama, teach various paths to union with Brahma: Is one true and another false, or are all saving paths? . . . Is it like the different roads going toward a village, all of which meet in the center?"

The Blessed One replied: "Vasettha, do you think that all these various paths lead aright?"

"I think so, Gotama."

"Would you be willing to assert that they all lead aright, Vasettha?"

"So I say, Gotama."

"But then, Vasettha, is there a single one of the Brahmans—or of their teachers, their pupils, or their ancestors back to the seventh generation—who has ever seen Brahma face to face?"

"No, indeed, Gotama." . . .

"Well, then, Vasettha, there are the ancient Rishis (sages) of the Brahmans; whose words are still chanted, uttered, or composed by the Brahmans of today, and did they ever say: 'We know and have seen where Brahma is, whence Brahma came, whither Brahma goes'?"

"Not so, Gotama." . . .

"And yet, Vasettha, these Brahmans pretend that they can show the path to union with that which they have not seen and which they know not, saying: This is the straight path, this is the direct way, which leads him, who acts according to it, into a state of union with Brahma. Now what think you, Vasettha, does it not follow that the talk of these Brahmans, versed though they be in the Three Vedas, is foolish talk?"

"Yes, Gotama, this being so, it follows that the talk of these Brahmans versed in the Three Vedas is indeed foolish talk."

"Vasettha, it is like a string of blind men clinging to one another, the foremost can not see the way, neither can the middle one, nor the hindmost. Just so, methinks, Vasettha, that the talk of the Brahmans versed in the Three Vedas, is but blind talk. The first sees not, the middle one sees not, the hindmost sees not. The talk, then, of these Brahmans turns out to be ridiculous, mere words, vain and empty. It is as if a man should say, 'How I long for, how I love the most beautiful woman in this land!' And people should ask him, 'Well, good friend! this most beautiful woman in the land whom you thus love and long for, do you know . . . her name, or her family name, whether she is tall or short, dark or of medium complexion, black or fair, or in what village or town or city she dwells?' But when so asked, he should answer, 'I do not know.' And when people should say to him, 'So then, good friend, whom you know not, neither have seen, how do you love and long for her?' And then when so asked, he should answer, 'Nevertheless, I love her.' Now what think you, Vasettha? Would it not turn out that the talk of such a man was foolish talk?"

"In sooth, Gotama, it would be so." . . .

"And just even so, Vasettha, the way to union with Brahma which the Brahmans are proclaiming without having seen Brahma or knowing anything about him, is just as foolish. Is it not so?"

"In sooth, Gotama, it is so." . . .

"Again, Vasettha. If this river Akiravati were full of water even to the brim and overflowing, and a man should come up and want to cross over because he had business on the other side, and he standing on this bank should say, Come hither, O further bank! come over to this side! Now what think you, Vasettha, would the further bank of the river, because of the man's invoking and praying and hoping and praising, come over to this side?"

"Certainly not, Gotama." . . .

"Now, Vasettha, when you have been among Brahmans, listening as they talked among themselves, learners and teachers and those aged and well stricken in years, what have you learned from them and of them? Is Brahma in possession of wives and wealth, or is he not?"

"He is not, Gotama."

"Is his mind full of anger, or is it free from anger?"

"Free from anger, Gotama."

"Is his mind full of malice or free from malice?"

"Free from malice, Gotama."

"Is his mind depraved, or pure?"

"It is pure, Gotama."

"Has he self-mastery, or has he not?"

"He has, Gotama."

"Now what think you, Vasettha? Are the Brahmans in possession of wives and wealth, or are they not?"

"They are, Gotama."

"Have they anger in their hearts?"

"They have, Gotama."

"Do they bear malice, or do they not?"

"They do, Gotama."

"Are they pure in heart or are they not?"

"They are not, Gotama."

"Now you say, Vasettha, that the Brahmans are in possession of wives and wealth, and that Brahma is not. Can there be agreement and likeness between the Brahmans with their wives and property and Brahma who has none of these things?"

"Certainly not, Gotama."

"Very good, Vasettha. But verily, that these Brahmans versed in the Three Vedas, who live married and wealthy should, after death when the body is dissolved, become united with Brahma who has none of these things—such a condition of things is impossible. . . . How can there be concord and likeness between Brahmans and Brahma?"

"There can not be, Gotama." . . .

"So, Vasettha, the Brahmans, versed though they be in the Three Vedas, while they rest in confidence, are really sinking. They think they are crossing over into some happier land, but so sinking they can only arrive at despair. Therefore, the threefold knowledge of the Brahmans in the Vedas is a waterless desert, their knowledge a pathless waste, their knowledge their destruction."

Thereupon the young Brahman Vasettha said to the Blessed One: "It has been told me, Gotama, that you know the way to a state of Union with Brahma. Can you teach us?" . . .

"Vasettha, supposing there was a man born in a certain village and who never to this time had left it, and people should ask him the way to this village. Would that man born and brought up there be in any doubt or uncertainty about the way?"

"Certainly not, Gotama. He would be perfectly familiar with every road leading to his native village." . . .

"Even so is it with Tathagata (Buddha), when asked about the path which leads to the world of Brahma, there can be neither doubt nor difficulty. For Brahma, the world of Brahma, the path which leadeth to the world of Brahma, I fully know. Yea, I know it even as one who was born there and lives there. . . .

"Know then, Vasettha, that from time to time a Tathagata is born into the world, a fully Enlightened One, blessed and worthy, abounding in wisdom and goodness, happy with knowledge of the worlds, unsurpassed as a guide to erring mortals, a teacher of gods and men, a Blessed Buddha. He thoroughly understands this universe, as though he saw it face to face. . . . The Truth does he proclaim both in its letter and in its spirit, lovely in its origin, lovely in its progress, lovely in its consummation. A higher life doth he make known in all its purity and in all its perfectness. . . .

"Now, Vasettha, how can a man's conduct be good? Herein, O Vasettha, by putting away all unkindness to sentient beings he abstains from destroying life. He lays aside the cudgel and sword and, full of humility and pity, he is compassionate and kind to all creatures that have life. Putting away the desire for things which are not his, he abstains from taking anything that is not freely given him. He has only what has been given him, therewith is he content, and he passes his life in honesty and in purity of heart. Putting away all thoughts of lust, he lives a life of chastity and purity. Putting away all thoughts of deceiving, he abstains from all prevarications; he speaks truthfully, from the truth he never swerves; faithful and trustworthy, he never injures his fellow men by deceit.

"Putting away all judgment of others, he abstains from slander. What he hears he repeats not elsewhere to raise a quarrel; what he hears elsewhere he repeats not here to raise a quarrel. Thus he brings together those who are divided, he encourages those who are friendly; he is a peacemaker, a lover of peace, impassioned for peace, a speaker of words that make for peace. Putting away all bitter thoughts, he abstains from harsh language. Whatever is humane, pleasant to the ear, kindly, reaching to the heart, urbane, acceptable to the people, appreciated by the people—such are the words he speaks. Putting away all foolish thoughts, he abstains from vain conversation. He speaks in season, he speaks truthfully, consistently, wisely, with restraint. He speaks only when it is appropriate for him to speak, words that are profitable, well sustained, well defined, full of wisdom.

"Besides being kind to all animate life, he refrains from injuring insects or even herbs. He takes but one meal a day; abstaining from food at all other times. He abstains from attending dances, concerts and theatrical shows. He abstains from wearing, using or adorning himself with garlands, scents and ointments, he abstains from large and soft beds. He abstains from accumulating silver or gold, from coveting great harvests, herds of cattle; he abstains from the getting of maids and women attendants, slaves either men or women; he abstains from gathering herds of sheep or goats, fowls or swine, elephants, cattle, horses, and mares. He abstains from the getting of fields and lands.

"He refrains from accepting commissions to carry messages, he refrains from all buying and selling, he abstains from the use of all trade deceptions, false weights, alloyed metals, false measures. He abstains from all bribery, cheating, fraud and crooked ways. He refrains from all banditry, killing or maiming, abducting, highway robbery, plundering villages, or obtaining money by threats of violence. These are the kinds of goodness he practices. . . .

"The true ascetic, he who is seeking the way to the Brahma World, lets his mind pervade all quarters of the world with thoughts of Love; first one quarter then the second quarter, then the third quarter and so the fourth quarter. And thus the whole wide world, above, below, around, and everywhere, does he continue to pervade with thoughts of love, far-reaching, beyond measure, all-embracing.

"Just, Vasettha, as a mighty trumpeter makes himself heard—and that without difficulty—in all four directions; even so of all things that have form or life, there is not one that he passes by or leaves aside; he regards them all with mind set free and filled with deep-felt love. Verily, Vasettha, this is the way to a state of union with Brahma. . . .

"Now what think you, Vasettha, will the ascetic be in possession of women and wealth, or will he not?"

"He will not, Gotama."

"Will he be full of anger, or will he be free from anger?"

"He will be free from anger, Gotama."

"Will his mind be full of malice, or free from malice?"

"Free from malice, Gotama."

"Will his mind be lustful or pure?"

"It will be pure, Gotama."

"Will he have self-mastery or will he not?"

"Surely he will, Gotama."

"Vasettha . . . is there then agreement and likeness between such a one and Brahma?"

"There is, Gotama."

"Very good, Vasettha!" . . .

And when the Blessed One had thus spoken, the two young Brahmans, Vasettha and Bharadvaga, addressed the Blessed One, saying:

"Most excellent, Lord, the words of thy mouth are most excellent! It is just as if a man were to set up what was thrown down, or to reveal that which was hidden away, or were to point out the right road to him who has gone astray, or were to bring a lamp into the darkness so that those who have eyes can see: just even so, Lord, the truth has been made known to us by the Blessed One. And we betake ourselves, Lord, to the Blessed One, to the Truth, and to the Brotherhood, as our refuge. May the Blessed One accept us as disciples, as true believers, from this day forth, as long as life shall last."

THE MAJJHIMA–NIKAYA

Buddha, it would seem, had no patience at all with the metaphysical issues which so exercised India's sages. The classic riddles of ontology, cosmology, and so forth, seemed to him pointless, and all the frantic efforts to solve them completely profitless. His sole concern was with man and man's life here on earth, with "misery and how to get rid of it." The proof is to be seen in this ancient sutta,[11] an extraordinarily illuminating document, and one of the most provocative in all of sacred literature. It is the sixty-third sutta in the Majjhima-Nikaya, *one of the larger collections of discourses in the "Basket of Doctrine."* [12]

Now it occurred to the venerable Malunkyaputta (*a would-be disciple*) that there were many problems which the Blessed One refused to elucidate—for example, whether or not the world is eternal, whether the world is finite or infinite, whether the soul is one thing and the body another, whether the saint does not exist after death, whether the saint both exists and does not exist after death, whether the saint neither exists nor does not exist after death. "These" (*said Malunkyaputta to himself*) "the Blessed One does not elucidate to me, and the fact does not please me. Therefore I will go to the Blessed One and inquire of him. If he will elucidate these problems to me, I shall join his

[11] And also in the one that follows.
[12] Reprinted by permission of the publishers from Henry Clarke Warren: *Buddhism in Translations*, Harvard Oriental Series, No. 3, Cambridge, Mass.: Harvard University Press, 8th Printing, 1922.

order, and if not, then I shall abandon religious training and return
to the lower life of a layman."

So the venerable Malunkyaputta arose at eventide from his seclusion, and drew near to where the Blessed One was; and having drawn
near and greeted the Blessed One, he sat down respectfully at one
side. And seated respectfully at one side, the venerable Malunkyaputta
spoke to the Blessed One as follows:

". . . If the Blessed One knows that the world is eternal, let the
Blessed One elucidate to me that the world is eternal; if the Blessed
One knows that the world is not eternal, let the Blessed One elucidate
to me that the world is not eternal. If the Blessed One does not know
either that the world is eternal or that the world is not eternal, the
only upright thing for one who does not know, or who has not that
insight, is to say, 'I do not know; I have not that insight.' "

(Then the Blessed One replied:) "Pray, Malunkyaputta, did I ever
say to you, 'Come, Malunkyaputta, lead the religious life under me,
and I will elucidate to you (all those matters).

"Nay, verily, Reverend Sir." . . .

"That being the case, vain man, whom are you so angrily denouncing? . . . Your attitude is like that of a man who has been
wounded by an arrow thickly smeared with poison, and when his
friends procure for him a physician or surgeon, he says, 'I will not
have this arrow taken out until I have learnt whether the man who
wounded me belonged to the warrior caste, or to the Brahmana caste,
or to the agricultural caste, or to the menial caste.'

"Or he says, 'I will not have this arrow taken out until I have
learnt whether the arrow which wounded me was an ordinary arrow,
or a claw-headed arrow, or an iron arrow, or a calf-tooth arrow.' That
man would die, Malunkyaputta, before he could learn any of these
things.

"In exactly the same way, Malunkyaputta, any one who should
say, 'I will not lead the religious life under the Blessed One until the
Blessed One elucidates so and so and so forth, that person would die
before the elucidation could be made to him.

"The religious life, Malunkyaputta, does not depend on the dogma
that the world is eternal; nor does the religious life, Malunkyaputta,
depend on the dogma that the world is not eternal. No matter what
the dogma . . . there still remain birth, old age, death, sorrow,

lamentation, misery, grief, and despair. And it is against these here on earth that I am prescribing. . . .

"Why, Malunkyaputta, have I not elucidated all those problems? Because, Malunkyaputta, they are profitless and have nothing to do with the fundamentals of religion. . . .

"But there are some matters which I have indeed elucidated. What are they? Misery, Malunkyaputta, have I elucidated; the origin of misery have I elucidated; the cessation of misery have I elucidated; and the path leading to the ending of misery have I elucidated. And why, Malunkyaputta, have I elucidated this? Because, Malunkyaputta, this does profit; it has to do with the fundamentals of religion; it tends to aversion, absence of passion, cessation, quiescence, knowledge, supreme wisdom, and Nirvana; therefore have I elucidated it. . . ."

Thus spake the Blessed One; and, delighted, the venerable Malunkyaputta applauded the speech of the Blessed One.

THE ITIVITTUKA

*Here is another sermon attributed to Buddha in which the ethical
nature of his religion is revealed with especial clearness. It is supposed
to have been addressed to those who had become his avowed disciples, to the* bhikkus, *"brethren," in the new order he had founded.
Characteristically, the discourse is studded with fragments of poetry,
for the early Buddhists found pleasure in putting into appropriate
verse the feelings of ecstasy which the new doctrines inspired. When
particularly happy in literary finish, or peculiarly rich in religious
feeling, such verses were handed on, from mouth to mouth, in the
small companies of the brethren and sisters.*

This particular sermon belongs in a collection known as the
Itivittuka.[13]

Brethren, for the monk
who is a learner not yet come
to mastery of mind, but who
dwells aspiring for peace from
the bond, making it a matter
concerning what is outside
the self, I see no other single
factor so helpful as friendship
with the kindly. Brethren,
one who is a friend of the
kindly abandons the unprofitable and makes the profitable
to occur.

The monk who has a kindly
    friend, who pays
Deference and reverence to
    him, who does
What friends advise,—if mindful and composed
Such in due course shall win all fetters' end.

[13] Reprinted—in somewhat shortened form—from F. L. Woodward, *Minor Anthologies of the Pali Canon, Part II* (Oxford Univ. Press, 1935).

Here, brethren, I discern a certain person with mind at peace to be such because I compass his thoughts with my mind; and, if at this moment this person were to make an end, he would be put just so into the heaven-world according to his deserts. What is the reason for that? His mind at peace. Indeed it is because of a mind at peace, brethren, that in this way certain beings, when body breaks up, after death arise again in the happy bourn, in the heaven-world.

> Here seeing a certain one with mind at peace,
> The Teacher 'mid the monks set forth this saying:
> "If at this time this person were to die,
> In the happy bourn he would arise again.
> Indeed the mind of him has come to peace.
> Thro' peace of mind men reach the happy bourn.
> As one lays down what he has taken up,
> So such an one, when body breaks up, strong
> In wisdom rises up in the heaven-world."

Brethren, if beings knew, as I know, the ripening of sharing gifts, they would not enjoy their use without sharing them, nor would the taint of stinginess obsess the heart and stay there. Even if it were their last bit, their last morsel of food, they would not enjoy its use without sharing it, if there were any one to receive it. But inasmuch, brethren, as beings do not know, as I know, the ripening of sharing gifts, therefore they enjoy their use without sharing them, and the taint of stinginess obsesses their heart and stays there.

> If only beings knew—as said the mighty sage—
> The ripening of sharing gifts, how great the fruit thereof,
> Putting away the taint of stinginess, with heart
> Made pure within, they would bestow in season due
> When great the fruit of charity on Aryans.
> And giving food as gift to those deserving much
> From man-state falling hence givers to heaven go.
> And they, to heaven gone, rejoice and there enjoy
> In the fullness of their hearts' desire the ripening
> Of sharing gifts, the fruit of their unselfishness.

Brethren, whatsoever grounds there be for good works undertaken with a view to rebirth, all of them are not worth one sixteenth part of that goodwill which is the heart's release; goodwill alone, which is the heart's release, shines and burns and flashes forth in surpassing them. Just as, brethren, the radiance of all the starry bodies is not worth one sixteenth part of the moon's radiance, but the moon's radiance shines and burns and flashes forth in surpassing them, even so, brethren, goodwill . . . flashes forth in surpassing good works undertaken with a view to rebirth.

Just as, brethren, in the last month of the rains, in autumn time, when the sky is opened up and cleared of clouds, the sun, leaping up into the firmament, drives away all darkness from the heavens and shines and burns and flashes forth,—even so, brethren, whatsoever grounds there be for good works . . . goodwill . . . flashes forth in surpassing them.

Just as, brethren, in the night at time of daybreak the star of healing shines and burns and flashes forth, even so, whatsoever grounds there be for good works undertaken with a view to rebirth, all of them are not worth one-sixteenth part of that goodwill which is the heart's release. Goodwill, which is the heart's release, alone shines and burns and flashes forth in surpassing them.

Brethren, there are two ethical teachings. . . . What two? "Look at evil as evil" is the first teaching. "Seeing evil as evil, be disgusted therewith, be cleansed of it, be freed of it" is the second teaching. These two teachings of the wayfarer take place one after the other.

> Of the wayfarer, the awakened one,
> Who hath compassion on all things that be,
> Behold the way of speech and teachings twain:
> "Evil behold for what it is, and then
> Conceive disgust for it: with heart made clean
> Of evil, ye shall make an end of ill."

. . . Brethren, there are these three persons found existing in the world. What three? The one who is like a drought, the one who rains locally, and the one who pours down everywhere.

And how, brethren, is a person like a drought?

Herein, brethren, a certain person is not a giver to all alike, no giver of food and drink, clothing and vehicle, flowers, scents and unguents, bed, lodging and lights to recluses and Brahmanas, to wretched and needy beggars. In this way, brethren, a person is like a drought.

And how, brethren, is a person like a local rainfall?

In this case a person is a giver to some, but to others he gives not; be they recluses and Brahmanas or wretched, needy beggars, he is no giver of food and drink . . . lodging and lights. In this way a person is like a local rainfall.

And how, brethren, does a person rain down everywhere?

In this case a certain person gives to all, be they recluses and Brahmanas or wretched, needy beggars; he is a giver of food and drink . . . lodging and lights. In this way a person rains down everywhere.

So these are the three sorts of persons found existing in the world.

Brethren, even if a monk should seize the hem of my garment and walk behind me step for step, yet if he be covetous in his desires, fierce in his longing, malevolent of heart, of mind corrupt, careless and unrestrained, not quieted but scatter-brained and uncontrolled in sense, that monk is far from me and I am far from him. . . .

Brethren, do ye live perfect in virtue, do ye live perfect in the performance of the obligations, restrained with the restraint of the obligations, perfect in the practice of right behaviour; seeing danger in the slightest faults, undertake and train yourselves in the training of the precepts. For him who so lives . . . so restrained . . . who undertakes the training of the precepts, what else remains to be done?

> Whether he walk or stand or rest or lie
> Or stretch his limbs or draw them in again,
> Let him do all these things composedly;
> Above, across, and back again returning—
> Whatever be one's bourn in all the world—
> Let him be one who views the rise-and-fall
> Of all compounded things attentively.
> So dwelling ardent, living a life of peace
> And not elated, but to calmness given,
> For mind's composure doing what is right,
> Ever and always training,—"ever intent"—
> That is the name men give to such a monk.

BUDDHIST PARABLES

I: THE BLIND MEN AND THE ELEPHANT

Gotama Buddha appears to have been an extraordinarily success-
ful teacher, in part no doubt because he was so given to using parables.
Few teachers in all of history ever made more frequent and effective
use of stories to illustrate the lessons they sought to impart. Here is
an excellent example, and one of the most familiar. It is taken from a
collection of sacred traditions called the Udana.[14]

On one occasion a number
of disciples went to the Blessed
One and said: "Sir, there are
living here in Savatthi many
wandering hermits and scholars
who indulge in constant dispute, some saying that the
world is infinite and eternal
and others that it is finite and
not eternal, some saying that
the soul dies with the body and
others that it lives on forever, and so forth. What, Sir, would you
say concerning them?"

The Blessed One answered: "Brethren, those disputatious fellows
are like unto blind men. . . . Once upon a time there was a raja in
this region who called to a certain man and said: 'Come thou, good
fellow, go and gather together in one place all the men in Savatthi
who were born blind.'

" 'Very good, sire,' replied that man, and in obedience to the raja
gathered together all the men born blind in Savatthi. And, having
done so, he went to the raja and said, 'Sire, all the men born blind in
Savatthi are assembled.'

" 'Then, my good man, show the blind men an elephant.'

[14] Translation by F. L. Woodward, *op. cit.*

" 'Very good, sire,' said the man, and did as he was told, and said to them, 'O blind, such as this is an elephant'; and to one man he presented the head of the elephant, to another its ears, to another a tusk, to another the trunk, the foot, back, tail and tuft of the tail, saying to each one that that was the elephant.

"Now, brethren, that man, having thus presented the elephant to the blind men, came to the raja and said, 'Sire, the elephant has been presented to the blind men. Do what is your will.'

"Thereupon, brethren, that raja went up to the blind men and said to each, 'Well, blind men, have you seen the elephant?'

" 'Yes, sire.'

" 'Then tell me, blind men, what sort of thing is an elephant?'

"Thereupon those who had been presented with the head an- swered, 'Sire, an elephant is like a pot.' And those who had observed an ear only replied, 'An elephant is like a winnowing-basket.' Those who had been presented with a tusk said it was a ploughshare. Those who knew only the trunk said it was a plough; they said the body was a granary; the foot, a pillar; the back, a mortar; the tail, a pestle; the tuft of the tail, just a besom.

"Then they began to quarrel, shouting, 'Yes, it is!' 'No, it is not!' 'An elephant is not that!' 'Yes, it's like that!' and so on, till they came to fisticuffs over the matter.

"Then, brethren, that raja was delighted with the scene.

"Just so are these wanderers holding other views, blind, unseeing, knowing not the profitable, knowing not the unprofitable. They know not dhamma. They know not what is not dhamma. In their ignorance of these things they are by nature quarrelsome, wrangling and dispu- tatious, each maintaining it is thus and thus."

Thereupon the Exalted One at that time, seeing the meaning of it, gave utterance to this verse of uplift:

O how they cling and wrangle, some who claim
Of Brahmana and recluse the honoured name!
For, quarreling, each to his view they cling.
Such folk see only one side of a thing.

II: THE FOLLY OF POSSESSIONS

Here is another illustration of Buddha's genius as a teacher. By the use of one short and irrefutable argument he succeeds in exploding the commonest of all human follies. This dialogue, like the last, is taken from the Udana.[15]

Thus have I heard: On a certain occasion the Exalted One was staying near Savatthi in East Park, at the storied house of Visakha, the mother of Migara.

Now at that time the dear and lovely grand-daughter of this Visakha chanced to die, and the woman came with clothes and hair still wet from washing to see the Exalted One. And the Exalted One said to her:

"Why, Visakha! How is it that you come here with clothes and hair still wet at an unseasonable hour?"

"O, sir, my dear and lovely grand-daughter is dead! That is why I come here, with hair and clothes still wet and at an unseasonable hour."

"Visakha, would you like to have as many sons and grandsons as there are men in Savatthi?"

"Yes, sir, I would indeed!"

"But how many men do you suppose die daily in Savatthi?"

"Ten, sir, or maybe nine, or eight. . . . Savatthi is never free from men dying, sir."

"What think you, Visakha? In such case would you ever be without wet hair and clothes?"

"Surely not, sir!" . . .

"Visakha, whoso have a hundred things beloved, they have a hundred sorrows. Whoso have ninety, eighty . . . thirty, twenty things beloved . . . whoso have ten . . . whoso have but one thing beloved, have but one sorrow. Whoso have no one thing beloved, they have no sorrow. Sorrowless are they and passionless. Serene are they, I declare."

> All griefs or lamentations whatso'er
> And divers forms of sorrow in the world,—
> Because of what is dear to these become.

[15] Translated by F. L. Woodward, *op. cit.*

Thing dear not being, these do not become.
Happy are they therefore and free from grief
To whom is naught at all dear in the world.
Wherefore aspiring for the griefless, sorrowless,
Make thou in all the world naught dear to thee.

III: THE FOLLY OF MOURNING

Here is one more of the great parables attributed to Buddha. Like the others, it may be apocryphal, but that is irrelevant. What is important is that this parable, like the rest, became a part of the Buddha tradition, and thus helped to make Buddhism a lamp for the feet of mankind.[16]

There was a rich man who found his gold suddenly transformed into ashes; and he took to his bed and refused all food. A friend, hearing of his sickness, visited the rich man and learned the cause of his grief. And the friend said: "Thou didst not make good use of thy wealth. When thou didst hoard it up, it was not better than ashes. Now heed my advice. Spread mats in the bazaar; pile up these ashes, and pretend to trade with them."

The rich man did as his friend had told him, and when his neighbors asked him, "Why sellest thou ashes?" he said: "I offer my goods for sale."

After some time a young girl, named Kisā Gotamī, an orphan and very poor, passed by, and seeing the rich man in the bazaar, said: "My lord, why pilest thou thus up gold and silver for sale?"

And the rich man said: "Wilt thou please hand me that gold and silver?" And Kisā Gotamī took up a handful of ashes, and lo! they changed back into gold.

Considering that Kisā Gotamī had the mental eye of spiritual knowledge and saw the real worth of things, the rich man gave her in marriage to his son, and he said: "With many, gold is no better than ashes, but with Kisā Gotamī ashes become pure gold."

And Kisā Gotamī had an only son, and he died. In her grief she carried the dead child to all her neighbors, asking them for medicine, and the people said: "She has lost her senses. The boy is dead."

[16] The version is taken from *The Gospel of Buddha*, by Paul Carus (Open Court, La Salle, Ill., 1917).

At length Kisā Gotamī met a man who replied to her request: "I cannot give thee medicine for thy child, but I know a physician who can."

And the girl said: "Pray tell me, sir; who is it?" And the man replied: "Go to Sakyamuni, the Buddha."

Kisā Gotamī repaired to the Buddha and cried: "Lord and Master, give me the medicine that will cure my boy."

The Buddha answered: "I want a handful of mustard-seed." And when the girl in her joy promised to procure it, the Buddha added: "The mustard-seed must be taken from a house where no one has lost a child, husband, parent, or friend."

Poor Kisā Gotamī now went from house to house, and the people pitied her and said: "Here is mustard-seed; take it!" But when she asked, "Did a son or daughter, a father or mother, die in your family?" they answered her: "Alas! the living are few, but the dead are many. Do not remind us of our deepest grief." And there was no house but some beloved one had died in it.

Kisā Gotamī became weary and hopeless, and sat down at the way-side, watching the lights of the city, as they flickered up and were extinguished again. At last the darkness of the night reigned everywhere. And she consdered the fate of men, that their lives flicker up and are extinguished. And she thought to herself: "How selfish am I in my grief! Death is common to all; yet in this valley of desolation there is a path that leads him to immortality who has surrendered all selfishness."

Putting away the selfishness of her affection for her child, Kisā Gotamī had the dead body buried in the forest. Returning to the Buddha, she took refuge in him and found comfort in the Dharma, which is a balm that will soothe all the pains of our troubled hearts.

The Buddha said:

"The life of mortals in this world is troubled and brief and combined with pain. For there is not any means by which those that have been born can avoid dying; after reaching old age there is death; of such a nature are living beings.

"As ripe fruits are early in danger of falling, so mortals when born are always in danger of death.

"As all earthen vessels made by the potter end in being broken, so is the life of mortals.

"Both young and adult, both those who are fools and those who are wise, all fall into the power of death; all are subject to death.

"Of those who, overcome by death, depart from life, a father cannot save his son, nor kinsmen their relations.

"Mark! while relatives are looking on and lamenting deeply, one by one mortals are carried off, like an ox that is led to the slaughter.

"So the world is afflicted with death and decay, therefore the wise do not grieve, knowing the terms of the world.

"In whatever manner people think a thing will come to pass, it is often different when it happens, and great is the disappointment; see, such are the terms of the world.

"Not from weeping nor from grieving will any one obtain peace of mind; on the contrary, his pain will be the greater and his body will suffer. He will make himself sick and pale, yet the dead are not saved by his lamentation.

"People pass away, and their fate after death will be according to their deeds.

"If a man live a hundred years, or even more, he will at last be separated from the company of his relatives, and leave the life of this world.

"He who seeks peace should draw out the arrow of lamentation, and complaint, and grief.

"He who has drawn out the arrow and has become composed will obtain peace of mind; he who has overcome all sorrow will become free from sorrow, and be blessed."

IV: SERMON AT THE MARRIAGE FEAST

There are many passages in the Buddhist scriptures which have a peculiarly familiar ring to Christian readers. Here, for example, is one closely recalling the story told in the second chapter of the Gospel of John *about the miracle performed at the marriage feast in Cana. How such parallels are to be explained is a matter of dispute. There was considerable intercourse between the Near and Far East in ancient times, and the Christian saga may have been influenced by the Buddhist, or vice versa. The latter may well be the case in this particular instance, for our story comes from an account of Buddha's life written not in Pali, or even in Sanskrit, but in Chinese.*

It is quoted here, however, not because it records a familiar miracle, but a unique sermon. A nobler epithalamium would be hard to find anywhere in sacred literature.[17]

There was a man in Jambunada who was to be married the next day, and he thought, "Would that the Buddha, the Blessed One, might be present at the wedding."

And the Blessed One passed by his house and met him, and when he read the silent wish in the heart of the bridegroom, he consented to enter.

When the Holy One appeared with the retinue of his many disciples, the host, whose means were limited, received them as best he could, saying: "Eat, my Lord, and all thy congregation, according to your desire."

While the holy men ate, the meats and drinks remained undiminished, and the host thought to himself: "How wondrous is this! I should have had plenty for all my relatives and friends. Would that I had invited them all."

When this thought was in the host's mind, all his relatives and friends entered the house; and although the hall in the house was small, there was room in it for all of them. They sat down at the table and ate, and there was more than enough for all of them.

The Blessed One was pleased to see so many guests full of good cheer and he quickened them and gladdened them with words of truth, proclaiming the bliss of righteousness:

"The greatest happiness which a mortal man can imagine is the bond of marriage that ties together two loving hearts. But there is a greater happiness still: it is the embrace of truth. Death will separate husband and wife, but death will never affect him who has espoused the truth.

"Therefore be married unto the truth and live with the truth in holy wedlock. The husband who loves his wife and desires for a union that shall be everlasting must be faithful to her so as to be like truth itself, and she will rely upon him and revere him and minister unto him. And the wife who loves her husband and desires a union that shall be everlasting must be faithful to him so as to be like truth itself; and he will place his trust in her, he will provide for her. Verily,

[17] Reprinted from *The Gospel of Buddha*, by Paul Carus (Open Court, Chicago, 1917).

I say unto you, their children will become like unto their parents and will bear witness to their happiness.

"Let no man be single, let every one be wedded in holy love to the truth. And when Mara, the destroyer, comes to separate the visible forms of your being, you will continue to live in the truth, and you will partake of the life everlasting, for the truth is immortal."

There was no one among the guests but was strengthened in his spiritual life, and recognized the sweetness of a life of righteousness; and they took refuge in the Buddha, the Dharma, and the Sangha.

THE DHAMMAPADA

One can readily understand why this little book has become the most widely known of all the Buddhist scriptures. It is an anthology of sayings couched in verse, a collection as wise as it is at times witty and as zestful as it is always profound. Here it is that one finds many of the maxims so often quoted by Western admirers of Buddhism: for example, "Let a man overcome anger by love . . . evil by good . . . greediness by generosity . . . the liar by truth."

We do not know by whom the DHAMMAPADA was composed, nor when, nor precisely where. Its contents, however, are clearly very ancient, and some of the stanzas may have been composed by Buddha himself. The work was probably intended originally as a textbook for young neophytes, and that is one of its main uses to this day. The sayings—423 altogether—are arranged in twenty-six groups, each group governing one of the main points in the dhamma *("doctrine") of Buddhism. The verses are uneven not alone in length and metre but also, of course, in meaningfulness. Many deal with abstruse details of the Buddhist system of self-culture and self-control, and these have been omitted from the version given below. Most of the repetitious verses have likewise been left out. What remains deserves the closest reading, for it contains as rich a wisdom and as high a morality as is to be found in any sacred writing on earth.*[18]

THE TWIN VERSES

All that we are is the result of what we have thought: it is founded on our thoughts, it is made up of our thoughts. If a man speaks or acts with an evil thought, pain follows him, as the wheel follows the foot of the ox that draws the carriage.

All that we are is the result of what we have thought: it is founded on our thoughts, it is made up of our thoughts. If a man speaks or acts with a pure thought, happiness follows him, like a shadow that never leaves him.

[17] Reprinted from *The Gospel of Buddha,* by Paul Carus (Open Court, La Salle, Ill., 1917).

"He abused me, he beat me, he defeated me, he robbed me"—in those who harbor such thoughts hatred will never cease. . . .

For hatred does not cease by hatred at any time: hatred ceases by love—this is an old rule.

The world does not know that we must all come to an end here; but those who know it, their quarrels cease at once.

He who lives looking for pleasures only, his senses uncontrolled, immoderate in his food, idle, and weak, Māra (the tempter) will certainly overthrow him, as the wind throws down a weak tree. . . .

He who wishes to put on the yellow dress [of a monk] without having cleansed himself from sin, who disregards also temperance and truth, is unworthy of the yellow dress.

But he who has cleansed himself from sin, is well grounded in all virtues, and endowed also with temperance and truth: he is indeed worthy of the yellow dress. . . .

As rain breaks through an ill-thatched house, passion will break through an unreflecting mind. . . .

The evil-doer mourns in this world, and he mourns in the next; he mourns in both. He mourns and suffers when he sees the evil result of his own work.

The virtuous man delights in this world, and he delights in the next; he delights in both. He delights and rejoices, when he sees the purity of his own work. . . .

The thoughtless man, even if he can recite a large portion of the law, but is not a doer of it, has no share in the priesthood, but is like a cow-herd counting the cows of others.

The follower of the law, even if he can recite only a small portion of the law, but, having forsaken passion and hatred and foolishness, possesses true knowledge and serenity of mind, he, caring for nothing in this world or that to come, has indeed a share in the priesthood.

ON EARNESTNESS

Earnestness is the path of immortality (Nirvāna), thoughtlessness the path of death. Those who are in earnest do not die, those who are thoughtless are as if dead already.

Having understood this clearly, those who are advanced in earnestness delight in earnestness, and rejoice in the knowledge of the elect. . . .

By rousing himself, by earnestness, by restraint and control, the wise man may make for himself an island which no flood can overwhelm.

Fools follow after vanity. The wise man keeps earnestness as his best jewel. . . .

Earnest among the thoughtless, awake among the sleepers, the wise man advances like a racer, leaving behind the hack. . . .

THOUGHT

As a fletcher makes straight his arrow, a wise man makes straight his trembling and unsteady thought, which is difficult to guard, difficult to hold back. . . .

It is good to tame the mind, which is difficult to hold in and flighty, rushing wherever it listeth; a tamed mind brings happiness.

Let the wise man guard his thoughts, for they are difficult to perceive, very artful, and they rush wherever they list: thoughts well guarded bring happiness. . . .

If a man's faith is unsteady, if he does not know the true law, if his peace of mind is troubled, his knowledge will never be perfect. . . .

Before long, alas! this body will lie on the earth, despised, without understanding, like a useless log.

Whatever a hater may do to a hater, or an enemy to an enemy, a wrongly-directed mind will do him greater mischief.

Not a mother, not a father, will do so much, nor any other relatives; a well-directed mind will do us greater service.

FLOWERS

Death carries off a man who is gathering flowers, and whose mind is distracted, as a flood carries off a sleeping village. . . .

As the bee collects nectar and departs without injuring the flower, or its color or scent, so let a sage dwell in his village. . . .

Like a beautiful flower, full of color, but without scent, are the fine but fruitless words of him who does not act accordingly. . . .

As many kinds of wreaths can be made from a heap of flowers, so many good things may be achieved by a mortal when once he is born.

The scent of flowers does not travel against the wind, nor that of sandal-wood, or of Tagara and Mallikā flowers; but the odor of good people travels even against the wind; a good man pervades every place. . . .

As on a heap of rubbish cast upon the highway the lily will grow full of sweet perfume and delight, thus among those who are mere rubbish the disciple of the truly enlightened Buddha shines forth by his knowledge above the blinded worldling.

THE FOOL

Long is the night to him who is awake; long is a mile to him who is tired; long is life to the foolish who do not know the true law.

If a traveller does not meet with one who is his better, or his equal, let him firmly keep to his solitary journey; there is no companionship with a fool.

"These sons belong to me, and this wealth belongs to me," with such thoughts a fool is tormented. He himself does not belong to himself; how much less sons and wealth?

The fool who knows his foolishness, is wise at least so far. But a fool who thinks himself wise, he is called a fool indeed.

If a fool be associated with a wise man even all his life, he will perceive the truth as little as a spoon perceives the taste of soup. . . .

As long as the evil deed done does not bear fruit, the fool thinks it is like honey; but when it ripens, then the fool suffers grief. . . .

And when the evil deed, after it has become known, turns to sorrow for the fool, then it destroys his bright lot, nay, it cleaves his head.

Let the fool wish for a false reputation, for precedence among the Bhikshus [monks], for lordship in the convents, for worship among other people!

THE WISE MAN

If you see a man who shows you what is to be avoided, who administers reproofs, and is intelligent, follow that wise man as you would one who tells of hidden treasures; it will be better, not worse, for him who follows him. . . .

Well-makers lead the water wherever they like; fletchers bend the arrow, carpenters bend a log of wood; wise people fashion themselves.

As a solid rock is not shaken by the wind, wise people falter not amidst blame and praise.

Wise people, after they have listened to the laws, become serene, like a deep, smooth, and still lake.

Good men indeed walk warily under all circumstances; good men speak not out of a desire for sensual gratification; whether touched by happiness or sorrow, wise people never appear elated or depressed.

If, whether for his own sake, or for the sake of others, a man wishes neither for a son, nor for wealth, nor for lordship, and if he does not wish for his own success by unfair means, then he is good, wise, and virtuous.

Few are there among men who arrive at the other shore [attain Nirvana]; the other people here run up and down the shore.

But those who, when the law has been well preached to them, follow the law, will pass over the dominion of death, however difficult to cross. . . .

Those whose mind is well grounded in the seven elements of knowledge, who without clinging to anything, rejoice in freedom from attachment, whose appetites have been conquered, and who are full of light, they are free even in this world.

THE VENERABLE

There is no suffering for him who has finished his journey, and abandoned grief, who has freed himself on all sides, and thrown off all fetters. . . .

Men who have no riches, who live on recognized food, who have perceived void and unconditioned freedom [Nirvāna], their path is difficult to understand, like that of birds in the air.

He whose appetites are stilled, who is not absorbed in enjoyment, who has perceived void and unconditioned freedom [Nirvāna], his path is difficult to understand, like that of birds in the air.

The gods even envy him whose senses, like horses well broken in by the driver, have been subdued, who is free from pride, and free from appetites; such a one who does his duty is tolerant like the earth, or like a threshold; he is like a lake without mud; no new births are in store for him.

His thought is quiet, quiet are his word and deed, when he has obtained freedom by true knowledge, when he has thus become a quiet man.

The man who is free from credulity, but knows the uncreated, who has cut all ties, removed all temptations, renounced all desires, he is the greatest of men.

In a hamlet or in a forest, on sea or on dry land, wherever venerable persons dwell, that place is delightful.

Forests are delightful; where the world finds no delight, there the passionless will find delight, for they look not for pleasures.

THE THOUSANDS

Even though a speech be a thousand words long, but made up of senseless words, one word of sense is better, which if a man hears, he becomes quiet. . . .

Though a man recite a hundred poems made up of senseless words, one word of the law is better, which if a man hears, he becomes quiet.

If one man conquer in battle a thousand times a thousand men, and if another conquer himself, he is the greatest of conquerors.

One's own self conquered is better than all other people; not even a god could change into defeat the victory of a man who has vanquished himself, and always lives under restraint.

If a man for a hundred years sacrifice month by month with a thousand, and if he but for one moment pay homage to a man whose soul is grounded in true knowledge, better is that homage than sacrifices for a hundred years. . . .

Whatever a man sacrifice in this world as an offering or as an oblation for a whole year in order to gain merit, the whole of it is not worth a quarter a farthing; reverence shown to the righteous is better.

He who always greets and constantly reveres the aged, four things will increase to him: life, beauty, happiness, power.

But he who lives a hundred years, ignorant and unrestrained, a life of one day is better if a man is wise and reflecting.

And he who lives a hundred years, idle and weak, a life of one day is better if a man has attained firm strength. . . .

And he who lives a hundred years, not seeing the highest law, a life of one day is better if a man sees the highest law.

EVIL

A man should hasten towards the good, and should keep his thought away from evil; if a man does what is good slothfully, his mind delights in evil. . . .

Even a good man sees evil days so long as his good deed does not ripen; but when his good deed ripens, then does the good man see good things.

Let no man think lightly of evil, saying in his heart, It will not come nigh unto me. Even by the falling of water-drops a water-pot is filled; the fool becomes full of evil, even if he gather it little by little.

Let a man avoid evil deeds, as a merchant, if he has few companions and carries much wealth, avoids a dangerous road; as a man who loves life avoids poison.

He who has no wound on his hand, may touch poison with his hand; poison does not affect one who has no wound; nor is there evil for one who does not commit evil.

If a man offend a harmless, pure, and innocent person, the evil falls back upon that fool, like light dust thrown up against the wind. . . .

Not in the sky, not in the midst of the sea, not if we enter into the clefts of the mountains, is there known a spot in the whole world where a man might be freed from an evil deed.

Not in the sky, not in the midst of the sea, not if we enter into the clefts of the mountains, is there known a spot in the whole world where death could not overcome the mortal.

PUNISHMENT

All men tremble at punishment, all men fear death; remember that you are like unto them, and do not kill, nor cause slaughter.

All men tremble at punishment, all men love life; remember that thou art like unto them, and do not kill, nor cause slaughter.

He who, seeking his own happiness, punishes or kills beings who also long for happiness, will not find happiness after death. . . .

Do not speak harshly to anyone; those who are spoken to will answer thee in the same way. Angry speech is painful: blows for blows will touch thee. . . .

As a cow-herd with his staff drives his cows into the stable, so do Age and Death drive the life of men. . . .

A fool does not know when he commits his evil deeds: but the wicked man burns by his own deeds, as if burnt by fire. . . .

Not nakedness, not platted hair, not dirt, not fasting, or lying on the earth, not rubbing with dust, not sitting motionless, can purify a mortal who has not overcome desires. . . .

Like a noble horse when touched by the whip, be ye strenuous and eager, and by faith, by virtue, by energy, by meditation, by discernment of the law, you will overcome this great pain, perfect in knowledge and in behavior, and never forgetful. . . .

OLD AGE

Look at this dressed-up lump, covered with wounds, joined together, sickly, full of many schemes, but which has no strength, no hold!

This body is wasted, full of sickness, and frail; this heap of corruption breaks to pieces, life indeed ends in death.

After one has looked at those gray bones, thrown away like gourds in the autumn, what pleasure is there left in life!

After a stronghold has been made of the bones, it is covered with flesh and blood, and there dwell in it old age and death, pride and deceit.

The brilliant chariots of kings are destroyed, the body also approaches destruction, but the virtue of good people never approaches destruction—thus do the good say to the good.

A man who has learnt little, grows old like an ox; his flesh grows, but his knowledge does not grow. . . .

SELF

Let each man direct himself first to what is proper, then let him teach others; thus a wise man will not suffer.

If a man make himself as he teaches others to be, then, being himself well subdued, he may subdue others; for one's own self is difficult to subdue.

Self is the lord of self, who else could be the lord? With self well subdued, a man finds a lord such as few can find. . . .

By one's self the evil is done, by one's self one suffers; by one's self evil is left undone, by one's self one is purified. The pure and the impure stand and fall by themselves, no one can purify another.

Let no one forget his own duty for the sake of another's, however great; let a man, after he has discerned his own duty, be always attentive to his duty.

THE WORLD

Do not follow the evil law! Do not live on in thoughtlessness! Do not follow false doctrine! Be not a friend of the world. . . .

Look upon the world as you would on a bubble, look upon it as you would on a mirage: the king of death does not see him who thus looks down upon the world.

Come, look at this world, glittering like a royal chariot; the foolish are immersed in it, but the wise do not touch it. . . .

This world is dark, few only can see here; a few only go to heaven, like birds escaped from the net. . . .

THE BUDDHA—THE AWAKENED

Even the gods envy those who are awakened and not forgetful, who are given to meditation, who are wise, and who delight in the repose of retirement from the world. . . .

Not to commit any sin, to do good, and to purify one's mind, that is the teaching of all the Awakened.

The Awakened call patience the highest penance, long-suffering the highest Nirvāna; for he is not an anchorite who strikes others, he is not an ascetic who insults others.

Not to blame, not to strike, to live restrained under the law, to be moderate in eating, to sleep and sit alone, and to dwell on the highest thoughts—this is the teaching of the Awakened. . . .

Men, driven by fear, go to many a refuge, to mountains and forests, to groves and sacred trees.

But that is not a safe refuge, that is not the best refuge; a man is not delivered from all pains after having gone to that refuge.

He who takes refuge with Buddha, the Law, and the Church; he who, with clear understanding, sees the four holy truths: pain, the origin of pain, the destruction of pain, and the eightfold holy way that leads to the quieting of pain;—that is the safe refuge, that is the best refuge; having gone to that refuge, a man is delivered from all pain. . . .

HAPPINESS

We live happily indeed, not hating those who hate us! among men who hate us we dwell free from hatred! We live happily indeed, free from ailments among the ailing! among men who are ailing let us dwell free from ailments!

We live happily indeed, free from greed among the greedy! among men who are greedy let us dwell free from greed!

We live happily indeed, though we call nothing our own! We shall be like the bright gods, feeding on happiness!

Victory breeds hatred, for the conquered is unhappy. He who has given up both victory and defeat, he, the contented, is happy. . . .

Health is the greatest of gifts, contentedness the best riches; trust is the best of relationships, Nirvāna the highest happiness. . . .

PLEASURE

Let no man ever cling to what is pleasant, or to what is unpleasant. Not to see what is pleasant is pain, and it is pain to see what is unpleasant.

Let, therefore, no man love anything; loss of the beloved is evil. Those who love nothing, and hate nothing, have no fetters.

From pleasure comes grief, from pleasures comes fear; he who is free from pleasure knows neither grief nor fear.

From affection comes grief, from affection comes fear; he who is free from affection knows neither grief nor fear. . . .

ANGER

Let a man leave anger, let him forsake pride, let him overcome all bondage! No sufferings befall the man who is not attached to name and form, and who calls nothing his own.

He who holds back rising anger like a rolling chariot, him I call a real driver; other people are but holding the reins.

Let a man overcome anger by love, let him overcome evil by good; let him overcome the greedy by liberality, the liar by truth!

Speak the truth, do not yield to anger; give, if thou art asked for little; by these three steps thou wilt go near the gods. . . .

This is an old saying, O Atula, this is not as if of to-day: "They blame him who sits silent, they blame him who speaks much, they also blame him who says little; there is no one on earth who is not blamed."

There never was, there never will be, nor is there now, a man who is always blamed, or a man who is always praised. . . .

Beware of bodily anger, and control thy body! Leave the sins of the body, and with thy body practise virtue!

Beware of the anger of the tongue, and control thy tongue! Leave the sins of the tongue, and practise virtue with thy tongue!

Beware of the anger of the mind, and control thy mind! Leave the sins of the mind, and practise virtue with thy mind!

The wise who control their body, who control their tongue, the wise who control their mind, are indeed well controlled.

IMPURITY

Let a wise man blow off the impurities of himself, as a smith blows off the impurities of silver, one by one, little by little, and from time to time.

As the impurity which springs from the iron, when it springs from it, destroys it; thus do a transgressor's own works lead him to the evil path.

The taint of prayers is non-repetition; the taint of houses, non-repair; the taint of complexion is sloth; the taint of a watchman, thoughtlessness.

Bad conduct is the taint of woman, niggardliness the taint of a benefactor; tainted are all evil ways, in this world and in the next.

But there is a taint worse than all taints—ignorance is the greatest taint. O mendicants! throw off that taint, and become pure! . . .

He who destroys life, who speaks untruth, who in the world takes what is not given him, who goes to another man's wife; and the man who gives himself to drinking intoxicating liquors, he, even in this world, digs up his own root. . . .

There is no fire like passion, there is no shark like hatred, there is no snare like folly, there is no torrent like greed.

The fault of others is easily perceived, but that of one's self is difficult to perceive; a man winnows his neighbor's faults like chaff, but his own fault he hides, as a cheat hides the bad die from the player.

If a man looks after the faults of others, and is always inclined to be offended, his own passions will grow, and he is far from the destruction of passions. . . .

THE JUST

A man is not just if he carries a matter by violence; no, he who distinguishes both right and wrong, who is learned and guides others, not by violence, but by the same law, being a guardian of the law and intelligent, he is called just.

A man is not learned because he talks much; he who is patient, free from hatred and fear, he is called learned. . . .

A man is not an elder because his head is gray; his age may be ripe, but he is called "Old-in-vain."

He in whom there is truth, virtue, pity, restraint, moderation, he who is free from impurity and is wise, he is called an elder.

An envious, stingy, dishonest man does not become respectable by means of much talking only, or by the beauty of his complexion. . . .

THE WAY

"All created things perish," he who knows and sees this becomes passive in pain; this is the way to purity.

"All created things are grief and pain," he who knows and sees this becomes passive in pain; this is the way that leads to purity.

"All forms are unreal," he who knows and sees this becomes passive in pain; this is the way that leads to purity.

He who does not rouse himself when it is time to rise, who, though young and strong, is full of sloth, whose will and thought are weak, that lazy and idle man never finds the way to knowledge.

Watching his speech, well restrained in mind, let a man never commit any wrong with his body! Let a man but keep these three roads of action clear, and he will achieve the way which is taught by the wise. . . .

"Here I shall dwell in the rain, here in winter and summer," thus the fool meditates, and does not think of death.

Death comes and carries off that man, honored for his children and flocks, his mind distracted, as a flood carries off a sleeping village.

Sons are no help, nor a father, nor relations; there is no help from kinsfolk for one whom death has seized.

A wise and well-behaved man who knows the meaning of this, should quickly clear the way that leads to Nirvāna.

THE DOWNWARD COURSE

He who says what is not, goes to hell; he also who, having done a thing, says I have not done it. After death both are equal: they are men with evil deeds in the next world. . . .

Better it would be to swallow a heated iron ball, like flaring fire, than that a bad unrestrained fellow should live on the charity of the land.

Four things does a reckless man gain who covets his neighbor's wife—demerit, an uncomfortable bed, thirdly, punishment, and lastly, hell.

There is demerit, and the evil way to hell: there is the short pleasure of the frightened in the arms of the frightened, and the king imposes heavy punishment; therefore let no man think of his neighbor's wife.

As a grass-blade, if badly grasped, cuts the arm, badly-practised asceticism leads to hell. . . .

They who fear when they ought not to fear, and fear not when they ought to fear, such men, embracing false doctrines, enter the evil path.

They who see sin where there is no sin, and see no sin where there is sin, such men, embracing false doctrines, enter the evil path.

They who see sin where there is sin, and no sin where there is no sin, such men, embracing the true doctrine, enter the good path.

THE ELEPHANT

Silently I endured abuse as the elephant in battle endures the arrow sent from the bow: for the world is ill-natured.

They lead a tamed elephant to battle, the king mounts a tamed elephant; the tamed is the best among men, he who silently endures abuse.

Mules are good, if tamed, and noble Sindhu horses, and elephants with large tusks; but he who tames himself is better still.

For with these animals does no man reach the untrodden country (Nirvāna), where a tamed man goes on a tamed animal—on his own well-tamed self. . . .

If a man becomes fat and a great eater, if he is sleepy and rolls himself about, that fool, like a hog fed on grains, is born again and again.

This mind of mine went formerly wandering about as it liked, as it listed, as it pleased; but I shall now hold it in thoroughly, as the rider who holds the hook holds in the furious elephant.

Be not thoughtless, watch your thoughts! Draw yourself out of the evil way, like an elephant sunk in mud. . . .

It is better to live alone: there is no companionship with a fool; let a man walk alone, let him commit no sin, with few wishes, like an elephant in the forest.

If the occasion arises, friends are pleasant; enjoyment is pleasant, whatever be the cause; a good work is pleasant in the hour of death; the giving up of all grief is pleasant. . . .

THIRST

The thirst of a thoughtless man grows like a creeper; he runs from life to life, like a monkey seeking fruit in the forest. . . .

Those who are slaves to passions, run down the stream of desires, as a spider runs down the web which he has made himself; when they have cut this, at last, wise people go onwards, free from cares, leaving all pain behind. . . .

If a man is tossed about by doubts, full of strong passions, and yearning only for what is delightful, his thirst will grow more and more, and he will indeed make his fetters strong.

Riches destroy the foolish, if they look not for the other shore;

the foolish by his thirst for riches destroys himself, as if he were destroying others.

The fields are damaged by weeds, mankind is damaged by passion: therefore a gift bestowed on the passionless brings great reward. . . .

THE BHIKSHU [19]

Restraint in the eye is good, and also in the ear, in the nose, in the tongue.

Restraint is good in action, and also in speech, in thought, in all things. A Bhikshu, restrained in all things, is freed from all pain.

He who controls his hand, he who controls his feet, he who controls his speech, he who is well controlled, he who delights inwardly, who is collected, who is solitary and content, him they call Bhikshu.

The Bhikshu who controls his mouth, who speaks wisely and calmly, who teaches the meaning and the law, his word is sweet. . . .

And this is the beginning here for a wise Bhikshu: watchfulness over the senses, contentedness, restraint under the law; keep noble friends whose life is pure, and who are not slothful.

Let him live in charity, let him be perfect in his duties; then in the fulness of delight he will make an end of suffering. . . .

THE BRAHMANA [20]

He who is thoughtful, blameless, settled, dutiful, without passions, and who has attained the highest end, him I call indeed a Brāhmana.

The sun is bright by day, the moon shines by night, the warrior is bright in his armor, the Brāhmana is bright in his meditation; but Buddha, the Awakened, is bright with splendor day and night. . . .

No one should attack a Brāhmana, but no Brāhmana, if attacked, should let himself fly at his aggressor! Woe to him who strikes a Brāhmana, more woe to him who flies at his aggressor! . . .

A man does not become a Brāhmana by his plaited hair, by his family, or by birth; in whom there is truth and righteousness, he is blessed, he is a Brāhmana.

What is the use of plaited hair, O fool! what of the raiment of

[19] Or *Bhikku*: Monk, mendicant, a religious devotee.
[20] Usually called "Brahmin" in English: a member of the priest class.

goatskins? Within thee there is ravening, but the outside thou makest clean. . . .

I do not call a man a Brāhmana because of his origin or of his mother. He is indeed arrogant, and he is wealthy: but the poor, who is free from all attachments, him I call indeed a Brāhmana. . . .

Him I call indeed a Brāhmana who, though he has committed no offence, endures reproach, stripes, and bonds: who has endurance for his force, and strength for his army. . . .

Him I call indeed a Brāhmana who is tolerant with the intolerant, mild with the violent, and free from greed among the greedy.

Him I call indeed a Brāhmana from whom anger and hatred, pride and hypocrisy have dropped like a mustard seed from the point of a needle. . . .

Him I call indeed a Brāhmana who calls nothing his own, whether it be before, behind, or between; who is poor, and free from the love of the world.

Him I call indeed a Brāhmana, the manly, the noble, the hero, the great sage, the conqueror, the indifferent, the accomplished, the awakened.

Him I call indeed a Brāhmana who knows his former abodes, who sees heaven and hell, has reached the end of births, is perfect in knowledge, a sage, and whose perfections are all perfect.

THE SURANGAMA SUTRA

This is perhaps the most renowned of all the Buddhist scriptures composed in Sanskrit. Its author is unknown by name, but all the evidence indicates that he lived in the first century A.D. Early in the eighth century it was smuggled out of Southern India, where it had been jealously cherished until then as a sort of magic talisman, and translated into Chinese. Its subsequent popularity there among the scholars led to the writing of some fifty-six known commentaries.

The term sutra is the Sanskrit equivalent of the Pali sutta, meaning "discourse." This one is purported to have been delivered by Buddha to his favorite disciple, Ananda, amid a host of other "brethren," in an effort to chart the road to "supreme enlightenment." That road is the practice of dhyana, "concentration of mind," and each step along its course is described in language both icily philosophical and flamingly religious. Lin Yutang has well compared the work to a combination of Locke's Essay On Human Understanding and the Gospel according to St. John.

First the sutra sets out to prove that all things perceived by the physical senses are transient and illusory, and that the truly real things can be known only through intuition. It follows, therefore, that to avoid all distress one must perfect one's powers of intuition; one must, by learning to see through and beyond the finite, gradually become at home only in the Infinite. Before any such talent can be attained, however, a man must be moral and kindly; he must live right before he can hope to think right. Buddha is most insistent on that point, and very specific, as the following selection makes plain.[21]

Then Ananda, rising in the midst of the assembly, straightened his robe, with the palms of his hands pressed together, knelt before the Lord Buddha. In the depths of his nature he was already enlightened and his heart was filled with happiness and compassion for all sentient beings and, especially, did he desire to benefit them by his newly

[21] Excerpted from a translation by Wai-tao and Dwight Goddard in *A Buddhist Bible*, edited by Dwight Goddard (Thetford, Vermont, 1938).

acquired wisdom. He addressed the Lord Buddha, saying:—Oh my Lord of Great Mercy! I have now seen the True Door for the attainment of Enlightenment, and have no more doubt about its being the only Door to Perfect Enlightenment. My Lord has taught us that those who are only starting the practice of Buddhahood and have not yet delivered themselves, but who already wish to deliver others, that this is a sign of Buddhahood. . . . Although I have not yet delivered myself, I already wish to deliver all sentient beings of this present existence. . . . What can I do to help them arrange a True Altar to Enlightenment within their minds so that they may be kept far away from all deceiving temptations and in whose progress there shall be no retrogression or discouragement in the attainment of Enlightenment?

In response to this appeal, the Blessed One addressed the assembly:—Ananda has just requested me to teach how to arrange a True Altar of Enlightenment to which sentient beings may come for deliverance and protection. Listen carefully as I explain it to you.

Ananda and all in this assembly! In explaining to you the rules of the Discipline, I have frequently emphasized three good lessons, namely, (1) the only way to keep the Precepts is first to be able to concentrate the mind; (2) by keeping the Precepts you will be able to attain Samadhi [mystical ecstasy]; (3) by means of Samadhi one develops intelligence and wisdom. Having learned these three good lessons, one has gained freedom from the intoxicants and hindrances.

Ananda, why is concentration of mind necessary before one can keep the Precepts? And why is it necessary to keep the Precepts before one can attain Samadhi? And why is the attainment of Samadhi necessary before one may attain true intelligence and wisdom? Let me explain this to you. All sentient beings in all the six realms of existence are susceptible to temptations and allurements. As they yield to these temptations and allurements, they fall into and become fast bound to the recurring cycles of deaths and rebirths. Being prone to yield to these temptations and allurements, one must, in order to free himself from their bondage and their intoxication, concentrate his whole mind in a resolution to resist them to the uttermost. The most important of these allurements are the temptations to yield to sexual thoughts, desires and indulgence, with all their following waste and bondage and suffering. Unless one can free himself from this bondage and these contaminations and exterminate these sexual lusts, there will be no escape from the following suffering, nor hope of advancement to enlightenment and peacefulness. No matter how keen you may be mentally, no matter how much you may be able to practice concentration, no matter to how high a degree of apparent Samadhi you may attain, unless you have wholly annihilated all sexual lusts, you will ultimately fall into the lower realms of existence. . . .

Therefore, Ananda, a man who tries to practice concentration without first attaining control of his lusts is like a man trying to bake bread out of a dough made of sand; bake it as long as he will, it will only be sand made a little hot. It is the same with sentient beings, Ananda. They can not hope to attain Buddhahood by means of an indecent body. How can they hope to attain the wonderful experience of Samadhi out of bawdiness? If the source is indecent, the outcome will be indecent; there will ever be a return to the never-ending recurrence of deaths and rebirths. Sexual lust leads to multiplicity; control of mind and Samadhi leads to enlightenment and the unitive life of Buddhahood. Multiplicity leads to strife and suffering; control of mind and concentration leads to the blissful peace of Samadhi and Buddhahood.

Inhibition of sexual thoughts and annihilation of sexual lusts is the path to Samadhi, and even the conception of inhibiting and annihilating must be discarded and forgotten. When the mind is under perfect control and all indecent thoughts excluded, then there may be a reasonable expectation for the Enlightenment of the Buddhas. Any other teaching than this is but the teaching of the evil Maras. This is my first admonition as to keeping the Precepts.

The next important hindrance and allurement is the tendency of all sentient beings of all the six realms of existence to gratify their pride of egoism. To gain this one is prone to be unkind, to be unjust and cruel, to other sentient beings. This tendency lures them into the bondage of deaths and rebirth, but if this tendency can be controlled they will no longer be lured into this bondage for right control of mind will enable them to keep the Precept of kindness to all animate life. The reason for practicing concentration and seeking to attain Samadhi is to escape from the suffering of life, but in seeking to escape from suffering ourselves, why should we inflict it upon others? Unless you can so control your minds that even the thought of brutal unkindness and killing is abhorrent, you will never be able to escape from the bondage of the world's life. No matter how keen you may be mentally, no matter how much you may be able to practice concentration, no matter to how high a degree of Samadhi you may attain, unless you have wholly annihilated all tendency to unkindness toward others, you will ultimately fall into the realms of existence where the evil ghosts dwell. . . .

You of this great Assembly ought to appreciate that those human beings who . . . kill sentient beings and eat the flesh . . . are not true disciples of Buddha. Therefore, Ananda, next to teaching the people of the last age to put away all sexual lust, you must teach them to put an end to all killing and brutal cruelty.

If one is trying to practice concentration and is still eating meat, he would be like a man closing his ears and shouting loudly and then asserting that he heard nothing. The more one conceals things, the more apparent they become. Pure and earnest monks and Saints, when walking a narrow path, will never so much as tread on the growing grass beside the path. How can a monk, who hopes to become a deliverer of others, himself be living on the flesh of other sentient beings?

Pure and earnest monks, if they are true and sincere, will never wear clothing made of silk, nor wear boots made of leather because it involves the taking of life. Neither will they indulge in eating milk or cheese because thereby they are depriving the young animals of that which rightly belongs to them. . . . To wear anything, or partake of anything for self-comfort, deceiving one's self as to the suffering it causes others or other sentient life, is to set up an affinity with that lower life which will draw them toward it. So all monks must be very careful to live in all sincerity, refraining from even the appearance of unkindness to other life. Even in one's speech and especially in one's teaching, one must practice kindness, for no teaching that is unkind can be the true teaching of Buddha. Unkindness is the murderer of the life of Wisdom. This is the second admonition of the Lord Buddha as to the keeping of the Precepts.

Then there is the Precept of not taking anything that does not rightfully belong to one, not coveting it or even admiring it. One must learn to keep this Precept in all sincerity if he is to hope for escape from the chain of deaths and rebirths. The purpose of your practice of concentration is to escape from the suffering of this mortal life. No matter how keen you may be mentally, no matter how much you may be able to practice concentration, no matter to how high a degree of apparent ecstasy you may attain, unless you refrain from covetousness and stealing, you will fall into the realm of heretics. . . .

For all these various reasons, I teach my bhikshu-brothers not to covet comforts and privileges, but to beg their food, not here and there, or now and then, but to make it a regular habit so that they will be better able to overcome the greediness and covetousness that hinders their progress toward enlightenment. I teach them not to cook their own food even, but to be dependent upon others for even the poorest living so that they will realize their oneness with all sentient life and are but sojourners in this triple world. . . .

If any of my disciples who are trying to practice concentration, do not abstain from stealing and covetousness, their efforts will be like trying to fill a leaking pot with water; no matter how long they try, they will never succeed. So all of you, my bhikshu disciples, with the exception of your poor garments and your begging bowls should have nothing more in possession. Even the food that is left over from your begging after you have eaten should be given to hungry sentient beings and should not be kept for the next meal. Moreover, you should look upon your own body, its flesh, blood and bone, as not being your own but as being one with the bodies of all other sentient beings and so be ever ready to sacrifice it for the common need. Even when men beat you and scold you, you must accept it patiently and, with hands pressed together, bow to them humbly. Furthermore, you should not accept one teaching, or one principle, that is easy and agreeable, and reject the rest of the Doctrine; you should accept all with equitable mind lest you misinterpret the Doctrine to the new converts. Thus living, the Lord Buddha will confirm your attainment as one who has acquired the true Samadhi. As you teach the Doctrine to others, be sure that your teaching is in agreement with the above so that it may be regarded as a true teaching of Buddha, otherwise it would be as heretical as the deceptive words of the goblin-heretics who are murderers of the life of Wisdom. This is the third admonition of the Lord Buddha as it relates to the Precepts.

Then there is the Precept of not deceiving nor telling lies. If the sentient beings of the six realms of existence should refrain from killing, stealing and adultery, and should refrain from even thinking about them, but should fail to keep the Precept of truthfulness . . . there would be no emancipation for them; they would . . . become prejudiced and egoistically assertive, and . . . lose their seed of Buddhahood. . . . They not only lose their own seed of Buddahood, they destroy the seed of Buddhahood in others. Such disciples progressively lose their nature of kindness and gradually lose the measure of understanding that they had attained and shall at last sink into the Sea of the Three Kinds of Suffering, namely, (1) the suffering of pain, (2) the loss of enjoyment, (3) the suffering of decay. They will not attain to Samadhi for a long, long time in after lives.

I urge all Saints and holy men to choose to be reborn in order to deliver all sentient beings.[22] You should make use of all manner of transformations, such as disciples, laymen, kings, lords, ministers, virgins, boy-eunuchs, and even as harlots, widows, adulterers, thieves, butchers, pedlers, etc., so as to be able to mingle with all kinds of people and to make known the true emancipation of Buddhism and the following peace of Samadhi. . . . To teach the world to observe the Precept of truthful sincerity, to practice concentration with sincerity and to attain a true ecstasy, this is the clear and true instruction of the Lord Buddha.

Therefore, Ananda, if any disciple does not abstain from deceit, he is like a man moulding human dung instead of carving sweet-smelling sandalwood. . . . But disciples whose lives are as straight as the chord of a bow will certainly attain Samandhi. They need never fear the wiles of the Maras. They are the disciples who are certain to attain the Savior's supreme understanding and insight. Any lesson or instruction that is in agreement with the foregoing can be relied upon as being a true teaching of the Lord Buddha. Differing from it, it is

[22] The doctrine of "bodhisattvaship," voluntarily abstaining from Nirvana and continuing in the cycle of rebirths until the world is saved, is an essential tenet of Mahayana Buddhism. A "bodhisattva" therefore corresponds somewhat to the Christian idea of "Saviour."

simply a false teaching of the heretics who have always been murderers of the Life of Wisdom. This is the fourth admonition of the Lord Buddha.

Ananda! As you have asked me as to the best method for concentrating the mind of those who have difficulty in following the common methods, I will now reveal to you the Lord Buddha's Secret Method for the attainment of saviorhood. But you must remember that it is of first importance to fully observe the Four Precepts as explained above. To become a savior, one must have a nature as pure and clear and repellent as frost and ice, so that no false growths of leaves and branches shall sprout out from the true Mind, such as the three poisons of lust, hatred and infatuation; or the four wickednesses of the mouth: falsehood, slander, obscene words, and flattery.

Ananda! If any of the disciples should be unable to overcome their old habits, you may teach them to recite this Dharani of mine. It is called The Supreme Dharani of the Radiating Brightness of the Lord Buddha's Crowning Experience. It is the invisible transcendental power that rays out from the Tathagata's Wisdom Eye manifesting the unconditioned Essential Mind of the Lord Buddha. It is the transcendental radio-activity of Power and Glory that was revealed in me at the time of my Highest Ecstasy, at the hour of my Perfect Enlightenment, as I sat amid the Lotus Blossoms under the Bodhi-tree. . . . Rest assured, all my Bhikshu Brothers in this great assembly, you who are earnestly seeking Supreme Attainment, rest assured that, by the power of this Great Dharani, you will attain Buddhahood.

THE LANKAVATARA SUTRA

This famed discourse comes down to us in its present form prob-ably from the first century A.D., *and gives the clearest short account of the metaphysical system underlying Mahayana Buddhism. The original Sanskrit text has long been lost, but there are Chinese trans-lations of it dating back as far as the fifth century. Though less vivid than the* SURANGAMA SUTRA, *it covers much the same ground with greater succinctness. It is far from easy to follow, however, especially for Western readers, and the selections quoted here are therefore few and brief. The last is regarded by scholars as perhaps the best de-scription of what the Mahayana Buddhists mean by Nirvana.*[23]

THE WAY TO NOBLE WISDOM

Then Mahamati asked the Blessed One, saying: What are the steps that will lead an awakened disciple toward the self-realization of Noble Wisdom?

The Blessed One replied: . . . The disciple must get into the habit of looking at things truthfully. He must recognize the fact that the world has no self-nature, that it is un-born, that it is like a passing cloud, like an imaginary wheel made by a revolving fire-brand . . . like the moon reflected in the ocean, like a vision, a mirage, a dream. He must come to understand that mind in its essence-nature has nothing to do with discrimination nor causation; he must not listen to discourses based on the imaginary terms of qualifications; he must understand that Universal Mind in its pure essence is a state of image-lessness, that it is only because of the accumulated defilements on its face that body-property-and-abode appear to be its manifestations, that in its own pure nature it is unaffected and unaffecting by such changes as rising, abiding and destruction; he must fully understand that all these things come with the awakening of the notion of an ego-soul and its conscious mind. Therefore, Mahamati, let those dis-

[23] Reprinted from a translation by Suzuki and Goddard in *A Buddhist Bible*, edited by Dwight Goddard (Thetford, Vermont, 1938).

ciples who wish to realize Noble Wisdom by following the Tathagata Vehicle desist from all discrimination and erroneous reasoning about such notions as the elements that make up the aggregates of personality and its sense-world or about such ideas as causation, rising, abiding and destruction, and exercise themselves in the discipline of dhyana that leads to the realization of Noble Wisdom.

THE WAY TO SELF-REALIZATION

Then said Mahamati to the Blessed One: Pray tell us more as to what constitutes the state of self-realization.

. . . The exalted state of self-realization as it relates to an earnest disciple is a state of mental concentration in which he seeks to identify himself with Noble Wisdom. In that effort he must seek to annihilate all vagrant thoughts and notions belonging to the externality of things, and all ideas of individuality and generality, of suffering and impermanence, and cultivate the noblest ideals of egolessness and emptiness and imagelessness; thus will he attain a realisation of truth that is free from passion and is ever serene. When this active effort at mental concentration is successful it is followed by a more passive, receptive state of Samadhi in which the earnest disciple will enter into the blissful abode of Noble Wisdom and experience its consummations in the transformations of Samapatti. This is an earnest disciple's first experience of the exalted state of realisation, but as yet there is no discarding of habit-energy nor escaping from the transformation of death.

Having attained this exalted and blissful state of realisation as far

as it can be attained by disciples, the Bodhisattva must not give himself up to the enjoyment of its bliss, for that would mean cessation,
but should think compassionately of other beings and keep ever fresh
his original vows; he should never let himself rest in nor exert himself
in the bliss of the Samadhis. . . .

To do all this the Bodhisattva should keep himself away from all
turmoil, social excitements and sleepiness; let him keep away from
the treatises and writings of worldly philosophers, and from the ritual
and ceremonies of professional priestcraft. Let him retire to a secluded
place in the forest and there devote himself to the practise of the
various spiritual disciplines, because it is only by so doing that he
will become capable of attaining in this world of multiplicities a true
insight into the workings of Universal Mind in its Essence. There
surrounded by his good friends the Buddhas, earnest disciples will
become capable of understanding the significance of the mind-system
and its place as a mediating agent between the external world and
Universal Mind and he will become capable of crossing the ocean
of birth-and-death which rises from ignorance, desire and deed.

Having gained a thorough understanding of the mind-system, the
three self-natures, the twofold egolessness, and established himself in
the measure of self-realisation that goes with that attainment, all of
which may be gained by his right-knowledge, the way will be clear
for the Bodhisattva's further advance along the stages of Bodhisattvahood. The disciple should then abandon the understanding of mind
which he has gained by right-knowledge, which in comparison with
Noble Wisdom is like a lame donkey, and entering on the eighth
stage of Bodhisattvahood, he should then discipline himself in Noble
Wisdom according to its three aspects.

These aspects are: First, imagelessness which comes forth when
all things belonging to discipleship, mastership, and philosophy are
thoroughly mastered. Second, the power added by all the Buddhas
by reason of their original vows including the identification of their
lives and the sharing of their merit with all sentient lives. Third, the
perfect self-realisation that thus far has only been realised in a
measure. As the Bodhisattva succeeds in detaching himself from viewing all things, including his own imagined egoness, in their phenom-
enality, and realises the states of Samadhi and Samapatti whereby he
surveys the world as a vision and a dream, and being sustained by
all the Buddhas, he will be able to pass on to the full attainment of

the Tathagata stage, which is Noble Wisdom itself. This is the triplicity of the noble life and being furnished with this triplicity the perfect self-realisation of Noble Wisdom has been attained.

THE NATURE OF NIRVANA

Then said Mahamati to the Blessed One: Pray tell us about Nirvana?

The Blessed One replied: The term, Nirvana, is used with many different meanings by different people. . . .

Those who are suffering or who fear suffering, think of Nirvana as an escape and a recompense. They imagine that Nirvana consists in the future annihilation of the senses and the sense-minds. They are not aware that Universal Mind and Nirvana are One, and that this life-and-death world and Nirvana are not to be separated. These ignorant ones, instead of meditating on the imagelessness of Nirvana, talk of different ways of emancipation. . . . They cling to the notion of Nirvana that is outside what is seen of the mind and, thus, go on rolling themselves along with the wheel of life and death. . . .

Some philosophers conceive Nirvana to be . . . a state where there is no recollection of the past or present, just as when a lamp is extinguished, or when a seed is burnt, or when a fire goes out. . . . But this is not Nirvana, because Nirvana does not consist in simple annihilation and vacuity.

Again, some philosophers . . . conceive being to be Nirvana, some non-being, while others conceive that all things and Nirvana are not to be distinguished from one another. Some, thinking that time is the creator and that as the rise of the world depends on time, they conceive that Nirvana consists in the recognition of time as Nirvana. Some think that there will be Nirvana when the "twenty-five" truths are generally accepted, or when the king observes the six virtues, and some religionists think that Nirvana is the attainment of paradise.

These views severally advanced by the philosophers with their various reasonings are not in accord with logic nor are they acceptable to the wise. They all conceive Nirvana dualistically and in some causal connection; by these discriminations philosophers imagine Nirvana, but where there is no rising and no disappearing, how can there be discrimination? Each philosopher relying on his own textbook from which he draws his understanding, sins against the truth, because truth is not where he imagines it to be. The only result is that it sets his mind to wandering about and becoming more confused as Nirvana is not to be found by mental searching, and the more his mind becomes confused the more he confuses other people.

As to the notion of Nirvana as held by disciples and masters who still cling to the notion of an ego-self, and who try to find it by going off by themselves into solitude: their notion of Nirvana is an eternity of bliss like the bliss of the Samadhis—for themselves. They recognise that the world is only a manifestation of mind and that all discriminations are of the mind, and so they forsake social relations and practise various spiritual disciplines and in solitude seek self-realisation of Noble Wisdom by self-effort. . . . Clinging to the bliss of the ecstasies, they pass to their Nirvana, but it is not the Nirvana of the Bodhisattvas.

Then said Mahamati to the Blessed One: Pray tell us, what is the Nirvana of the Bodhisattvas?

The Blessed One replied: Mahamati, this assurance is not an assurance of numbers nor logic; it is not the mind that is to be assured but the heart. The Bodhisattva's assurance comes with the unfolding insight that follows passion-hindrances cleared away, knowledge-hindrance purified, and egolessness clearly perceived and patiently accepted. As the mortal-mind ceases to discriminate, there is no more thirst for life, no more sex-lust, no more thirst for learning, no more thirst for eternal life; with the disappearance of these fourfold thirsts, there is no more accumulation of habit-energy; with no more accumulation of habit-energy the defilements on the face of Universal Mind clear away, and the Bodhisattva attains self-realisation of Noble Wisdom that is the heart's assurance of Nirvana.

There are Bodhisattvas here and in other Buddha-lands, who are sincerely devoted to the Bodhisattva's mission and yet who cannot wholly forget the peace of Nirvana—for themselves. The teaching of Nirvana is revealed according to a hidden meaning for the sake of such disciples, that they may be inspired to exert themselves in the Bodhisattva's mission of emancipation for all beings. . . . In the perfect self-realisation of Noble Wisdom the Bodhisattva realises that for Buddhas there is no Nirvana.

The death of a Buddha, the great Parinirvana, is neither destruction nor death, else would it be birth and continuation. If it were destruction, it would be an effect-producing deed, which it is not.

Neither is it a vanishing nor an abandonment, neither is it attainment, nor is it of no attainment; neither is it of one significance nor of no significance, for there is no Nirvana for the Buddhas.

The Tathagata's Nirvana is where it is recognised that there is nothing but what is seen of the mind itself; is where, recognising the nature of the self-mind, one no longer cherishes the dualisms of discrimination; is where there is no more thirst nor grasping; is where there is no more attachment to external things. Nirvana is where the thinking-mind with all its discriminations, attachments, aversions and egoism is forever put away; is where logical measures, as they are seen to be inert, are no longer seized upon; is where even the notion of truth is treated with indifference because of its causing bewilderment; is where, getting rid of the four propositions, there is insight into the abode of Reality. Nirvana is where the twofold passions have subsided and the twofold hindrances are cleared away and the twofold egolessness is patiently accepted; is where, by the attainment of the "turning-about" in the deepest seat of consciousness, self-realisation of Noble Wisdom is fully entered into—that is the Nirvana of the Tathagatas.

Nirvana is where the manifestation of Noble Wisdom expresses itself in Perfect Love for all; it is where the manifestation of Perfect Love expresses itself in Noble Wisdom for the enlightenment of all;—there, indeed, is Nirvana!

There are two classes of those who may not enter the Nirvana of the Tathagatas: there are those who have abandoned the Bodhisattva ideals, saying, they are not in conformity with the sutras, the codes of morality, nor with emancipation. Then there are the true Bodhisattvas who, on account of their original vows made for the sake of all beings, saying, "So long as they do not attain Nirvana, I will not attain it myself," voluntarily keep themselves out of Nirvana. But no beings are left outside by the will of the Tathagatas; some day each and every one will be influenced by the wisdom and love of the Tathagatas of Transformation to lay up a stock of merit and ascend the stages. But, if they only realised it, they are already in the Tathagata's Nirvana for, in Noble Wisdom, all things are in Nirvana from the beginning.

THE SHRADDHOTPADA SHASTRA

This shastra ("commentary") is said to have been written by the great Indian theologian, Ashvagosha (first century A.D.), who is often described as the St. Paul of Buddhism. It is a treatise on faith: whence it arises, how it grows, and whither it can lead. The passage quoted below is taken from the fourth chapter, and summarizes what kind of faith is necessary in order to attain the bliss of Buddhahood, and the ways in which it can best be practiced.

The Sanskrit original no longer exists, and the work has survived through a Chinese version made in the sixth century. It is said to be an exceptionally elegant translation, and enjoys great prestige among Mahayana Buddhists.[24]

There are four kinds of faith: First, the novice disciple must have faith in the fundamental, ultimate Principle of things, that it is perfect Wisdom and perfect Compassion, and perfect Oneness. He should think joyfully of his own identity with its pure Mind-Essence. Second, the disciple should have abounding faith in Buddhahood. This means that he should cherish a sincere faith in the merits and virtues of the Buddhas, that he should constantly remember them to feel his fellowship with them, to make offerings to them of adoration and gifts, to seek instruction and guidance from them. Third, the disciple should have an unshakable faith in the wisdom, the

[24] English translation by Wai-tao and Goddard, in *A Buddhist Bible*, edited by Dwight Goddard (Thetford, Vermont, 1938).

compassion, the power of the Dharma ("Doctrine"). This means he should look to it and rely upon it as an infallible guide in his practice of its ideals. Fourth, the disciple should have an unfeigned, affectionate and abounding faith in the Brotherhood of Wandering Monks, caring for them, supplying their few needs, looking to them for instruction and sympathy in their own practice, that they may perfect their faith and move toward Buddhahood together.

There are six ways of practicing faith. First, there is the Way of Charity. Second, the Way of unselfish kindness in Keeping the Precepts. Third, the Way of Patience and Humility. Fourth, the Way of Zeal and Perseverance. Fifth, the Way of Tranquillity, stopping all discriminating thoughts and quietly realizing Truth itself. Sixth, the Way of Wisdom.

First, the Way of Charity. The purpose of this practice is to eradicate one's own stinginess and cupidity. To effect this one should train himself to be generous. If any one comes to him begging, he should give him money or things as he has particular need, with discretion and kindness, as much as he can up to his ability and the other's need, so that the begging ones may be relieved and go away cheerful. Or, if the disciple come upon one in danger or hardship or an extremity of any kind, he should encourage him and help him as much as he can. Or, if one should come seeking instruction in the Dharma, he should humbly and patiently interpret it to him using expedient means, as much as he can interpret with clearness according to his ability. The disciple should practice Charity simply and unostentatiously, with no ulterior motive in mind of ambition, self-interest, reward, or praise, keeping in mind only this that the giving and receiving shall both tend in the direction of Enlightenment from them both alike and equally.

Second, the Way of Keeping the Precepts. The purpose of this practice is to get rid of all selfish grasping after comforts, delights, and self-interests. It means not to kill any sentient being, not to steal, not to commit adultery, not to deceive nor slander nor to utter malicious words nor to flatter. If he is a layman, it means keeping away from all greedy actions, envy, cheating, mischief, injustice, hatred, anger, and all heretical views. If he is a Bhikshu (monk), it means he should avoid all vexatious and annoying acts, he should keep away from the turmoil and activities of the worldly life and live in solitude and quietness, practicing begging and disciplining himself to be content with least desires. He should feel regret over any slight fault and should always act with prudence and attentiveness. He should not neglect any of the Lord Buddha's instruction, and should be always ready to defend any one suffering under suspicion or slander so as to restrain them from falling into further evil.

Third, the Way of Patience. This means to practice patience when vexed or annoyed by others and to restrain any rising thoughts of ill-will or vengeance. It means being patient when overtaken by any affront to one's pride, personal losses, criticisms, or praise, or flattery; it means being patient and undisturbed by either happiness or suffering, comfort or discomfort.

Fourth, the Way of Zeal. The purpose of this discipline is to restrain oneself from yielding to temptations to laziness and weariness. It disciplines one not to relax one's effort when one meets success and praise, but to ever renew one's resolution to seek enlightenment. It should strengthen one to keep far away from temptations to timidity or false modesty. One should ever remember past sufferings borne because of evil committed carelessly and to no benefit to himself, and by these recollections to renew his zeal and preseverance to make diligent practicing of all kinds of meritorious and virtuous deeds that will benefit both others and himself and keep himself free from suffering in the future. In spite of his being a Bhikshu he may be suffering from unmatured karma of previous lives and thus still be open to the attacks of evil influences, or still be entangled in worldly affairs, or the responsibilities of a family life, or under some chronic illness or disability. In the face of all such burdensome hindrances, he should be courageous and zealous and unceaselessly diligent in his practicings during the day, and in the six watches of the night should be on his guard against idle thoughts by constantly repeating adorations to all the Buddhas with zeal and sincerity, beseeching the Buddhas to abide in the world to turn the Dharma wheel, to support all right efforts to practice, to encourage all kind acts, to awaken faith in the faithless, to encourage right vows and to return all merit for the Enlightenment of all sentient beings. Unless one is zealous and persevering in his practice, he will not be able to keep himself from increasing hindrances to cultivating his root of devotion.

Fifth, the Way of Tranquillity. The purpose of this discipline is twofold, to bring to a standstill all disturbing thoughts, and all discriminating thoughts are disturbing, to quiet all engrossing moods and emotions so that it will be possible to concentrate the mind for the practice of meditation and realization, and thus to be able to follow the practice willingly and gladly. Secondly, when the mind is tranquillized by stopping all thought, to practice "reflection" or meditation not in a discriminating way but in a more intellectual way of realizing the meaning and significance of one's thoughts and experiences, and also to follow this part of the practice willingly and gladly. By this twofold practice of "stopping and realizing," one's faith, that is already awakened, will become developed and gradually the two aspects of this practice will merge into one another—the mind perfectly tranquil but most active in realization. In the past, one naturally has had confidence in his faculty of discrimination, but this is now to be eradicated and ended.

For those who are practicing "stopping," they should retire to some quiet place, or better live in some quiet place, sitting erect and with earnest and zestful purpose seek to quiet and concentrate the mind. While one may at first think of his breathing, it is not wise to continue it very long, nor to let the mind rest on any particular appearances or sights, or conceptions arising from the senses, such as the primal elements of earth, water, fire and ether, nor to let it rest on any of the lower mind's perceptions, particularizations, discriminations, moods or emotions. All kinds of ideation are to be discarded as fast as they arise, even the notions of controlling and discarding are to be gotten rid of. One's mind should become like a mirror, reflecting things but not judging them nor retaining them. Conceptions of themselves have no substance, let them rise and pass away unheeded. Conceptions arising from the senses and lower mind, will not take form of themselves, unless they are grasped by the attention, but if they are ignored there will be no appearing and no disappearing. The same is true of conditions outside the mind: they should not be permitted to engross one's attention nor hinder one's practice. As the mind can not be absolutely vacant, as thoughts rising from the senses and discriminating mind are discarded and ignored, one must supply their place by right mentation. The question then arises, what is right mentation? The reply is: right mentation is the realization of the mind itself, of its pure undifferentiated Essence. Even when we sit quietly with the mind fixed on its pure Essence, there should be no lingering notions of self, of self realizing, or any phenomena of realization.

Pure Mind-Essence is ungraspable of any rising or appearing of individuation.

Sixth, the Way of Wisdom. The purpose of this discipline is to bring one into the habit of applying the insight that has come to him by the preceding ways of discipline. Even when one is rising, standing, walking, doing something, stopping, one should constantly concentrate his mind on the act and the doing of it, not on his relation to it or its character or its value. One should think: there is walking, there is doing, there is stopping, there is realizing; not, I am walking, I am doing this, it is a good thing, it is disagreeable, it is I who am gaining merit, it is I who am realizing how wonderful it is. Then come vagrant thoughts, feelings of elation or defeat and failure and unhappiness. Instead of all this, one should simply practice concentration of the mind on the act itself, understanding it to be an expedient means for attaining tranquillity of mind, realization, insight and Wisdom, and to follow the practice in faith, willingness and gladness. After long practice the bondage of old habits becomes weakened and disappears, and in its place appear confidence, satisfaction, awareness and tranquillity.

What is this practice of Wisdom designed to accomplish? There are three classes of conditions that hinder one from advancing along the path to Enlightenment: first, the allurements arising from the senses and external conditions and the discriminating mind; second, the inner conditions of the mind, its thoughts, desires and moods; these the earlier practices are designed to eliminate. The third class are the instinctive and fundamental, insidious and persistent, urgings, the will-to-live and enjoy, the will-to-protect one's life and personality, the will-to-propagate, which give rise to greed and lust, fear and anger, infatuation and pride of egoism. The practice of the Wisdom Paramita is designed to control and eliminate these fundamental and instinctive hindrances. By means of it the mind gradually becomes clearer, more luminous, more peaceful. Insight clears, faith deepens and broadens, until they merge into the inconceivable Samadhi of the Mind's Pure Essence. As one continues the practice of Wisdom, one less and less yields to thoughts of comfort or discomfort, faith becomes surer, more pervasive, beneficent, joyous, and fear of retrogression vanishes.

But do not think that these consummations are to be attained easily or quickly; many rebirths may be necessary, many asamkyas of kalpas may have to elapse. So long as doubt, unbelief, slanders, evil conduct, hindrances of karma, weakness of faith, pride, laziness, a disturbed mind, persist, or their shadows linger, there can be no attainment of the Samadhi of the Buddhas. But once attained, in the luminous brightness of highest Samadhi, one will be able to realize with all the Buddhas the perfect unity of all sentient beings with Buddhahood's Dharmakaya. In the pure Dharmakaya, there is no dualism, neither shadow of differences. All sentient beings, if they are able to realize it, are already in Nirvana. The Mind's pure Essence is Highest Samadhi. The Mind's Pure Essence is *anuttara-samyak-sambodh*, is Prajna Paramita, Highest Perfect Wisdom.

INTRODUCTION

Confucianism was until recently the state religion of China, and it still commands the devotion of untold millions in that land. Originally it was a system of morals engrafted upon the crude nature-worship that had been China's real religion from the very earliest times. The author of this system was Kung-fu-tze (Latinized as Confucius, 551–478 B.C.), a sage who devoted all his days to the public weal. China was then in a state of chaos because the ancient feudal order was breaking up, and there was increasing lawlessness, corruption, and distress. The need of the hour was a set of values to which the people could cling, a morality around which they could rebuild their lives. It was to this need that Confucius applied himself.

He failed, of course. Though he did work out such a morality, he was unable to get it accepted by more than a handful of disciples. Over two centuries had to elapse before the worth of his teachings was acknowledged, and then it was only because they had in the meantime been thoroughly warped. From a cry for human righteousness they had been reduced largely to a plea for social regimentation.

Confucius polarized his system around two virtues: duty and love. Social well-being was possible, he declared, only if each individual performed his social obligations. These he grouped under five heads: the obligations of (1) rulers and subjects, (2) parents and children, (3) husbands and wives, (4) elder and younger children, (5) friend and friend. In each case there were set proprieties to be observed, conventions established by Nature and hallowed by history.

Dutifulness alone, however, was not enough. In addition there had to be affection (jin), a comprehensive term which included char-

ity, justice, courage, loyalty, and general righteousness. "Jin is love for all mankind."

Confucius was fundamentally a humanist. Like Buddha, he was what we would call an agnostic, admitting ignorance as to the gods and indifference toward religious rites. Supreme blessedness, he insisted, had to be found here on earth, not in heaven, and among men, not shades. To prove it could indeed be found here, he pointed to ancient records which told of a Golden Age that had once existed because men had been truly dutiful and full of jin. He devoted much of his life to compiling and editing those records, making of them five books which he called the "Classics." Later generations added four more books, one containing Confucius's own traditional sayings, and these together with the Classics became the scriptural canon of the Confucian religion.

THE SHU KING

The first of the Five Classics, the YU KING, *is a book of magic spells, and therefore outside the pale of this Anthology. We begin with the second, the* SHU KING, *which contains a number of passages deserving quotation. This Classic is a collection of ancient Chinese chronicles, and quite dull on the whole. It was compiled by Confucius because of his veneration for the past and his anxiety to preserve all he could of its records. Most of the documents are mere catalogues of monarchs and battles, and in their monotony, redundance, and childish prating they recall the chronicles of Assyria. Intermingled, however, are passages of an altogether different quality, full of moral counsel and genuinely prophetic in eloquence. For example—*

I: THE CAUTIONS OF THE GREAT YU

This passage—from Book III, Part III, of the SHU KING—*records the remonstrances uttered by five brothers of a lazy and dissipated monarch named Thai Khang (2188–2160 B.C.). They repeat the testament left by the founder of their dynasty, Yu, who was one of the greatest of China's kings. (It was Yu, according to tradition, who reduced the Yang-tze floods by cutting gorges through the mountains so that the river could reach the sea.) The testament may have come down in the form of a series of runes, for it is thus that those brothers recite it.*[1]

The first said,

> "It was the lesson of our great ancestor:
> The people should be cherished,
> And not looked down upon.
> The people are the root of a country;
> The root firm, the country is tranquil.
> When I look at all under heaven,

[1] This and the succeeding excerpts are taken from the translation of the *Shu King* by James Legge in *The Sacred Books of the East*, vol. iii (The Clarendon Press, Oxford).

211

Of the simple men and simple women,
Any one may surpass me.
If the One man (*the king*) err repeatedly,
Should dissatisfaction be waited for till it appears?
Before it is seen, it should be guarded against.
In my dealing with the millions of the people,
I should feel as much anxiety as if I were driving
      six horses with rotten reins.
The ruler of men—
How should he be but reverent of his duties?"

The second said,

    "It is in the Lessons:
When the palace is a wild of
    lust,
And the country is a wild for
    hunting;
When spirits are liked, and
    music is the delight;
When there are lofty roofs and
    carved walls—
The existence of any one of
    these things
Has never been but the prelude
    to ruin."

The third said,

    "There was the lord of Thao and Thang,
Who possessed this region of Chi.
Now we have fallen from his ways,
And thrown into confusion his rules and laws;
The consequence is extinction and ruin."

The fourth said,

    "Brightly intelligent was our ancestor,
Sovereign of the myriad regions.
He had canons, he had patterns,
Which he transmitted to his posterity.

The standard stone and the equalizing quarter
Were in the royal treasury.
Wildly have we dropped the clue he gave us,
Overturning our temple, and extinguishing our
    sacrifices."

The fifth said,

"Oh! whither shall we turn?
The thoughts in my breast make me sad.
All the people are hostile to us;
On whom can we rely?
Anxieties crowd together in our hearts;
Thick as are our faces, they are covered with blushes.
We have not been careful of our virtue;
And though we repent, we can not overtake the past.'

II: THE PRONOUNCEMENT OF CHUNG-HUI

This—from Book II, Part IV—is the first of a series of such "pro-nouncements" preserved in the SHU KING. *Chung-hui, to whom it is attributed, was the minister of Thang the Glorious, the legendary founder of the Shang dynasty in 1766 B.C.*

Our king did not approach to dissolute music and women; he did not seek to accumulate property and wealth. To great virtue he gave great offices, and to great merit great rewards. He employed others as if their excellences were his own; he was not slow to change his errors. Rightly indulgent and rightly benevolent, from the display of such virtue, confidence was reposed in him by the millions of the people. . . .

Show favor to the able and right-principled among the princes, and aid the virtuous; distinguish the loyal, and let the good have free course. Absorb the weak, and punish the wilfully blind; take their States from the disorderly, and deal summarily with those going to ruin. When you thus accelerate the end of what is of itself ready to perish, and strengthen what is itself strong to live, how will the States all flourish! When a sovereign's virtue is daily being renewed, he is cherished throughout the myriad regions; when his mind is full only of himself, he is abandoned by the nine branches of his kindred.

Exert yourself, O king, to make your virtue still more illustrious, and set up the standard of the Mean before the people. Order your affairs by righteousness; order your heart by propriety; so shall you transmit a grand example to posterity. I have heard the saying, "He who finds instructors for himself comes to the supreme dominion; he who says that others are not equal to himself comes to ruin. He who likes to put questions becomes enlarged; he who uses only his own views becomes smaller than he was." Oh! he who would take care for the end must be attentive to the beginning. There is establishment for the observers of propriety, and overthrow for the blinded and wantonly indifferent. To revere and honor the path prescribed by Heaven is the way ever to preserve the favoring appointment of Heaven.

III: THE PRONOUNCEMENT OF THANG

Thang (literally "The Glorious One"), having led a successful insurrection against the cruel king of Hsia, returned from the field of battle to make the following "grand announcement to the myriad regions":

The king said, "Ah! ye multitudes of the myriad regions, listen clearly to the announcement of me, the One man.[2] The great God has conferred even on the inferior people a moral sense, compliance with which would show their nature invariably right. To make them tranquilly pursue the course which it would indicate is the work of the sovereign.

"The king of Hsia extinguished his virtue, and played the tyrant, extending his oppression over you, the people of the myriad regions. Suffering from his cruel injuries, and unable to endure the wormwood and poison, you protested with one accord your innocence to the spirits of heaven and earth. The way of Heaven is to bless the good, and make the bad miserable. It sent down calamities on the House of Hsia, to make manifest its guilt. Therefore I, the little child, charged with the decree of Heaven and its bright terrors, did not dare to forgive the criminal. I presumed to use a dark-colored victim-bull, and, making clear announcement to the Spiritual Sovereign in the high heavens, requested leave to deal with the ruler of Hsia as a criminal.

[2] "The One man" has occurred before, in the Songs of the Five Sons, as a designation of the sovereign. It continues to be so to the present day.

Then I sought for the great Sage, with whom I might unite my strength, to request the favor of Heaven for you, my multitudes. High Heaven truly showed its favor to the inferior people, and the criminal has been degraded and subjected. What Heaven appoints is without error—brilliantly now, like the blossoming of plants and trees, the millions of the people show a true reviving.

"It is given to me, the One man, to secure the harmony and tranquillity of your States and clans; and now I know not whether I may not offend against the Powers above and below. I am fearful and trembling, as if I were in danger of falling into a deep abyss. Throughout all the regions that enter on a new life under me, do not, ye princes, follow lawless ways; make no approach to insolence and dissoluteness; let every one be careful to keep his statutes, that so we may receive the favor of Heaven. The good in you I will not dare to keep concealed; and for the evil in me I will not dare to forgive myself. I will examine these things in harmony with the mind of God. When guilt is found anywhere in you who occupy the myriad regions, let it rest on me, the One man. When guilt is found in me, the One man, it shall not attach to you who occupy the myriad regions.

"Oh! let us attain to be sincere in these things, and so we shall likewise have a happy consummation."

IV: THE INSTRUCTIONS OF I-YIN

I-Yin was the chief minister of Thang the Glorious, and lived to offer the following "Instructions" to the latter's grandson and successor. Tradition describes I-Yin as "a great sage" and one of the most noteworthy of the ancient royal counsellors.

Now your Majesty is entering on the inheritance of his virtue; all depends on how you commence your reign. To set up love, it is for you to love your relations; to set up respect, it is for you to respect your elders. The commencement is in the family and the State; the consummation is in all within the four seas.

Oh! the former king began with careful attention to the bonds that hold men together. He listened to expostulation, and did not seek to resist it; he conformed to the wisdom of the ancients; occupying the highest position, he displayed intelligence; occupying an inferior position, he displayed his loyalty; he allowed the good qualities of the men whom he employed, and did not seek that they should have every talent; in the government of himself, he seemed to think that he could never sufficiently attain. It was thus he arrived at the possession of the myriad regions. How painstaking was he in these things!

He extensively sought out wise men, who should be helpful to you, his descendant and heir. He laid down the punishments for officers, and warned those who were in authority, saying, "If you dare to have constant dancing in your palaces, and drunken singing in your chambers—that is called the fashion

of sorcerers; if you dare to set your hearts on wealth and women, and abandon yourselves to wandering about or to the chase—that is called the fashion of extravagance; if you dare to despise sage words, to resist the loyal and upright, to put far from you the aged and virtuous, and to seek the company of precocious youths—that is called the fashion of disorder. Now if a high noble or officer be addicted to one of these three fashions with their ten evil ways, his family will surely come to ruin; if the prince of a country be so addicted, his State will surely come to ruin. The minister who does not try to correct such vices in the sovereign shall be punished with branding." These rules were minutely inculcated also on the sons of officers and nobles in their lessons.

Oh! do you, who now succeed to the throne, revere these warnings in your person. Think of them!—sacred counsels of vast importance, admirable words forcibly set forth! The ways of God are not invariable: on the good-doer he sends down all blessings, and on the evil-doer he sends down all miseries. Do you but be virtuous, be it in small things or in large, and the myriad regions will have cause for rejoicing. If you be not virtuous, be it in small things or in large, the myriad regions will not have cause for rejoicing. If you be not virtuous, be it in large things or in small, it will bring the ruin of your ancestral temple.

I-Yin again made an announcement to the king, saying, "Oh! Heaven has no partial affection; only to those who are reverent does it show affection. The people are not constant to those whom they cherish; they cherish only him who is benevolent. The spirits do not always accept the sacrifices that are offered to them; they accept only the sacrifices of the sincere. A place of difficulty is the Heaven-conferred seat. When there are those virtues, good government is realized; when they are not, disorder comes. To maintain the same principles as those who secured good government will surely lead to prosperity; to pursue the courses of disorder will surely lead to ruin. He who at last, as at first, is careful as to whom and what he follows is a truly intelligent sovereign. The former king was always zealous in the reverent cultivation of his virtue, so that he was the fellow of God. Now, O king, you have entered on the inheritance of his excellent line; fix your inspection on him.

"Your course must be as when in ascending high you begin from where it is low, and when in traveling far you begin from where it is near. Do not slight the occupations of the people; think of their difficulties. Do not yield to a feeling of repose on your throne; think of its perils. Be careful for the end at the beginning. When you hear words that are distasteful to your mind, you must inquire whether they be not right; when you hear words that accord with your own views, you must inquire whether they be not contrary to what is right. Oh! what attainment can be made without anxious thought? what achievement can be made without earnest effort? Let the One man be greatly good, and the myriad regions will be rectified by him.

"When the sovereign does not with disputatious words throw the old rules of government into confusion, and the minister does not, for favor and gain, continue in an office whose work is done, then the country will lastingly and surely enjoy happiness."

V: THE CHARGE TO YUEH

*A certain king named Hsiao-Yi took as his chief counsellor a
recluse named Yueh, whose virtue had been made known to him in
a dream. In appointing him, the ruler gave Yueh the following
charge, and received the subsequent response:*

"Morning and evening present your instructions to aid my virtue.
Suppose me a weapon of steel—I will use you for a whetstone. Suppose
me crossing a great stream—I will use you for a boat with its oars.
Suppose me in a year of great drought—I will use you as a copious
rain. Open your mind, and enrich my mind. Be you like medicine,
which must distress the patient, in order to cure his sickness. Think
of me as one walking barefoot, whose feet are sure to be wounded,
if he do not see the ground.

"Do you and your companions all cherish the same mind to assist
your sovereign, that I may follow my royal predecessors, and tread in
the steps of my high ancestor, to give repose to the millions of the
people. Oh! respect this charge of mine; so shall you bring your work
to a good end." . . .

Yueh, having received his charge, and taken the presidency of all
the officers, he presented himself before the king, and said, "Oh!
intelligent kings act in reverent accordance with the ways of Heaven.
The founding of States and the setting up of capitals, the appointing
of sovereign kings, of dukes and other nobles, with their great officers
and heads of departments, were not designed to minister to the idleness and pleasures of one, but for the good government of the people.
It is Heaven which is all-intelligent and observing; let the sage king
take it as his pattern. Then his ministers will reverently accord with
him, and the people consequently will be well governed.

"It is the mouth that gives occasion for shame; they are the coat
of mail and helmet that give occasion to war. The upper robes and
lower garments for reward should not be lightly taken from their
chests; before spear and shield are used, one should examine himself.
If your Majesty will be cautious in regard to these things, and, believing this about them, attain to the intelligent use of them, your
government will in everything be excellent. Good government and
bad depend on the various officers. Offices should not be given to
men because they are favorites, but only to men of ability. Dignities

should not be conferred on men of evil practices, but only on men of worth.

"Anxious thought about what will be best should precede your movements, which also should be taken at the time proper for them. Indulging the consciousness of being good is the way to lose that goodness; being vain of one's ability is the way to lose the merit it might produce.

"For all affairs let there be adequate preparation; with preparation there will be no calamitous issue. Do not open the door for favorites, from whom you will receive contempt. Do not be ashamed of mistakes, and go on to make them crimes. Let your mind rest in its proper objects, and the affairs of your government will be pure. Officiousness in sacrificing is called irreverence; and multiplying ceremonies leads to disorder. To serve the spirits acceptably in this way is difficult."

The king said, "Excellent! your words, O Yueh, should indeed be put in practice by me. If you were not so good in counsel, I should not have heard these rules for my conduct." Yueh did obeisance with his head to the ground, and said, "It is not the knowing that is difficult, but the doing. But since your Majesty truly knows this, there will not be the difficulty, and you will become really equal in complete virtue to our first king. Wherein I, Yueh, refrain from speaking what I ought to speak, the blame will rest with me. . . ."

Yueh said, "O king, a ruler should seek to learn much from his ministers, with a view to establish his affairs; but to learn the lessons of the ancients is the way to attain this. That the affairs of one, not making the ancients his masters, can be perpetuated for generations, is what I have not heard.

"In learning there should be a humble mind and the maintenance of a constant earnestness; in such a case the learner's improvement will surely come. He who sincerely cherishes these things will find all truth accumulating in his person. Teaching is the half of learning; when a man's thoughts from first to last are constantly fixed on learning, his virtuous cultivation comes unperceived.

"Survey the perfect pattern of our first king; so shall you forever be preserved from error. Then shall I be able reverently to meet your views, and on every side to look out for men of eminence to place in the various offices. . . ."

VI: THE GREAT PLAN

The following is from the most celebrated item in the SHU KING, the so-called "Great Plan" recorded in Book IV, Part V. This "Great Plan," a synopsis of the principles underlying the order of the universe and the nature of good government, is said to have been divinely revealed to that worthiest of kings, the great Yu. It touches on physics, astrology, magic, morals, politics and religion, all in order to show the sovereign how he can best bring happiness to the people. Here is one of its nine divisions, that summarizing the "principles of royal perfection"—

The sovereign, having established in himself the highest degree and pattern of excellence, concentrates in his own person the five sources of happiness, and proceeds to diffuse them, and give them to the multitudes of the people. Then they, on their part, embodying your perfection, will give it back to you, and secure the preservation of it. Among all the multitudes of the people there will be no unlawful confederacies, and among men in office there will be no bad and selfish combinations; let the sovereign establish in himself the highest pattern of excellence.

"Among all the multitudes of the people there will be those who have ability to plan and to act, and who keep themselves from evil: do you keep such in mind; and there will be those who, not coming up to the highest point of excellence, yet do not involve themselves in evil: let the sovereign receive such. And when a placid satisfaction appears in their countenances, and they say, 'Our love is fixed on virtue,' do you then confer favor on them; those men will in this way advance to the perfection of the sovereign. Do not let him oppress the friendless and childless, nor let him fear the high and distinguished. When men in office have ability and administrative power, let them be made still more to cultivate their conduct; and the prosperity of the country will be promoted. All such right men, having a competency, will go on in goodness. If you can not cause them to have what they love in their families, they will forthwith proceed to be guilty of crime. As to those who have not the love of virtue, although you confer favors and emoluments on them, they will only involve you in the guilt of employing the evil.

> "Without deflection, without unevenness,
> Pursue the royal righteousness.
> Without selfish likings,
> Pursue the royal way.
> Without selfish dislikings,
> Pursue the royal path.
> Avoid deflection, avoid partiality;
> Broad and long is the royal way.
> Avoid partiality, avoid deflection;
> Level and easy is the royal way.
> Avoid perversity, avoid one-sidedness;
> Correct and straight is the royal way.
> Ever seek for this perfect excellence,
> Ever turn to this perfect excellence."

He went on to say, "This amplification of the royal perfection contains the unchanging rule, and is the great lesson; yea, it is the lesson of God. All the multitudes of the people, instructed in this amplification of the perfect excellence, and carrying it into practice, will thereby approximate to the glory of the Son of Heaven, and say, 'The Son of Heaven is the parent of the people, and so becomes the sovereign of all under the sky.' "

VII: THE FINAL PRONOUNCEMENT

Here is the closing passage—Book XXX, Part V—of the SHU KING. *It records the speech of the Marquis of Chin, a feudal ruler in the seventh century* B.C., *who had learned the cost of listening to false ministers.*

The duke said, "Ah! my officers, listen to me without noise. I solemnly announce to you the most important of all sayings. It is this which the ancients have said, 'Thus it is with all people—they mostly love their ease. In reproving others there is no difficulty, but to receive reproof, and allow it to have free course—this is difficult.' The sorrow of my heart is that the days and months have passed away, and it is not likely they will come again, so that I might pursue a different course. . . .

"I have deeply thought and concluded. Let me have but one resolute minister, plain and sincere, without other ability, but having a straightforward mind, and possessed of generosity, regarding the talents of others as if he himself possessed them; and when he finds accomplished and sage men, loving them in his heart more than his mouth expresses, really showing himself able to bear them: such a minister would be able to preserve my descendants and people, and would indeed be a giver of benefits.

"But if the minister, when he finds men of ability, be jealous and hates them; if, when he finds accomplished and sage men, he oppose them and does not allow their advancement, showing himself really not able to bear them; such a man will not be able to protect my descendants and people; and will he not be a dangerous man?

"The decline and fall of a State may arise from one man. The glory and tranquility of a State may also arise from the goodness of one man."

THE SHI KING

The third of the Five Classics is an anthology of ancient hymns and poetic eulogies compiled by Confucius and considered by him of supreme importance. "If you fail to study the Shi," he declared, "you are unfit to engage in learned discourse." His enthusiasm, however, is hard to share, especially by readers who can study the work only through translations. Even in the original most of the poems make little sense, and the innumerable learned commentaries on them succeed only in making that little even less. When tortured into English, they seem to make no sense at all. For that reason, and also because the rest of the poems, those relatively meaningful, have little of any ethical import, only one is quoted here. It is a poem recalling certain Psalms in the Old Testament, fervent, forthright, and supremely religious.[3]

WARNING TO GOVERNORS

God has reversed his usual course of procedure,
And the lower people are full of distress.
The words which you utter are not right;
The plans which you form are not far-reaching.
As there are not sages, you think you have no guidance;—
You have no real sincerity.
Thus your plans do not reach far,
And I therefore strongly admonish you.

Heaven is now sending down calamities;—
Do not be so complacent.
Heaven is now producing such movements;—
Do not be so indifferent.
If your words were harmonious,
The people would become united.
If your words were gentle and kind,
The people would be settled.

[3] Translated by James Legge in *The Chinese Classics*, Vol. IV (Trubner & Co., London, 1871).

Though my duties are different from yours,
I am your fellow-servant.
I come to advise with you,
And you hear me with contemptuous indifference.
My words are about the present urgent affairs;—
Do not think them matter for laughter.
The ancients had a saying;—"Consult the gatherers of
    grass and firewood."

Heaven is now exercising oppression;—
Do not in such a way make a mock of things.
An old man, I speak with entire sincerity;
But you, my juniors, are full of pride.
It is not that my words are those of age,
But you make a joke of what is sad.
But the troubles will multiply like flames,
Till they are beyond help or remedy.

Heaven is now displaying its anger;—
Do not be either boastful or flattering,
Utterly departing from all propriety of demeanour,
Till good men are reduced to personators of the dead.
The people now sigh and groan,
And we dare not examine into the causes of their trouble.
The ruin and disorder are exhausting all their means of living,
And we show no kindness to our multitudes.

Heaven enlightens the people,
As the bamboo flute responds to the earthen whistle;

As two half-maces form a whole one;
As you take a thing, and bring it away in your hand,
Bringing it away, without any more ado.
The enlightenment of the people is very easy.
They have now many perversities;—
Do not you set up your perversity before them.

Good men are a fence;
The multitudes of the people are a wall;
Great states are screens;
Great families are buttresses;
The cherishing of virtue secures repose;
The circle of the king's relatives is a fortified wall.
We must not let the fortified wall get destroyed;
We must not let the king be solitary and consumed with terrors.

Revere the anger of heaven,
And presume not to make sport or be idle.
Revere the changing moods of heaven,
And presume not to drive about at your pleasure.
Great heaven is intelligent,
And is with you in all your goings.
Great heaven is clear-seeing,
And is with you in your wanderings and indulgences.

THE LI-KI

This Classic is a book of rites, and lists the social and sacerdotal practices which Confucius venerated so highly. He believed them to have originated with the earliest of the Imperial dynasties—traditionally dated 2205–1766 B.C.—and his one concern was to see them revived and perpetuated. Taken as a whole, the LI-KI is flat and tedious, an antiquarian's catalogue, yet it does not entirely lack flashes of religious insight and zeal. The proof is to be seen in the following selections.[4]

THE FUNCTIONS OF THE RULER

Heaven produces the seasons. Earth produces all the sources of wealth. Man is begotten by his father, and instructed by his teacher. The ruler correctly uses these four agencies, and therefore he stands in the place where there is no error.

Hence the ruler is he to whose brightness men look; he does not seek to brighten men. It is he whom men support; he does not seek to support men. It is he whom men serve; he does not seek to serve men. If the ruler were to seek to brighten men he would fall into errors. If he were to seek to nourish men, he would be unequal to the task. If he were to seek to serve men, he would be giving up his position. Therefore the people imitate the ruler and we have their self-government; they nourish the ruler, and they find their security in doing so; they serve the ruler, and find

[4] Reprinted from the translation by James Legge in *The Sacred Books of the East*, vols. XXVII and XXVIII (The Clarendon Press, Oxford, 1885).

226

their distinction in doing so. Thus it is by the universal application of the rules of propriety that the lot and duty of different classes are fixed; thus it is that men acting contrary to those rules would all have to account death a boon, and life an evil.

Therefore the ruler, making use of the wisdom of others, will put away the cunning to which that wisdom might lead him; using their courage, he will put away passion; and using their benevolence, he will put away covetousness.

Therefore when it is said that the ruler, being a sage, can look on all under the sky as one family, and on all in the middle states as one man, this does not mean that he will do so on premeditation and purpose. He must know men's feelings, lay open to them what they consider right, show clearly to them what is advantageous, and comprehend what are their calamities. Being so furnished, he is then able to effect the thing.

THE MEANING OF SACRIFICE

Of all the methods for the good ordering of men, there is none more urgent than the use of ceremonies. Ceremonies are of five kinds, and there is none of them more important than sacrifices.

Sacrifice is not a thing coming to a man from without; it issues from within him, and has its birth in his heart. When the heart is deeply moved, expression is given to it by ceremonies; and hence, only men of ability and virtue can give complete exhibition to the idea of sacrifice.

The sacrifices of such men have their own blessing;—not indeed what the world calls blessing. Blessing here means perfection;—it is the name given to the complete and natural discharge of all duties. When nothing is left incomplete or improperly discharged;—this is what we call perfection, implying the doing everything that should be done in one's internal self, and externally the performance of everything according to the proper method. There is a fundamental agreement between a loyal subject in his service of his ruler and a filial son in his service of his parents. In the supernal sphere there is a compliance with what is due to the repose and expansion of the energies of nature; in the external sphere, a compliance with what is due to rulers and elders; in the internal sphere, the filial service of parents;—all this constitutes what is called perfection.

It is only the able and virtuous man who can attain to this perfection; and can sacrifice when he has attained to it. Hence in the sacrifices of such a man he brings into exercise all sincerity and good faith, with all right-heartedness and reverence; he offers the proper things; accompanies them with proper rites; employs the soothing of music; does everything suitably to the season. Thus intelligently does he offer his sacrifices, without seeking for anything to be gained by them:--- such is the heart and mind of a filial son.

MAN'S EMOTIONS

What are the emotions of men? They are joy, anger, sadness, fear, love, disliking, and liking. These seven feelings belong to men without their learning them. What are "the things which men consider right"? Kindness on the part of the father, and filial duty on that of the son; gentleness on the part of the elder brother, and obedience on that of the younger; righteousness on the part of the husband, and submission on that of the wife; kindness on the part of elders, and deference on that of juniors; with benevolence on the part of the ruler, and loyalty on that of the minister;—these ten are the things which men consider to be right.

Truthfulness in speech and the cultivation of harmony constitute what are called "the things advantageous to men." Quarrels, plundering, and murders are "the things disastrous to men."

Hence when a ruler would regulate the seven feelings of men, cultivate the ten virtues that are right, promote truthfulness of speech, and the maintenance of harmony, show his value for kindly consideration and complaisant courtesy, and put away quarrelling and plundering: if he neglect the rules of propriety, how shall he succeed?

The things which men greatly desire are comprehended in meat and drink and sexual pleasure; those which they greatly dislike are comprehended in death, exile, poverty, and suffering. Thus liking and disliking are the great elements in men's minds. But men keep them hidden in their minds, where they cannot be fathomed or measured. The good and the bad of them being in their minds, and no outward manifestations of them being visible, if it be wished to determine these qualities in one uniform way, how can it be done without the rules of propriety?

THE ANALECTS OF CONFUCIUS

This, the LUN-YU, *is the chief of the "Four Books of the Philosophers," and the most widely known work in all of Chinese literature. It is a collection of the sayings of Confucius, and though lacking inner arrangement, it succeeds in giving us our most comprehensive understanding of his gospel. That gospel, we see, was a pure secularism. Confucius was concerned primarily with man's life here on earth, and with the practical ways calculated to make that life happy and fruitful. He was, as has already been said, a social philosopher, not a religious prophet. Despite this, however, what he taught was in many respects supremely ennobling and in the truest sense inspired.*

No precise date can be assigned to this work, but it was probably compiled by some disciple, or group of disciples, not long after Confucius died. Since then its words have been pored over and memorized, discussed and venerated, as thoroughly as the words of Jesus—and by many more millions. To zealots, the aphorisms of the Chinese sage may sound disappointingly flat, and to mystics disgustingly obvious. But to people with a taste for cool wisdom and hard sense, they make refreshing, even exciting, reading.[5]

BOOK ONE: ON LEARNING

"To learn," said the Master, "and then to practice opportunely what one has learnt—does not this bring with it a sense of satisfaction?

"To have associates in study coming to one from distant parts—does not this also mean pleasure in store?

"And are not those who, while not comprehending all that is said, still remain not unpleased to hear, men of the superior order? . . ."

The Scholar Tsang once said of himself: "On three points I examine myself daily, *viz.*, whether in looking after other people's interests, I have not been acting whole-heartedly; whether, in my intercourse with friends, I have not been true; and whether, after teaching, I have not myself been practicing what I have taught. . . ."

[5] The selections here are reprinted—with some rearrangement—from the text translated by William Jennings, *The Sacred Books of the East, op. cit.*

"If the great man be not grave, he will not be revered, neither can his learning be solid.

"Give prominent place to loyalty and sincerity.

"Have no associates in study who are not advanced somewhat like yourself. . . ."

Sayings of the Scholar Yu:

"For the practice of the Rules of Propriety, one excellent way is to be natural. This naturalness became a great grace in the practice of kings of former times; let every one, small or great, follow their example.

"It is not, however, always practicable; and it is not so in the case of a person who does things naturally, knowing that he should act so, and yet who neglects to regulate his acts according to the Rules.

"When truth and right are hand in hand, a statement will bear repetition. When respectfulness and propriety go hand in hand, disgrace and shame are kept afar-off. Remove all occasion for alienating those to whom you are bound by close ties, and you have them still to resort to."

A Saying of the Master:

"The man of greater mind who, when he is eating, craves not to eat to the full; who has a home, but craves not for comforts in it; who is active and earnest in his work and careful in his words; who makes toward men of high principle, and so maintains his own rectitude—that man may be styled a devoted student."

Tsze-kung asked, "What say you, sir, of the poor who do not cringe and fawn; and what of the rich who are without pride and haughtiness?" "They are passable," the Master replied; "yet they are scarcely in the same category as the poor who are happy, and the rich who love propriety. . . ."

"It does not greatly concern me," said the Master, "that men do not know me; my great concern is, my not knowing them."

BOOK TWO: GOOD GOVERNMENT

Sayings of the Master:

"Let a ruler base his government upon virtuous principles, and he will be like the pole-star, which remains steadfast in its place, while all the host of stars turn toward it.

"The 'Book of Odes' contains three hundred pieces, but one expression in it may be taken as covering the purport of all, *viz.*, Unswerving mindfulness.

"To govern simply by statute, and to reduce all to order by means of pains and penalties, is to render the people evasive, and devoid of any sense of shame.

"To govern upon principles of virtue, and to reduce them to order by the Rules of Propriety would not only create in them the sense of shame, but would moreover reach them in all their errors.

"When I attained the age of fifteen, I became bent upon study. At thirty, I was a confirmed student. At forty, naught could move me from my course. At fifty, I comprehended the will and decrees of Heaven. At sixty, my ears were attuned to them. At seventy, I could follow my heart's desires, without overstepping the lines of rectitude. . . ."

Tsze-kung put a question relative to government. In reply the Master mentioned three essentials: sufficient food, sufficient armament, and the people's confidence.

"But," said the disciple, "if you can not really have all three, and one has to be given up, which would you give up first?"

"The armament," he replied.

"And if you are obliged to give up one of the remaining two, which would it be?"

"The food," said he. "Death has been the portion of all men from of old. Without the people's trust nothing can stand. . . ."

Ki K'ang was consulting him about the direction of public affairs.

Confucius answered him, "A director should be himself correct. If you, sir, as a leader show correctness, who will dare not to be correct?"

Ki K'ang, being much troubled on account of robbers abroad, consulted Confucius on the matter. He received this reply: "If you, sir, were not covetous, neither would they steal, even were you to bribe them to do so."

Ki K'ang, when consulting Confucius about the government, said, "Suppose I were to put to death the disorderly for the better encouragement of the orderly—what say you to that?"

"Sir," replied Confucius, "in the administration of government why resort to capital punishment? Covet what is good, and the people will be good. The virtue of the noble-minded man is as the wind, and that of inferior men as grass; the grass must bend, when the wind blows upon it."

Tsze-chang asked how otherwise he would describe the learned official who might be termed influential.

"What, I wonder, do you mean by one who is influential?" said the Master.

"I mean," replied the disciple, "one who is sure to have a reputation throughout the country, as well as at home."

"That," said the Master, "is reputation, not influence. The influential man, then, if he be one who is genuinely straightforward and loves what is just and right, a discriminator of men's words, and an observer of their looks, and in honor careful to prefer others to himself—will certainly have influence, both throughout the country and at home. The man of mere reputation, on the other hand, who speciously affects philanthropy, though in his way of procedure he acts contrary to it, while yet quite evidently engrossed with that virtue—will certainly have reputation, both in the country and at home. . . ."

The Master was on a journey to Wei, and Yen Yu was driving him. "What multitudes of people!" he exclaimed. Yen Yu asked him, "Seeing they are so numerous, what more would you do for them?"

"Enrich them," replied the Master.

"And after enriching them, what more would you do for them?"

"Instruct them."

"Were any one of our princes to employ me," he said, "after a twelvemonth I might have made some tolerable progress; but give me three years, and my work should be done."

Again, "How true is that saying, 'Let good men have the management of a country for a century, and they would be adequate to cope with evil-doers, and thus do away with capital punishments.'"

Again, "Suppose the ruler to possess true kingly qualities, then surely after one generation there would be good-will among men."

Again, "Let a ruler but see to his own rectitude, and what trouble will he then have in the work before him? If he be unable to rectify himself, how is he to rectify others? . . ."

"Learned officials," said he, "who hanker after a home life, are not worthy of being esteemed as such."

Again, "In a country under good government, speak boldly, act boldly. When the land is ill-governed, though you act boldly, let your words be moderate."

Again, "Men of virtue will needs be men of words—will speak out— but men of words are not necessarily men of virtue. They who care for their fellow-men will needs be bold, but the bold may not necessarily be such as care for their fellow-men. . . ."

"If you observe what things people usually take in hand, watch their motives, and note particularly what it is that gives them satisfaction, shall they be able to conceal from you what they are? Conceal themselves, indeed!

"Be versed in ancient lore, and familiarize yourself with the modern; then may you become teachers.

"The great man is not a mere receptacle."

In reply to Tsze-kung respecting the great man:

"What he first says, as a result of his experience, he afterward follows up.

"The great man is catholic-minded, and not one-sided. The common man is the reverse.

"Learning, without thought, is a snare; thought, without learning, is a danger.

"Where the mind is set much upon heterodox principles—there truly and indeed is harm. . . ."

To the disciple Tsze-lu the Master said, "Shall I give you a lesson about knowledge? When you know a thing, maintain that you know it; and when you do not, acknowledge your ignorance. This is characteristic of knowledge."

Tsze-chang was studying with an eye to official income. The Master addressed him thus: "Of the many things you hear, hold aloof from those that are doubtful, and speak guardedly with reference to the rest; your mistakes will then be few. Also, of the many courses you see adopted, hold aloof from those that are risky, and carefully follow the others; you will then seldom have occasion for regret. Thus, being seldom mistaken in your utterances, and having few occasions for regret in the line you take, you are on the high road to your preferment."

To a question put to him by Duke Ngai as to what should be done in order to render the people submissive to authority, Confucius replied, "Promote the straightforward, and reject those whose courses are crooked, and the thing will be effected. Promote the crooked and reject the straightforward, and the effect will be the reverse."

When Ki K'ang asked of him how the people could be induced to show respect, loyalty, and willingness to be led, the Master answered, "Let there be grave dignity in him who has the oversight of them, and they will show him respect; let him be seen to be good to his own parents, and kindly in disposition, and they will be loyal to him; let him promote those who have ability, and see to the instruction of those who have it not, and they will be willing to be led. . . .

"It is moral cowardice to leave undone what one perceives to be right to do."

BOOK FOUR: SOCIAL VIRTUE

Sayings of the Master:

"It is social good feeling that gives charm to a neighborhood. And where is the wisdom of those who choose an abode where it does not abide?

"Those who are without it can not abide long, either in straitened or in happy circumstances. Those who possess it find contentment in it. Those who are wise go after it as men go after gain.

"Only they in whom it exists can have right likings and dislikings for others.

"Where the will is set upon it, there will be no room for malpractices.

"Riches and honor are what men desire; but if they arrive at them by improper ways, they should not continue to hold them. Poverty and low estate are what men dislike; but if they arrive at such a condition by improper ways, they should not refuse it.

"If the 'superior man' make naught of social good feeling, how shall he fully bear that name?

"Not even whilst he eats his meal will the 'superior man' forget what he owes to his fellow-men. Even in hurried leave-takings, even in moments of frantic confusion, he keeps true to this virtue.

"I have not yet seen a lover of philanthropy, nor a hater of mis-anthropy—such, that the former did not take occasion to magnify that virtue in himself, and that the latter, in his positive practice of philan-thropy, did not, at times, allow in his presence something savoring of misanthropy.

"Say you, is there any one who is able for one whole day to apply the energy of his mind to this virtue? Well, I have not seen any one whose energy was equal to it. It may be there are such, but I have never met with them.

"The faults of individuals are peculiar to their particular class and surroundings; and it is by observing their faults that one comes to understand the condition of their good feelings toward their fellows.

"One may hear the right way in the morning, and at evening die.

"The scholar who is intent upon learning the right way, and who is yet ashamed of poor attire and poor food, is not worthy of being discoursed with.

"The masterly man's attitude to the world is not exclusively this or that: whatsoever is right, to that he will be a party.

"The masterly man has an eye to virtue, the common man, to earthly things; the former has an eye to penalties for error—the latter, to favor.

"Where there is habitual going after gain, there is much ill-will. . . ."

"Men of loftier mind manifest themselves in their equitable deal-ings; small-minded men in their going after gain.

"When you meet with men of worth, think how you may attain to their level; when you see others of an opposite character, look within, and examine yourself.

"A son, in ministering to his parents, may on occasion offer gentle remonstrances; when he sees that their will is not to heed such, he should nevertheless still continue to show them reverent respect, never obstinacy; and if he have to suffer, let him do so without murmuring.

"Whilst the parents are still living, he should not wander far; or, if a wanderer, he should at least have some fixed address.

"If for three years he do not veer from the principles of his father, he may be called a dutiful son.

"A son should not ignore the years of his parents. On the one hand, they may be a matter for rejoicing that they have been so many, and on the other, for apprehension that so few remain.

"People in olden times were loth to speak out, fearing the disgrace of not being themselves as good as their words.

"Those who keep within restraints are seldom losers.

"To be slow to speak, but prompt to act, is the desire of the 'superior man.'

"Virtue dwells not alone; she must have neighbors."

An observation of Tse-yu:

"Officiousness, in the service of princes, leads to disgrace; among friends, to estrangement."

CHARACTERISTICS OF CONFUCIUS

Said the Master:

"I am a transmitter and not an originator, and one who believes in and loves the ancients.

"What find you indeed in me? a quiet brooder and memorizer; a student never satiated with learning; an unwearied monitor of others!

"The things which weigh heavily upon my mind are these—failure to improve in the virtues, failure in discussion of what is learnt, inability to walk according to knowledge received as to what is right and just, inability also to reform what has been amiss."

In his hours of recreation and refreshment the Master's manner was easy and unconstrained, affable and winning. . . .

"Concentrate the mind," said he, "upon the Good Way.

"Maintain firm hold upon Virtue.

"Rely upon Philanthropy.

"Find recreation in the Arts.

"I have never withheld instruction from any, even from those who have come for it with the smallest offering.

"No subject do I broach, however, to those who have no eager desire to learn; no encouraging hint do I give to those who show no anxiety to speak out their ideas; nor have I anything more to say to those who, after I have made clear one corner of the subject, can not from that give me the other three. . . ."

As to wealth, he remarked, "If wealth were an object that I could go in quest of, I should do so even if I had to take a whip and do grooms' work. But seeing that it is not, I go after those objects for which I have a liking. . . ."

"With a meal of coarse rice," said the Master, "and with water to drink, and my bent arm for my pillow—even thus can I find happiness. Riches and honors without righteousness are to me as fleeting clouds. . . .

"As I came not into life with any knowledge of it," he said, "and as my likings are for what is old, I busy myself in seeking knowledge there."

Strange occurrences, exploits of strength, deeds of lawlessness, references to mystical things—such-like matters the Master avoided in conversation.

"Let there be," he said, "three men walking together: from that number I should be sure to find my instructors; for what is good in them I should choose out and follow, and what is not good I should modify. . . ."

To his disciples he once said, "Do you look upon me, my sons, as keeping anything secret from you? I hide nothing from you. I do nothing that is not manifest to your eyes, my disciples. That is so with me."

Four things there were which he kept in view in his teaching—scholarliness, conduct of life, honesty, faithfulness.

"It is not given to me," he said, "to meet with a genius; let me behold a man of superior mind, and that will suffice. Neither is it given to me to meet with a holy man; let me but see a man of constancy, and it will suffice. It is difficult for persons who have constancy, when they pretend to have that which they are destitute of, to be full when they are empty, to do things on a grand scale when their means are contracted!"

When the Master fished with hook and line, he did not also use a net. When out with his bow, he would never shoot at game in cover.

"Some there may be," said he, "who do things in ignorance of what they do. I am not of these. There is an alternative way of knowing things, *viz*: to sift out the good from the many things one hears, and follow it; and to keep in memory the many things one sees. . . ."

When the Master was in company with any one who sang, and who sang well, he must needs have the song over again, and after that would join in it.

"Although in my letters," he said, "I may have none to compare with me, yet in my personification of the 'superior man' I have not as yet been successful.

" 'A Sage and a Philanthropist?' How should I have the ambition?" said he. "All that I can well be called is this—An insatiable student, an unwearied teacher; this, and no more." "Exactly what we, your disciples, can not by any learning manage to be," said Kung-si Hwa.

Once when the Master was seriously ill, Tsze-lu requested to be allowed to say prayers for him. . . . "My prayer has been going on a long while," said the Master. . . .

In his own village, Confucius presented a somewhat plain and simple appearance, and looked unlike a man who possessed ability of speech.

But in the ancestral temple, and at Court, he spoke with the fluency and accuracy of a debater, but ever guardedly. . . .

At his meals he would enter into discussions; and when reposing afterward he would not utter a word.

Even should his meal consist only of coarse rice and vegetable broth or melons, he would make an offering, and never fail to do so religiously.

He would never sit on a mat that was not straight.

After a feast among his villagers, he would wait before going away until the old men had left. . . .

Ki K'ang once sent him a present of some medicine. He bowed, and received it; but remarked, "Until I am quite sure of its properties I must not venture to taste it."

Once when the stabling was destroyed by fire, he withdrew from the Court, and asked, "Is any person injured?"—without inquiring as to the horses. . . .

If a friend died, and there were no near relatives to take him to, he would say, "Let him be buried from my house. . . ."

ON THE SUPERIOR MAN

"The nobler-minded man," he remarked, "will be agreeable even when he disagrees; the small-minded man will agree and be disagreeable. . . .

"The superior man is exacting of himself; the common man is exacting of others.

"A superior man has self-respect, and does not strive; is sociable, yet no party man.

"He does not promote a man because of his words, nor pass over the words because of the man. . . .

"The superior man deliberates upon how he may walk in truth, not upon what he may eat. The farmer may plow, and be on the way to want: the student learns, and is on his way to emolument. To live a right life is the concern of men of nobler minds: poverty gives them none. . . .

"The superior man may not be conversant with petty details, and yet may have important matters put into his hands. The inferior man may not be charged with important matters, yet may be conversant with the petty details. . . ."

Tsze-kung was consulting him, and asked, "What say you of a person who was liked by all in his village?"

"That will scarcely do," he answered.

"What, then, if they all disliked him?"

"That, too," said he, "is scarcely enough. Better if he were liked by the good folk in the village, and disliked by the bad."

"The superior man," he once observed, "is easy to serve, but difficult to please. Try to please him by the adoption of wrong principles and you will fail. Also, when such a one employs others, he uses them according to their capacity. The inferior man is, on the other hand, difficult to serve, but easy to please. Try to please him by the adoption of wrong principles, and you will succeed. And when he employs others he requires them to be fully prepared for everything."

Again, "The superior man can be high without being haughty. The inferior man can be haughty if not high.

"The firm, the unflinching, the plain and simple, the slow to speak," said he once, "are approximating toward their duty to their fellow-men."

Tsze-lu asked how he would characterize one who might fitly be called an educated gentleman. The Master replied, "He who can properly be so-called will have in him a seriousness of purpose, a habit of controlling himself, and an agreeableness of manner: among his friends and associates the seriousness and the self-control, and among his brethren the agreeableness of manner. . . ."

"Superior men," said the Master, "are modest in their words, profuse in their deeds."

Again, "There are three attainments of the superior man which are beyond me—the being sympathetic without anxiety, wise without skepticism, brave without fear. . . ."

During his residence in the State of Ch'in, his followers, owing to a famine, became so weak and ill that not one of them could stand. Tsze-lu, with indignation pictured on his countenance, exclaimed, "And is a gentleman to suffer starvation?"

"A gentleman," replied the Master, "will endure it unmoved, but a common person breaks out in excesses under it. . . ."

PRACTICAL WISDOM

"Not to speak to a man," said he, "to whom you ought to speak, is to lose your man; to speak to one to whom you ought not to speak, is to lose your words. Those who are wise will not lose their man, nor yet their words. . . ."

Other sayings of the Master:

"They who care not for the morrow will the sooner have their sorrow.

"Ah, 'tis hopeless! I have not yet met with the man who loves Virtue as he loves Beauty.

"Be generous yourself, and exact little from others; then you banish complaints.

"If a number of students are all day together, and in their conversation never approach the subject of righteousness, but are fond merely of giving currency to smart little sayings, they are difficult indeed to manage. . . .

"Good-fellowship is more to men than fire and water. I have seen men stepping into fire and into water, and meeting with death thereby; I have not yet seen a man die from planting his steps in the path of good-fellowship.

"Rely upon good nature. 'Twill not allow precedence even to a teacher. . . .

"There are," said he, "three kinds of friendships which are profitable, and three which are detrimental. To make friends with the upright, with the trustworthy, with the experienced, is to gain benefit; to make friends with the subtly perverse, with the artfully pliant, with the subtle in speech, is detrimental."

Again, "There are three kinds of pleasure which are profitable, and three which are detrimental. To take pleasure in going regularly through the various branches of Ceremonial and Music, in speaking of others' goodness, in having many worthy wise friends, is profitable. To take pleasure in wild bold pleasures, in idling carelessly about, in the too jovial accompaniments of feasting, is detrimental."

Again, "Three errors there be, into which they who wait upon their superior may fall: (1) to speak before the opportunity comes to them to speak, which I call heedless haste; (2) refraining from speaking when the opportunity has come, which I call concealment; and (3) speaking, regardless of the mood he is in, which I call blindness."

Again, "Three things a superior should guard against: (1) against the lusts of the flesh in his earlier years while the vital powers are not fully developed and fixed; (2) against the spirit of combativeness when he has come to the age of robust manhood and when the vital powers are matured and strong, and (3) against ambitiousness when old age has come on and the vital powers have become weak and decayed.

"Three things also such a man greatly reveres: (1) the ordinances of Heaven, (2) great men, (3) words of sages. . . ."

Tsze-chang asked Confucius about the virtue of philanthropy. His answer was, "It is the being able to put in practice five qualities, in any place under the sun."

"May I ask, please, what these are?" said the disciple.

"They are," he said, "dignity, indulgence, faithfulness, earnestness, kindness. If you show dignity you will not be mocked; if you are indulgent you will win the multitude; if faithful, men will place their trust in you; if earnest, you will do something meritorious; and if kind, you will be enabled to avail yourself amply of men's services. . . ."

"Does a gentleman," asked Tsze-lu, "make much account of bravery?"

"Righteousness he counts higher," said the Master. "A gentleman who is brave without being just may become turbulent; while a common person who is brave and not just may end in becoming a highwayman."

Tsze-kung asked, "I suppose a gentleman will have his aversions as well as his likings?"

"Yes," replied the Master, "he will dislike those who talk much about other people's ill-deeds. He will dislike those who, when occupying inferior places, utter defamatory words against their superiors. He will dislike those who, though they may be brave, have no regard for propriety. And he will dislike those hastily decisive and venturesome spirits who are nevertheless so hampered by limited intellect.

"And you, too, Tsze-kung," he continued, "have your aversions, have you not?"

"I dislike," said he, "those plagiarists who wish to pass for wise persons. I dislike those people who wish their lack of humility to be taken for bravery. I dislike also those divulgers of secrets who think to be accounted straightforward."

"Of all others," said the Master, "women-servants and men-servants are the most difficult people to have the care of. Approach them in a familiar manner, and they take liberties; keep them at a distance, and they grumble."

Again, "When a man meets with odium at forty, he will do so to the end."

TEACHINGS OF VARIOUS DISCIPLES

"The learned official," said Tsze-chang, "who when he sees danger ahead will risk his very life, who when he sees a chance of success is mindful of what is just and proper, who in his religious acts is mindful of the duty of reverence, and when in mourning thinks of his loss, is indeed a fit and proper person for his place."

Again he said, "If a person hold to virtue but never advance in it, and if he have faith in right principles and do not build himself up in them, how can he be regarded either as having such, or as being without them?"

Tsze-hia's disciples asked Tsze-chang his views about intercourse with others. "What says your Master?" he rejoiced. "He says," they replied, " 'Associate with those who are qualified, and repel from you such as are not.' " Tsze-chang then said, "That is different from what I have learnt. A superior man esteems the worthy and wise, and bears them all. He makes much of the good and capable, and pities the incapable. Am I eminently worthy and wise?—who is there then among men whom I will not bear with? Am I not worthy and wise?—others will be minded to repel me: I have nothing to do with repelling them."

Sayings of Tsze-hia:

"Even in inferior pursuits there must be something worthy of contemplation, but if carried to an extreme there is danger of fanaticism; hence the superior man does not engage in them.

"The student who daily recognizes how much he yet lacks, and as the months pass forgets not what he has succeeded in learning, may undoubtedly be called a lover of learning.

"Wide research and steadfast purpose, eager questioning and close reflection—all this tends to humanize a man.

"As workmen spend their time in their workshops for the perfecting of their work, so superior men apply their minds to study in order to make themselves thoroughly conversant with their subjects.

"When an inferior man does a wrong thing, he is sure to gloss it over.

"The superior man is seen in three different aspects; look at him from a distance, he is imposing in appearance; approach him, he is gentle and warm-hearted; hear him speak, he is acute and strict.

"Let such a man have the people's confidence, and he will get much work out of them; so long, however, as he does not possess their confidence they will regard him as grinding them down.

"When confidence is reposed in him, he may then with impunity administer reproof; so long as it is not, he will be regarded as a detractor.

"Where there is no over-stepping of barriers in the practice of the higher virtues, there may be freedom to pass in and out in the practice of the lower ones. . . ."

Further observations of Tsze-hia:

"In the public service devote what energy and time remain to study. After study devote what energy and time remain to the public service."

THE LAST SAYINGS

"None can be a superior man," said the Master, "who does not recognize the decrees of Heaven.

"None can have stability in him without knowledge of the proprieties.

"None can know a man without knowing his utterances."

THE TA HSIO

The TA HSIO, *or "Great Learning," is another of the Four Books of the Philosophers. It is a capsule summary of the teachings of Confucius which has been endlessly annotated, interpreted, and expatiated on by Chinese scholars. The original text is supposed to have been dictated by the sage to a disciple named Tsang, who in turn dictated a commentary to one of his disciples. Though neither document is particularly illuminating to the casual reader, both are curious, and therefore deserving of at least brief quotation.*[6]

1. The Great Learning teaches (the importance of) establishing illustrious virtue, improving the population, and achieving the highest excellence. . . .

2. The ancients who wished to establish illustrious virtue set out first to govern their states properly. . . .

(*Commentary*—In the Announcement of KIANG it is written: "Act as if you were watching over an infant." If a mother is genuinely anxious to satisfy the wants of her child, she will come near to succeeding even though she does not know what precisely those wants may be.)

. . . . Wishing to govern their States properly, they first regulated their own families. . . .

(*Commentary*—One who is unable to instruct his own family cannot possibly instruct a whole state, for the one is the other in microcosm. In both there must be filial piety (wherewith the sovereign is served), fraternal submission (wherewith the elders and officials are served), and kindness (wherewith the people are served). . . .)

. . . . Wishing to regulate their own families, they first cultivated their own persons. . . .

(*Commentary*—On the bathing-tub of Thang the following words were inscribed: "If you can one day improve yourself, do so every day. Yea, let there be daily improvement.")

[6] The arrangement is made from a translation printed (without acknowledgment) in *The Sacred Books and Early Literature of the East*, edited by Charles F. Horne, Ph.D. (Park, Austin and Lipscomb, New York and London, 1917).

. . . . Wishing to regulate their own persons, they first clarified their own minds. . . .

(*Commentary*—The meaning may be thusly illustrated: If a man allows himself to be ruled by passion, his conduct will be wrong. This is true whether the passion be fear or love or sorrow or distress. When the mind is not clear, we look but do not see, we hear but do not understand, we eat but do not know the taste.)

. . . . Wishing to clarify their minds, they first sought to be sincere in their thoughts. . . .

(*Commentary*—i.e., they permitted no self-deception, for even worse is it to deceive oneself than to deceive others.)

. . . . Wishing to be sincere in their thoughts, they first so investigated things that they extended their knowledge to the utmost. . . .

(*Commentary*—i.e., we must investigate the nature of all things which we encounter, for all things do have their nature, and the mind of intelligent man is certainly capable of discerning that nature. On this account the book entitled *Learning for Adults* begins by instructing the learner to persist in investigating the principles inhering in all things, for such persistence will in time make one the possessor of a wide and wondrous comprehension. Then the qualities of all things, whether external or internal, whether obvious or subtle, will all be apprehended, and the mind will be perfectly intelligent. Such is the "investigation of things" which leads to the "perfection of knowledge.")

3. Things being investigated, knowledge became perfect. Their knowledge being perfect, their thoughts were sincere. Their thoughts being sincere, their minds were naturally clarified. Their minds being clarified, their persons were cultivated. Their persons being cultivated, their families were regulated. Their families being regulated, their States were properly governed. . . .

(*Commentary*—From the example of one loving family, the entire State can become loving, and from its courtesies the entire State can become courteous. On the other hand, the ambition and wickedness of the One Man (ruler) can reduce the whole State to rebellious disorder, for such is the nature of influence. This verifies the adage: "Quarrels can be settled by a single sentence, and kingdoms ruined by One Man.")

. . . . Their States being properly governed, the whole Empire was made tranquil and happy. . . .

(*Commentary*—To govern properly, a ruler must venerate the aged, respect the elders, and show compassion to the young and helpless. If he does these things, his people will do likewise. . . . Whatever a man dislikes in his superiors, let him not show the same to his inferiors; and whatever he dislikes in his inferiors, let him not show the same to his superiors.)

4. From the emperor down to the mass of the people, cultivation of the individual is the one thing which is fundamental.

THE GOLDEN MEAN OF TSESZE

This work, traditionally ascribed to Tsesze, the grandson of Confucius, is probably the best introduction to Confucianism as a moral philosophy. Its central emphasis is on reasonableness as a guide to conduct, on the Middle Way as the highest ideal. The measure of all things, it insists, is man, for "truth does not depart from human nature." Therefore to be true to God, a man must be true to his own kind, and instead of worrying about Heaven, he ought to take care of the earth.

In its present form the book appears to be a composite of two different works, one a sustained philosophical essay and the other a collection of Confucian comments on the Golden Mean. The following selections comprise about three-quarters of the entire document.[7]

I: THE CENTRAL HARMONY

(I) What is God-given is what we call human nature. To fulfil the law of our human nature is what we call the moral law. The cultivation of the moral law is what we call culture.

The moral law is one from whose operation we cannot escape for an instant in all our existence. A law from which we may escape is not the moral law. Wherefore it is that the moral man (or the superior man) watches diligently over what his eyes cannot see and is in fear and awe of what his ears cannot hear.

There is nothing more evident than that which cannot be seen by the eyes and nothing more palpable than that which cannot be perceived by the senses. Wherefore the moral man watches diligently over his secret thoughts.

When the passions, such as joy, anger, grief, and pleasure, have not awakened, that is our *central* self, or moral being (*chung*). When these passions awaken and each and all attain due measure and degree, that

[7] Reprinted from a translation by Ku Hungming as rearranged by Lin Yutang in *The Wisdom of Confucius*. (Copyright, 1938, by Random House, Inc.) Reprinted by permission of Random House.

is *harmony,* or the moral order *(ho).* Our central self or moral being is the great basis of existence, and *harmony* or moral order is the universal law in the world.

When our true central self and harmony are realised, the universe then becomes a cosmos and all things attain their full growth and development.

II: THE GOLDEN MEAN

(II) Confucius remarked: "The life of the moral man is an exemplification of the universal moral order (*chung-yung,* usually translated as "the Mean"). The life of the vulgar person, on the other hand, is a contradiction of the universal moral order.

"The moral man's life is an exemplification of the universal order, because he is a moral person who unceasingly cultivates his true self or moral being. The vulgar person's life is a contradiction of the universal order, because he is a vulgar person who in his heart has no regard for, or fear of, the moral law."

(III) Confucius remarked: "To find the central clue to our moral being which unites us to the universal order, that indeed is the highest human attainment. For a long time, people have seldom been capable of it."

(IV) Confucius remarked: "I know now why the moral life is not practiced. The wise mistake moral law for something higher than what it really is; and the foolish do not know enough what moral law really is. I know now why the moral law is not understood. The noble natures want to live too high, high above their moral ordinary self; and ignoble natures do not live high enough, i.e., not up to their moral ordinary true self. There is no one who does not eat and drink. But few there are who really know flavor. . . ."

(IX) Confucius remarked: "A man may be able to put a country in order, be able to spurn the honors and emoluments of office, be able to trample upon bare, naked weapons; with all that he is still not able to find the central clue in his moral being."

(X) Tselu asked what constituted strength of character.

Confucius said: ". . . To be patient and gentle, ready to teach, returning not evil for evil; that is the strength of character of the people of the southern countries. It is the ideal place for the moral man. To lie under arms and meet death without regret; that is the strength of character of the people of the northern countries. It is the ideal of brave men of your type. Wherefore the man with the true strength of moral character is one who is gentle, yet firm. How unflinching is his strength! When there is moral social order in the country, if he enters

public life he does not change from what he was when in retirement. When there is no moral social order in the country, he is content unto death. How unflinching is his strength!"

(XI) Confucius remarked: "There are men who seek for the abstruse and strange and live a singular life in order that they may leave a name to posterity. This is what I never would do. There are again good men who try to live in conformity with the moral law, but who, when they have gone half way, throw it up. I never could give it up. Lastly, there are truly moral men who unconsciously live a life in entire harmony with the universal moral order and who live unknown to the world and unnoticed of men without any concern. It is only men of holy, divine natures who are capable of this."

III: MORAL LAW EVERYWHERE

(XII) The moral law is to be found everywhere, and yet it is a secret.

The simple intelligence of ordinary men and women of the people may understand something of the moral law; but in its utmost reaches there is something which even the wisest and holiest of men cannot understand. The ignoble natures of ordinary men and women of the people may be able to carry out the moral law; but in its utmost reaches even the wisest and holiest of men cannot live up to it.

Great as the Universe is, man is yet not always satisfied with it. For there is nothing so great but the mind of the moral man can conceive of something still greater which nothing in the world can hold. There is nothing so small but the mind of the moral man can conceive of something still smaller which nothing in the world can split. . . .

Confucius remarked: "The power of spiritual forces in the Universe—how active it is everywhere! Invisible to the eyes, and impalpable to the senses, it is inherent in all things, and nothing can escape its operation."

It is the fact that there are these forces which makes men in all countries fast and purify themselves, and with solemnity of dress institute services of sacrifice and religious worship. Like the rush of mighty waters, the presence of unseen Powers is felt; sometimes above us, sometimes around us.

In the *Book of Songs* it is said:

> "The presence of the Spirit:
> It cannot be surmised,
> How may it be ignored!"

Such is the evidence of things invisible that it is impossible to doubt the spiritual nature of man.

IV: THE HUMANISTIC STANDARD

(XIII) Confucius said: . . . "When a man carries out the principles of conscientiousness and reciprocity he is not far from the moral law. What you do not wish others should do unto you, do not do unto them.

"There are four things in the moral life of a man, not one of which I have been able to carry out in my life. To serve my father as I would expect my son to serve me: that I have not been able to do. To serve my sovereign as I would expect a minister under me to serve me: that I have not been able to do. To act towards my elder brothers as I would expect my younger brother to act towards me: that I have not been able to do. To be the first to behave towards friends as I would expect them to behave towards me: that I have not been able to do.

"In the discharge of the ordinary duties of life and in the exercise of care in ordinary conversation, whenever there is shortcoming, never fail to strive for improvement, and when there is much to be said, always say less than what is necessary; words having respect to actions and actions having respect to words. Is it not just this thorough genuiness and absence of pretense which characterizes the moral man?"

(XIV) The moral life of man may be likened to traveling to a distant place: one must start from the nearest stage. It may also be likened to ascending a height: one must begin from the lowest step. . . .

(XV) The moral man conforms himself to his life circumstances; he does not desire anything outside of his position. Finding himself in a position of wealth and honor, he lives as becomes one living in a position of wealth and honor. Finding himself in a position of poverty and humble circumstances, he lives as becomes one living in a position of poverty and humble circumstances. Finding himself in uncivilized countries, he lives as becomes one living in uncivilized countries. Finding himself in circumstances of danger and difficulty, he acts according to what is required of a man under such circumstances. In one word, the moral man can find himself in no situation in life in which he is not master of himself.

In a high position he does not domineer over his subordinates. In a subordinate position he does not court the favors of his superiors. He puts in order his own personal conduct and seeks nothing from others; hence he has no complaint to make. He complains not against God, nor rails against men.

Thus it is that the moral man lives out the even tenor of his life calmly waiting for the appointment of God, whereas the vulgar person takes to dangerous courses, expecting the uncertain chances of luck.

Confucius remarked: "In the practice of archery we have something resembling the principle in a moral man's life. When the archer misses the center of the target, he turns round and seeks for the cause of his failure within himself."

V: CERTAIN MODELS

(XVI) Confucius remarked: "There was the Emperor Shun. He was perhaps what may be considered a truly great intellect. Shun had a natural curiosity of mind and he loved to inquire into ordinary conversation. He ignored the bad (words?) and broadcast the good.

Taking two extreme counsels, he took the mean between them and applied them in dealings with his people. This was the characteristic of Shun's great intellect."

(XVII) Confucius remarked: "The Emperor Shun might perhaps be considered in the highest sense of the word a pious man. In moral qualities he was a saint. In dignity of office he was the ruler of the empire. In wealth all that the wide world contained belonged to him. After his death his spirit was sacrificed to in the ancestral temple, and his children and grandchildren preserved the sacrifice for long generations.

"Thus it is that he who possesses great moral qualities will certainly attain to corresponding high position, to corresponding great prosperity, to corresponding great name, to corresponding great age.

"For God in giving life to all created things is surely bountiful to them according to their qualities. Hence the tree that is full of life He fosters and sustains, while that which is ready to fall He cuts off and destroys. . . ."

VI: ETHICS AND POLITICS

(XX) Duke Ai (ruler of Lu, Confucius' native state) asked what constituted good government.

Confucius replied: ". . . With the right men, the growth of good government is as rapid as the growth of vegetation is in the right soil. Indeed, good government is like a fast-growing plant. The conduct of government, therefore, depends upon the men. The right men are obtained by the ruler's personal character. . . .

"Therefore it is necessary for a man of the governing class to set about regulating his personal conduct and character. In considering how to regulate his personal conduct and character, it is necessary for him to do his duties toward those nearly related to him. In considering how to do his duties toward those nearly related to him, it is necessary for him to understand the nature and organization of human society. In considering the nature and organization of human society it is necessary for him to understand the laws of God.

"The duties of universal obligation are five, and the moral qualities by which they are carried out are three. The duties are those between ruler and subject, between father and son, between husband and wife, between elder brother and younger, and those in the intercourse between friends. These are the five duties of universal obligation. Wisdom, compassion and courage—these are the three universally recognized moral qualities of man. It matters not in what way men come to the exercise of these moral qualities, the result is one and the same.

"Some men are born with the knowledge of these moral qualities; some acquire it as the result of education; some acquire it as the result of hard experience. But when the knowledge is acquired, it comes to one and the same thing. Some exercise these moral qualities naturally and easily; some because they find it advantageous to do so; some with effort and difficulty. But when the achievement is made it comes to one and the same thing."

Confucius went on to say: "Love of knowledge is akin to wisdom. Strenuous attention to conduct is akin to compassion. Sensitiveness to shame is akin to courage.

"When a man understands the nature and use of these three moral qualities, he will then understand how to put in order his personal conduct and character. When a man understands how to put in order his personal conduct and character, he will understand how to govern men. When a man understands how to govern men, he will then understand how to govern nations and empires.

"For every one called to the government of nations and empires there are nine cardinal directions to be attended to:

1. Cultivating his personal conduct.
2. Honoring worthy men.
3. Cherishing affection for, and doing his duty toward, his kindred.
4. Showing respect to the high ministers of state.
5. Identifying himself with the interests and welfare of the whole body of public officers.
6. Showing himself as a father to the common people.
7. Encouraging the introduction of all useful arts.
8. Showing tenderness to strangers from far countries.
9. Taking interest in the welfare of the princes of the Empire. . . ."

VII: BEING ONE'S TRUE SELF

"If the people in inferior positions do not have confidence in those above them, government of the people is an impossibility. There is only one way to gain confidence for one's authority: if a man is not trusted by his friends, he will not have confidence in those above him. There is only one way to be trusted by one's friends: if a man is not affectionate toward his parents, he will not be trusted by his friends. There is only one way to be affectionate toward one's parents: if a man, looking into his own heart, is not true to himself, he will not be affectionate toward his parents. There is only one way for a man to be true to himself. If he does not know what is good, a man cannot be true to himself.

"Being true to oneself is the law of God. Try to be true to oneself is the law of man.

"He who is naturally true to himself is one who, without effort, hits upon what is right, and without thinking understands what he wants to know, whose life is easily and naturally in harmony with the moral law. Such a one is what we call a saint or a man of divine nature. He who learns to be his true self is one who finds out what is good and holds fast to it.

"In order to learn to be one's true self, it is necessary to obtain a wide and extensive knowledge of what has been said and done in the world; critically to inquire into it; carefully to ponder over it; clearly to sift it; and earnestly to carry it out.

"It matters not what you learn; but when you once learn a thing, you must never give it up until you have mastered it. It matters not what you inquire into, but when you inquire into a thing, you must never give it up until you have thoroughly understood it. It matters not what you try to think out, but when you once try to think out a thing you must never give it up until you have got what you want. It matters not what you try to sift out, but when you once try to sift out a thing, you must never give it up until you have sifted it out clearly and distinctly. It matters not what you try to carry out, but when you once try to carry out a thing you must never give it up until you have done it thoroughly and well. If another man succeed by one effort, you will use a hundred efforts. If another man succeed by ten efforts, you will use a thousand efforts.

"Let a man really proceed in this manner, and, though dull, he will surely become intelligent; though weak, he will surely become strong."

(XXI) To arrive at understanding from being one's true self is called nature, and to arrive at being one's true self from understanding is called culture. He who is his true self has thereby understanding, and he who has understanding finds thereby his true self.

VIII: THOSE WHO ARE THEIR ABSOLUTE TRUE SELVES

(XXII) Only those who are their absolute true selves in the world can fulfil their own nature; only those who fulfil their own nature can fulfil the nature of others; only those who fulfil the nature of others can fulfil the nature of things; those who fulfil the nature of things are worthy to help Mother Nature in growing and sustaining life; and those who are worthy to help Mother Nature in growing and sustaining life are the equals of Heaven and Earth.

(XXIII) The next in order are those who are able to attain to the apprehension of a particular branch of study. By such studies, they are also able to apprehend the truth. Realization of the true self compels expression; expression becomes evidence; evidence becomes clarity or luminosity of knowledge; clarity or luminosity of knowledge activates; active knowledge becomes power and power becomes a pervading influence. Only those who are absolutely their true selves in this world can have pervading influence. . . .

(XXV) Truth means the fulfilment of our self; and moral law means following the law of our being. Truth is the beginning and end (the substance) of material existence. Without truth there is no material existence. It is for this reason that the moral man values truth.

Truth is not only the fulfilment of our own being; it is that by which things outside of us have an existence. The fulfilment of our being is moral sense. The fulfilment of the nature of things outside of us is intellect. These, moral sense and intellect, are the powers or faculties of our being. They combine the inner or subjective and outer or objective use of the power of the mind. Therefore, with truth, everything done is right.

(XXVI) Thus absolute truth is indestructible. Being indestructible, it is eternal. Being eternal, it is self-existent. Being self-existent, it is infinite. Being infinite, it is vast and deep. Being vast and deep, it is transcendental and intelligent. It is because it is vast and deep that it contains all existence. It is because it is transcendental and intelligent that it embraces all existence. In vastness and depth it is like the Earth. In transcendental intelligence it is like Heaven. Infinite and eternal, it is the Infinite itself.

Such being the nature of absolute truth, it manifests itself without

being seen; it produces effects without motion; it accomplishes its ends
without action.

The principle in the course and operation of nature may be
summed up in one word: because it obeys only its own immutable
law, the way in which it produces the variety of things is unfathomable. . . .

IX: EULOGY ON CONFUCIUS

(XXVII) Oh, how great is the divine moral law of the Sage. Overflowing and illimitable, it gives birth and life to all created things and
towers high up to the very heavens. How magnificent it is! How imposing the three hundred principles and three thousand rules of conduct! They await the man who can put the system into practice.
Hence it is said: Unless there be the highest moral character, the
highest moral law cannot be realized.

Wherefore the moral man, while honoring the greatness and
power of his moral nature, yet does not neglect inquiry and pursuit of
knowledge. While broadening the scope of his knowledge, he yet seeks
to exhaust the mystery of the small things. While seeking to attain the
highest understanding he yet orders his conduct according to the
middle course (literally "chungyung."). Going over what he has already learned, he gains some new knowledge. Earnest and simple, he
respects and obeys the laws and usages of social life (li).

Therefore, when in a position of authority, he is not proud; in a
subordinate position, he is not insubordinate. When there is moral
social order in the country, what he speaks will bring prosperity to the
nation; and when there is no moral social order in the country, his
silence will ensure forbearance for himself.[8]

In the *Book of Songs* it is said:

> "With wisdom and good sense,
> He guards his life from harm."

That is the description of the moral man. . . .

Every system of moral laws must be based upon the man's own
consciousness, verified by the common experience of mankind, tested

[8] Here we see the connection between the realization of the true self and harmony
with the outside world, between "sincerity" and "harmony."

by due sanction of historical experience and found without error, applied to the operations and processes of nature in the physical universe and found to be without contradiction, laid before the gods without question or fear, and able to wait a hundred generations and have it confirmed without a doubt by a Sage of posterity. The fact that he is able to confront the spiritual powers of the universe without any fear shows that he understands the laws of God. The fact that he is prepared to wait a hundred generations for confirmation from the Sage of posterity without any misgiving shows that he understands the laws of man.

Wherefore it is that it is true of the really great moral man that every move he makes becomes an example for generations; every act he does becomes a model for generations and every word he utters becomes a guide for generations. Those who are far away look up to him, while those who are near do not decrease their respect for him. In the *Book of Songs* it is said:

> "There they found no fault of him,
> Here they never tire of him;
> Thus from day to day and night to night
> They will perpetuate his praise!"

There never was a moral man who did not answer this description and who yet could obtain timely recognition throughout the world. . . .

X: EPILOGUE

In the *Book of Songs* it is said:

> "Over her brocaded robe,
> She wore a plain and simple dress,"

in that way showing her dislike of the loudness of its color and magnificence. Thus the ways of the moral man are unobtrusive and yet they grow more and more in power and evidence; whereas the ways of the vulgar person are ostentatious, but lose more and more in influence until they perish and disappear.

The life of the moral man is plain, and yet not unattractive; it is simple, and yet full of grace; it is easy, and yet methodical. He knows that accomplishment of great things consists in doing little things well. He knows that great effects are produced by small causes. He knows the evidence and reality of what cannot be perceived by the senses. Thus he is enabled to enter into the world of ideas and morals.

In the *Book of Songs*, it is said:

> "How deep the fish may dive below,
> And yet it is quite clearly seen."

Therefore the moral man must examine into his own heart and see that he has no cause for self-reproach, that he has no evil thought in his mind. Wherein the moral man is superior to other men consists even in those things that people do not notice.

In the *Book of Songs* it is said:

> "In your secret chamber even you are judged;
> See you do nothing to blush for,
> Though but the ceiling looks down upon you."

Therefore the moral man, even when he is not doing anything, is serious; and, even when he does not speak, is truthful.

In the *Book of Songs* it is said:

> "All through the solemn rite not a word was spoken,
> And yet all strife was banished from their hearts."

Hence the moral man, without the inducement of rewards, is able to make the people good; and without the show of anger, to awe them into fear more than if he had used the most dreadful instruments of punishment.

In the *Book of Songs* it is said:

> "He makes no show of his moral worth,
> Yet all the princes follow in his steps."

Hence the moral man, by living a life of simple truth and earnestness, alone can help to bring peace and order in the world.

In the *Book of Songs* it is said:

"I keep in mind the fine moral qualities
Which make no great noise or show."

Confucius remarked: "Among the means for the regeneration of mankind, those made with noise and show are of the least importance."
In another place in the *Book of Songs,* it is said:

"His virtue is light as hair."

Still a hair is something material. "The workings of Almighty God
have neither sound nor smell." That is the highest development of our
moral nature.

THE HSIAO KING

The HSIAO KING, *or "Classic of Filial Piety," is the prime scripture of Confucianism as an organized creed. Though ostensibly derived from the Master himself, and therefore called a* king, *not a* shu, *the work is obviously of far lesser and later authorship. It seeks to base the entire religion on respect for parents, a principle easily turned into worship of ancestors. Since such a worship naturally fostered conservatism, submissiveness, and a generally stable order, the rulers of China were quick to seize on the* HSIAO KING *and declare it a most sacred book. An official text was published in 722 A.D. with notations by the Emperor Hsuan, and thenceforth no document in the Confucian canon was shown higher governmental favor. Its influence has continued to pervade Chinese life and thought almost to the present day.*

The work is quite brief, consisting of twenty-eight "chapters," many of which are no longer than a paragraph. Its style, as the following typical passages will reveal, is simple, forthright, and most engaging.[9]

I: THE SOURCE OF ALL VIRTUES

Once upon a time Confucius was sitting in his study, having his disciple Tseng Ts'an to attend upon him. He asked Tseng Ts'an: "Do you know by what virtue and power the good emperors of old made the world peaceful, the people to live in harmony with one another, and the inferior contented under the control of their superiors?" To this Tseng Ts'an, rising from his seat, replied: "I do not know this, for I am not clever." Then said Confucius: "The duty of children to their parents is the fountain whence all other virtues spring, and also the starting-point from which we ought to begin our education. Now take your seat, and I will explain this. Our body and hair and skin are all derived from our parents, and therefore we have no right to injure any of them in the least. This is the first duty of a child.

"To live an upright life and to spread the great doctrines of human-

[9] The translation is by Ivan Chen, *The Book of Filial Duty* (New York, E. P. Dutton, 1920; John Murray, London).

ity must win good reputation after death, and reflect great honour upon our parents. This is the last duty of a son.

"Hence the first duty of a son is to pay a careful attention to every want of his parents. The next is to serve his government loyally; and the last to establish a good name for himself.

"So it is written in the Ta Ya: 'You must think of your ancestors and continue to cultivate the virtue which you inherit from them.' "

II: THE PRACTICAL DUTY OF MAN

On hearing what Confucius said about filial duty, Tseng Tze remarked: "How great is the use of filial duty!" Here Confucius continued: "Filial duty is the constant doctrine of heaven, the natural righteousness of earth, and the practical duty of man. Every member of the community ought to observe it with the greatest care. We do what is dictated by heaven and what is good for the general public in order to organize the community. On this account our education is widespread, though it is not compulsory, and our government is sound, though it is not rigorous. The effect of education upon the minds of the people was well known to the good emperors of old. They made every person love his parents by loving their own parents first. They induced every person to cultivate his virtue by expounding the advantages of virtue to him. They behaved themselves respectfully and humbly, so that the people might not quarrel with one another. They trained the people with ceremonial observances, and educated them with music so that they might live in harmony. They told the people what things they liked or disliked to see done, so that they might understand what they were forbidden to do."

In the Shih King it is thus written: "The dignified statesman is always the subject of the attention of the people."

III: THE PRACTICAL DUTY OF RULERS

The good emperors of old ruled the Empire by means of filial duty, and dared not neglect the ministers of their vassal states. How much less the dukes, marquises, earls, viscounts, and barons! They thereby gained the goodwill of all their vassal states, which sent their deputies to represent them in any sacrifice offered to the ancestors of their Supreme Master. This is what we mean by saying that the good emperors of old governed the world by filial duty.

As to the vassal states, their rulers dared not treat widowers and widows with insolence; how then could they dare act so towards the literary class and the people? Hence they gained the goodwill of their subjects, and the latter would join them in offering sacrifices to their ancestors.

Now we may say a word about a family. If the head of a family do not act haughtily towards his servant, he cannot act so to his wife and children. Hence he will gain the goodwill of all his people, and they will help him in the fulfilment of his filial duty. In such a family the parents must feel happy when they are living, and their spirits must come to enjoy the sacrifice when they are dead. By the principle of filial duty the whole world can be made happy and all calamities and dangers can be averted. Such was the government of the Empire by the enlightened rulers of old, in accordance with the principle of filial duty.

In the Shih King it is thus written: "If you adorn yourself with the highest virtue, the whole world will follow you."

IV: THE MIRACLE OF THE BAMBOO SHOOTS

Meng Tsung, who lived in the Chin Dynasty, lost his father when young. His mother was very ill, and one winter's day she longed to taste a soup made of bamboo shoots, but Meng could not procure any. At last he went into the bamboo grove, and clasping the bamboos with his hands, wept bitterly. His filial love moved nature, and the ground slowly opened, sending forth several shoots, which he gathered and carried home. He made a soup of them, which his mother tasted, and immediately recovered from her malady.

V: WHAT IF THE PARENTS ARE WRONG?

Tseng Tze said: "I have heard all that you said about parental love, filial love, reverence to elders, how to treat parents every day, and how to please them by making oneself known for good conduct; and now I will venture to ask you whether it is filial that a son should obey every command of his father, whether right or wrong?"

"What do you say?—what do you say?" replied Confucius. "Once upon a time there was a certain emperor who would have lost his empire through his wickedness but that he had seven good ministers who often checked his illegal actions by strong protests; there was also a feudal baron who would have lost his feudal estate through wantonness, but for the fact that he had five good men who often made strong remonstrances to him; and there was also a statesman who would have brought frightful calamity upon his family, but for the fact that he had three good servants who often strongly advised him not to do what he ought not.

"If a man has a good friend to resist him in doing bad actions, he will have his reputation preserved; so if a father has a son to resist his wrong commands, he will be saved from committing serious faults.

"When the command is wrong, a son should resist his father, and a minister should resist his august master.

"The maxim is, 'Resist when wrongly commanded.' Hence how can he be called filial who obeys his father when he is commanded to do wrong?"

THE BOOKS OF MENCIUS

Fully five generations passed before the cult of Kung Fu-tze, or Confucius, became a popular religion, and then it was largely because of labors of a devotee named Mang-tze, or Mencius. The latter, born in 372 (or 385) B.C., remained a cloistered scholar during the first half of his life, but then suddenly plunged himself into worldly affairs as a sort of evangelical politician. He could see China falling into chaos, "the royal ordinances violated, the multitudes oppressed, and the supplies of food and drink flowing away like water," and he said to himself, "If Heaven wishes that tranquillity be restored, who is there besides me to bring it about?" Accordingly, in imitation of the Master whose teachings he so greatly revered, he went searching for a royal patron who might allow him to try and organize a model government.

More than twenty years he carried on that search, and though he never found the perfect patron, he did at least manage to influence a lot of imperfect ones. During all that while, he continued to go up and down the country denouncing kings and courtiers, oppressors and mountebanks, until at last, losing heart, he returned once more to seclusion. From then until his death twenty years later he devoted himself to organizing his opinions, dictating them to disciples who eventually edited them in seven books.

Mencius's chief contribution, and the secret of the ultimate popularity of his works, lay in the stress he placed on the ideal of democracy. Though agreeing with Confucius that monarchism was established by God, he insisted that the individual monarch must be established by the people. "Heaven," said Mencius, "sees as the people see; Heaven hears as the people hear." Consequently, unlike Confucius, he could quite countenance the idea of rebellion—so long as there was no other recourse, and the purpose was the good of the people.

Mencius was in essence a devoutly romantic populist, believing that all men are equal in that all are innately good. Said he: "The sense of mercy is in all mortals; the sense of shame is in all mortals; the sense of courtesy and respect is in all mortals; the sense of right

*and wrong is in all mortals." In each, however, there is a greater and
lesser self, and a man's worth depends on which of these he cultivates. The greater self is the one with which he is born, his "air of
the early dawn," and if he clings to this, keeps breathing it in, then
he becomes truly a great man no matter how mean his worldly station. For what is greatness but "to dwell in love, to stand in probity,
to walk in righteousness, and . . . to labor for the good the people?"*

*These convictions led Mencius to develop a whole theory of what
he called "benevolent government," and that theory became to China
much what "democracy" became much later to certain Western lands
—an ideal to be at least believed in, if not always practiced. Mencius's
books were made compulsory reading in the schools, and committed
to memory by all Chinese pupils. That they were noble books, and in
a sense genuinely religious, can be judged from such typical passages
as those quoted below.[10]*

FROM BOOK I:

Mencius went to see king Hwuy of Leang. The king said, "Venerable sir, since you have not counted it far to come here, a distance of a
thousand le, may I presume that you are likewise provided with
counsels to profit my kingdom?" Mencius replied, "Why must your
Majesty use that word profit? What I am 'likewise' provided with, are
counsels to benevolence and righteousness, and these are my only
topics.

"If your Majesty says, 'What is to be done to profit my kingdom?'
the great officers will say, 'What is to be done to profit our families?'
and the inferior officers and the common people will say, 'What is to
be done to profit our persons?' Superiors and inferiors will try to snatch
this profit, the one from the other, and . . . if righteousness be put
last, and profit be put first, each will not be satisfied without trying
to snatch all.

"There never has been a man trained to benevolence who neglected
his parents. There never has been a man trained to righteousness who
made his sovereign an after consideration.

"Let your Majesty also say, 'Benevolence and righteousness, and
these shall be the only themes.' Why must you use that word—
'profit'?"

[10] Translated by Charles A. Wong.

Mencius, another day, saw king Hwuy of Leang. The king went and stood with him by a pond, and, looking round at the large geese and deer, said, "Do wise and good princes also find pleasure in these things?"

Mencius replied, "Being wise and good, they have pleasure in these things. If they are not wise and good, though they have these things, they do not find pleasure."

King Hwuy of Leang said, "I wish quietly to receive your instructions."

Mencius replied, "Is there any difference between killing a man with a stick and with a sword?" The king said, "There is no difference." "Is there any difference between doing it with a sword and with the style of government?" "There is no difference," was the reply.

Mencius then said, "In your kitchen there is fat meat; in your stables there are fat horses. But your people have the look of hunger, and on the wilds there are those who have died of famine. This is leading on beasts to devour men. Beasts devour one another, and men hate them for doing so. When a prince, being the parent of his people, administers his government so as to be chargeable with leading on beasts to devour men, where is that parental relation to the people?"

The king, Seuen, of Ts'e asked, "Was it so, that the park of king Wan contained seventy square le?" Mencius replied, "It is so in the records."

"Was it so large as that?" exclaimed the king. "The people," said Mencius, "still looked on it as small." The king added, "My park contains only forty square le, and the people still look on it as large. How is this?" "The park of king Wan," was the reply, "contained seventy square le, but the grass-cutters and fuel-gatherers had the privilege of entrance into it; so also had the catchers of pheasants and hares. He shared it with the people, and was it not with reason that they looked on it as small?

"When I first arrived at the borders of your state, I inquired about the great prohibitory regulations, before I would venture to enter it; and I heard that inside the border-gates there was a park of forty square le, and that he who killed a deer in it was held guilty of the same crime as if he had killed a man. Thus those forty square le are a pitfall in the middle of the kingdom. Is it not with reason that the people look upon them as large?"

FROM BOOK II:

"When one by force subdues men, they do not submit to him in heart. They submit because their strength is not adequate to resist. When one subdues men by virtue, in their hearts' core they are pleased, and sincerely submit, as was the case with the seventy disciples in their submission to Confucius. What is said in the Book of Poetry,

'From the west, from the east,
From the south, from the north,
There was not one who thought of refusing submission,'

is an illustration of this."

Mencius said, "All men have a mind which cannot bear to see the sufferings of others. . . . My meaning may be illustrated thus:—even nowadays, if men suddenly see a child about to fall into a well, they will without exception experience a feeling of alarm and distress.

"From this case we may perceive that the feeling of commiseration is essential to man, that the feeling of shame and dislike is essential to man, that the feeling of modesty and complaisance is essential to man, and that the feeling of approving and disapproving is essential to man.

"The feeling of commiseration is the principle of benevolence. The feeling of shame and dislike is the principle of righteousness. The feeling of modesty and complaisance is the principle of propriety. The feeling of approving and disapproving is the principle of knowledge."

"From the want of benevolence and the want of wisdom will ensue the entire absence of propriety and righteousness;—he who is in such a case must be the servant of other men. To be the servant of men and yet ashamed of such servitude is like a bow-maker's being ashamed to make bows, or an arrow-maker's being ashamed to make arrows.

"If he be ashamed of his case, his best course is to practice benevolence.

"The man who would be benevolent is like the archer. The archer adjusts himself and then shoots. If he misses, he does not murmur against those who surpass him. He simply turns round and seeks the cause of his failure in himself."

Mencius said, "When any one told Tsze-loo that he had a fault, he rejoiced.

"The great Shun had a still greater delight in what was good. He regarded virtue as the common property of himself and others, giving up his own way to follow that of others, and delighting to learn from others to practice what was good.

"To take example from others to practice virtue, is to help them in the same practice. Therefore, there is no attribute of the superior man greater than his helping men to practice virtue."

FROM BOOK IV:

Mencius said, "With those who do violence to themselves, it is impossible to speak. With those who throw themselves away, it is impossible to do anything. To disown in his conversation propriety and righteousness, is what we mean by doing violence to one's self. To say—'I am not able to dwell in benevolence or pursue the path of righteousness,' is what we mean by throwing one's self away.

"Benevolence is the tranquil habitation of man, and righteousness is his straight path.

"Alas for them who leave the tranquil dwelling empty and do not reside in it, and who abandon the right path and do not pursue it!"

Mencius said, "When those occupying inferior situations do not obtain the confidence of the sovereign, they cannot succeed in governing the people. There is a way to obtain the confidence of the sovereign:—if one is not trusted by his friends, he will not obtain the confidence of his sovereign. There is a way of being trusted by one's friends:—if one do not serve his parents so as to make them pleased, he will not be trusted by his friends. There is a way to make one's parents pleased:—if one, on turning his thoughts inwards, finds a want of sincerity, he will not give pleasure to his parents. There is a way to the attainment of sincerity in one's self:—if a man do not understand what is good, he will not attain sincerity in himself.

"Therefore, sincerity is the way of heaven. To think how to be sincere is the way of man.

"Never has there been one possessed of complete sincerity, who did not move others. Never has there been one who had not sincerity who was able to move others."

Mencius said, "Of all the parts of a man's body there is none more excellent than the pupil of the eye. The pupil cannot be used to hide a man's wickedness. If within the breast all be correct, the pupil is bright. If within the breast all be not correct, the pupil is dull.

"Listen to a man's words and look at the pupil of his eye. How can a man conceal his character?"

Kung-sun Ch'ow said, "Why is it that the superior man does not himself teach his son?"

Mencius replied, "The circumstances of the case forbid its being done. The teacher must inculcate what is correct. When he inculcates what is correct and his lessons are not practiced, he follows them up with being angry. When he follows them up with being angry, then, contrary to what should be, he is offended with his son. At the same time, the pupil says, 'My master inculcates in me what is correct, and he himself does not proceed in a correct path.' The result of this is, that father and son are offended with each other. When father and son come to be offended with each other, the case is evil.

"The ancients exchanged sons, and one taught the son of another.

"Between father and son, there should be no reproving admonitions to what is good. Such reproofs lead to alienation, and than alienation there is nothing more inauspicious."

Mencius said, "When scholars are put to death without any crime, the great officers are justified in quitting the country. When the people are slaughtered without any crime, the scholars are justified in quitting it.

"If the sovereign be benevolent, all will be benevolent. If the sovereign be righteous, all will be righteous. . . .

"Men must be decided on what they will *not* do, and then they are able to act with vigour in what they ought to do.

"The great man does not think beforehand of his words that they may be sincere, not of his actions that they may be resolute;—he simply speaks and does what is right.

"The great man is he who does not lose his child's-heart.

"That whereby man differs from the lower animals is but small. The mass of people cast it away, while superior men preserve it.

"He who loves others is constantly loved by them. He who respects others is constantly respected by them.

"Here is a man who treats me in a perverse and unreasonable manner. The superior man in such a case will turn round upon himself—'I must have been wanting in benevolence; I must have been wanting in propriety:—how should this have happened to me?'

"He examines himself, and is specially benevolent. He turns round upon himself, and is specially observant of propriety. The perversity and unreasonableness of the other, however, are still the same. The superior man will again turn round on himself—'I must have been failing to do my utmost.'

"He turns round upon himself, and proceeds to do his utmost, but still the perversity and unreasonableness of the other are repeated. On this the superior man says, 'This is a man utterly lost indeed! Since he conducts himself so, what is there to choose between him and a brute? Why should I go to contend with a brute?' "

FROM BOOK V:

Wan Chang asked Mencius saying, "I venture to ask the principles of friendship." Mencius replied, "Friendship should be maintained without any presumption on the ground of one's superior age, or station, or the circumstances of his relatives. Friendship with a man is friendship with his virtue, and does not admit of assumptions of superiority.

"Respect shown by inferiors to superiors is called giving to the noble the observance due to rank. Respect shown by superiors to inferiors is called giving honour to talents and virtue. The rightness in each case is the same."

Mencius said to Wan Chang, "The scholar whose virtue is most distinguished in a village shall make friends of all the virtuous scholars in the village. The scholar whose virtue is most distinguished throughout a state shall make friends of all the virtuous scholars of that state. The scholar whose virtue is most distinguished throughout the empire shall make friends of all the virtuous scholars of the empire.

"When a scholar feels that his friendship with all the virtuous scholars of the empire is not sufficient to satisfy him, he proceeds to ascend to consider the men of antiquity. He repeats their poems, and reads their books, and as he does not know what they were as men, to ascertain this he considers their history. This is to ascend and make friends of the men of antiquity."

FROM BOOK VI:

The philosopher Kaou said, "Man's nature is like the willow, and righteousness is like a cup or a bowl. Fashioning benevolence and righteousness out of man's nature is like making cups and bowls out of the willow."

Mencius replied, "Can you, leaving untouched the nature of the willow, make with it cups and bowls? You must do violence and injury to the willow, before you can make cups and bowls with it. If you must do violence and injury to the willow in order to make cups and bowls with it, on your principles you must in the same way do violence and injury to humanity in order to fashion from it benevolence and righteousness! Your words, alas! would certainly lead all men on to reckon benevolence and righteousness to be calamities."

The philosopher Kaou said, "Man's nature is like water whirling round in a corner. Open a passage for it to the east, and it will flow to the east; open a passage for it to the west, and it will flow to the west. Man's nature is indifferent to good and evil, just as the water is indifferent to the east and west."

Mencius replied, "Water indeed will flow indifferently to the east or west, but will it flow indifferently up or down? The tendency of man's nature to good is like the tendency of water to flow downwards. There are none but have this tendency to good, just as all water flows downwards.

"Now by striking water and causing it to leap up, you may make it go over your forehead, and, by damming and leading it, you may force it up a hill;—but are such movements according to the nature of water? It is the force applied which causes them. When men are made to do what is not good, their nature is dealt with in this way."

Mencius said, "This is what I mean in saying that the nature is good. If men do what is not good, the blame cannot be imputed to their natural powers. The feeling of commiseration belongs to all men; so does that of shame and dislike; and that of reverence and respect; and that of approving and disapproving. The feeling of commiseration implies the principle of benevolence; that of shame and dislike, the principle of righteousness; that of reverence and respect, the principle of propriety; and that of ap-proving and disapproving the principle of knowledge. Benevolence, righteousness, propriety, and knowledge are not infused into us from without. We are certainly furnished with them. And a different view is simply from want of reflection. Hence it is said, 'Seek and you will find them. Neglect and you will lose them.' Men differ from one another in regard to them;— some as much again as others, some five times as much, and some to an incalculable amount:—it is because they cannot carry out fully their natural powers."

Mencius said, "In good years the children of the people are most of them good, while in bad years the most of them abandon themselves to evil. It is not owing to their natural powers conferred by heaven that they are thus different. The abandonment is owing to the circumstances through which they allow their minds to be ensnared and drowned in evil.

"There now is barley.—Let it be sown and covered up; the ground being the same, and the time of sowing likewise the same, it grows rapidly up, and when the full time is come, it is all found to be ripe. Although there may be inequalities of produce, that is owing to the difference of the soil, as rich or poor, to the unequal nourishment afforded by the rains and dews, and to the different ways in which man has performed his business in reference to it.

"Thus all things which are the same in kind are like to one another; —why should we doubt in regard to man, as if he were a solitary exception to this? The sage and we are the same in kind."

Mencius said, "The trees of the New mountain were once beautiful. Being situated, however, in the borders of a large state, they were hewn down with axes and bills;—and could they retain their beauty? Still through the activity of the vegetative life day and night, and the nourishing influence of the rain and dew, they were not without buds and sprouts springing forth, but then came the cattle and goats and browsed upon them. To these things is owing the bare and stript appearance of the mountain, which when people see, they think it was never finely wooded. But is this the nature of the mountain?

"And so also of what properly belongs to man;—shall it be said that the mind of any man was without benevolence and righteousness? The way in which a man loses his proper goodness of mind is like the way in which the trees are denuded by axes and bills. Hewn down day after day, can it—the mind—retain its beauty? But there is a development of its life day and night, and in the calm air of the morning, just between night and day, the mind feels in a degree those desires and aversions which are proper to humanity, but the feeling is not strong, and it is fettered and destroyed by what takes place during the day. This fettering taking place again and again, the restorative influence of the night is not sufficient to preserve the proper goodness of the mind; and when this proves insufficient for that purpose, the nature becomes not much different from that of the irrational animals, which when people see, they think that it never had those powers which I assert. But does this condition represent the feelings proper to humanity?"

Mencius said, "It is not to be wondered at that the king is not wise! Suppose the case of the most easily growing thing in the world;—if you let it have one day's genial heat, and then expose it for ten days to cold, it will not be able to grow. It is but seldom that I have an audience of the king, and when I retire, there come all those who act upon him like the cold. Though I succeed in bringing out some buds of goodness, of what avail is it!

"Now chess-playing is but a small art, but without his whole mind being given, and his will bent to it, a man cannot succeed at it. Chess Ts'ew is the best chess-player in all the kingdom. Suppose that he is teaching two men to play.—The one gives to the subject his whole mind and bends to it all his will, doing nothing but listening to Chess Ts'ew. The other, although he seems to be listening to him, has his whole mind running on a swan which he thinks is approaching, and wishes to bend his bow, adjust the string to the arrow, and shoot it. Although he is learning along with the other, he does not come up to him. Why?—because his intelligence is not equal? Not so."

Mencius said, "I like fish and I also like bear's paws. If I cannot have the two together, I will let the fish go, and take the bear's paws. So, I like life, and I also like righteousness. If I cannot keep the two together, I will let life go and choose righteousness.

"I like life indeed, but there is that which I like more than life, and therefore I will not seek to possess it by any improper ways. I dislike death indeed, but there is that which I dislike more than death, and therefore there are occasions when I will not avoid danger.

"If among the things which man likes there were nothing which he liked more than life, why should he not use every means by which he could preserve it? If among the things which man dislikes there were nothing which he disliked more than death, why should he not do everything by which he could avoid danger?

"There are cases when men by a certain course might preserve life, and they do not employ it; when by certain things they might avoid danger, and they will not do them.

"Therefore, men have that which they like more than life, and that which they dislike more than death. They are not men of distinguished talents and virtue only who have this mental nature. All men have it; what belongs to such men is simply that they do not lose it.

"Here are a small basket of rice and a platter of soup, and the case is one in which the getting them will preserve life, and the want of them will be death;—if they are offered with an insulting voice, even a tramp will not receive them, or if you first tread upon them, even a beggar will not stoop to take them.

"And yet a man will accept of ten thousand chung, without any consideration of propriety or righteousness. What can the ten thousand chung add to him? When he takes them, is it not that he may obtain beautiful mansions, that he may secure the services of wives and concubines, or that the poor and needy of his acquaintance may be helped by him?

"In the former case the offered bounty was not received, though it would have saved from death, and now the emolument is taken for the sake of beautiful mansions. The bounty that would have preserved from death was not received, and the emolument is taken to get the service of wives and concubines. The bounty that would have saved from death was not received, and the emolument is taken that one's poor and needy acquaintance may be helped by him. Was it then not possible likewise to decline this? This is a case of what is called— 'Losing the proper nature of one's mind.' "

The disciple Kung-too said, "All are equally men, but some are great men, and some are little men;—how is this?" Mencius replied, "Those who follow that part of themselves which is great are great men; those who follow that part which is little are little men."

Mencius said, "Benevolence subdues its opposite just as water subdues fire. Those, however, who nowadays practice benevolence do it as if with one cup of water they could save a whole wagon-load of fuel which was on fire, and when the flames were not extinguished, were to say that water cannot subdue fire. This conduct, moreover, greatly encourages those who are not benevolent. The final issue will simply be this—the loss of that small amount of benevolence."

A man of Jin asked the disciple Uh-loo, saying, "Is an observance of the rules of propriety in regard to eating, or the eating, the more important?" The answer was, "The observance of the rules of propriety is the more important."

"Is the gratifying the appetite of sex, or the doing so only according to the rules of propriety, the more important?" The answer again was, "The observance of the rules of propriety in the matter is the more important."

The man pursued, "If the result of eating only according to the rules of propriety will be death by starvation, while by disregarding those rules we may get food, must they still be observed in such a case? If according to the rule that he shall go in person to meet his wife a man cannot get married, while by disregarding that rule he may get married, must he still observe the rule in such a case?"

Uh-loo was unable to reply to these questions, and the next day he went to Tsow, and told them to Mencius, Mencius said, "What difficulty is there in answering these inquiries?

"If you do not adjust them at their lower extremities, but only put their tops on a level, a piece of wood an inch square may be made to be higher than the pointed peak of a high building.

"Gold is heavier than feathers;—but does that saying have reference, on the one hand, to a single clasp of gold, and, on the other, to a wagon-load of feathers?

"If you take a case where the eating is of the utmost importance and the observing the rules of propriety is of little importance, and compare the things together, why stop with saying merely that the eating is more important? So, taking the case where the gratifying the appetite of sex is of the utmost importance and the observing the rules of propriety is of little importance, why stop with merely saying that the gratifying the appetite is the more important?

"Go and answer him thus, 'If, by twisting your elder brother's arm, and snatching from him what he is eating, you can get food for yourself, while, if you do not do so, you will not get anything to eat, will you so twist his arm? If by getting over your neighbour's wall, and dragging away his virgin daughter, you can get a wife, while if you do not do so, you will not be able to get a wife, will you so drag her away?' "

The prince of Loo wanting to commit the administration of his government to the disciple Yo-ching, Mencius said, "When I heard of it, I was so glad that I could not sleep."

Kung-sun Ch'ow asked, "Is Yo-ching a man of vigour?" and was answered, "No." "Is he wise in council?" "No." "Is he possessed of much information?" "No."

"What then made you so glad that you could not sleep?"

"He is a man who loves what is good."

"Is the love of what is good sufficient?"

"The love of what is good is more than a sufficient qualification for the government of the empire;—how much more is it so for the state of Loo!"

FROM BOOK VII:

Mencius said, "There is an appointment for everything. A man should receive submissively what may be correctly ascribed thereto. Therefore, he who has the true idea of what is heaven's appointment will not stand beneath a precipitous wall. Death sustained in the discharge of one's duties may correctly be ascribed to the appointment of heaven. Death under handcuffs and fetters cannot correctly be so ascribed.

"All things are already complete in us.

"If one acts with a vigorous effort at the law of reciprocity, when he seeks for the realization of perfect virtue, nothing can be closer than his approximation to it.

"To act without understanding, and to do so habitually without examination, pursuing the proper path all the life without knowing its nature;—this is the way of multitudes.

"Kindly words do not enter so deeply into men as a reputation for kindness. Good government does not lay hold of the people so much as good instructions. Good government is feared by the people, while good instructions are loved by them. Good government gets the people's wealth, while good instructions get their heart.

"Men who are possessed of intelligent virtue and prudence in affairs will generally be found to have been in sickness and troubles. They are the friendless minister and concubine's son, who keep their hearts under a sense of peril, and use deep precautions against calamity. On this account they become distinguished for their intelligence.

"To stand in the centre of the empire, and tranquillize the people within the four seas;—the superior man delights in this, but the highest enjoyment of his nature is not here.

"What belongs by his nature to the superior man cannot be increased by the largeness of his sphere of action, nor diminished by his dwelling in poverty and retirement;—for this reason, that it is determinately apportioned to him by heaven.

"What belong by his nature to the superior man are benevolence, righteousness, propriety, and knowledge. These are rooted in his heart; their growth and manifestation are a mild harmony appearing in the countenance, a rich fullness in the back, and the character imparted to the four limbs. Those limbs understand to arrange themselves, without being told."

Mencius said, "The principle of the philosopher Yang was—'Each one for himself.' Though he might have benefited the whole empire by plucking out a single hair, he would not have done it. The philosopher Mih loves all equally. If by rubbing smooth his whole body from the crown to the heel, he could have benefited the empire, he would have done it. Tsze-moh holds a medium between these. By holding that medium, he is nearer the right. But by holding it without leaving room for the exigency of circumstances, it becomes like their holding their one point. The reason why I hate that holding to one point is the injury it does to the way of right principle. It takes up one point and disregards a hundred others.

"The hungry think any food sweet, and the thirsty think the same of any drink, and thus they do not get the right taste of what they eat and drink. The hunger and thirst, in fact, injure their palate. And is it only the mouth and belly which are injured by hunger and thirst? Men's minds are also injured by them. If a man can prevent the evils of hunger and thirst from being any evils to his mind, he need not have any sorrow about not being up with other men.

"To feed a scholar and not love him, is to treat him as a pig. To love him and not respect him, is to keep him as a domestic animal. Honouring and respecting are what exist before any offering of gifts. If there be honouring and respecting without the reality of them, a superior man may not be retained by such empty demonstrations."

Kung-sun Ch'ow said, "Lofty are your principles and admirable, but to learn them may well be likened to ascending the heavens, something which cannot be reached. Why not adapt your teachings so as to cause learners to consider them attainable, and so daily exert themselves?"

Mencius said, "A great artificer does not, for the sake of a stupid workman, alter or do away with the marking line. E did not, for the sake of a stupid archer, change his rule for drawing the bow.

"The superior man draws the bow, but does not discharge the arrow. The whole thing seems to leap before the learner. Such is his standing exactly in the middle of the right path. Those who are able, follow him."

Mencius said, "There are men who say—'I am skilful at marshalling troops, I am skilful at conducting a battle!'—They are great criminals. If the sovereign of a state love benevolence, he will have no enemy in the empire.

"A carpenter or a carriage-maker may give a man the circle and square, but cannot make him skilful in the use of them.

"Anciently, the establishment of the frontier-gates was to guard against violence. Nowadays, it is to exercise violence.

"If men of virtue and ability be not confided in, a state will become empty and void. Without the rules of propriety and distinctions of right, the high and the low will be thrown into confusion. Without the great principles of government and their various business, there will not be wealth sufficient for the expenditure.

"Anciently, men of virtue and talents by means of their own enlightenment made others enlightened. Nowadays, it is tried, while they are themselves in darkness, and by means of that darkness, to make others enlightened.

"There are the foot-paths along the hills;—if suddenly they be used, they become roads; and if as suddenly they are not used, the wild grass fills them up. Now, the wild grass fills up your mind.

"Words which are simple, while their meaning is far-reaching, are good words. Principles which, as held, are compendious, while their application is extensive, are good principles. The words of the superior man do not go below the girdle, but great principles are contained in them. The principle which the superior man holds is that of personal cultivation, but the empire is thereby tranquillized. The disease of men is this:—that they neglect their own fields, and go to weed the fields of others, and that what they require from others is great, while what they lay upon themselves is light.

"Those who give counsel to the great should despise them, and not look at their pomp and display. Halls several times eight cubits high, with beams projecting several cubits;—these, if my wishes were to be realized, I would not have. Food spread before me over ten cubits square, and attendant girls to the amount of hundreds;—these, though my wishes were realized, I would not have. Pleasure and wine, and the dash of hunting, with thousands of chariots following after me;—these, though my wishes were realized, I would not have. What they esteem are what I would have nothing to do with; what I esteem are the rules of the ancients. Why should I stand in awe of them?"

THE GOSPEL OF MO-TI

Of all the Chinese sages, MO-TI *(sometimes Latinized into Micius) is the one who comes closest to being in the ordinary sense a religious prophet. He lived somewhen during the century between Confucius and Mencius, and taught a doctrine sharply opposed to theirs. Mo-ti had no use for secularism, looked with contempt on politics, and questioned all social distinctions. He was an extremist, an ascetic, a believer in heavenly spirits and earthly saints, a preacher of Love, Truth, and Goodness as absolutes to be practiced all the time. It was said of him that he would "wear his head and heels off to help mankind," and of his disciples that they would "go through fire, walk on knives, and accept death" rather than do harm. Some writers have likened Mo-ti to Diogenes, others to Jesus—and still others to Don Quixote.*

It might be assumed that such a teacher would find few followers, especially among a people as realistic as the Chinese are supposed to be. The fact is, however, that for some two centuries his influence rivalled that of Confucius, and the cult of Mo-ti all but became the official religion. Then of a sudden it waned and disappeared—why, no one can quite explain.

The doctrine of Mo-ti was preserved in seventy-one essays of which a number have been lost. Here are a few typical selections.[11]

ON THE NECESSITY OF STANDARDS

Mo-ti said: To accomplish anything whatsoever one must have standards. None has yet accomplished anything without them. The gentlemen fulfilling their duties as general and councillors have their standards. Even the artisans performing their tasks have their standards. The artisans make square objects according to the square, circular objects according to the compasses; they draw straight lines with the carpenter's line and find the perpendicular by a pendulum. All

[11] Reprinted from a translation by Y. P. Mei, in *The Wisdom of China and India*, edited by Lin Yutang (copyright, 1942, by Random House, Inc.). Reprinted by permission of Random House.

artisans, whether skilled or unskilled, employ these five standards. Only, the skilled workers are accurate. Though the unskilled labourers have not attained accuracy, yet they do better by following these standards than otherwise. Thus all artisans follow the standards in their work.

Now, the government of the empire and that of the large states do not observe their standards. This shows the governors are even less intelligent than the artisans.

What, then, should be taken as the proper standard in government? How will it do for everybody to imitate his parents? There are numerous parents in the world but few are magnanimous. For everybody to imitate his parents is to imitate the unmagnanimous. Imitating the unmagnanimous cannot be said to be following the proper standard. How will it do for everybody to follow his teacher? There are numerous teachers in the world but few are magnanimous. For everybody to imitate his teacher is to imitate the unmagnanimous. Imitating the unmagnanimous cannot be taken as following the proper standard. . . .

ON UNIVERSAL LOVE

Mo-ti said: The purpose of the magnanimous [12] is to be found in procuring benefits for the world and eliminating its calamities.

But what are the benefits of the world and what its calamities?"

Mo-ti said: Mutual attacks among states, mutual usurpation among houses, mutual injuries among individuals; the lack of grace and loyalty between ruler and ruled, the lack of affection and filial piety between father and son, the lack of harmony between elder and younger brothers—these are the major calamities in the world.

But whence did these calamities arise, out of mutual love?

Mo-ti said: They arise out of want of mutual love. At present feudal lords have learned only to love their own states and not those of others. Therefore they do not scruple about attacking other states. The heads of houses have learned only to love their own houses and not those of others. Therefore they do not scruple about usurping other houses. And individuals have learned only to love themselves and not

[12] *Jen*, variously translated as "benevolence," "charity," "love," "kindness." *Jenjen* philosophically means the "true man" in Confucianism, and in general usage the "good, kind man." Throughout this translation the word "magnanimous" refers to *jen*.

others. Therefore they do not scruple about injuring others. When feudal lords do not love one another there will be war on the fields. When heads of houses do not love one another they will usurp one another's power. When individuals do not love one another they will injure on another. When ruler and ruled do not love one another they will not be gracious and loyal. When father and son do not love each other they will not be affectionate and filial. When elder and younger brothers do not love each other they will not be harmonious. When nobody in the world loves any other, naturally the strong will over-power the weak, the many will oppress the few, the wealthy will mock the poor, the honoured will

disdain the humble, the cun-ning will deceive the simple. Therefore all the calamities, strifes, complaints, and hatred in the world have arisen out of want of mutual love. Therefore the benevolent disapproved of this want.

Now that there is disap-proval, how can we have the condition altered?

Mo-ti said: It is to be al-tered by the way of universal love and mutual aid.

But what is the way of uni-versal love and mutual aid?

Mo-ti said: It is to regard the state of others as one's own, the houses of others as one's own, the persons of others as one's self. When feudal lords love one another there will be no more war; when heads of houses love one another there will be no more mutual usurpation; when individuals love one another there will be no more mutual injury. When ruler and ruled love each other they will be gracious and loyal; when father and son love each other they will be affectionate and filial; when elder and younger brothers love each other they will be harmonious. When all the people in the world love one another, then the strong will not overpower the weak, the many will not oppress the few, the wealthy will not mock the poor, the honoured will not disdain the humble, and the cunning will not deceive the simple. And it is all due to mutual love that calamities, strifes, complaints, and hatred are prevented from arising. Therefore the benevolent exalt it.

But the gentlemen of the world would say: "So far so good. It is of course very excellent when love becomes universal. But it is only a difficult and distant ideal."

Mo-ti said: This is simply because the gentlemen of the world do not recognize what is to the benefit of the world, or understand what is its calamity. Now, to besiege a city, to fight in the fields, or to achieve a name at the cost of death—these are what men find difficult. Yet when the superior encourages them, the multitude can do them. Besides, universal love and mutual aid is quite different from these. Whoever loves others is loved by others; whoever benefits others is benefited by others; whoever hates others is hated by others; whoever injures others is injured by others. Then, what difficulty is there with it (universal love)? Only, the ruler fails to embody it in his government and the ordinary man in his conduct.[13]

   .   .   .   .

Yet the objection is not all exhausted. It is asked: "It may be a good thing, but can it be of any use?"

Mo-ti replied: If it were not useful then even I would disapprove of it. But how can there be anything that is good but not useful? Let us consider the matter from both sides. Suppose there are two men. Let one of them hold to partiality and the other to universality. Then the advocate of partiality would say to himself, how can I take care of my friend as I do of myself, how can I take care of his parents as my own? Therefore when he finds his friend hungry he would not feed him, and when he finds him cold he would not clothe him. In his illness he would not minister to him, and when he is dead he would not bury him. Such is the word and such is the deed of the advocate of partiality. The advocate of universality is quite unlike this both in word and in deed. He would say to himself, I have heard that to be a superior man one should take care of his friend as he does of himself, and take care of his friend's parents as his own. Therefore

---

[13] This is half of Mo-ti's second essay on "Universal Love," and what follows is the third. He goes on to prove his point by illustrations from ancient history and answers criticisms of Universal Love as "impracticable," etc. The idea of Universal Love is closely connected with "the will of Heaven" and is further developed all through Mo-ti's works.

when he finds his friend hungry he would feed him, and when he finds him cold he would clothe him. In his sickness he would serve him, and when he is dead he would bury him. Such is the word and such is the deed of the advocate of universality.

These two persons then are opposed to each other in word and also in deed. Suppose they are sincere in word and decisive in deed so that their word and deed are made to agree like the two parts of a tally, and that there is no word but what is realized in deed, then let us consider further: Suppose a war is on, and one is in armour and helmet ready to join the force, life and death are not predictable. Or suppose one is commissioned a deputy by the ruler to such far countries like Pa, Yüeh, Ch'i and Ching, and the arrival and return are quite uncertain. Now (under such circumstances) let us inquire upon whom would one lay the trust of one's family and parents. Would it be upon the universal friend or upon the partial friend? It seems to me, on occasions like these, there are no fools in the world. Even if he is a person who objects to universal love, he will lay the trust upon the universal friend all the same. This is verbal objection to the principle but actual selection by it—this is self-contradiction between one's word and deed. It is incomprehensible, then, why people should object to universal love when they hear it.

Yet the objection is still not exhausted. It raises the question, when one does not think in terms of benefits and harm to one's parents, would it be filial piety?

Mo-ti replied: Now let us inquire about the plans of the filial sons for their parents. I may ask, when they plan for their parents, whether they desire to have others love or hate them? Judging from the whole doctrine (of filial piety), it is certain that they desire to have others love their parents. Now, what should I do first in order to attain this? Should I first love others' parents in order that they would love my parents in return, or should I first hate others' parents in order that they would love my parents in return? Of course I should first love others' parents in order that they would love my parents in return. Hence those who desire to be filial to one another's parents, if they have to choose (between whether they should love or hate others' parents), had best first love and benefit others' parents. Would any one suspect that all the filial sons are stupid and incorrigible (in loving their own parents)? We may again inquire about it. It is said in the "Ta Ya" among the books of the ancient kings: "No idea is not given its due value; no virtue is not rewarded. When a peach is thrown to us, we would return with a prune." This is to say whoever loves others will be loved and whoever hates others will be hated. It is then quite incomprehensible why people should object to universal love when they hear it.

A disciple said to Mo-ti: "Though you love universally the world cannot be said to be benefited; though I do not love (universally) the world cannot be said to be injured. Since neither of us has accomplished anything, what makes you then praise yourself and blame me?" Mo-ti answered: Suppose a conflagration is on. One person is fetching water to extinguish it, and another is holding some fuel to reinforce it. Neither of them has yet accomplished anything, but which one do you value? The disciple answered that he approved of the intention of the person who fetches water and disapproved of the intention of the person who holds fuel. Mo-ti said: (In the same manner) do I approve of my intention and disapprove of yours.

The same disciple said to Mo-ti: "For all the righteousness that you do, men do not help you and ghosts do not bless you. Yet you keep on doing it. You must be demented." Mo-ti said: Suppose you have here two employees. One of them works when he sees you but will not work when he does not see you. The other one works whether he sees you or not. Which of the two would you value? The disciple said that he wuld value him that worked whether he saw him or not. Mo-ti then said: Then you are valuing him who is demented.

ON THE CRIMINALITY OF WAR

The murder of one person is called unrighteous and incurs the death penalty. Following this argument, the murder of ten persons will be ten times as unrighteous and there should be ten death penalties; the murder of a hundred persons will be a hundred times as unrighteous and there should be a hundred death penalties. All the gentlemen of the world know that they should condemn these things, calling them unrighteous. But when it comes to the great unrighteousness of attacking states, they do not know that they should condemn it. On the contrary, they applaud it, calling it righteous. And they are really ignorant of its being unrighteous. Hence they have recorded their judgment to bequeath to their posterity. If they did know that it is unrighteous, then why would they record their false judgment to bequeath to posterity?

Now, if there were a man who, upon seeing a little blackness, should say it is black, but, upon seeing much, should say it is white; then we should think he could not tell the difference between black and white. If, upon tasting a little bitterness one should say it is bitter, but, upon tasting much, should say it is sweet; then we should think he could not tell the difference between bitter and sweet. Now, when a little wrong is committed people know that they should condemn it, but when such a great wrong as attacking a state is committed, people do not know that they should condemn it. On the contrary, it is applauded, called righteous. Can this be said to be knowing the difference between the righteous and unrighteous? Hence we know the gentlemen of the world are confused about the difference between righteousness and unrighteousness. . . .

Now, about a country going to war. If it is in winter it will be too cold; if it is summer it will be too hot. So it should be neither in winter nor in summer. If it is in spring it will take people away from sowing and planting; if it is in autumn it will take people away from reaping and harvesting. Should they be taken away in either of these seasons, innumerable people would die of hunger and cold. And, when the army sets out, the bamboo arrows, the feather flags, the house tents, the armour, the shields, the sword hilts—innumerable quantities of these will break and rot and never come back. The spears, the lances, the swords, the poniards, the chariots, the carts—innumerable quantities of these will break and rot and never come back. Then innumerable horses and oxen will start out fat and come back lean or will not return at all. And innumerable people will die because their food will be cut off and cannot be supplied on account of the great distances of the roads. And innumerable people will be sick and die of the constant danger and the irregularity of eating and drinking and the extremes of hunger and over-eating. Then, the army will be lost in large numbers or entirely; in either case the number will be innumerable. And this means the spirits will lose their worshippers, and the number of these will also be innumerable.

Why then does the government deprive the people of their opportunities and benefits to such a great extent? It has been answered: "I covet the fame of the victor and the possessions obtainable through the conquest. So I do it."

Mo-ti said: But when we consider the victory as such, there is nothing useful about it. When we consider the possessions obtained through it, it does not even make up for the loss. Now about the siege of a city of three *li* or a *kuo* of seven *li*—if these could be obtained without the use of weapons or the killing of lives, it would be all right. But (as a matter of fact) those killed must be counted by the ten thousand, those widowed or left solitary must be counted by the thousand, before a city of three *li* or a *kuo* of seven *li* could be captured. Moreover the states of ten thousand chariots now have empty towns to be counted by the thousand, which can be entered without conquest; and their extensive lands to be counted by the ten thousand (of *mu*), which can be cultivated without conquest. So, land is abundant but people are few. Now to pursue the people to death and aggravate the danger feared by both superiors and subordinates in order to obtain an empty city—this is to give up what is needed and to treasure what is already in abundance. Such an undertaking is not in accordance with the interest of the country. . . .

Mo-ti said: What does the world now praise to be good? Is not an act praised because it is useful to Heaven on high, to the spirits in the middle sphere, and to the people below? Certainly no other reason is needed for praise than to be useful to Heaven on high, to the spirits in the middle, and to the people below. Even the stupid would say it is praiseworthy when it is helpful to Heaven on high, to the spirits in the middle, and to the people below. And what the world agrees on is just the way of the sage-kings.

Now to capture a state and to destroy an army, to disturb and torture the people, and to set at naught the aspirations of the sages by confusion—is this intended to bless Heaven? But the people of Heaven are gathered together to besiege the towns belonging to Heaven. This is to murder men of Heaven and dispossess the spirits of their altars and to ruin the state and to kill the sacrificial animals. It is then not a blessing to Heaven on high. Is it intended to bless the spirits? But men of Heaven are murdered, spirits are deprived of their sacrifices, the earlier kings [14] are neglected, the multitude are tortured and the people are scattered; it is then not a blessing to the spirits in the middle. Is it intended to bless the people? But the blessing of the people by killing them off must be very meagre. And when we cal-

---

[14] Meaning the ancestral spirits of the state.

culate the expense, which is the root of the calamities of living, we find the property of innumerable people is exhausted. It is, then, not a blessing to the people below either.

Have we not heard it said that, when a warring state goes on an expedition, of the officers there must be several hundred, of the common people there must be several thousand, and of the soldiers and prisoners there must be ten thousand, before the army can set out? It may last for several years, or at the shortest, several months. So, the superior will have no time to attend to their offices, the farmers will have no time to sow or reap, the women will have no time to weave or spin: that is, the state will lose its men and the people will neglect their vocations. Besides, the chariots will break and horses will be exhausted. As to tents, army supplies, and soldiers' equipment—if one-fifth of these can remain (after the war) it would already be beyond expectation. Moreover, innumerable men will be missing and lost on the way, and will become sick from the long distances, meagre rations, hunger and cold, and die in the ditches. Now the calamity to the people and the world is tremendous. Yet the rulers enjoy doing it. This means they enjoy injuring and exterminating the people; is this not perversity?

ON THE WILL OF HEAVEN

Now, what does Heaven desire and what does it abominate? Heaven desires righteousness and abominates unrighteousness. . . . But how do we know Heaven desires righteousness and abominates unrighteousness? For, with righteousness the world lives and without it the world dies; with it the world becomes rich and without it the world becomes poor; with it the world becomes orderly and without it the world becomes chaotic. And Heaven likes to have the world live and dislikes to have it die, likes to have it rich and dislikes to have it poor, and likes to have it orderly and dislikes to have it disorderly. Therefore we know Heaven desires righteousness and abominates unrighteousness. . . .

To obey the will of Heaven is to accept righteousness as the standard. To oppose the will of Heaven is to accept force as the standard. Now what will the standard of righteousness do?

Mo-ti said: He who rules a large state does not attack small states: he who rules a large house does not molest small houses. The strong does not plunder the weak. The honoured does not disdain the humble. The clever does not deceive the stupid. This is beneficial to Heaven above, beneficial to the spirits in the middle sphere, and beneficial to the people below. Being beneficial to these three it is beneficial to all. So the most excellent name is attributed to such a man and he is called sage-king.

The standard of force is different from this. It is contradictory to this in word and opposed to this in deed like galloping with back to back. Leading a large state, he whose standard is force, attacks small states; leading a large house he molests small houses. The strong plunders the weak, the honoured disdains the humble. The clever deceives the stupid. This is not beneficial to Heaven above, or to the spirits in the middle sphere, or to the people below. Not being beneficial to these three, it is beneficial to none. So, the most evil name in the world is attributed to him and he is called the wicked king.

Mo-ti said: The will of Heaven to me is like the compasses to the wheelwright and the square to the carpenter. The wheelwright and the carpenter measure all the square and circular objects with their square and compasses and accept those that fit as correct, and reject those that do not fit as incorrect. The writings of the gentry of the world of the present day cannot be all loaded (in a cart), and their doctrines cannot be exhaustively enumerated. They endeavour to convince the feudal lords on the one hand and the scholars on the other. But from magnanimity and righteousness they are far off. How do we know? Because I have the most competent standard in the world to measure them with. . . .

And hence Mo-ti said: If the gentry of the world really desire to follow the way and benefit the people, they must not disobey the will of Heaven, the origin of magnanimity and righteousness.

Now that we must obey the will of Heaven, what does the will of Heaven desire and what does it abominate? Mo-ti said: The will of Heaven abominates the large state which attacks small states, the large house which molests small houses, the strong who plunder the weak, the clever who deceive the stupid, and the honoured who disdain the humble—these are what the will of Heaven abominates. On the other hand, it desires people having energy to work for each other, those knowing the way to teach each other, and those possessing wealth to share with each other. And it desires the superior diligently to attend to government and the subordinates diligently to attend to their work. . . .

Heaven loves the whole world universally. Everything is prepared for the good of man. Even the tip of a hair is the work of Heaven. Substantial may be said of the benefits that are enjoyed by man. Yet there is no service in return. And they do not even know this to be unmagnanimous and unfortunate. This is why I say the gentry understand only trifles and not things of importance. .

THE SCRIPTURES OF TAOISM

THE TAO TEH KING
THE WRITINGS OF CHUANG-TZE

INTRODUCTION

Taoism is a mystical philosophy founded in China in the sixth century B.C., *which eventually became a religious cult and still survives as such throughout that land. There is no estimating the number of its adherents, since virtually all Taoists are also Confucianists, and millions are Buddhists to boot. The only Chinese professing a single and exclusive religion are the relatively few who adhere to Islam or Christianity.*

The creator of Taoism as a system of thought was a sage named Lao-Tze (circa 604–524 B.C.), the reputed author of the TAO TEH KING. Like Confucius, who was his younger contemporary, Lao-Tze was bitterly troubled by the conditions of the day, the lawlessness, misery, and moral confusion engendered by the breakdown of the ancient feudal order. He was entirely a mystic, however, not a rationalist, and therefore looked for salvation in a program of spiritual rather than practical reform. He believed that behind and beyond all existence lay an infinite, impersonal, and imperturbable essence called Tao. *This was the Ultimate Reality, and real happiness, said Lao-Tze, could come only to those who made themselves deliberately and consciously a part of it. One had to get down to fundamentals, and these were not the moral niceties and social proprieties spoken of by Confucius. They were the imponderable values inherent in Life itself, the transcendant virtues of eternal Nature. The wise man, therefore, is he who forgets the world and its ways, he who shuns society and returns to the life primeval.*

Lao-Tze's gospel was thus closely akin to Buddha's, and to that of the Brahman mystic who composed the UPANISHADS. *It was part and parcel, indeed, of a type of supra-rational thinking so common throughout history that Aldous Huxley has well named it "the Perennial Philosophy." Even the Chinese, traditionally a most realistic folk, found it not without some appeal. At any rate, they did preserve the little book entitled* TAO TEH KING *in which that gospel was first expounded to them.*

Its influence was slight until some two centuries after Lao-Tze's death, when a philosopher named Chuang-Tze gave the gospel fresh currency in China. Chuang-Tze was a brilliant polemicist as well as profound thinker, and his writings attracted wide attention. He made scathing sport of the Confucianists with their petty moralism and fussy regulations, arguing that the whole duty of man was to "resolve all mental energy into abstraction, and all physical energy into inaction." Everything would come out right, he insisted, if people simply sat back, did nothing, and let Nature take its course. He succeeded in winning a considerable following of hermits.

But inaction is hard to sustain, and eventually those hermits could not resist a temptation to try and help Nature along. They began to dabble in alchemy and other magical arts, hoping thus to ferret out Nature's hidden secrets and use them to mankind's advantage. This inevitably attracted royal as well as popular interest, and within a century of Chuang-Tze's death the Taoist adepts became little more than a pack of professional magicians.

Finally, around the second century A.D., *the movement developed into a regular religion with Lao-Tze as its chief god, a multitude of temples, a powerful priesthood, and an elaborate ritual of its own. In recent years the Taoist temples have been allowed to fall into neglect, the priests are in beggarly circumstances, and the ritual has largely degenerated into mere fortune-telling and exorcism. But the religion still claims to draw its inspiration from the books of Lao-Tze and Chuang-Tze, and these certainly belong among the world's great scriptures.*

THE TAO TEH KING

The TAO TEH KING *is the basic scripture of the Taoist religion. It is a small book of some five thousand characters divided into eighty-one chapters, and though primarily mystical, it contains much that is ethically cogent and impressive. The virtues which it commends are seemingly negative, yet—at least as a corrective—highly salutary. It counsels man to empty himself of material desires, for thus alone can he avoid frustration and attain spiritual contentment. The sage refuses to identify his happiness with this thing or that, and as a result he never loses his happiness. Because he does not set his heart on specific ambitions, they never escape him, and thus it is as though he actually realized them. Because "he does not live for Self . . . his Self achieves perfection."*

Even a hasty reader will find much in this scripture to bring him up short and provoke at least inward questionings. Careful ones may discover in it enough to re-orient their whole thinking. For that reason most of the TAO TEH KING *has been included in this Anthology, the only omissions being the distinctly metaphysical passages.[1]*

ACTION WITHOUT DEEDS

Exalt not the wise,[2]
    So that the people shall not scheme and contend;
Prize not rare objects,
    So that the people shall not steal;
Shut out from sight the things of desire,
    So that the people's hearts shall not be disturbed.

Therefore in the government of the Sage:
    He keeps empty their hearts [3]

[1] Translation (and footnotes) by Lin Yutang, *The Wisdom of China and India* (Random House, New York, 1942).
[2] Exalting the wise in government is a typically Confucianist idea.
[3] "Empty-heart" in the Chinese language means "open-mindedness," or "humility," a sign of the cultured gentleman. Throughout this book, "empty" and "full" are used as meaning "humility" and "pride" respectively.

Makes full their bellies,
Discourages their ambitions,
Strengthens their frames;
So that the people may be purified of their thoughts and desires.
And the cunning ones shall not presume to interfere.[4]
By action without deeds
May all live in peace.

THE CHARACTER OF TAO

Tao is all-pervading,[5]
And its use is inexhaustible!
Fathomless!
Like the fountain head of
all things.
Its sharp edges rounded off,
Its tangles untied,
Its light tempered,
Its turmoil submerged,
Yet crystal clear like still water
it seems to remain.
I do not know whose Son
it is,
An image of what existed
before God.

LIVING FOR OTHERS

The universe is everlasting.
The reason the universe is everlasting
Is that it does not live for Self.[6]
Therefore it can long endure.

Therefore the Sage puts himself last,
And finds himself in the foremost place;

[4] *Wei,* "to act," frequently used in this book to denote "interfere." *Wu-wei,* or "inaction" practically means non-interference, for it is the exact equivalent of "*laissez-faire.*"

[5] *Ch'ung,* "empty," "mild," "formless," "filling all space." Another reading, *chung,* "Tao is an empty vessel."

[6] Gives life to others through its transformations.

Regards his body as accidental,
And his body is thereby preserved.
Is it not because he does not live for Self
That his Self achieves perfection?

WATER

The best of men is like water;
Water benefits all things
And does not compete with them.
It dwells in (the lowly) places that all disdain,—
Wherein it comes near to the Tao.

In his dwelling, (the Sage) loves the (lowly) earth;
In his heart, he loves what is profound;
In his relations with others, he loves kindness;
In his words, he loves sincerity;
In government, he loves peace;
In business affairs, he loves ability;
In his actions, he loves choosing the right time.
It is because he does not contend
That he is without reproach.

THE DANGER OF OVERWEENING SUCCESS

Stretch (a bow) [7] to the very full,
And you will wish you had stopped in time.
Temper a (sword-edge) to its very sharpest,
And the edge will not last long.
When gold and jade fill your hall,
You will not be able to keep them safe.
To be proud with wealth and honor
Is to sow the seeds of one's own downfall.
Retire when your work is done,
Such is Heaven's way.

[7] Throughout Lao-Tze, the idea of *ying*, "fullness" or "filled to the brim" associated with pride, is condemned as the opposite of "emptiness" or "humility," because success contains the seeds of downfall.

EMBRACING THE ONE

In embracing the One [8] with your soul,
  Can you never forsake the Tao?
In controlling your vital force to achieve gentleness,
  Can you become like the new-born child?
In cleansing and purifying your Mystic vision,
  Can you strive after perfection?
In loving the people and governing the kingdom,
  Can you rule without interference?
In opening and shutting the Gates of Heaven,
  Can you play the part of the Female? [9]
In comprehending all knowledge,
  Can you renounce the mind?

To give birth, to nourish,
To give birth without taking possession,
To act without appropriation,
To be chief among men without managing them—
This is the Mystic Virtue.

THE UTILITY OF NOT-BEING

Thirty spokes unite around the nave;
  From their not-being (losing of their individuality)
    Arises the utility of the wheel.
Mould clay into a vessel;
  From its not-being (in the vessel's hollow)
    Arises the utility of the vessel.
Cut out doors and windows in the house (-wall),
  From their not-being (empty space) arises the utility
    of the house.
Therefore by the existence of things we profit.
And by the non-existence of things we are served.

[8] The babe as symbol of innocence, a common imagery found also in Chuang-Tze; sometimes the imagery of the "new-born calf" is used.
[9] The *Yin*, the receptive, the passive, the quiet.

THE SENSES

The five colors blind the eyes of man;
The five musical notes deafen the ears of man;
The five flavors dull the taste of man;
Horse-racing, hunting and chasing madden the minds of
      man;
Rare, valuable goods keep their owners awake at night.

Therefore the Sage:
   Provides for the belly and not for the eye.[10]
   Hence, he rejects the one and accepts the other.

PRAISE AND BLAME

"Favor and disgrace cause one dismay;
What we value and what we fear are as if within our Self."

What does this mean:
"Favor and disgrace cause one dismay?"
Those who receive a favor from above
   Are dismayed when they receive it,
   And dismayed when they lose it.

What does this mean:
"What we value and what we fear [11] are as if within our Self"?
We have fears because we have a self.[12]
When we do not regard that self as self,
What have we to fear?

Therefore he who values the world as his self
   May then be entrusted with the government of the world;
And he who loves the world as his self—
   The world may then be entrusted to his care.

[10] "Belly" here refers to the inner self, the unconscious, the instinctive; the "eye" refers to the external self or the sensuous world.
[11] Interpreted as life and death.
[12] Lit. "body."

KNOWING THE ETERNAL LAW

Attain the utmost in Humility; [13]
Hold firm to the basis of Quietude.

The myriad things take shape and rise to activity,
    But I watch them fall back to their repose.
Like vegetation that luxuriantly grows
    But returns to the root (soil) from which it springs.

To return to the root is Repose;
    It is called going back to one's Destiny.
Going back to one's Destiny is to find the Eternal Law.
    To know the Eternal Law is Enlightenment.
And not to know the Eternal Law
    Is to court disaster.

He who knows the Eternal Law is tolerant;
Being tolerant, he is impartial;
Being impartial, he is kingly;
Being kingly, he is in accord with Nature;
Being in accord with Nature, he is in accord with Tao;
Being in accord with Tao, he is eternal,
And his whole life is preserved from harm.

RULERS

Of the best rulers
    The people (only) know that they exist;
The next best they love and praise;
The next they fear;
And the next they revile.
    When they do not command the people's faith,
    Some will lose faith in them,
    And then they resort to oaths!
But (of the best) when their task is accomplished, their
    work done,
    The people all remark, "We have done it ourselves."

[13] *Hsü:* emptiness, void. But in actual usage, this "emptiness" has no other meaning than "humility." Both "humility" and "quietude" are central Taoist ideas.

REALIZE THE SIMPLE SELF

Banish wisdom, discard knowledge,
  And the people shall profit a hundredfold;
Banish "love," discard "justice,"
  And the people shall recover love of their kin;
Banish cunning, discard "utility,"
  And the thieves and brigands shall disappear.
As these three touch the externals and are inadequate;
  The people have need of what they can depend upon:
    Reveal thy Simple Self,
    Embrace thy Original Nature,
    Check thy selfishness,
    Curtail thy desires.[14]

THE WORLD AND I

Banish learning, and vexations end.
  Between "Ah!" and "Ough!"
  How much difference is there?
Between "good" and "evil"
  How much difference is there?
That which men fear
  Is indeed to be feared;
But, alas, distant yet is the dawn (of awakening)!

The people of the world are merry-making,
  As if eating of the sacrificial offerings,
  As if mounting the terrace in spring;
I alone am mild, like one unemployed,
  Like a new-born babe that cannot yet smile,
  Unattached, like one without a home.

The people of the world have enough and to spare,
But I am like one left out,
  My heart must be that of a fool,
  Being muddled, nebulous!

[14] The eight characters in these four lines sum up practical Taoist teachings.

The vulgar are knowing, luminous;
　　I alone am dull, confused.
The vulgar are clever, self-assured;
　　I alone, depressed.
Patient as the sea,
　　Adrift, seemingly aimless.

The people of the world all have a purpose;
　　I alone appear stubborn and uncouth.
I alone differ from the other people,
　　And value drawing sustenance from the Mother.

FUTILITY OF CONTENTION

To yield is to be preserved whole.
To be bent is to become straight.
To be hollow is to be filled.
To be tattered is to be renewed.

To be in want is to possess.
To have plenty is to be confused.

Therefore the Sage embraces the One,[15]
And becomes the model of the world.
He does not reveal himself,
   And is therefore luminous.
He does not justify himself,
   And is therefore far-famed.
He does not boast of himself,
   And therefore people give him credit.
He does not pride himself,
   And is therefore the ruler among men.

It is because he does not contend
That no one in the world can contend against him.

Is it not indeed true, as the ancients say,
   "To yield is to be preserved whole?"
Thus he is preserved and the world does him homage.

IDENTIFICATION WITH TAO

Nature says few words:
Hence it is that a squall lasts not a whole morning.
A rainstorm continues not a whole day.
Where do they come from?
From Nature.
Even Nature does not last long (in its utterances),
   How much less should human beings?

Therefore it is that:
   He who follows the Tao is identified with the Tao.
   He who follows Virtue (*Teh*) is identified with Virtue.
   He who abandons (Tao) is identified with abandonment
      (of Tao).
He who is identified with Tao—
   Tao is also glad to welcome him.

[15] The Absolute, to which transient attributes revert.

He who is identified with Virtue—
    Virtue is also glad to welcome him.
He who is identified with abandonment—
    Abandonment is also glad to welcome him.
He who has not enough faith
    Will not be able to command faith from others.

THE DREGS AND TUMORS OF VIRTUE

He who stands on tiptoe does not stand (firm);
He who strains his strides does not walk (well);
He who reveals himself is not luminous;
He who justifies himself is not far-famed;
He who boasts of himself is not given credit;
He who prides himself is not chief among men.
    These in the eyes of Tao
    Are called "the dregs and tumors of Virtue,"
        Which are things of disgust.
Therefore the man of Tao spurns them.

ON STEALING THE LIGHT

A good runner leaves no track.
A good speech leaves no flaws for attack.
A good reckoner makes use of no counters.
A well shut door makes use of no bolts,
    And yet cannot be opened.
A well-tied knot makes use of no rope,
    And yet cannot be untied.

Therefore the Sage is good at helping men;
    For that reason there is no rejected (useless) person.
He is good at saving things;
    For that reason there is nothing rejected.[16]
    —This is called stealing [17] the Light.

[16] The Sage uses each according to his talent.
[17] *Hsi*, to enter or secure by devious means such as invasion, attack at night, penetration, etc. The idea is cunningly to make use of knowledge of nature's law to obtain the best results.

Therefore the good man is the Teacher of the bad.
And the bad man is the lesson of the good.

He who neither values his teacher
    Nor loves the lesson
Is one gone far astray,
    Though he be learned.
    —Such is the subtle secret.

WARNING AGAINST INTERFERENCE

There are those who will con-
    quer the world
And make of it (what they
    conceive or desire).
  I see that they will not suc-
    ceed.
(For) the world is God's own
    Vessel
It cannot be made (by human
    interference).
  He who makes it spoils it.
  He who holds it loses it.
For: Some things go forward,
  Some things follow behind;
  Some blow hot,
  And some blow cold;
  Some are strong,
  And some are weak;
  Some may break,
  And some may fall.

      Hence the Sage eschews excess,
               eschews extravagance,
               eschews pride.

WARNING AGAINST THE USE OF FORCE

He who by Tao purposes to help the ruler of men
Will oppose all conquest by force of arms.

For such things are wont to rebound.
Where armies are, thorns and brambles grow.
The raising of a great host
Is followed by a year of dearth.[18]

Therefore a good general effects his purpose and stops.
    He dares not rely upon the strength of arms;
Effects his purpose and does not glory in it;
Effects his purpose and does not boast of it;
Effects his purpose and does not take pride in it;
    Effects his purpose as a regrettable necessity;
    Effects his purpose but does not love violence.
(For) things age after reaching their prime.
That (violence) would be against the Tao.
And he who is against the Tao perishes young.

WEAPONS OF EVIL

Of all things, soldiers are instruments of evil,
    Hated by men.
Therefore the religious man (possessed of Tao) avoids
    them.
The gentleman favors the left in civilian life,
But on military occasions favors the right.

Soldiers are weapons of evil.
    They are not the weapons of the gentleman.
When the use of soldiers cannot be helped,
    The best policy is calm restraint.

Even in victory, there is no beauty,
And who calls it beautiful
    Is one who delights in slaughter.
He who delights in slaughter
    Will not succeed in his ambition to rule the world. . . .

The slaying of multitudes should be mourned with sorrow.
A victory should be celebrated with the Funeral Rite.

[18] These six lines are by Waley, for they cannot be improved upon.

KNOWING ONESELF

He who knows others is learned;
    He who knows himself is wise.
He who conquers others has power of muscles;
    He who conquers himself is strong.
He who is contented is rich.
    He who is determined has strength of will.
He who does not lose his center endures,
He who dies yet (his power) remains has long life.

THE RHYTHM OF LIFE

He who is to be made to dwindle (in power)
    Must first be caused to expand.
He who is to be weakened
    Must first be made strong,
He who is to be laid low
    Must first be exalted to power.
He who is to be taken away from
    Must first be given,
    —This is the Subtle Light.

Gentleness overcomes strength:
    Fish should be left in the deep pool,
    And sharp weapons of the state should be left
        Where none can see them.

QUALITIES OF THE TAOIST

When the highest type of men hear the Tao (truth),
    They practice it diligently.
When the mediocre type hear the Tao,
    They seem to be aware and yet unaware of it.
When the lowest type hear the Tao,
    They break into loud laughter,—
        If it were not laughed at, it would not be Tao.

Therefore there is the established saying:
  "Who understands Tao seems dull of comprehension;
  Who is advanced in Tao seems to slip backwards;
  Who moves on the even Tao (Path) seems to go up and down."

Superior virtue appears like a hollow (valley);
Sheer white appears like tarnished;
Great character appears like insufficient;
Solid character appears like infirm;
Pure worth appears like contaminated.
  Great space has no corners;
  Great talent takes long to mature;
  Great music is faintly heard;
  Great Form has no contour;
  And Tao is hidden without a name.
It is this Tao that is adept at lending (its power) and bringing fulfil-
  ment.

THE VIOLENT MAN

  Others have taught this maxim,
  Which I shall teach also:
  "The violent man shall die a violent death."
  This I shall regard as my spiritual teacher.

THE SOFTEST SUBSTANCE

  The softest substance of the world
  Goes through the hardest.
  That which-is-without-form penetrates that-which-has-no-crevice;
  Through this I know the benefit of taking no action.
  The teaching without words
  And the benefit of taking no action
    Are without compare in the universe.

BE CONTENT

  Fame or one's own self, which does one love more?
  One's own self or material goods, which has more worth?
  Loss (of self) or possession (of goods), which is the greater evil?

Therefore: he who loves most spends most,
  He who hoards much loses much.
The contented man meets no disgrace;
Who knows when to stop runs into no danger—
He can long endure.

CALM QUIETUDE

The highest perfection is like imperfection,[19]
  And its use is never impaired.
The greatest abundance seems meagre,
  And its use will never fail.
What is most straight appears devious;
The greatest cleverness appears like stupidity;
The greatest eloquence seems like stuttering.
Movement overcomes cold,
(But) keeping still overcomes heat.
Who is calm and quiet becomes the guide for the universe.

RACING HORSES

When the world lives in accord with Tao,
Racing horses are turned back to haul refuse carts.
When the world lives not in accord with Tao,
Cavalry abounds in the countryside.

There is no greater curse than the lack of contentment.
No greater sin than the desire for possession.
Therefore he who is contented with contentment shall be
    always content.

PURSUIT OF KNOWLEDGE

Without stepping outside one's doors,
  One can know what is happening in the world,
Without looking out of one's windows,
  One can see the Tao of Heaven.

[19] Because it assumes fluid form according to circumstances.

The farther one pursues knowledge,
  The less one knows.
Therefore the Sage knows without running about,
  Understands without seeing,
  Accomplishes without doing.

CONQUERING THE WORLD BY INACTION

The student of knowledge (aims at) learning day by day;
The student of Tao (aims at) losing day by day.
  By continual losing
  One reaches doing nothing.
  By doing nothing everything is done.
He who conquers the world often does so by doing nothing.[20]
When one is compelled to do something,[21]
The world is already beyond his conquering.

THE PEOPLE'S HEARTS

The Sage has no decided opinions and feelings,[22]
But regards the people's opinions and feelings as his own.

The good ones I declare good;
The bad ones I also declare good.
  That is the goodness of Virtue.
The honest ones I believe;
The liars I also believe;
  That is the faith of Virtue.

The Sage dwells in the world peacefully, harmoniously.
The people of the world are brought into a community of heart,
And the Sage regards them all as his own children.

[20] By moral influence.
[21] By ordering people about.
[22] *Hsin*, Lit. "heart." Both thinking and feeling are denoted by this word. It is impossible to say a "decided heart."

THE PRESERVER OF LIFE

Out of life, death enters.
The organs of life are thirteen; [23]
The organs of death are (also) thirteen.
What send man to death in this life are also (these) thirteen.
    How is it so?
Because of the intense activity of multiplying life.

It has been said that he
    who is a good pre-
    server of his life
    Meets no tigers or wild
    buffaloes on land,
    Is not vulnerable to
    weapons in the field
    of battle.
The horns of the wild
    buffalo are powerless
    against him;
The paws of the tiger are
    useless against him;
The weapons of the sol-
    dier cannot avail
    against him.
    How is it so?
Because he is beyond
    death.[24]

STEALING THE ABSOLUTE

There was a beginning of the universe
    Which may be regarded as the Mother of Universe.
From the Mother, we may know her sons.
    After knowing the sons, keep to the Mother.
    Thus one's whole life may be preserved from harm.

[23] According to Han Fei, the four limbs and nine external cavities. Another ortho-dox reading is "three-tenths," but this makes less sense.
[24] Lit. "deathless."

Stop its apertures,
Close its doors,
And one's whole life is without toil.

Open its apertures,
Be busy about its affairs,

And one's whole life is beyond redemption.
He who can see the small is clear-sighted;
He who stays by gentility is strong.
    Use the light,
    And return to clear-sightedness—
Thus cause not yourself later distress.
—This is to steal the Absolute.

BRIGANDAGE

If I were possessed of Austere Knowledge,
Walking on the Main Path (Tao),
I would avoid the by-paths.
    The Main Path is easy to walk on,
    Yet people love the small by-paths.

The (official) courts are spic and span,
(While) the fields go untilled,
And the granaries are very low.
(Yet) clad in embroidered gowns,
And carrying fine swords,
Surfeit with good food and drinks,
(They are) splitting with wealth and possessions.
    —This is to lead the world toward brigandage.
    Is it not the corruption of Tao?

THE INDIVIDUAL AND THE STATE

Who is firmly established is not easily shaken.
Who has a firm grasp does not easily let go.
From generation to generation his ancestral sacrifices
    Shall be continued without fail.

Cultivated in the individual, Virtue will become genuine;
Cultivated in the family, Virtue will become abundant;
Cultivated in the village, Virtue will multiply;
Cultivated in the state, Virtue will prosper;
Cultivated in the world, Virtue will become universal.

Therefore:
  According to (the virtue of) the individual, judge the individual;
  According to (the virtue of) the family, judge the family;
  According to (the virtue of) the village, judge the village;
  According to (the virtue of) the state, judge the state;
  According to (the virtue of) the world, judge the world.
  How do I know the world is so.
  From within myself.

THE VIRTUES OF THE CHILD

Who is rich in virtue
Is like a child.
  No poisonous insects sting him,
  No wild beasts attack him,
  And no birds of prey pounce upon him.
His bones are soft, his sinews tender, yet his grip is strong.
Not knowing the union of male and female, yet his organs are complete,
    plete,
  Which means his vigor is unspoiled.
Crying the whole day, yet his voice never runs hoarse,
  Which means his (natural) harmony is perfect.
To know harmony is to be in accord with the eternal,
(And) to know eternity is called discerning.
(But) to improve upon life is called an ill-omen;
To let go the emotions through impulse is called assertiveness.
[For) things age after reaching their prime;
That (assertiveness) would be against Tao.
And he who is against Tao perishes young.

BEYOND HONOR AND DISGRACE

He who knows does not speak;
He who speaks does not know.
    Fill up its apertures,
    Close its doors,
    Dull its edges,
    Untie its tangles,
    Soften its light,
    Submerge its turmoil,
    —This is the Mystic Unity.

Then love and hatred cannot touch him.
Profit and loss cannot reach him.
Honor and disgrace cannot affect him.
Therefore is he always the honored one of the world.

THE ART OF GOVERNMENT

    The more prohibitions there are, the poorer the people become.
The more sharp weapons there are,
    The more prevailing chaos there is in the state.
The more skills of technique,
    The more cunning things are produced.
The greater the number of statutes,
    The greater the number of thieves and brigands.

Therefore the Sage says:
    I do nothing and the people are reformed of themselves.
    I love quietude and the people are righteous of themselves.
    I deal in no business and the people grow rich by themselves.
    I have no desires and the people are simple and honest by them-
       selves.

LAZY GOVERNMENT

When the government is lazy and dull,
    Its people are unspoiled;
When the government is efficient and smart,
    Its people are discontented.

Disaster is the avenue of fortune,
(And) fortune is the concealment for disaster.
   Who would be able to know its ultimate results?
(As it is), there would never be the normal,
   But the normal would (immediately) revert to the deceitful,
   And the good revert to the sinister.
Thus long has mankind gone astray!

Therefore the Sage is square (has firm principles), but not cutting
      (sharp-cornered),
   Has integrity but does not hurt (others),[25]
   Is straight, but not high-handed,
   Bright, but not dazzling.

BE SPARING

In managing human affairs, there is no better rule than to be sparing,[26]
To be sparing is to forestall;
To forestall is to be prepared and strengthened;
To be prepared and strengthened is to be ever-victorious;
To be ever-victorious is to have infinite capacity;
He who has infinite capacity is fit to rule a country,
And the Mother (principle) of a ruling country can long endure.
   This is to be firmly rooted, to have deep strength,
   The road to immortality and enduring vision.

RULING A BIG COUNTRY

   Rule a big country as you would fry small fish.

Who rules the world in accord with Tao
   Would find that the spirits lose their power.
It is not that the spirits lose their power,
   But that they cease to do people harm.
It is not (only) that they cease to do people harm,
   The Sage (himself) also does no harm to the people.
When both do not do each other harm,
   Virtue (power) flows towards them.

[25] In removing corruption by artificial laws and statutes and punishments.
[26] Never do too much.

BIG AND SMALL COUNTRIES

A big country (must be like) the delta low-regions,
  Being the concourse of the world,
  (And) the Female of the world.
The Female overcomes the Male by quietude,
And achieves the lowly position by quietude.

Therefore if a big country places itself below a small country,
  It absorbs the small country;
(And) if a small country places itself below a big country,
  It absorbs the big country.
Therefore some place themselves low to absorb (others),
Some are (naturally) low and absorb (others).
  What a big country wants is but to shelter others,
  And what a small country wants is but to be able to come in and be
    sheltered.
Thus (considering) that both may have what they want,
  A big country ought to place itself low.

THE GOOD MAN'S TREASURE

Tao is the mysterious secret of the universe,
The good man's treasure,
And the bad man's refuge.
  Beautiful sayings can be sold at the market,
  Noble conduct can be presented as a gift.
Though there be bad people,
Why reject them?

Therefore on the crowning of an emperor,
  On the appointment of the Three Ministers,
  Rather than send tributes of jade and teams of four horses,
  Send in the tribute of this Tao.
Wherein did the Ancients prize this Tao?
Did they not say, "to search for the guilty ones and pardon them?"
  Therefore is (Tao) the treasure of the world.

DIFFICULT AND EASY

Accomplish do-nothing.
Attend to no-affairs.
Taste the flavorless.
Whether it is big or small, many or few,
Requite hatred with Virtue.
    Deal with the difficult while
        yet it is easy;
    Deal with the big while yet
        it is small.
The difficult (problems) of the
      world
    Must be dealt with while
        they are yet easy;
The great (problems) of the
      world
    Must be dealt with while
        they are yet small.
Therefore the Sage by never
    dealing with great (prob-
    lems)
    Accomplish greatness.

He who lightly makes a promise
    Will find it often hard to keep his faith.
He who makes light of many things
    Will encounter many difficulties.
Hence even the Sage regards things as difficult,
    And for that reason never meets with difficulties.

BEGINNING AND END

That which lies still is easy to hold;
    That which is not yet manifest is easy to forestall;
That which is brittle (like ice) is easy to melt;
    That which is minute is easy to scatter.
Deal with a thing before it is there;

Check disorder before it is rife.
> A tree with a full span's girth begins from a tiny sprout;
> A nine-storied terrace begins with a clod of earth.
> A journey of a thousand *li* begins at one's feet.

He who acts, spoils;
He who grasps, lets slip.
Because the Sage does not act, he does not spoil,
Because he does not grasp, he does not let slip.
> The affairs of men are often spoiled within an ace of completion,
> By being careful at the end as at the beginning
> Failure is averted.

Therefore the Sage desires to have no desire,
> And values not objects difficult to obtain.
Learns that which is unlearned,
> And restores what the multitude have lost.
That he may assist in the course of Nature
> And not presume to interfere.

THE GRAND HARMONY

The Ancients who knew how to follow the Tao
> Aimed not to enlighten the people,
> But to keep them ignorant.
The reason it is difficult for the people to live in peace
> Is because of too much knowledge.
Those who seek to rule a country by knowledge
> Are the nation's curse.
Those who seek not to rule a country by knowledge
> Are the nation's blessing.
Those who know these two (principles)
> Also know the Ancient Standard,
And to know always the Ancient Standard
> Is called the Mystic Virtue.
When the Mystic Virtue becomes clear, far-reaching,
> And things revert back (to their source),
> Then and then only emerges the Grand Harmony.

THE LORDS OF THE RAVINES

How did the great rivers and seas become the Lords of the Ravines?
By being good at keeping low.
That was how they became the Lords of the Ravines.
Therefore in order to be the chief among the people,
   One must speak like their inferiors.
In order to be foremost among the people,
   One must walk behind them.
Thus it is that the Sage stays above,
   And the people do not feel his weight;
Walks in front,
   And the people do not wish him harm.
Then the people of the world are glad to uphold him forever.
Because he does not contend,
No one in the world can contend against him.

THE THREE TREASURES

All the world says: my teaching (Tao) greatly resembles folly.
   Because it is great; therefore it resembles folly.
If it did not resemble folly,
   It would have long ago become petty indeed!

I have Three Treasures;
Guard them and keep them safe:
   The first is Love.
   The second is, Never too much.
   The third is, Never be the first in the world.
Through Love, one has no fear;
Through not doing too much, one has amplitude (of reserve power);
Through not presuming to be the first in the world,
   One can develop one's talent and let it mature.

If one forsakes love and fearlessness,
    forsakes restraint and reserve power,
    forsakes following behind and rushes in front,
He is dead!

For love is victorious in attack,
  And invulnerable in defense.
Heaven arms with love
  Those it would not see destroyed.

THE VIRTUE OF NOT-CONTENDING

The brave soldier is not violent;
The good fighter does not lose his temper;
The great conqueror does not fight (on small issues);
The good user of men places himself below others.
—This is the Virtue of not contending,
  Is called the capacity to use men,
  Is reaching to the height of being
    Mated to Heaven, to what was of old.

CAMOUFLAGE

There is the maxim of military strategists;
  I dare not be the first to invade, but rather be the invaded.
  Dare not press forward an inch, but rather retreat a foot.
That is, to march without formations,
  To roll not up the sleeves,
  To charge not in frontal attacks,
  To arm without weapons.[27]
There is no greater catastrophe than to underestimate the enemy.
To underestimate the enemy might entail the loss of my treasures.
  Therefore when two equally matched armies meet,
It is the man of sorrow [28] who wins.

THEY KNOW ME NOT

My teachings are very easy to understand and very easy to practise,
But no one can understand them and no one can practise them.
  In my words there is a principle.
  In the affairs of men there is a system.

[27] Or to feel like being in this condition, i.e., the subjective condition of humility. This is entirely consistent with Lao-Tze's philosophy of camouflage, the earliest in the world. Cf. "great eloquence is like stuttering," etc.
[28] Who hates killing. The corrected text of Yü Yüeh would make this read, "The man who yields wins."

Because they know not these,
They also know me not.
    Since there are few that know me,
Therefore I am distinguished.
Therefore the Sage wears a coarse cloth on top
    And carries jade within his bosom.

SICK-MINDEDNESS

Who knows that he does not know is the highest;
Who (pretends to) know what he does not know is sick-minded.
And who recognizes sick-mindedness as sick-mindedness is not sick-
    minded.
    The Sage is not sick-minded.
    Because he recognizes sick-mindedness as sick-mindedness,
    Therefore he is not sick-minded.

ON PUNISHMENT

When people have no fear of force,[29]
    Then (as is the common practice) great force descends upon them.

Despise not their dwellings,
Dislike not their progeny.
    Because you do not dislike them,
    You will not be disliked yourself.
Therefore the Sage knows himself, but does not show himself,
    Loves himself, but does not exalt himself.
Therefore he rejects the one (force) and accepts the other (gentility).

Who is brave in daring (you) kill,
Who is brave in not daring (you) let live.
In these two,
    There is some advantage and some disadvantage.
    (Even if) Heaven dislikes certain people,
    Who would know (who are to be killed and) why?

[29] *Wei*, military force or authority; sometimes also used in connection with "God's anger." Another interpretation, "when the people have no fear of God, then God's anger descends upon them." But this fits in not so well with the context. See next two chapters on the futility of punishment, especially the first two lines, Ch. 74.

Therefore even the Sage regards it as a difficult question.
  Heaven's Way (Tao) is good at conquest without strife,
  Rewarding (vice and virtue) without words,
  Making its appearance without call,
  Achieving results without obvious design.
The Heaven's Net is broad and wide,[30]
With big meshes, yet letting nothing slip through.

The people are not afraid of death;
Why threaten them with death?
  Supposing that the people *are* afraid of death,
  And we can seize and kill the unruly,
  Who would dare to do so?
Often it happens that the executioner is killed.
And to take the place of the executioner
  Is like handling the hatchet for the master carpenter.
He who handles the hatchet for the master carpenter
  Seldom escapes injury to his hands.

When people are hungry,
It is because their rulers eat too much tax-grain.
  Therefore the unruliness of hungry people
  Is due to the interference of their rulers.
  That is why they are unruly.
The people are not afraid of death,
Because they are anxious to make a living.
That is why they are not afraid of death.
  It is those who interfere not with their living
  That are wise in exalting life.

HARD AND SOFT

When man is born, he is tender and weak;
  At death, he is hard and stiff.
When the things and plants are alive, they are soft and supple;
When they are dead, they are brittle and dry.
  Therefore hardness and stiffness are the companions of death,
  And softness and gentleness are the companions of life.

[30] This has now become a Chinese proverb for "virtue always rewarded, vice always punished."

Therefore when an army is headstrong, it will lose in battle.
When a tree is hard, it will be cut down.
 The big and strong belong underneath.
 The gentle and weak belong at the top.

BENDING THE BOW

The Tao (way) of Heaven,
Is it not like the bending of a bow?
 The top comes down and the bottom-end goes up,
 The extra (length) is shortened, the insufficient (width) is ex-
  panded.
It is the Way of Heaven to take away from those that have too much
And give to those that have not
  enough.
 Not so with man's way:
 He takes away from those
  that have not
 And gives it as tribute to
  those that have too much.
Who can have enough and to
  spare to give to the entire
  world?
Only the man of Tao.
Therefore the Sage acts, but
  does not possess,
 Accomplishes but lays claim
  to no credit,
 Because he has no wish to
  seem superior.

NOTHING WEAKER THAN WATER

 There is nothing weaker than water
 But none is superior to it in overcoming the hard,
 For which there is no substitute.
  That weakness overcomes strength
  And gentleness overcomes rigidity,
  No one does not know;
  No one can put into practice.

Therefore the Sage says:
"Who receives unto himself the calumny of the world
Is the preserver of the state.
Who bears himself the sins of the world
Is the king of the world."
Straight words seem crooked.

PEACE SETTLEMENTS

Patching up a great hatred is sure to leave some hatred behind.
How can this be regarded as satisfactory?
Therefore the Sage holds the left tally,[31]
And does not put the guilt on the other party.
The virtuous man is for patching up;
The vicious is for fixing guilt.
But "the way of Heaven is impartial
It sides only with the good man." [32]

THE SMALL UTOPIA

(Let there be) a small country with a small population,
Where the supply of goods are tenfold or hundredfold, more than they
can use.
Let the people value their lives and not migrate far.
Though there be boats and carriages,
None be there to ride them.
Though there be armor and weapons,
No occasion to display them.

Let the people again tie ropes for reckoning,
Let them enjoy their food,
Beautify their clothing,
Be satisfied with their homes,
Delight in their customs.
The neighboring settlements overlook one another
So that they can hear the barking of dogs and crowing of cocks of
their neighbors,
And the people till the end of their days shall never have been outside
their country.

[31] Sign of inferiority in an agreement.
[32] An ancient quotation appearing in many ancient texts.

THE WAY OF HEAVEN

True words are not fine-sounding;
  Fine-sounding words are not true.
A good man does not argue;
  He who argues is not a good man.
The wise one does not know many things;
  He who knows many things is not wise.
The Sage does not accumulate (for himself):
  He lives for other people,
  And grows richer himself;
  He gives to other people,
  And has greater abundance.
The Tao of Heaven
  Blesses, but does not harm.
The Way of the Sage
  Accomplishes, but does not contend.

THE WRITINGS OF CHUANG-TZE

What Mang-tze (Mencius) did for Confucianism, that Chuang-tze did for Taoism. It was primarily through the latter's writings that the strange doctrine of old Lao-tze became popular, and China acquired her second great religion. Little is known concerning Chuang-tze's career, for in keeping with his principles, he appears to have shunned office and avoided acclaim. He lived some two centuries after Lao-tze, and is reported to have died in 272 B.C.

The following selections are taken from the thirty-three small "books" bearing Chuang-tze's name, and they make rich reading. They are at once profound and brilliant, abstruse and simple. They crackle with paradox, bristle with irony, indulge in the sheerest fantasy, yet somehow inspire respect, even awe. Their central teaching may impress some readers as nihilistic nonsense, and others as mystic supersense; in either case, it will at least impress. For Chuang-tze was obviously one of those rare religious geniuses who could not merely reach high for thoughts but come to earth with words. Whether a great sage or a superb fool, he was certainly a supreme stylist.[33]

ALL THINGS ARE ONE

Great knowledge embraces the whole: small knowledge, a part only. Great speech is universal: small speech is particular.

For whether when the mind is locked in sleep or whether when in waking hours the body is released, we are subject to daily mental perturbations,—indecision, want of penetration, concealment, fretting fear, and trembling terror. Now like a javelin the mind flies forth, the arbiter of right and wrong. Now like a solemn covenanter it remains firm, the guardian of rights secured. Then, as under autumn and winter's blight, comes gradual decay, a passing away, like the flow of water, never to return. Finally, the block when all is choked up like an old drain,—the failing mind which shall not see light again.

Joy and anger, sorrow and happiness, caution and remorse, come

[33] Translation (but not headings) by Herbert A. Giles, in his *Chuang Tzu, Mystic, Moralist, and Social Reformer* (Kelly & Walsh, 1889).

upon us by turns, with ever-changing mood. They come like music from hollowness, like mushrooms from damp. Daily and nightly they alternate within us, but we cannot tell whence they spring. Can we then hope in a moment to lay our finger upon their very cause?

But for these emotions I should not be. But for me, they would have no scope. So far we can go; but we do not know what it is that brings them into play. 'Twould seem to be a soul; but the clue to its existence is wanting. That such a power operates is credible enough, though we cannot see its form. It has functions without form.

Take the human body with all its manifold divisions. Which part of it does a man love best? Does he not cherish all equally, or has he a preference? Do not all equally serve him? And do these servitors then govern themselves, or are they subdivided into rulers and subjects? Surely there is some soul which sways them all.

But whether or not we ascertain what are the functions of this soul, it matters but little to the soul itself. For coming into existence with this mortal coil of mine, with the exhaustion of this mortal coil its mandate will also be exhausted. To be harassed by the wear and tear of life, and to pass rapidly through it without possibility of arresting one's course,—is not this pitiful indeed? To labour without ceasing, and then, without living to enjoy the fruit, worn out, to depart, suddenly, one knows not whither,—is not that a just cause for grief?

What advantage is there in what men call not dying? The body decomposes, and the mind goes with it. This is our real cause for sorrow. Can the world be so dull as not to see this? Or is it I alone who am dull and others not so?

Speech is not mere breath. It is differentiated by meaning. Take away that, and you cannot say whether it is speech or not. Can you even distinguish it from the chirping of young birds?

But how can TAO be so obscured that we speak of it as true and false? And how can speech be so obscured that it admits the idea of contraries? How can TAO go away and yet not remain? How can speech exist and yet be impossible?

TAO is obscured by our want of grasp. Speech is obscured by the gloss of this world.

There is nothing which is not objective: there is nothing which is not subjective. But it is impossible to start from the objective. Only from subjective knowledge is it possible to proceed to objective knowledge.

When subjective and objective are both without their correlates, that is the very axis of TAO. And when that axis passes through the centre at which all infinities converge, positive and negative alike blend into an infinite ONE.

Therefore it is that, viewed from the standpoint of TAO, a beam and a pillar are identical. So are ugliness and beauty, greatness, wickedness, perverseness, and strangeness. Separation is the same as construction: construction is the same as destruction. Nothing is subject either to construction or to destruction, for these conditions are brought together into ONE.

Only the truly intelligent understand this principle of the identity of all things. They do not view things as apprehended by themselves, subjectively; but transfer themselves into the position of the things viewed. And viewing them thus they are able to comprehend them, nay, to master them;—and he who can master them is near. So it is that to place oneself in subjective relation with externals, without consciousness of their objectivity,—this is TAO. But to wear out one's intellect is an obstinate adherence to the individuality of things, not recognizing the fact that all things are ONE. . .

Yeh Ch'ueh asked Wang I, saying, "Do you know for certain that all things are subjectively the same?"

"How can I know?" answered Wang I. "Do you know what you do not know?"

"How can I know?" replied Yeh Ch'ueh. "But can then nothing be known?"

"How can I know?" said Wang I. "Nevertheless, I will try to tell you. How can it be known that what I call knowing is not really not knowing, and that what I call not knowing is not really knowing? Now I would ask you this. If a man sleeps in a damp place, he gets lumbago and dies. But how about an eel? And living up in a tree is precarious and trying to the nerves;—but how about monkeys? Of the man, the eel, and the monkey, whose habitat is the right one, absolutely? Human beings feed on flesh, deer on grass, centipedes on snakes, owls and crows on mice. Of these four, whose is the right taste, absolutely? Monkey mates with monkey, the buck with the doe; eels consort with fishes, while men admire Mao Ch'iang and Li Chi, at the sight of whom fishes plunge deep down in the water, birds soar high in the air, and deer hurry away. Yet who shall say which is the correct standard of beauty? In my opinion, the standard of human virtue, and of positive and negative, is so obscured that it is impossible to actually know it as such."

"If you then," asked Yeh Ch'ueh, "do not know what is bad for you, is the perfect man equally without this knowledge?"

"The perfect man," answered Wang I, "is a spiritual being. Were the ocean itself scorched up, he would not feel hot. Were the Milky Way frozen hard, he would not feel cold. Were the mountains to be riven with thunder, and the great deep to be thrown up by storm, he would not tremble. In such case, he would mount upon the clouds of heaven, and driving the sun and the moon before him, would pass beyond the limits of this external world, where death and life have no more victory over man;—how much less what is bad for him?"

ALL LIFE IS A DREAM

Those who dream of a banquet, wake to lamentation and sorrow. Those who dream of lamentation and sorrow wake to join the hunt. While they dream, they do not know that they dream. Some will even interpret the very dream they are dreaming; and only when they awake do they know it was a dream. By and by comes the Great Awakening, and then we find out that this life is really a great dream. Fools think they are awake now, and flatter themselves they know if they are really princes or peasants. Confucius and you are both dreams; and I who say you are dreams,—I am but a dream myself. This is a paradox. Tomorrow a sage may arise to explain it; but that to-morrow will not be until ten thousand generations have gone by. . . .

Once upon a time, I, Chuang Tze, dreamt I was a butterfly, fluttering hither and thither, to all intents and purposes a butterfly. I was conscious only of following my fancies as a butterfly, and was unconscious of my individuality as a man. Suddenly, I awaked, and there I lay, myself again. Now I do not know whether I was then a man dreaming I was a butterfly, or whether I am now a butterfly dreaming I am a man.

THE WORTH OF THE WORTHLESS

Hui Tze said to Chuang Tze, "Sir, I have a large tree, of a worthless kind. Its trunk is so irregular and knotty that it cannot be measured out for planks; while its branches are so twisted as to admit no geometrical subdivision whatever. It stands by the roadside, but no carpenter will look at it. And your words, sir, are like that tree;—big and useless, not wanted by anybody."

"Sir," rejoined Chuang Tze, "have you never seen a wild cat, crouching down in wait for its prey? Right and left it springs from bough to bough, high and low alike,—until perchance it gets caught in a trap or dies in a snare. On the other hand, there is the yak with its great huge body. It is big enough in all conscience, but it cannot catch mice.

"Now if you have a big tree and are at a loss what to do with it, why not plant it in the domain of non-existence, whither you might betake yourself to inaction by its side, to blissful repose beneath its shade? There it would be safe from the axe and from all other injury; for being of no use to others, itself would be free from harm."

Tze Ch'i of Nan-poh was travelling on the Shang mountain when he saw a large tree which astonished him very much. A thousand chariot teams could have found shelter under its shade.

"What tree is this?" cried Tze Ch'i. "Surely it must have unusually fine timber." Then looking up, he saw that its branches were too crooked for rafters; while as to the trunk he saw that its irregular grain made it valueless for coffins. He tasted a leaf, but it took the skin off his lips; and its odour was so strong that it would make a man as it were drunk for three days together.

"Ah!" said Tze Ch'i. "This tree is good for nothing, and that is how it has attained this size. A wise man might well follow its example."

THE MIDDLE COURSE

My life has a limit, but my knowledge is without limit. To drive the limited in search of the limitless, is fatal; and the knowledge of those who do this is fatally lost.

In striving for others, avoid fame. In striving for self, avoid disgrace. Pursue a middle course. Thus you will keep a sound body, and a sound mind, fulfil your duties, and work out your allotted span.

THE WISE COOK

Prince Hui's cook was cutting up a bullock. Every blow of his hand, every heave of his shoulders, every tread of his foot, every thrust of his knee, every *whshh* of rent flesh, every *chhk* of the chopper, was in perfect harmony,—rhythmical like the dance of the Mulberry Grove, simultaneous like the chords of the Ching Shou.

"Well done!" cried the Prince. "Yours is skill indeed."

"Sire," replied the cook; "I have always devoted myself to TAO. It is better than skill. When I first began to cut up bullocks, I saw before me simply whole bullocks. After three years' practice, I saw no more whole animals. And now I work with my mind and not with my eye. When my senses bid me stop, but my mind urges me on, I fall back upon eternal principles. I follow such openings or cavities as there may be, according to the natural constitution of the animal. I do not attempt to cut through joints: still less through large bones.

"A good cook changes his chopper once a year,—because he cuts. An ordinary cook, once a month,—because he hacks. But I have had this chopper nineteen years, and although I have cut up many thousand bullocks, its edge is as if fresh from the whetstone. For at the joints there are always interstices, and the edge of a chopper being without thickness, it remains only to insert that which is without thickness into such an interstice. By these means the interstices will be enlarged, and the blade will find plenty of room. It is thus that I have kept my chopper for nineteen years as though fresh from the whetstone.

"Nevertheless, when I come upon a hard part where the blade meets with a difficulty, I am all caution. I fix my eye on it. I stay my hand, and gently apply my blade, until with a *hwah* the part yields like earth crumbling to the ground. Then I take out my chopper, and stand up, and look around, and pause, until with an air of triumph I wipe my chopper and put it carefully away."

"Bravo!" cried the Prince. "From the words of this cook I have learnt how to take care of my life."

WHY FEAR DEATH?

Four men were conversing together, when the following resolution was suggested: "Whosoever can make inaction the head, life the back-bone, and death the tail, of his existence,—that man shall be admitted to friendship with us." The four looked at each other and smiled; and tacitly accepting the conditions, became friends forthwith.

By and by, one of them, named Tze Yu, fell ill, and another, Tze Ssu, went to see him. "Verily God is great!" said the sick man. "See how he has doubled me up. My back is so hunched that my viscera are at the top of my body. My cheeks are level with my navel. My shoulders are higher than my neck. My hair grows up towards the sky. The whole economy of my organism is deranged. Nevertheless, my mental equilibrium is not disturbed." So saying, he dragged himself painfully to a well, where he could see himself, and continued, "Alas, that God should have doubled me up like this!"

"Are you afraid?" asked Tze Ssu.

"I am not," replied Tze Yu. "What have I to fear? Ere long I shall be decomposed. My left shoulder will become a cock, and I shall herald the approach of morn. My right shoulder will become a cross-bow, and I shall be able to get broiled duck. My buttocks will become wheels; and with my soul for a horse, I shall be able to ride in my own chariot. I obtained life because it was my time: I am now parting with it in accordance with the same law. Content with the natural sequence of these states, joy and sorrow touch me not. I am simply, as the ancients expressed it, hanging in the air, unable to cut myself down, bound with the trammels of material existence. But man has ever given way before God: why, then, should I be afraid?"

By and by, another of the four, named Tze Lai, fell ill, and lay gasping for breath, while his family stood weeping around. The fourth friend, Tze Li, went to see him. "Chut!" cried he to the wife and children; "begone! you balk his decomposition." Then, leaning against the door, he said, "Verily, God is great! I wonder what he will make of you now. I wonder whither you will be sent. Do you think he will make you into rat's liver or into the shoulders of a snake?"

"A son," answered Tze Lai, "must go whithersoever his parents bid him. Nature is no other than a man's parents. If she bid me die quickly, and I demur, then I am an unfilial son. She can do me no wrong. TAO gives me this form, this toil in manhood, this repose in old age, this rest in death. And surely that which is such a kind arbiter of my life is the best arbiter of my death.

"Suppose that the boiling metal in a smelting-pot were to bubble up and say, 'Make of me an Excalibur'; I think the caster would reject that metal as uncanny. And if a sinner like myself were to say to God, 'Make of me a man, make of me a man'; I think he too would reject me as uncanny. The universe is the smelting-pot, and God is the caster. I shall go whithersoever I am sent, to wake unconscious of the past, as a man wakes from a dreamless sleep."

THE SIN OF CIVILIZATION

Horses have hoofs to carry them over frost and snow; hair, to protect them from wind and cold. They eat grass and drink water, and fling up their heels over the champaign. Such is the real nature of horses. Palatial dwellings are of no use to them.

One day Poh Loh appeared, saying, "I understand the management of horses."

So he branded them, and clipped them, and pared their hoofs, and put halters on them, tying them up by the head and shackling them by the feet, and disposing them in stables, with the result that two or three in every ten died. Then he kept them hungry and thirsty, trotting them and galloping them, and grooming, and trimming, with the misery of the tasselled bridle before and the fear of the knotted whip behind, until more than half of them were dead.

The potter says, "I can do what I will with clay. If I want it round, I use compasses; if rectangular, a square."

The carpenter says, "I can do what I will with wood. If I want it curved, I use an arc; if straight, a line."

But on what grounds can we think that the natures of clay and wood desire this application of compasses and square, of arc and line? Nevertheless, every age extols Poh Loh for his skill in managing horses, and potters and carpenters for their skill with clay and wood. Those who *govern* the empire make the same mistake.

Now I regard government of the empire from quite a different point of view.

The people have certain natural instincts;—to weave and clothe themselvs, to till and feed themselves. These are common to all humanity, and all are agreed thereon. Such instincts are called "Heaven-sent."

And so in the days when natural instincts prevailed, men moved quietly and gazed steadily. At that time, there were no roads over mountains, nor boats, nor bridges over water. All things were produced, each for its own proper sphere. Birds and beasts multiplied; trees and shrubs grew up. The former might be led by the hand; you could climb up and peep into the raven's nest. For then man dwelt with birds and beasts, and all creation was one. There were no distinctions of good and bad men. Being all equally without knowledge, their virtue could not go astray. Being all equally without evil desires, they were in a state of natural integrity, the perfection of human existence.

But when sages appeared, tripping people over charity and fettering with duty to one's neighbour, doubt found its way into the world. And then, with their gushing over music and fussing over ceremony, the empire became divided against itself.

Were the natural integrity of things left unharmed, who could make sacrificial vessels? Were white jade left unbroken, who could make the regalia of courts? Were TAO not abandoned, who could introduce charity and duty to one's neighbour? Were man's natural

instincts his guide, what need would there be for music and ceremonies? Were the five colours not confused, who would practise deco-
ration? Were the five notes not confused, who would adopt the six
pitch-pipes?

Destruction of the natural integrity of things, in order to produce
articles of various kinds,—this is the fault of the artisan. Annhilation
of TAO in order to practise charity and duty to one's neighbour,—
this is the error of the sage.

Horses live on dry land, eat grass and drink water. When pleased,
they rub their necks together. When angry, they turn round and kick
up their heels at each other. Thus far only do their natural dispositions
carry them. But bridled and bitted, with a plate of metal on their
foreheads, they learn to cast vicious looks, to turn the head to bite,
to resist, to get the bit out of the mouth or the bridle into it. And thus
their natures become depraved,—the fault of Poh Loh.

In the days of Ho Hsu the people did nothing in particular when
at rest, and went nowhere in particular when they moved. Having
food, they rejoiced; having full bellies, they strolled about. Such were
the capacities of the people. But when the sages came to worry them
with ceremonies and music in order to rectify the form of government,
and dangled charity and duty to one's neighbour before them in order
to satisfy their hearts,—then the people began to develop a taste for
knowledge and to struggle one with the other in their desire for gain.
This was the error of the sages.

LET PEOPLE ALONE

There has been such a thing as letting mankind alone; there has
never been such a thing as governing mankind.

Letting alone springs from fear lest men's natural dispositions be
perverted and their virtue laid aside. But if their natural dispositions
be not perverted, nor their virtue laid aside, what room is there left
for government?

Because men are made to rejoice and to sorrow and to displace
their centre of gravity, they lose their steadiness, and are unsuccessful
in thought and action. And thus it is that the idea of surpassing others
first came into the world, followed by the appearance of such men as
Robber Che, Tseng, and Shih, the result being that the whole world

could not furnish enough rewards for the good nor distribute punishments enough for the evil among mankind. And as this great world is not equal to the demand for rewards and punishments; and as, ever since the time of the Three Dynasties downwards, men have done nothing but struggle over rewards and punishments,—what possible leisure can they have had for adapting themselves to the natural conditions of their existence?

Besides, over-refinement of vision leads to debauchery in colour; over-refinement of hearing leads to debauchery in sound; over-refinement of charity leads to confusion in virtue; over-refinement of duty towards one's neighbour leads to perversion of principle; over-refinement of ceremonial leads to divergence from the true object; over-refinement of music leads to lewdness of thought; over-refinement of wisdom leads to an extension of mechanical art; and over-refinement of shrewdness leads to an extension of vice.

If people adapt themselves to the natural conditions of existence, the above eight may be or may not be; it matters not. But if people do not adapt themselves to the natural conditions of existence, then these eight become hindrances and spoilers, and throw the world into confusion.

In spite of this, the world reverences and cherishes them, thereby greatly increasing the sum of human error. And not as a passing fashion, but with admonitions in words, with humility in prostrations, and with the stimulus of music and song. What then is left for me?

Therefore, for the perfect man who is unavoidably summoned to power over his fellows, there is naught like inaction. By means of inaction he will be able to adapt himself to the natural conditions of existence. And so it is that he who respects the state as his own body is fit to support it, and he who loves the state as his own body is fit to govern it. And if I can refrain from injuring my internal economy, and from taxing my powers of sight and hearing, sitting like a corpse while my dragon-power is manifested around, in profound silence while my thunder-voice resounds, the powers of heaven responding to every phase of my will, as under the yielding influence of inaction all things are brought to maturity and thrive,—what leisure then have I to set about governing the world?

Ts'ui Chu asked Lao Tze, saying, "If the empire is not to be governed, how are men's hearts to be kept in order?"

"Be careful," replied Lao Tze, "not to interfere with the natural goodness of the heart of man. Man's heart may be forced down or stirred up. In each case the issue is fatal.

"By gentleness, the hardest heart may be softened. But try to cut and polish it,—'twill glow like fire or freeze like ice. In the twinkling of an eye it will pass beyond the limits of the Four Seas. In repose, profoundly still; in motion, far away in the sky. No bolt can bar, no bond can bind,—such is the human heart."

GET IN TUNE WITH GOD

When water is still, it is like a mirror, reflecting the beard and the eyebrows. It gives the accuracy of the water-level, and the philosopher makes it his model. And if water thus derives lucidity from stillness, how much more the faculties of the mind? The mind of the sage being in repose becomes the mirror of the universe, the speculum of all creation.

Repose, tranquillity, stillness, inaction,—these were the levels of the universe, the ultimate perfection of TAO. Therefore wise rulers and sages rest therein. Resting therein they reach the unconditioned, from which springs the conditioned; and with the conditioned comes order. Again, from the unconditioned comes repose, and from repose comes movement, and from movement comes attainment. Further, from repose comes inaction, and from inaction comes potentiality of action. And inaction is happiness; and where there is happiness no cares can abide, and life is long. . . .

To fully apprehend the scheme of the universe, this is called the great secret of being in accord with GOD, whereby the empire is so administered that the result is in accord with man. To be in accord with man is human happiness; to be in accord with God is the happiness of God.

Appeal to arms is the lowest form of virtue. Rewards and punishments are the lowest form of education. Ceremonies and laws are the lowest form of government. Music and fine clothes are the lowest form of happiness. Weeping and mourning are the lowest form of grief. These five should follow the movements of the mind.

The ancients indeed cultivated the study of accidentals, but they did not allow it to precede that of essentials. The prince precedes, the minister follows. The father precedes, the son follows. The elder brother precedes, the younger follows. Seniors precede, juniors follow. Men precede, women follow. Husbands precede, wives follow. Distinctions of rank and precedence are part of the scheme of the universe, and the sage adopts them accordingly. In point of spirituality, heaven is honourable, earth is lowly. Spring and summer precede autumn and winter: such is the order of the seasons. In the constant production of all things, there are phases of existence. There are the extremes of maturity and decay, the perpetual tide of change. And if heaven and earth, divinest of all, admit of rank and precedence, how much more man?

In the ancestral temple, parents rank before all; at court, the most honourable; in the village the elders; in matters to be accomplished, the most trustworthy. Such is the order which appertains to TAO. He who in considering TAO disregards this order, thereby disregards TAO; and he who in considering TAO disregards TAO,—whence will he secure TAO?

Therefore, those of old who apprehended TAO, first apprehended God. TAO came next, and then charity and duty to one's neighbour, and then the functions of public life, and then forms and names, and then employment according to capacity, and then distinctions of good and bad, and then discrimination between right and wrong, and then rewards and punishments. Thus wise men and fools met with their dues; the exalted and the humble occupied their proper places. And the virtuous and the worthless being each guided by their own natural instincts, it was necessary to distinguish capabilities, and to adopt a corresponding nomenclature, in order to serve the ruler, nourish the ruled, administer things generally, and elevate self. Where knowledge and plans are of no avail, one must fall back upon the natural. This is perfect peace, the acme of good government. . . .

Lao Tze said, "TAO is not too small for the greatest, nor too great for the smallest. Thus all things are embosomed therein; wide indeed its boundless capacity, unfathomable its depth.

"Form, and virtue, and charity, and duty to one's neighbour, these are the accidentals of the spiritual. Except he be a perfect man, who shall determine their place? The world of the perfect man, is not that vast? And yet it is not able to involve him in trouble. All struggle for power, but he does not join. Though discovering nothing false, he is not tempted astray. In spite of the utmost genuineness, he still confines himself to essentials.

"He thus places himself outside the universe, beyond all creation, where his soul is free from care. Apprehending TAO, he is in accord with virtue. He leaves charity and duty to one's neighbour alone. He treats ceremonies and music as adventitious. And so the mind of the perfect man is at peace.

"Books are what the world values as representing TAO. But books are only words, and the valuable part of words is the thought therein contained. That thought has a certain bias which cannot be conveyed in words, yet the world values words as being the essence of books. But though the world values them, they are not of value; as that sense in which the world values them is not the sense in which they are valuable.

"That which can be seen with the eye is form and colour; that which can be heard with the ear is sound and noise. But alas! the people of this generation think that form, and colour, and sound, and noise, are means by which they can come to understand the essence of TAO. This is not so. And as those who know do not speak, while those who speak do not know, whence should the world derive its knowledge?"

CONFUCIUS AND LAO TZE

Confucius had lived to the age of fifty-one without hearing TAO, when he went south to P'ei, to see Lao Tze.

Lao Tze said, "So you have come, sir, have you? I hear you are considered a wise man up north. Have you got TAO?"

"Not yet," answered Confucius.

"In what direction," asked Lao Tze, "have you sought for it?"

"I sought it for five years," replied Confucius, "in the science of numbers, but did not succeed."

"And then? . . ." continued Lao Tze.

"Then," said Confucius, "I spent twelve years seeking for it in the doctrine of the Yin and Yang, also without success."

"Just so," rejoined Lao Tze. "Were TAO something which could be presented, there is no man but would present it to his sovereign, or to his parents. Could it be imparted or given, there is no man but would impart it to his brother or give it to his child. But this is impossible, for the following reason. Unless there is a suitable endowment within, TAO will not abide. Unless there is outward correctness, TAO will not operate. The external being unfitted for the impression of the internal, the true sage does not seek to imprint. The internal being unfitted for the reception of the external, the true sage does not seek to receive.

"Reputation is public property; you may not appropriate it in excess. Charity and duty to one's neighbour are as caravanserais established by wise rulers of old; you may stop there one night, but not for long, or you will incur reproach.

"The perfect men of old took their road through charity, stopping a night with duty to their neighbour, on their way to ramble in transcendental space. Feeding on the produce of non-cultivation, and establishing themselves in the domain of no obligations, they enjoyed their transcendental inaction. Their food was ready to hand; and being under no obligations to others, they did not put any one under obligation to themselves. The ancients called this the outward visible sign of an inward and spiritual grace.

"Those who make wealth their all in all, cannot bear loss of money. Those who make distinction their all in all, cannot bear loss of fame. Those who affect power will not place authority in the hands of others. Anxious while holding, distressed if losing, yet never taking warning from the past and seeing the folly of their pursuit,—such men are the accursed of God.

"Resentment, gratitude, taking, giving, censure of self, instruction of others, power of life and death,—these eight are the instruments of right; but only he who can adapt himself to the vicissitudes of fortune, without being carried away, is fit to use them. Such a one is an upright man among the upright. And he whose heart is not so constituted,—the door of divine intelligence is not yet opened for him."

Confucius visited Lao Tze, and spoke of charity and duty to one's neighbour.

Lao Tze said, "The chaff from winnowing will blind a man's eyes so that he cannot tell the points of the compass. Mosquitoes will keep a man awake all night with their biting. And just in the same way this talk of charity and duty to one's neighbour drives me nearly crazy. Sir! strive to keep the world to its own original simplicity. And as the wind bloweth where it listeth, so let virtue establish itself. Wherefore such undue energy, as though searching for a fugitive with a big drum?

"The snow-goose is white without a daily bath. The raven is black without daily colouring itself. The original simplicity of black and of white is beyond the reach of argument. The vista of fame and reputation is not worthy of enlargement. When the pond dries up and the fishes are left upon dry ground, to moisten them with the breath or to damp them with a little spittle is not to be compared with leaving them in the first instance in their native rivers and lakes."

On returning from this visit to Lao Tze, Confucius did not speak for three days. A disciple asked him, saying, "Master, when you saw Lao Tze, in what direction did you admonish him?"

"I saw a dragon," replied Confucius, "—a dragon which by convergence showed a body, by radiation became colour, and riding upon the clouds of heaven, nourished the two principles of creation. My mouth was agape: I could not shut it. How then do you think I was going to admonish Lao Tze?"

THE NATURAL AND THE ARTIFICIAL

It was the time of autumn floods. Every stream poured into the river, which swelled in its turbid course. The banks receded so far from one another that it was impossible to tell a cow from a horse.

Then the Spirit of the River laughed for joy that all the beauty of the earth was gathered to himself. Down with the stream he journeyed east, until he reached the ocean. There, looking eastwards and seeing no limit to its waves, his countenance changed. And as he gazed over the expanse, he sighed and said to the Spirit of the Ocean, "A vulgar proverb says that he who has heard but part of the truth thinks no one equal to himself. And such a one am I.

"When formerly I heard people detracting from the learning of Confucius or underrating the heroism of Poh I, I did not believe. But now that I have looked upon your inexhaustibility—alas for me, had I not reached your abode, I should have been for ever a laughing-stock to those of comprehensive enlightenment!"

To which the Spirit of the Ocean replied, "You cannot speak of ocean to a well-frog,—the creature of a narrower sphere. You cannot speak of ice to a summer insect,—the creature of a season. You cannot speak of TAO to a pedagogue: his scope is too restricted. But now that you have emerged from your narrow sphere and have seen the great ocean, you know your own insignificance, and I can speak to you of great principles.

"Dimensions are limitless; time is endless. Conditions are not invariable; terms are not final. Thus, the wise man looks into space, and does not regard the small as too little, nor the great as too much; for he knows that there is no limit to dimension. He looks back into the past, and does not grieve over what is far off, nor rejoice over what is near; for he knows that time is without end. He investigates fullness and decay, and does not rejoice if he succeeds, nor lament if he fails; for he knows that conditions are not invariable. He who clearly apprehends the scheme of existence, does not rejoice over life, nor repine at death; for he knows that terms are not final.

"What man knows is not to be compared with what he does not know. The span of his existence is not to be compared with the span of his non-existence.

"I have heard say, the man of TAO has no reputation; perfect virtue acquires nothing; the truly great man ignores self;—this is the height of self-discipline."

"But how then," asked the Spirit of the River, "are the internal and external extremes of value and worthlessness, of greatness and smallness, to be determined?"

"From the point of view of TAO," replied the Spirit of the Ocean, "there are no such extremes of value or worthlessness. Men individually value themselves and hold others cheap. The world collectively withholds from the individual the right of appraising himself.

"If we say that a thing is great or small because it is relatively great or small, then there is nothing in all creation which is not great, nothing which is not small.

"The life of man passes by like a galloping horse, changing at every turn, at every hour. What should he do, or what should he not do, other than let his decomposition go on?"

"If this is the case," retorted the Spirit of the River, "pray what is the value of TAO?"

"Those who understand TAO," answered the Spirit of the Ocean, "must necessarily apprehend the eternal principles above mentioned and be clear as to their application. Consequently, they do not suffer any injury from without.

"The man of perfect virtue cannot be burnt by fire, nor drowned in water, nor hurt by frost or sun, nor torn by wild bird or beast. Not that he makes light of these; but that he discriminates between safety and danger.

"Happy under prosperous and adverse circumstances alike, cautious as to what he discards and what he accepts;—nothing can harm him.

"Therefore it has been said that the natural abides within, the artificial without. Virtue abides in the natural. Knowledge of the action of the natural and of the artificial has its root in the natural, its development in virtue. And thus, whether in motion or at rest, whether in expansion or in contraction, there is always a reversion to the essential and to the ultimate."

"What do you mean," inquired the Spirit of the River, "by the natural and the artificial?"

"Horses and oxen," answered the Spirit of the Ocean, "have four feet. That is the natural. Put a halter on a horse's head, a string through a bullock's nose,—that is the artificial.

"Therefore it has been said, do not let the artificial obliterate the natural; do not let will obliterate destiny; do not let virtue be sacrificed to fame. Diligently observe these precepts without fail, and thus you will revert to the divine."

EACH IN ITS OWN WAY

The walrus envies the centipede; the centipede envies the snake; the snake envies the wind; the wind envies the eye; the eye envies the mind.

The walrus said to the centipede, "I hop about on one leg, but not very successfully. How do you manage all these legs you have?"

"I don't manage them," replied the centipede. "Have you never seen saliva? When it is ejected, the big drops are the size of pearls, the small ones like mist. They fall promiscuously on the ground and cannot be counted. And so it is that my mechanism works naturally, without my being conscious of the fact."

The centipede said to the snake, "With all my legs I do not move as fast as you with none. How is that?"

"One's natural mechanism," replied the snake, "is not a thing to be changed. What need have I for legs?"

The snake said to the wind, "I can manage to wriggle along, but I have a form. Now you come blustering down from the north sea to bluster away to the south sea, and you seem to be without form. How is that?"

"'Tis true," replied the wind, "that I bluster as you say; but any one who can point at me or kick at me, excels me. On the other hand, I can break huge trees and destroy large buildings. That is my strong point. Out of all the small things in which I do not excel I make one great one in which I do excel. And to excel in great things is given only to the sages."

WHAT IS TRUE HAPPINESS?

Is perfect happiness to be found on earth, or not? Are there those who can enjoy life, or not? If so, what do they do, what do they affect, what do they avoid, what do they rest in, accept, reject, like, and dislike?

What the world esteems comprises wealth, rank, old age, and goodness of heart. What it enjoys comprises comfort, rich food, fine clothes, beauty, and music. What it does not esteem comprises poverty, want of position, early death, and evil behaviour. What it does not enjoy comprises lack of comfort for the body, lack of rich food for the palate, lack of fine clothes for the back, lack of beauty for the eye, and lack of music for the ear. If men do not get these, they are greatly miserable. Yet from the point of view of our physical frame, this is folly.

Wealthy people who toil and moil, putting together more money than they can possibly use,—from the point of view of our physical frame, is not this going beyond the mark?

Officials of rank who turn night into day in their endeavours to compass the best ends;—from the point of view of our physical frame, is not this a divergence?

Man is born to sorrow, and what misery is theirs whose old age with dulled faculties only means prolonged sorrow! From the point of view of our physical frame, this is going far astray.

Patriots are in the world's opinion admittedly good. Yet their goodness does not enable them to enjoy life; and so I know not whether theirs is veritable goodness or not. If the former, it does not enable them to enjoy life; if the latter, it at any rate enables them to cause others to enjoy theirs.

It has been said, "If your loyal counsels are not attended to, depart quietly without resistance." Thus, when Tze Hsu resisted, his physical frame perished; yet had he not resisted, he would not have made his name. Is there then really such a thing as this goodness, or not?

As to what the world does and the way in which people are happy now, I know not whether such happiness be real happiness or not. The happiness of ordinary persons seems to me to consist in slavishly following the majority, as if they could not help it. Yet they all say they are happy.

But I cannot say that this is happiness or that it is not happiness. Is there then, after all, such a thing as happiness?

I make true pleasure to consist in inaction, which the world regards as great pain. Thus it has been said, "Perfect happiness is the absence of happiness; perfect renown is the absence of renown."

Now in this sublunary world of ours it is impossible to assign positive and negative absolutely. Nevertheless, in inaction they can be so assigned. Perfect happiness and preservation of life are to be sought for only in inaction.

Let us consider. Heaven does nothing; yet it is clear. Earth does nothing; yet it enjoys repose. From the inaction of these two proceed all the modifications of things. How vast, how infinite is inaction, yet without source! How infinite, how vast, yet without form!

The endless varieties of things around us all spring from inaction. Therefore it has been said, "Heaven and earth do nothing, yet there is nothing which they do not accomplish." But among men, who can attain to inaction?

THE FOLLY OF MOURNING

When Chuang Tze's wife died, Hui Tze went to condole. He found the widower sitting on the ground, singing, with his legs spread out at a right angle, and beating time on a bowl.

"To live with your wife," exclaimed Hui Tze, "and see your eldest son grow up to be a man, and then not to shed a tear over her corpse, —this would be bad enough. But to drum on a bowl, and sing; surely this is going too far."

"Not at all," replied Chuang Tze. "When she died, I could not help being affected by her death. Soon, however, I remembered that she had already existed in a previous state before birth, without form, or even substance; that while in that unconditioned condition, substance was added to spirit; that this substance then assumed form; and that the next stage was birth. And now, by virtue of a further change, she is dead, passing from one phase to another like the sequence of spring, summer, autumn, and winter. And while she is thus lying asleep in eternity, for me to go about weeping and wailing would be to proclaim myself ignorant of these natural laws. Therefore I refrain."

THE DEAD ARE HAPPY

Chuang Tze one day saw an empty skull, bleached but still preserving its shape. Striking it with his riding whip, he said, "Wert thou once some ambitious citizen whose inordinate yearnings brought him to this pass?—some statesman who plunged his country into ruin and perished in the fray?—some wretch who left behind him a legacy of shame?—some beggar who died in the pangs of hunger and cold? Or didst thou reach this state by the natural course of old age?"

When he had finished speaking, he took the skull, and placing it under his head as a pillow, went to sleep. In the night, he dreamt that the skull appeared to him and said, "You speak well, sir; but all you say has reference to the life of mortals, and to mortal troubles. In death there are none of these. Would you like to hear about death?"

Chuang Tze having replied in the affirmative, the skull began:— "In death, there is no sovereign above, and no subject below. The workings of the four seasons are unknown. Our existences are bounded only by eternity. The happiness of a king among men cannot exceed that which we enjoy."

Chuang Tze, however, was not convinced, and said, "Were I to prevail upon God to allow your body to be born again, and your bones and flesh to be renewed, so that you could return to your parents, to your wife, and to the friends of your youth,—would you be willing?"

At this, the skull opened its eyes wide and knitted its brows and said, "How should I cast aside happiness greater than that of a king, and mingle once again in the toils and troubles of mortality?'"

THE SECRET OF LIFE

"A drunken man who falls out of a cart, though he may suffer, does not die. His bones are the same as other people's; but he meets his accident in a different way. His spirit is in a condition of security. He is not conscious of riding in the cart; neither is he conscious of falling out of it. Ideas of life, death, fear, etc., cannot penetrate his breast; and so he does not suffer from contact with objective existences. And if such security is to be got from wine, how much more is it to be got from God. It is in God that the sage seeks his refuge, and so he is free from harm."

THE WAY OF THE ARTIST CARPENTER

Ch'ing, the chief carpenter, was carving wood into a stand for hanging musical instruments. When finished, the work appeared to those who saw it as though of supernatural execution. And the prince of Lu asked him, saying, "What mystery is there in your art?"

"No mystery, your Highness," replied Ch'ing; "and yet there is something.

"When I am about to make such a stand, I guard against any diminution of my vital power. I first reduce my mind to absolute quiescence. Three days in this condition, and I become oblivious of any reward to be gained. Five days, and I become oblivious of any fame to be acquired. Seven days, and I become unconscious of my four limbs and my physical frame. Then, with no thought of the Court present to my mind, my skill becomes concentrated, and all disturbing elements from without are gone. I enter some mountain forest. I search for a suitable tree. It contains the form required, which is afterwards elaborated. I see the stand in my mind's eye, and then set to work. Otherwise, there is nothing. I bring my own natural capacity into relation with that of the wood. What was suspected to be of supernatural execution in my work was due solely to this."

THE PARABLE OF THE STRANGE BIRD

When Chuang Tze was wandering in the park at Tiao-ling, he saw a strange bird which came from the south. Its wings were seven feet across. Its eyes were an inch in circumference. And it flew close past Chuang Tze's head to alight in a chestnut grove.

"What manner of bird is this?" cried Chuang Tze. "With strong wings it does not fly away. With large eyes it does not see."

So he picked up his skirts and strode towards it with his cross-bow, anxious to get a shot. Just then he saw a cicada enjoying itself in the shade, forgetful of all else. And he saw a mantis spring and seize it, forgetting in the act its own body, which the strange bird immediately pounced upon and made its prey. And this it was which had caused the bird to forget its own nature.

"Alas!" cried Chuang Tze with a sigh, "how creatures injure one another. Loss follows the pursuit of gain."

So he laid aside his bow and went home, driven away by the park-keeper who wanted to know what business he had there.

THE PARABLE OF THE CONCUBINES

The innkeeper had two concubines, one beautiful, the other ugly. The latter he loved; the former, he hated.

Yang Tze asked how this was; whereupon one of the inn servants said, "The beautiful one is so conscious of her beauty that one does not think her beautiful. The ugly one is so conscious of her ugliness that one does not think her ugly."

"Note this, my disciples!" cried Yang Tze. "Be virtuous, but without being consciously so; and wherever you go, you will be beloved."

THE MAN WHO FISHED FOR FUN

When Wen Wang was on a tour of inspection in Tsang, he saw an old man fishing. But his fishing was not real fishing, for he did not fish to catch fish, but to amuse himself.

So Wen Wang wished to employ him in the administration of government, but feared lest his own ministers, uncles, and brothers, might object. On the other hand, if he let the old man go, he could not bear to think of the people being deprived of such an influence.

Accordingly, that very morning he informed his ministers, saying, "I once dreamt that a sage of a black colour and with a large beard, riding upon a parti-coloured horse with red stockings on one side, appeared and instructed me to place the administration in the hands of the old gentleman of Tsang, promising that the people would benefit greatly thereby."

The ministers at once said, "It is a command from your Highness' father."

"I think so," answered Wen Wang. "But let us try by divination."

"It is a command from your Highness' late father," said the ministers, "and may not be disobeyed. What need for divination?"

So the old man of Tsang was received and entrusted with the administration. He altered none of the existing statutes. He issued no unjust regulations. And when, after three years, Wen Wang made another inspection, he found all dangerous organizations broken up, the officials doing their duty as a matter of course, while the use of measures of grain was unknown within the four boundaries of the state. There was thus unanimity in the public voice, singleness of official purpose, and identity of interests to all.

So Wen Wang appointed the old man Grand Tutor; and then, standing with his face to the north, asked him, saying, "Can such government be extended over the empire?"

The old man of Tsang was silent and made no reply. He then abruptly took leave, and by the evening of that same day had disappeared, never to be heard of again.

CAN ONE OWN TAO?

Shun asked Ch'eng, saying, "Can one get TAO so as to have it for one's own?"

"Your very body," replied Ch'eng, "is not your own. How should TAO be?"

"If my body," said Shun, "is not my own, pray whose is it?"

"It is the delegated image of God," replied Ch'eng. "Your life is not your own. It is the delegated harmony of God. Your individuality is not your own. It is the delegated adaptability of God. Your posterity is not your own. It is the delegated exuviae of God. You move, but know not how. You are at rest, but know not why. You taste, but know not the cause. These are the operation of God's laws. How then should you get TAO so as to have it for your own?"

THE PLACE OF TAO

Tung Kuo Tze asked Chuang Tze, saying, "What you call TAO,—where is it?"

"There is nowhere," replied Chuang Tze, "where it is not."

"Tell me one place at any rate where it is," said Tung Kuo Tze.

"It is in the ant," replied Chuang Tze.

"Why go so low down?" asked Tung Kuo Tze.

"It is in a tare," said Chuang Tze.

"Still lower," objected Tung Kuo Tze.

"It is in potsherd," said Chuang Tze.

"Worse still!" cried Tung Kuo Tze.

"It is in ordure," said Chuang Tze. And Tung Kuo Tze made no reply.

"Sir," continued Chuang Tze, "your question does not touch the essential. When Huo, inspector of markets, asked the managing director about the fatness of pigs, the test was always made in parts least likely to be fat. Do not therefore insist in any particular direction;

for there is nothing which escapes. Such is perfect TAO; and such also is ideal speech. *Whole, entire, all,* are three words which sound differently but mean the same. Their purport is ONE.

"Try to reach with me the palace of Nowhere, and there, amidst the identity of all things, carry your discussions into the infinite. Try to practise with me inaction, wherein you may rest motionless, without care, and be happy. For thus my mind becomes an abstraction. It wanders not, and yet is not conscious of being at rest. It goes and comes and is not conscious of stoppages. Backwards and forwards without being conscious of any goal. Up and down the realms of infinity, wherein even the greatest intellect would fail to find an end.

"That which makes things the things they are, is not limited to such things. The limits of things are their own limits in so far as they are things. The limits of the limitless, the limitlessness of the limited, —these are called fullness and emptiness, renovation and decay. TAO causes fullness and emptiness, but it is not either. It causes renovation and decay, but it is not either. It causes beginning and end, but it is not either. It causes accumulation and dispersion, but it is not either."

THE PARABLE OF THE STICKLEBACK

Chuang Tze's family being poor, he went to borrow some corn from the prince of Chien-ho.

"Yes," said the prince. "I am just about collecting the revenue of my fief, and will then lend you three hundred ounces of silver. Will that do?"

At this Chuang Tze flushed with anger and said, "Yesterday, as I was coming along, I heard a voice calling me. I looked round, and in the cart-rut I saw a stickleback.

"'And what do you want, stickleback?' said I.

"'I am a denizen of the eastern ocean,' replied the stickleback. 'Pray, sir, a pint of water to save my life.'

"'Yes,' said I. 'I am just going south to visit the princes of Wu and Yueh. I will bring you some from the west river. Will that do?'

"At this the stickleback flushed with anger and said, 'I am out of my element. I have nowhere to go. A pint of water would save me. But to talk to me like this,—you might as well put me in a dried-fish shop at once.'"

THE FOLLY OF SPLENDID FUNERALS

When Chuang Tze was about to die, his disciples expressed a wish to give him a splendid funeral. But Chuang Tze said, "With heaven and earth for my coffin and shell; with the sun, moon, and stars as my burial regalia; and with all creation to escort me to the grave,— are not my funeral paraphernalia ready to hand?"

"We fear," argued the disciples, "lest the carrion kite should eat the body of our Master"; to which Chuang Tze replied, "Above ground I shall be food for kites; below I shall be food for mole-crickets and ants. Why rob one to feed the other?"

THE GOSPEL OF LAO TZE

Nan Yung took some provisions, and after a seven days' journey arrived at the abode of Lao Tze.

"Have you come from Keng Sang Ch'u?" said the latter.

"I have," replied Nan Yung.

"But why," said Lao Tze, "bring all these people with you?"

Nan Yung looked back in alarm, and Lao Tze continued, "Do you not understand what I say?"

Nan Yung bent his head abashed, and then looking up, said with a sigh, "I have now forgotten how to answer, in consequence of missing what I came to ask."

"What do you mean?" said Lao Tze.

"If I do not know," replied Nan Yung, "men call me a fool. If I do know, I injure myself. If I am not charitable, I injure others. If I am, I injure myself. If I do not do my duty to my neighbour, I injure others. If I do it, I injure myself. My trouble lies in not seeing how to escape from these three dilemmas. On the strength of my connexion with Keng Sang, I would venture to ask advice."

"When I saw you," said Lao Tze, "I knew in the twinkling of an eye what was the matter with you. And now what you say confirms my view. You are confused, as a child that has lost its parents. You would fathom the sea with a pole. You are astray. You are struggling to get back to your natural self, but cannot find the way. Alas! alas!"

Nan Yung begged to be allowed to remain, and set to work to cultivate the good and eliminate the evil within him. At the expiration of ten days, with sorrow in his heart, he again sought Lao Tze.

"Have you thoroughly cleansed yourself?" said Lao Tze. "But this grieved look . . . There is some evil obstruction yet.

"If the disturbances are external, do not be always combating them, but close the channels to the mind. If the disturbances are internal, do not strive to oppose them, but close all entrance from without. If the disturbances are both internal and external, then you will not even be able to hold fast to TAO, still less practise it."

"If a rustic is sick," said Nan Yung, "and another rustic goes to see him; and if the sick man can say what is the matter with him,—then he is not seriously ill. Yet my search after TAO is like swallowing drugs which only increase the malady. I beg therefore merely to ask the art of preserving life."

"The art of preserving life," replied Lao Tze, "consists in being able to keep all in ONE, to lose nothing, to estimate good and evil without divination, to know when to stop, and how much is enough, to leave others alone and attend to oneself, to be without cares and without knowledge,—to be in fact as a child. A child will cry all day and not become hoarse, because of the perfection of its constitutional harmony. It will keep its fist tightly closed all day and not open it, because of the concentration of its virtue. It will gaze all day without taking off its eyes, because its sight is not attracted by externals. In motion, it knows not whither it is bound; at rest, it is not conscious of doing anything; but unconsciously adapts itself to the exigencies of its environment. This is the art of preserving life."

"Is this then the virtue of the perfect man?" cried Nan Yung.

"Not so," said Lao Tze. "I am, as it were, but breaking the ice.

"The perfect man shares the food of this earth, but the happiness of God. He does not incur trouble either from men or things. He does not join in censuring, in plotting, in toadying. Free from care he comes, and unconscious he goes;—this is the art of preserving life."

"This then is perfection?" inquired Nan Yung.

"Not yet," said Lao Tze. "I specially asked if you could be as a child. A child acts without knowing what it does; moves without knowing whither. Its body is like a dry branch; its heart like dead ashes. Thus, good and evil fortune find no lodgment therein; and there where good and evil fortune are not, how can the troubles of mortality be?

"Those whose hearts are in a state of repose give forth a divine radiance, by the light of which they see themselves as they are. And only by cultivating such repose can man attain to the constant.

"Those who are constant are sought after by men and assisted by God. Those who are sought after by men are the people of God; those who are assisted by God are his chosen children.

"To study this is to study what cannot be learnt. To practise this is to practise what cannot be accomplished. To discuss this is to discuss what can never be proved. Let knowledge stop at the unknowable. That is perfection. And for those who do not follow this, God will destroy them!

"With such defences for the body, ever prepared for the unexpected, deferential to the rights of others,—if then calamities overtake you, these are from God, not from man. Let them not disturb what you have already achieved. Let them not penetrate into the soul's abode. For there resides the will. And if the will knows not what to will, it will not be able to will.

"Whatsoever is not said in all sincerity, is wrongly said. And not to be able to rid oneself of this vice is only to sink deeper towards perdition.

"Those who do evil in the open light of day,—men will punish them. Those who do evil in secret,—God will punish them. Who fears both man and God, he is fit to walk alone. Those who are devoted to the internal, in practice acquire no reputation. Those who are devoted to the external, strive for pre-eminence among their fellows. Practice without reputation throws a halo around the meanest. But he who strives for pre-eminence among his fellows, he is as a huckster whose weariness all perceive though he himself puts on an air of gaiety.

"He who is naturally in sympathy with man, to him all men come. But he who forcedly adapts, has no room even for himself, still less for others. And he who has no room for others, has no ties. It is all over with him.

"TAO informs its own subdivisions, their successes and their failures. What is feared in sub-division is separation. What is feared in separation, is further separation. Thus, to issue forth without return, this is development of the supernatural. To issue forth and attain the goal, this is called death. To be annihilated and yet to exist, this is convergence of the supernatural into ONE. To make things which have form appear to all intents and purposes formless,—this is the sum of all things.

"Birth is not a beginning; death is not an end. There is existence without limitation; there is continuity without a starting-point. Existence without limitation is space. Continuity without a starting-point is time. There is birth, there is death, there is issuing forth, there is entering in. That through which one passes in and out without seeing its form, that is the Portal of God.

"The Portal of God is non-existence. All things sprang from non-existence. Existence could not make existence existence. It must have proceeded from non-existence, and non-existence and nothing are ONE. Herein is the abiding-place of the sage.

"The knowledge of the ancients reached the highest point,—the time before anything existed. This is the highest point. It is exhaustive. There is no adding to it.

"The second best was that of those who started from existence. Life was to them a misfortune. Death was a return home. There was already separation. . . .

"Man's life is as the soot on a kettle. Yet men speak of the subjective point of view. But this subjective point of view will not bear the test. It is a point of knowledge we cannot reach.

"At the winter sacrifice, the tripe may be separated from the great toe; yet these cannot be separated. He who looks at a house, visits the ancestral hall, and even the latrines. Thus every point is the subjective point of view.

"Let us try to formulate this subjective point of view. It originates with life, and, with knowledge as its tutor, drifts into the admission of right and wrong. But one's own standard of right is the standard, and others have to adapt themselves to it. Men will die for this. Such people look upon the useful as appertaining to wisdom, the useless as appertaining to folly; upon success in life as honorable, upon failure as dishonourable. The subjective point of view is that of the present generation, who like the cicada and the young dove see things only from their own standpoint.

"If a man treads upon a stranger's toe in the market-place, he apologizes on the score of hurry. If an elder brother does this, he is quit with an exclamation of sympathy. And if a parent does so, nothing whatever is done.

"Therefore it has been said, 'Perfect politeness is not artificial; perfect duty to one's neighbour is not a matter of calculation; perfect wisdom takes no thought; perfect charity recognizes no ties; perfect trust requires no pledges.'

"Discard the stimuli of purpose. Free the mind from disturbances. Get rid of entanglements to virtue. Pierce the obstructions to TAO.

"Honours, wealth, distinction, power, fame, gain,—these six stimulate purpose.

"Mien, carriage, beauty, arguments, influence, opinions,—these six disturb the mind.

"Hate, ambition, joy, anger, sorrow, pleasure,—these six are entanglements to virtue.

"Rejecting, adopting, receiving, giving, knowledge, ability,—these six are obstruction to TAO.

"If these twenty-four be not allowed to run riot, then the mind will be duly ordered. And being duly ordered, it will be in repose. And being in repose, it will be clear of perception. And being clear of perception, it will be unconditioned. And being unconditioned, it will be in that state of inaction by which there is nothing which cannot be accomplished."

THE GATHAS
THE VENDIDAD
THE YASNA

AHURA MAZDA

INTRODUCTION

Zoroastrianism, the ancient religion of Persia, survives today almost solely among the Parsees of India, who number barely 100,000. Because of its theological distinctiveness, however, and its historical importance, it clearly ranks among the world's major religions.

Tradition attributes its founding to a certain Zoroaster, or Zarathushtra, who is said to have lived in the sixth century B.C., and was perhaps a native of the Iranian province now known as Azerbaijan. If the teachings associated with his name were truly his, he was one of the greatest prophets of all time, for he sought to convert his people from a primitive nature worship to a most advanced ethical cult.

According to this cult, the whole universe is dominated by two primal forces, Good and Evil, and the task of mankind is to choose between them. Good is represented by Ahura Mazda (Ormuzd), the "Lord of Light," who manifested himself through six deified virtues, Truth, Piety, Kindness, Health, and so forth. Evil, on the other hand, is represented by Angra Mainyu (Ahriman), the "Hostile Spirit," who is abetted by a horde of demons, among them the old nature gods. The field of battle between these two forces is the present world, and the conflict must continue until at last Evil is utterly routed, after which there will ensue a general Resurrection, a Final Judgment, and then an endless era of Universal Peace. Meanwhile all men are necessarily fighting on one side or the other, and deciding their individual fate accordingly. He who devotes himself throughout life to the service of Ahura Mazda will at death enter right into Paradise. The rest will be ushered into a sort of Purgatory, or else be plunged straight into Hell.

Serving Ahura Mazda entails more than shouting his praises. It

361

means working for his victory, laboring to spread the Light of which he is the symbol. Specifically it means warring against all marauders, hunting down all wild things, clearing fields, building barns, bridging streams—in short, furthering civilization. There was little ritualism in this religion, and no mysticism or metaphysics. It was altogether a pragmatic faith, demanding "goodly thoughts, goodly words, goodly deeds," and nothing more—or less.

Such was Zoroastrianism according to the most ancient texts called the GATHAS. *As was inevitable, however, the religion could not long retain so high a character. Ordinary men were not content to believe in abstract principles; they wanted concrete gods, comforting myths, and comfortable rites. So they got them. The old pagan worship reasserted itself, gradually modifying the prophet's faith, until finally Zoroastrianism became almost entirely a priest's religion. It began to acknowledge many gods besides Ahura Mazda, and also a host of semi-divinities, among them Zoroaster himself. More and more rites were introduced, and countless strange taboos. The daily life of the believer became one unbroken round of pious ceremonialism. Nevertheless something remained of the original doctrine, a deep and strong ethical undertone which has persisted down to the present day.*

The great age of Zoroastrianism was the sixth to the fourth centuries B.C., *when it dominated the Persian Empire, and that Empire dominated much of the civilized world. Historians believe it profoundly influenced Judaism at that time—Judea was then a part of the Persian Empire—planting seeds which later flowered in the Biblical and Apocryphal doctrines of Heaven, Hell, Satan, Armageddon, the Final Judgment, and the Messianic Age. If this is true, much of the Zoroastrian theology may be said to survive today, not alone in Judaism, but also in Christianity and Mohammedanism.*

The basic scriptures of this religion, known collectively as the Avesta, were largely destroyed during the Greek, Mohammedan, and Mongol invasions of Persia. The fragment that has been preserved consists of the oldest and most sacred texts called the GATHAS, *which are included in a liturgical collection known as the* YASNA; *an appendix called the Vispered; a priestly code akin to Leviticus which is called the Vendidad; and a series of hymns called* YASHTS. *In addition there are many secondary scriptures written in Pahlavi, a later Persian language; but these are primarily apocalyptic in nature, and almost bare of ethical import. For that reason the following selections are taken solely from the Avesta.*

THE GATHAS

The core of the Avesta, the Zoroastrian holy canon, consists of five long metrical passages known as the GATHAS, "psalms." These are obviously very ancient, dating perhaps from the time of Zarathustra himself (circa 600 B.C.), and they bring out the ethical nature of his gospel in its primitive starkness and grandeur. There is almost no reference to the elaborate ritualism and sacerdotal organization which became so important later on. The emphasis is all on the prophetic elements in the religion, on the basic beliefs concerning the rôle of man in the cosmic drama of Existence. The universe is seen as one vast battle-ground whereon Ahura Mazda, the Wise Spirit (i.e., civilization), struggles to rout Angra Mainyu, the Lie Demon (i.e., Barbarism). Man, alone of all created things, is free to choose sides, and he manifests his choice by means of deeds rather than words. If he settles down, tends the cattle, improves the earth, and aids his fellows, then he is patently a follower of Ahura Mazda—and certain to share in the Final Triumph. If, on the contrary, he persists in being a vicious and wasteful nomad, then he is as patently a follower of Satan —and sure to land in eternal Hell.

The style of the GATHAS is so archaic, and the text in part so mutilated, that they are not readily intelligible to the modern reader. For that reason the verses have been freely rearranged in the first selection given below, and some of the more abstruse phrases have been broadly paraphrased. The second and third selections, however, are translated verbatim.[1]

I

When Zarathustra, by looking at nature with his own eye,
And fathoming its meaning with his own mind,
Did comprehend Mazda . . . and realize
He was both the First and Last of Creation,
The Father of Righteousness,

[1] By J. H. Moulton, in his *Early Zoroastrianism* (Allen & Unwin, London, 1913). By permission of the Hibbert Trust.

The true creator of Justice,
The Ruling Lord of all that is done. . . .
(*Then did Zarathustra declare:*) I pray thee, O Ahura Mazda,
Thou who dost watch with thy sharp and shining eyes,
Over all who ask questions, and
Over all who seek to exert authority,
Tell me, O Ahura Mazda, with the tongue of thy mouth,
What is the command for the enlightened,
That I may cause all men to
    choose aright. . . .
Thou, O Mazda,
Didst shape matter and spirit,
Didst establish body and
    breath,
And deeds and doctrines
    whereby thoughtful men
    might attain true faith,
Therefore tell me, O Ahura
    Mazda, what is to be
And what is not to be,
In order that I may know and
    ponder on the better
    course,
And gain therefrom the due
    reward.

O Ahura Mazda, I ask thee
    concerning the present
    and the future,
How shall the righteous man be dealt with,
And how the wicked,
At the time of the Final Judgement?

I ask thee, O Ahura, what shall be the punishments
Of them that serve the Evil One,
Of them that cannot make their living
Save through violence to cattle and herdsmen.
O Ahura Mazda, I ask thee whether the well-disposed,
The one who strives to improve the houses,

The villages,
The clans and provinces,
Through Justice,
Can he become at all like thee?
And when?
And by what deeds?
　　Tell me, O Lord, that I may no longer be deluded,
Be thou to us an instructor of Good Disposition?

　　(And Ahura Mazda answered:) O well-dispcsed believer,
Hearken not to the followers of the Evil One,
For these seek to wreck houses,
Raze villages,
Despoil clans and provinces;
They can cause only disaster and death.
So fight them with all your weapons!

　　The righteous alone shall be saved
From destruction and eternal darkness,
From foul food and the worst curses,
At the time of the End of Days.
But ye wicked ones, beware,
For to these will ye be delivered,
Because of your evil spirit!

　　He who serveth Ahura Mazda in mind and deed,
To him shall be granted the bliss of divine fellowship,
And fullness of Health,
Immortality,
Justice and Power,
And the Good Disposition.

　　The man who is well-disposed, he comprehends this,
Even as does Mazda, who is All Wise.
It is such a one who weds justice to authority,
It is the well-disposed man who most surely prospers,
And is a companion to Ahura Mazda.

Yasna xxxi

II

This I ask thee, tell me truly, Ahura—as to prayer, how it should be? O Mazda, might one like thee teach it to his friend such as I am, and through friendly Right give us support, that Good Thought may come unto us? . . .

This I ask thee, tell me truly, Ahura. Who is by generation the Father of Right, at the first? Who determined the path of sun and stars? Who is it by whom the moon waxes and wanes again? This, O Mazda, and yet more, I am fain to know.

This I ask thee, tell me truly, Ahura. Who upheld the earth beneath and the firmament from falling? Who the waters and the planets? Who yoked swiftness to winds and clouds? Who is, O Mazda, creator of Good Thought?

This I ask thee, tell me truly, Ahura. What artist made light and darkness? What artist made sleep and waking? Who made morning, noon, and night, that call the understanding man to his duty?

This I ask thee, tell me truly, Ahura—whether what I shall proclaim is verily the truth. Will Right with its actions give aid at the last? Will Piety? Will Good Thought announce from thee the Dominion? For whom hast thou made the pregnant cow [2] that brings good luck?

This I ask thee, tell me truly, Ahura. Who created together with Dominion the precious Piety? Who made by wisdom the son obedient to his father? I strive to recognize by these things thee, O Mazda, creator of all things through the holy spirit.

This I ask thee, tell me truly, Ahura. I would keep in mind thy design, O Mazda, and understand aright the maxims of life which I ask of Good Thought and Right. How will my soul partake of the good that gives increase? . . .

This I ask thee, tell me truly, Ahura. Who among those with whom I would speak is a righteous man, and who a liar? On which side is the enemy? On this, or is he the enemy, the Liar, who opposes thy blessings? How shall it be with him? Is he not to be thought of as an enemy?

This I ask thee, tell me truly, Ahura—whether we shall drive the Lie away from us to those who being full of disobedience will not

[2] The symbol of good fortune.

strive after fellowship with Right, nor trouble themselves with counsel of Good Thought.

This I ask thee, tell me truly, Ahura—whether I could put the Lie into the hands of Right, to cast her down by the words of thy lore, to work a mighty destruction among the Liars, to bring torments upon them and enmities, O Mazda.

This I ask thee, tell me truly, Ahura—if thou hast power over this to ward it off from me through Right, when the two opposing hosts [3] meet in battle according to those decrees which thou wilt firmly establish. Whether is it of the twain that thou wilt give victory?

This I ask thee, tell me truly, Ahura. Who is victorious to protect by thy doctrine all that are? By vision assure me how to set up the judge that heals the world.[4] Then let him have Obedience coming with Good Thought unto every man whom thou desirest, O Mazda.

This I ask thee, tell me truly, Ahura—whether through you I shall attain my goal, O Mazda, even attachment unto you, and that my voice may be effectual, that Welfare and Immortality may be ready to unite according to that promise with him who joins himself with Right.

Yasna, xliv

III

Zarathustra: Can my soul count on any one for help? Who is there found for my herd, who for myself a protector indeed, at my call other than Right and thyself, O Mazda Ahura, and the Best Thought?

How, O Mazda, should one desire the luck-bringing cattle, one who would fain it should come to him together with the pasture?
Mazda: They that live uprightly according to the Right among the many that look upon the sun, these when they stand in the judgment I will settle in the dwelling of the wise.
Zarathustra: So this reward shall come to him through the Right, O Mazda, the reward which by the Dominion and Good thought he promised, whosoever by the power of his Destiny prospers the neighboring possession that now the Liar holds.

I will worship you with praise, O Mazda Ahura, joined with Right

---

[3] The hosts of Mazdayasnians and Daevayasnians; or perhaps rather the spiritual forces in the great Armageddon that precedes the Renovation.
[4] This seems to be Zarathustra himself—he is praying for a vision that may openly confirm his designation as a prophet.

and Best Thought and Dominion, that they, desired of pious men, may stand as Judges on the path of the obedient unto the House of Song.

Assured by you, O Mazda Ahura and Right, are the pointings of the hand—since you are well disposed to your prophet—which shall bring us to bliss, together with visible manifest help.

The prophet Zarathustra, who as thy friend, O Mazda and the Right, lifts up his voice with worship—may the Creator of Wisdom teach me his ordinances through Good Thought, that my tongue may have a pathway.

For you I will harness the swiftest steeds, stout and strong, by the prompting of your praise, that ye may come hither, O Mazda, Right and Good Thought. May ye be ready for my help!

With verses that are recognized as those of pious zeal I will come before you with outstretched hands, O Mazda, before you, O thou Right, with the worship of the faithful man, before you with all the capacity of Good Thought.

With these prayers I would come and praise you, O Mazda and thou Right, with actions of Good Thought. If I be master of my own destiny as I will, then will I take thought for the portion of the wise in the same.

Those actions that I shall achieve, and those done aforetime, and those, O Good Thought, that are precious in the sight, the rays of the sun, the bright uprisings of the days, all is for your praise, O thou Right and Mazda Ahura.

Your praiser, Mazda, will I declare myself and be, so long, O right, as I have strength and power. May the Creator of the world accomplish through Good Thoughts its fulfilment of all that most perfectly answers to his will!

Yasna 1

THE VENDIDAD

The most revered of the Zoroastrian scriptures, after the GATHAS, *is the Book of Law called the* VENDIDAD. *It contains some twenty-two chapters, many of relatively late origin, and all essentially sacerdotal in character. Their main concern is with rite rather than right, with sacramental correctness rather than moral probity. As the following passages will reveal, however, the priests who composed the book were not completely unillumined by the original Prophet's flame.[5]*

I

With these words the holy Ahura Mazda rejoiced the holy Zarathustra: "Purity is for man, next to life, the greatest good, that purity, O Zarathustra, that is in the religion of Mazda for him who cleanses his own self with good thoughts, words, and deeds."

O Maker of the material world, thou Holy One! This Law, this fiend-destroying Law of Zarathustra, by what greatness, goodness, and fairness is it great, good, and fair above all other utterances?

Ahura Mazda answered: "As much above all other floods as is the sea Vouru-kasha, so much above all other utterances in greatness, goodness, and fairness is this Law, this fiend-destroying Law of Zarathustra.

"As much as a great stream flows swifter than a slender rivulet,

[5] The translations are by James Darmesteter, in *The Sacred Books of the East,* vol. iv (The Clarendon Press, Oxford, 1895).

so much above all other utterances in greatness, goodness, and fairness is this Law, this fiend-destroying Law of Zarathustra.

"As high as the great tree stands above the small plants it overshadows, so high above all other utterances in greatness, goodness, and fairness is this Law, this fiend-destroying Law of Zarathustra.

"As high as heaven is above the earth that it compasses around, so high above all other utterances is this Law, this fiend-destroying Law of Mazda.

"Therefore, he will apply to the Ratu, he will apply to the *Sraosha-varez*; whether for a *draona*-service that should have been undertaken and has not been undertaken; or for a *draona* that should have been offered up and has not been offered up; or for a *draona* that should have been entrusted and has not been entrusted.

"The Ratu has power to remit him one-third of his penalty: if he has committed any other evil deed, it is remitted by his repentance; if he has committed no other evil deed, he is absolved by his repentance forever and ever."

Ch. V, 5

II

He that does not restore a loan to the man who lent it steals the thing and robs the man. This he doeth every day, every night, as long as he keep in his house his neighbor's property, as though it were his own. . . .

Verily I say it unto thee, O Spitama Zarathustra! the man who has a wife is far above him who lives in continence; he who keeps a house is far above him who has none; he who has children is far above the childless man; he who has riches is far above him who has none.

And of two men, he who fills himself with meat receives in him Good Thought much better than he who does not do so; the latter is all but dead; the former is above him by the worth of a man.

This man can strive against the onsets of death; he can strive against the well-darted arrow; he can strive against the winter fiend, with thinnest garment on; he can strive against the wicked tyrant and smite him on the head. . . .

Ch. iv, 1, 3*b*

III

How many are the sins that men commit and that, being committed and not confessed, nor atoned for, make their committer a *Peshotanu?*

Ahura Mazda answered: "There are five such sins, O holy Zarathustra! It is the first of these sins that men commit when a man teaches one of the faithful another faith, another law, a lower doctrine, and he leads him astray with a full knowledge and conscience of the sin: the man who has done the deed becomes a *Peshotanu.*

"It is the second of these sins when a man gives bones too hard or food too hot to a shepherd's dog or to a housedog;

"If the bones stick in the dog's teeth or stop in his throat; or if the food too hot burn his mouth or his tongue, he may come to grief thereby; if he come to grief thereby, the man who has done the deed becomes a *Peshotanu.*

"It is the third of these sins when a man smites a bitch big with young or affrights her by running after her, or shouting or clapping with the hands;

"If the bitch fall into a hole, or a well, or a precipice, or a river, or a canal, she may come to grief thereby; if she come to grief thereby, the man who has done the deed becomes a *Peshotanu.*

"It is the fourth of these sins when a man has intercourse with a woman who has the whites or sees the blood, the man that has done the deed becomes a *Peshotanu.*

"It is the fifth of these sins when a man has intercourse with a woman quick with child, whether the milk has already come to her breasts or has not yet come: she may come to grief thereby; if she come to grief thereby, the man who has done the deed becomes a *Peshotanu.*

"If a man come near unto a damsel, either dependent on the chief of the family or not dependent, either delivered unto a husband or not delivered, and she conceives by him, let her not, being ashamed of the people, produce in herself the menses, against the course of nature, by means of water and plants.

"And if the damsel, being ashamed of the people, shall produce in herself the menses against the course of nature, by means of water and plants, it is a fresh sin as heavy as the first.

"If a man come near unto a damsel, either dependent on the chief of the family or not dependent, either delivered unto a husband or not delivered, and she conceives by him, let her not, being ashamed of the people, destroy the fruit in her womb.

"And if the damsel, being ashamed of the people, shall destroy the fruit in her womb, the sin is on both the father and herself, the murder is on both the father and herself; both the father and herself shall pay the penalty for wilful murder.

"If a man come near unto a damsel, either dependent on the chief of the family or not dependent, either delivered unto a husband or not delivered, and she conceives by him, and she says, 'I have conceived by thee'; and he replies, 'Go then to the old woman and apply to her for one of her drugs, that she may procure thee miscarriage';

"And the damsel goes to the old woman and applies to her for one of her drugs, that she may procure her a miscarriage; and the old woman brings her some *Banga*, or *Shaeta*, a drug that kills in the womb, or one that expels out of the womb, or some other of the drugs that produce miscarriage, and the man says, 'Cause thy fruit to perish!' and she causes her fruit to perish; the sin is on the head of all three, the man, the damsel, and the old woman.

"If a man come near unto a damsel, either dependent on the chief of the family or not dependent, either delivered unto a husband or not delivered, and she conceives by him, so long shall he support her, until the child be born.

"If he shall not support her, so that the child comes to grief, for want of proper support, he shall pay for it the penalty for wilful murder."

O Maker of the material world, thou Holy One! If she be near her time, which is the worshiper of Mazda that shall support her?

Ahura Mazda answered: "If a man come near unto a damsel, either dependent on the chief of the family or not dependent, either delivered unto a husband or not delivered, and she conceives by him, so long shall he support her, until the child be born.

"If he shall not support her . . .

"It lies with the faithful to look in the same way after every pregnant female, either two-footed or four-footed, two-footed woman or four-footed bitch."

Ch. xv, 1–2

THE YASNA

The following excerpt is taken from the YASNA, *the collection of seventy-two psalms—including the* GATHAS—*which forms the chief liturgical work in the Avesta. These hymns are still regularly recited in the preparation and offering of the sacred drink made of the juice of the* haoma *plant mixed with milk and aromatic spices. Most of the psalms are mere repetitions of sacerdotal formulae, but this one* (Yasna xii) *is strikingly meaningful. It is generally regarded as the summary of the Zoroastrian creed.*[6]

I drive the Daevas (demons) hence; I confess as a Mazda-worshipper of the order of Zarathustra, estranged from the Daevas, devoted to the lore of the Lord, a praiser of the bountiful Immortals; and to Ahura Mazda, the good and endowed with good possessions, I attribute all things good, to the Holy One, the resplendent, to the glorious, whose are all things whatsoever which are good; whose is the kine, whose is Asha (the righteous order pervading all things pure), whose are the stars, in whose lights the glorious beings and objects are clothed.

And I choose Piety, the bounteous and the good, mine may she be. And therefore I loudly deprecate all robbery and violence against the sacred kine, and all drought to the wasting of the Mazdayasnian villages.

Away from their thoughts do I wish to lead the thought of wandering at will, away the thought of free nomadic pitching of the tent,

[6] Translated by L. H. Mills in *The Sacred Books of the East*, vol. xxxi (The Clarendon Press, Oxford, 1887).

for I wish to remove all wandering from their kine which abide in steadfastness upon this land; and bowing down in worship to Righteousness I dedicate my offerings with praise so far as that. Never may I stand as a source of wasting, never as a source of withering to the Mazdayasnian villages, not for the love of body or of life. . . .

Off, off, do I abjure the Daevas and all possessed by them, the sorcerers and all that hold to their devices, and every existing being of the sort; their thoughts do I abjure, their words and actions, and their seed that propagate their sin; away do I abjure their shelter and their headship, and the iniquitous of every kind who act as Rakhshas act! . . .

A Mazda-worshipper I am, of Zarathustra's order; so do I confess, as a praiser and confessor, and I therefore praise aloud the well-thought thought, the word well spoken, and the deed well done.

Yet, I praise at once the faith of Mazda, the faith which has no faltering utterance, the faith that wields the felling halberd, the faith of kindred marriage, the holy creed, which is the most imposing, best, and most beautiful of all religions which exist, and of all that shall in future come to knowledge, Ahura's faith, the Zarathustrian creed. Yea, to Ahura Mazda do I ascribe all good, and such shall be the worship of the Mazdayasnian belief!

THE SCRIPTURES OF JUDAISM

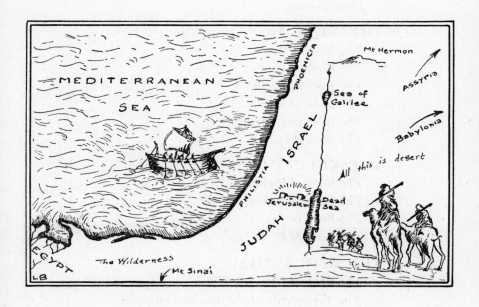

THE TORAH
   Exodus
   Leviticus
   Deuteronomy

THE NEVI'IM
   The Book of Amos
   The Book of Hosea
   The Book of Isaiah
   The Book of Micah
   The Book of Jeremiah
   The Second Isaiah

THE KETUBIM
   The Book of Psalms
   The Book of Proverbs
   The Book of Job
   The Book of Ecclesiastes

THE APOCRYPHA
   The Book of Jesus ben Sirach
   The Testaments of the Twelve Patriarchs

THE TALMUD
   From the Mishna
   From the Gemara

INTRODUCTION

In a quantitative sense, Judaism is a very minor faith today, the entire Jewish community comprising—since the recent fearful persecutions—barely a half of one percent of the world's population. Qualitatively, however, it is one of the most important, for, being basic to Islam as well as Christianity, it colors the religious life of perhaps fifty percent of mankind.

The origins of Judaism go back to a primitive Semitic cult imported into Canaan by certain nomadic tribesmen called Hebrews. This was a pastoral cult associated with a desert spirit named Yahveh (Jehovah), but it gradually assumed agricultural trappings, thus enabling Yahveh to crowd out the native Canaanite gods. The religion then was hardly to be distinguished from that of any other semi-barbaric folk, for it was still fundamentally tribal and ritualistic.

Around the eighth century B.C., however, it began to acquire a new character at the hands of fiery exhorters called nevi'im ("prophets") who preached two revolutionary doctrines: (a) Yahveh was not a tribal deity, but the One and Only God of all mankind; (b) what He demanded of his worshippers was not ritual piety but righteous conduct. Neither doctrine was completely novel—see, for example, the Egyptian HYMNS TO ATON, p. 38 above—but both had never before been stated so clearly and with such vehemence. During some two centuries, from Amos to Jeremiah, a campaign was waged which made Judaism fundamentally a prophetic religion.

In order to survive, however, the religion had to be "organized," and this need brought the priests back into power. They effected a compromise between their sacerdotal practices and the prophetic ideals, producing the BOOK OF DEUTERONOMY (622 B.C.), a law code in which the ethical spirit was given a ritual body. Shortly thereafter

(586 B.C.) *the Jews were deported to Babylonia, a land where priestcraft was inordinately strong, and this encouraged further compromises. But the ethicism of the prophets managed to persist, as did also their universalism, and both these principles leavened most of the scriptures which became cardinal to the Jewish faith.*

The holiest of those scriptures were eventually formed into a canon consisting of three divisions: the TORAH *("Law"), the* NEVI'IM *("Prophets"), and the* KETUBIM *("Writings"). The Christians called this canon the "Old Testament," but the Jews referred to it as the Tanak. Certain later and therefore less venerable texts were put into a secondary group now known as the* APOCRYPHA. *Finally a great literature of pious interpretation arose called the* TALMUD, *and this too became sacred to the Jews. In all these various writings there is so marked a stress on the importance of ethics in the scheme of salvation that they form a particularly vital portion of an Anthology such as this.*

THE TORAH

This, the most ancient and hallowed portion of the Jewish scriptures, consists of the so-called "Five Books of Moses." Critical scholars are agreed that these books—Genesis, Exodus, Leviticus, Numbers, and Deuteronomy—are not actually Mosaic, but rather a mosaic, being made up of a number of different sacred traditions reflecting the widely divergent religious and social attitudes of as many different periods in Hebraic history. This heterogeneity explains the numerous discrepancies within the TORAH, and the difficulties of those who have sought equal worth in all of its commands. What is true of all ancient scriptures is especially true of the TORAH: to be rationally appreciated it must be intelligently studied rather than literally believed. It is more than a haphazard compilation of bizarre tales and bewildering fiats, more than a disjointed miscellany of myths, genealogies, visions, and legal codes. It is the first part of a great and coherent epic that tells of one people's confused, faltering, but indomitable struggle to achieve a nobler life in a happier world.

Owing to the limitations of this Anthology, the quotations are confined here to the three books in the TORAH which are especially rich in ethical material.

EXODUS

Here, in the second of the "Five Books of Moses," we find the earliest recorded laws of the Jews. The initial passage contains the "Ten Commandments," the core of the entire TORAH, and historically the most important moral code in the world. It appears to have been part of a "Covenant" containing the statutes adopted by the Hebrews after they ceased to be desert nomads and settled in Canaan. Such statutes would naturally have been learned from the native Canaanites, who in turn almost certainly learned them from their close kinsmen, the Babylonians. Characteristically, however, the Hebrews gave a distinct ethical slant to all their ordinances, as can be seen if the follow-

ing passages are compared with the CODE OF HAMMURAPI *quoted on p. 17 above.*[1]

And God spoke all these words, saying:

I am the LORD thy God, who brought thee out of the land of Egypt, out of the house of bondage.

Thou shalt have no other gods before Me. Thou shalt not make unto thee a graven image, nor any manner of likeness, of any thing that is in heaven above, or that is in the earth beneath, or that is in the water under the earth; thou shalt not bow down unto them, nor serve them; for I the LORD thy God am a jealous God, visiting the iniquity of the fathers upon the children unto the third and fourth generation of them that hate Me; and showing mercy unto the thousandth generation of them that love Me and keep My commandments.

Thou shalt not take the name of the LORD thy God in vain; for the LORD will not hold him guiltless that taketh His name in vain.

Remember the sabbath day, to keep it holy. Six days shalt thou labour, and do all thy work; but the seventh day is a sabbath unto the LORD thy God, in it thou shalt not do any manner of work, thou, nor thy son, nor thy daughter, nor thy man-servant, nor thy maid-servant, nor thy cattle, nor the stranger that is within thy gates; for in six days the LORD made heaven and earth, the sea, and all that in them is, and rested on the seventh day; wherefore the LORD blessed the sabbath day, and hallowed it.

Honour thy father and thy mother, that thy days may be long upon the land which the LORD thy God giveth thee.

Thou shalt not murder.

Thou shalt not commit adultery.

Thou shalt not steal.

Thou shalt not bear false witness against thy neighbour.

[1] This and the succeeding Biblical passages are reprinted from the standard Jewish translation of *The Holy Scriptures* (Jewish Publication Society of America, Philadelphia, 1917).

Thou shalt not covet thy neighbour's house; thou shalt not covet thy neighbour's wife, nor his man-servant, nor his maid-servant, nor his ox, nor his ass, nor any thing that is thy neighbour's.

20: 1–14

He that smiteth a man, so that he dieth, shall surely be put to death. And if a man lie not in wait, but God cause it to come to hand; then I will appoint thee a place whither he may flee.

And if a man come presumptuously upon his neighbour, to slay him with guile; thou shalt take him from Mine altar, that he may die.

And he that smiteth his father, or his mother, shall be surely put to death.

And he that stealeth a man, and selleth him, or if he be found in his hand, he shall surely be put to death.

And he that curseth his father or his mother, shall surely be put to death.

And if men contend, and one smite the other with a stone, or with his fist, and he die not, but keep his bed; if he rise again, and walk abroad upon his staff, then shall he that smote him be quit; only he shall pay for the loss of his time, and shall cause him to be thoroughly healed.

And if a man smite his bondman or his bondwoman, with a rod, and he die under his hand, he shall surely be punished. . . .

21: 12–20

And if men strive together, and hurt a woman with child, so that her fruit depart, and yet no harm follow, he shall be surely fined, according as the woman's husband shall lay upon him; and he shall pay as the judges determine. But if any harm follow, then thou shalt give life for life, eye for eye, tooth for tooth, hand for hand, foot for foot, burning for burning, wound for wound, stripe for stripe.

And if a man smite the eye of his bondman, or the eye of his bondwoman, and destroy it, he shall let him go free for his eye's sake. And if he smite out his bondman's tooth, or his bondwoman's tooth, he shall let him go free for his tooth's sake.

And if an ox gore a man or a woman, that they die, the ox shall be surely stoned, and its flesh shall not be eaten; but the owner of the ox shall be quit. But if the ox was wont to gore in time past, and warning hath been given to its owner, and he hath not kept it in, but it hath killed a man or a woman; the ox shall be stoned, and its owner also shall be put to death. . . .

21: 22–29

And if a man shall open a pit, or if a man shall dig a pit and not cover it, and an ox or an ass fall therein, the owner of the pit shall make it good; he shall give money unto the owner of them, and the dead beast shall be his. . . .

21: 33–34

If a man cause a field or vineyard to be eaten, and shall let his beast loose, and it feed in another man's field; of the best of his own field, and of the best of his own vineyard, shall he make restitution.

If fire break out, and catch in thorns, so that the shocks of corn, or the standing corn, or the field are consumed; he that kindled the fire shall surely make restitution.

If a man deliver unto his neighbour money or stuff to keep, and it be stolen out of the man's house; if the thief be found, he shall pay double. If the thief be not found, then the master of the house shall come near unto God, to see whether he have not put his hand unto his neighbour's goods. For every matter of trespass, whether it be for ox, for ass, for sheep, for raiment, or for any manner of lost thing, whereof one saith: 'This is it,' the cause of both parties shall come before God; he whom God shall condemn shall pay double unto his neighbour.

If a man deliver unto his neighbour an ass, or an ox, or a sheep, or any beast, to keep, and it die, or be hurt, or driven away, no man seeing it; the oath of the Lord shall be between them both, to see whether he have not put his hand unto his neighbour's goods; and the owner thereof shall accept it, and he shall not make restitution. But if it be stolen from him, he shall make restitution unto the owner thereof. If it be torn in pieces, let him bring it for witness; he shall not make good that which was torn. . . .

And if a man entice a virgin that is not betrothed, and lie with her, he shall surely pay a dowry for her to be his wife. If her father utterly refuse to give her unto him, he shall pay money according to the dowry of virgins.

Thou shalt not suffer a sorceress to live.

Whosoever lieth with a beast shall surely be put to death. . . .

And a stranger shalt thou not wrong, neither shalt thou oppress him; for ye were strangers in the land of Egypt. Ye shall not afflict any widow, or fatherless child. If thou afflict them in any wise—for if they cry at all unto Me, I will surely hear their cry— My wrath shall wax hot, and I will kill you with the sword; and your wives shall be widows, and your children fatherless.

If thou lend money to any of My people, even to the poor with thee, thou shalt not be to him as a creditor; neither shall ye lay upon him interest. If thou at all take thy neighbour's garment to pledge, thou shalt restore it unto him by that the sun goeth down; for that is his only covering, it is his garment for his skin; wherein shall he sleep? and it shall come to pass, when he crieth unto Me, that I will hear; for I am gracious. . . .

22: 3–28

Thou shalt not utter a false report; put not thy hand with the wicked to be an unrighteous witness. Thou shalt not follow a multitude to do evil; neither shalt thou bear witness in a cause to turn aside after a multitude to pervert justice; neither shalt thou favour a poor man in his cause.

If thou meet thine enemy's ox or his ass going astray, thou shalt surely bring it back to him again.

If thou see the ass of him that hateth thee lying under its burden, thou shalt forbear to pass by him; thou shalt surely release it with him.

Thou shalt not wrest the judgment of thy poor in his cause. Keep thee far from a false matter; and the innocent and righteous slay thou not; for I will not justify the wicked. And thou shalt take no gift; for a gift blindeth them that have sight, and perverteth the words of the righteous. And a stranger shalt thou not oppress; for ye know the heart of a stranger, seeing ye were strangers in the land of Egypt.

23: 1–9

LEVITICUS

This is primarily a book of sacerdotal laws and practices, and is said to reflect the influence of the priest-ridden Babylonians in whose midst the Jews were held captive from 586 to 536 B.C. But even here one finds the characteristic stress on the ethical, piety being always identified with probity, and rite with right. "Ye shall be holy," the people are commanded—and then told that holiness is social decency.

And the LORD spoke unto Moses, saying: Speak unto all the congregation of the children of Israel, and say unto them:

Ye shall be holy; for I the LORD your God am holy. Ye shall fear every man his mother, and his father, and ye shall keep My sabbaths: I am the LORD your God. Turn ye not unto the idols, nor make to yourselves molten gods: I am the LORD your God. . . .

And when ye reap the harvest of your land, thou shalt not wholly reap the corner of thy field, neither shalt thou gather the gleaning of thy harvest. And thou shalt not glean thy vineyard, neither shalt thou gather the fallen fruit of thy vineyard; thou shalt leave them for the poor and for the stranger: I am the LORD your God. Ye shall not steal; neither shall ye deal falsely, nor lie one to another. And ye shall not swear by My name falsely, so that thou profane the name of thy God: I am the LORD. Thou shalt not oppress thy neighbour, nor rob him; the wages of a hired servant shall not abide with thee all night until the morning. Thou shalt not curse the deaf, nor put a stumbling-block before the blind, but thou shalt fear thy God: I am the LORD. Ye shall do no unrighteousness in judgment; thou shalt not respect the person of the poor, nor favour the person of the mighty; but in righteousness shalt thou judge thy neighbour. Thou shalt not go up and down as a talebearer among thy people; neither shalt thou stand idly by the blood of thy neighbour: I am the LORD. Thou shalt not hate thy brother in thy heart; thou shalt surely rebuke thy neighbour, and not bear sin because of him. Thou shalt not take vengeance, nor bear any grudge against the children of thy people, but thou shalt love thy neighbour as thyself: I am the LORD. . . .

19: 1–19

Turn ye not unto the ghosts, nor unto familiar spirits; seek them not out, to be defiled by them: I am the LORD your God. Thou shalt rise up before the hoary head, and honour the face of the old man, and thou shalt fear thy God: I am the LORD. And if a stranger sojourn with thee in your land, ye shall not do him wrong. The stranger that sojourneth with you shall be unto you as the home-born among you, and thou shalt love him as thyself; for ye were strangers in the land of Egypt: I am the LORD your God. Ye shall do no unrighteousness in judgment, in meteyard, in weight, or in measure. Just balances, just weights, a just ephah, and a just hin, shall ye have: I am the LORD your God, who brought you out of the land of Egypt. And ye shall observe all My statutes, and all Mine ordinances, and do them: I am the LORD. . . .

19: 31–37

Whatsoever man there be that curseth his father or his mother shall surely be put to death; he hath cursed his father or his mother; his blood shall be upon him. And the man that committeth adultery with another man's wife, even he that committeth adultery with his neighbour's wife, both the adulterer and the adulteress shall surely be put to death. And the man that lieth with his father's wife—he hath uncovered his father's nakedness—both of them shall surely be put to death; their blood shall be upon them. And if a man lie with his daughter-in-law, both of them shall surely be put to death; they have wrought corruption; their blood shall be upon them. And if a man lie with mankind, as with womankind, both of them have committed abomination: they shall surely be put to death; their blood shall be upon them. And if a man take with his wife also her mother, it is wickedness: they shall be burnt with fire, both he and they; that there be no wickedness among you. And if a man lie with a beast, he shall surely be put to death; and ye shall slay the beast. And if a woman approach unto any beast, and lie down thereto, thou shalt kill the woman, and the beast: they shall surely be put to death; their blood shall be upon them. And if a man shall take his sister, his father's daughter, or his mother's daughter, and see her nakedness, and she see his nakedness: it is a shameful thing; and they shall be cut off in the sight of the children of their people: he hath uncovered his sister's nakedness; he shall bear his iniquity. And if a man shall lie with a woman having her sickness, and shall uncover her nakedness—he hath nade naked her fountain, and she hath uncovered the fountain of her blood—both of them shall be cut off from among their people. And thou shalt not uncover the nakedness of thy mother's sister, nor of thy father's sister; for he hath made naked his near kin; they shall bear their iniquity. And if a man shall lie with his uncle's wife— he hath uncovered his uncle's nakedness—they shall bear their sin; they shall die childless. And if a man shall take his brother's wife, it is impurity: he hath uncovered his brother's nakedness; they shall be childless.

20: 9—21

DEUTERONOMY

According to tradition, this book contains the discourses delivered by Moses just before his death; but modern commentators believe it must have been composed at a much later date. Its language and spirit show the distinct influence of the succession of prophets beginning with Amos, and external evidence indicates that the document was published for the first time in 622 B.C. There is a striking lack of emphasis on the ritual laws, and an even more striking insistence on the importance of the moral ones. God is described not as a tribal deity gluttonous for flatteries and sacrifices, but as a Universal Ruler demanding most of all that men show kindness toward one another. If to be humane is a mark of wisdom, then this book is one of the wisest in the entire literature of mankind. For, as the following selections will make plain, Deuteronomy is—considering its age—phenomenally humane.

WHAT DOTH THE LORD REQUIRE?

And now, Israel, what doth the LORD thy God require of thee, but to fear the LORD thy God, to walk in all His ways, and to love Him, and to serve the LORD thy God with all thy heart and with all thy soul; to keep for thy good the commandments of the LORD, and His statutes, which I command thee this day? Behold, unto the LORD thy God belongeth the heaven, and the heaven of heavens, the earth, with all that therein is. Only the LORD had a delight in thy fathers to love them, and He chose their seed after them, even you, above all peoples, as it is this day. Circumcise therefore the foreskin of your heart, and be no more stiffnecked. For the Lord your God, He is God of gods, and Lord of lords, the great God, the mighty, and the awful, who regardeth not persons, nor taketh reward. He doth execute justice for the fatherless and widow, and loveth the stranger, in giving him food and raiment. Love ye therefore the stranger; for ye were strangers in the land of Egypt. Thou shalt fear the Lord thy God; Him shalt thou serve; and to Him shalt thou cleave, and by His name shalt thou swear. He is thy glory, and He is thy God, that hath done for thee these great and tremendous things, which thine eyes have seen.

10: 12–20

CONCERNING JUDGES

Judges and officers shalt thou make thee in all thy gates, which the Lord thy God giveth thee, tribe by tribe; and they shall judge the people with righteous judgment. Thou shalt not wrest judgment; thou shalt not respect persons; neither shalt thou take a gift; for a gift doth blind the eyes of the wise, and pervert the words of the righteous. Justice, justice shalt thou follow, that thou mayest live, and inherit the land which the Lord thy God giveth thee.

16: 18–20

AGAINST IDOLATRY

When thou art come into the land which the Lord thy God giveth thee, thou shalt not learn to do after the abominations of those nations. There shall not be found among you any one that maketh his son or his daughter to pass through the fire, one that useth divination, a soothsayer, or an enchanter, or a sorcerer, or a charmer, or one that consulteth a ghost or a familiar spirit, or a necromancer. For whosoever doeth these things is an abomination unto the Lord; and because of these abominations the Lord thy God is driving them out from before thee. Thou shalt be whole-hearted with the Lord thy

God. For these nations, that thou art to dispossess, hearken unto soothsayers, and unto diviners; but as for thee, the Lord thy God hath not suffered thee so to do. A prophet will the Lord thy God raise up unto thee, from the midst of thee, of thy brethren, like unto me; unto him ye shall hearken.

18: 9–15

CONCERNING WITNESSES

One witness shall not rise up against a man for any iniquity, or for any sin, in any sin that he sinneth; at the mouth of two witnesses, or at the mouth of three witnesses, shall a matter be established. If an unrighteous witness rise up against any man to bear perverted witness against him; then both the men, between whom the controversy is, shall stand before the Lord, before the priests and the judges that shall be in those days. And the judges shall inquire diligently; and, behold, if the witness be a false witness, and hath testified falsely against his brother; then shall ye do unto him, as he had purposed to do unto his brother; so shalt thou put away the evil from the midst of thee. And those that remain shall hear, and fear, and shall henceforth commit no more any such evil in the midst of thee.

19: 15–20

THE WICKED SON

If a man have a stubborn and rebellious son, that will not hearken to the voice of his father, or the voice of his mother, and though they chasten him, will not hearken unto them; then shall his father and his mother lay hold on him, and bring him out unto the elders of his city, and unto the gate of his place; and they shall say unto the elders of his city: 'This our son is stubborn and rebellious, he doth not hearken to our voice; he is a glutton, and a drunkard.' And all the men of his city shall stone him with stones, that he die; so shalt thou put away the evil from the midst of thee; and all Israel shall hear, and fear.

21: 18–21

SUNDRY LAWS

Thou shalt not see thy brother's ox or his sheep driven away, and hide thyself from them; thou shalt surely bring them back unto thy brother. And if thy brother be not nigh unto thee, and thou know him not, then thou shalt bring it home to thy house, and it shall be with thee until thy brother require it, and thou shalt restore it to him. And so shalt thou do with his ass; and so shalt thou do with his garment; and so shalt thou do with every lost thing of thy brother's, which he hath lost, and thou hast found; thou mayest not hide thyself.

Thou shalt not see thy brother's ass or his ox fallen down by the way, and hide thyself from them; thou shalt surely help him to lift them up again.

A woman shall not wear that which pertaineth unto a man, neither shall a man put on a woman's garment; for whosoever doeth these things is an abomination unto the Lord thy God.

If a bird's nest chance to be before thee in the way, in any tree or on the ground, with young ones or eggs, and the dam sitting upon the young, or upon the eggs, thou shalt not take the dam with the young; thou shalt in any wise let the dam go, but the young thou mayest take unto thyself; that it may be well with thee, and that thou mayest prolong thy days.

When thou buildest a new house, then thou shalt make a parapet for thy roof, that thou bring not blood upon thy house, if any man fall from thence. . . .

Thou shalt not plow with an ox and an ass together. Thou shalt not wear a mingled stuff, wool and linen together.

22: 1–10

No man shall take the mill or the upper millstone to pledge; for he taketh a man's life to pledge.

If a man be found stealing any of his brethren of the children of Israel, and he deal with him as a slave, and sell him; then that thief shall die; so shalt thou put away the evil from the midst of thee.

24: 6–7

When thou dost lend thy neighbour any manner of loan, thou shalt not go into his house to fetch his pledge. Thou shalt stand without, and the man to whom thou dost lend shall bring forth the pledge without unto thee. And if he be a poor man, thou shalt not sleep with his pledge; thou shalt surely restore to him the pledge when the sun goeth down, that he may sleep in his garment, and bless thee; and it shall be righteousness unto thee before the LORD thy God.

Thou shalt not oppress a hired servant that is poor and needy, whether he be of thy brethren, or of thy strangers that are in thy land within thy gates. In the same day thou shalt give him his hire, neither shall the sun go down upon it; for he is poor, and setteth his heart upon it; lest he cry against thee unto the LORD, and it be sin in thee.

The fathers shall not be put to death for the children, neither shall the children be put to death for the fathers; every man shall be put to death for his own sin.

Thou shalt not pervert the justice due to the stranger, or to the fatherless; nor take the widow's raiment to pledge. But thou shalt remember that thou wast a bondman in Egypt, and the LORD thy God redeemed thee thence; therefore I command thee to do this thing.

When thou reapest thy harvest in thy field, and hast forgot a sheaf in the field, thou shalt not go back to fetch it; it shall be for the stranger, for the fatherless, and for the widow; that the LORD thy God may bless thee in all the work of thy hands.

When thou beatest thine olive-tree, thou shalt not go over the boughs again; it shall be for the stranger, for the fatherless, and for the widow. When thou gatherest the grapes of thy vineyard, thou shalt not glean it after thee; it shall be for the stranger, for the fatherless, and for the widow. And thou shalt remember that thou wast a bondman in the land of Egypt; therefore I command thee to do this thing.

24: 10–22

THEY WHO ARE CURSED

Cursed be the man that maketh a graven or molten image, an abomination unto the LORD, the work of the hands of the craftsman, and setteth it up in secret. And all the people shall answer and say: Amen.

Cursed be he that dishonoureth his father or his mother. And all the people shall say: Amen.

Cursed be he that removeth his neighbour's landmark. And all the people shall say: Amen.

Cursed be he that maketh the blind to go astray in the way. And all the people shall say: Amen.

Cursed be he that perverteth the justice due to the stranger, fatherless, and widow. And all the people shall say: Amen.

Cursed be he that lieth with his father's wife; because he hath uncovered his father's skirt. And all the people shall say: Amen.

Cursed be he that lieth with any manner of beast. And all the people shall say: Amen.

Cursed be he that lieth with his sister, the daughter of his father, or the daughter of his mother. And all the people shall say: Amen.

Cursed be he that lieth with his mother-in-law. And all the people shall say: Amen.

Cursed be he that smiteth his neighbour in secret. And all the people shall say: Amen.

Cursed be he that taketh a bribe to slay an innocent person. And all the people shall say: Amen.

Cursed be he that confirmeth not the words of this law to do them. And all the people shall say: Amen.

28: 15–26

THE NEVI'IM

The second grand division of the Jewish Bible contains the books of the NEVI'IM, the "Prophets." In the beginning those prophets were probably in a class with the witch-doctors and medicine men of all other primitive races. By the eighth century B.C. however, their character had completely changed. They had somehow become men whose distinction lay in their moral courage rather than their magical craft, men who sought to sway the populace by dint of preaching ideals rather than casting spells. They ceased to be mere foretellers and became forthtellers.

This change occurred gradually of course, and signs of it are clearly observable in the stories told about certain prophets who lived long before the eighth century. Once the Hebrews overran the Land of Canaan, they naturally tended to forsake their stark old desert way of life. Formerly they had all been poor and therefore equal; but now, settled in fertile places, some among them grew rich, and sharp social distinctions resulted. Formerly they had been remote from civilization, so their wants had been simple and their morals correspondingly stern; but now, surrounded by citified races, they learned to crave luxuries, and their standards grew more and more lax. And it was apparently these things that first goaded the prophets to become more than mere thaumaturgists. Being anxious to maintain the old religion, they were necessarily disquieted by all new fashions, and took to denouncing them with increasing passion. They became the voice of Israel's conscience, the chronic "troublers" in the land; and though ideologically reactionaries, practically they proved themselves revolutionists.

THE BOOK OF AMOS

With Amos, who lived in the first half of the eighth century, B.C., the evolution of the Hebrew prophet from conjurer to reformer becomes complete. He was apparently the first whose greatness was seen to lie primarily in what he had to say, and whose words were *therefore remembered to the exclusion of almost all else about the man. The little book containing his utterances is one of the marvels of literature both because of its subject matter and style. Amos was no more than a peasant by calling, a mere casual laborer in a remote hill-country; yet he managed to voice ideas so startlingly advanced for his day that he deserves to be ranked with the supreme sages of all time. Briefly, his ideas were these: (1) God cares for all peoples, not just the Israelites; (2) He will show the latter no special favor unless they show special diligence in following His ways; (3) His ways are the ways of righteousness, and they can be followed only by doing good, not by performing rites; (4) unless the Israelites do follow them, and at once, God Himself will devour their land.*

Leaving his flocks, Amos went down into the fat valley-lands where the people had become most corrupt, and he cried:

The words of Amos, who was among the herdmen of Tekoa, which he saw concerning Israel in the days of Uzziah king of Judah, and in the days of Jeroboam the son of Joash king of Israel, two years before the earthquake:

And he said:
The LORD roareth from Zion,
And uttereth His voice from Jerusalem;
And the pastures of the shepherds shall mourn,
And the top of Carmel shall wither. . . .
Because they sell the righteous for silver,
And the needy for a pair of shoes;
That pant after the dust of the earth on the head of the poor,
And turn aside the way of the humble;
And a man and his father go unto the same maid,
To profane My holy name;
And they lay themselves down beside every altar

Upon clothes taken in pledge,
And in the house of their God they drink
The wine of them that have been fined. . . .

1: 1–2; 2: 6–8

They know not to do right, saith the LORD,
Who store up violence and robbery in their palaces.
Therefore thus saith the Lord GOD:
An adversary, even round about the land!
And he shall bring down thy strength from thee,
And thy palaces shall be spoiled.
Thus saith the LORD:
As the shepherd rescueth out of the mouth of the lion
Two legs, or a piece of an ear,
So shall the children of Israel that dwell in Samaria
Escape with the corner of a couch, and the leg of a bed.

3: 10–12

Hear ye this word which I take up for a lamentation over you, O house of Israel:

The virgin of Israel is fallen,
She shall no more rise;
She is cast down upon her land,
There is none to raise her up.

For thus saith the Lord GOD: The city that went forth a thousand shall have a hundred left, and that which went forth a hundred shall have ten left, of the house of Israel.

For thus saith the LORD unto the house of Israel:

Seek ye Me, and live; . . .
Seek the LORD, and live—
Lest He break out like fire in the house of Joseph,
And it devour, and there be none to quench it in Beth-el—
Ye who turn justice to wormwood,
And cast righteousness to the ground;
Him that maketh the Pleiades and Orion,
And bringeth on the shadow of death in the morning,

And darkeneth the day into night;
That calleth for the waters of the sea,
And poureth them out upon the face of the earth;
The Lord is His name;
That causeth destruction to flash upon the strong,
So that destruction cometh upon the fortress. . . .
Because ye trample upon the poor,
And take from him exactions of wheat;
Ye have built houses of hewn stone,
But ye shall not dwell in them,
Ye have planted pleasant vineyards,
But ye shall not drink the wine thereof.
For I know how manifold are your transgressions,
And how mighty are your sins;
Ye that afflict the just, that take a ransom,
And that turn aside the needy in the gate. . . .

Seek good, and not evil, that ye may live;
And so the Lord, the God of hosts, will be with you,
        as ye say.
Hate the evil, and love the good,
And establish justice in the gate;
It may be that the Lord, the God of hosts,
Will be gracious unto the remnant of Joseph. . . .

I hate, I despise your feasts,
And I will take no delight in your solemn assemblies.
Yea, though ye offer me burnt-offerings and your meal-
        offerings,
I will not accept them;
Neither will I regard the peace-offerings of your fat
        beasts.
Take thou away from Me the noise of thy songs;
And let Me not hear the melody of thy psalteries.
But let justice well up as waters,
And righteousness as a mighty stream.

                                              5: 1–24

Then Amaziah the priest of Beth-el sent to Jeroboam king of
Israel, saying: 'Amos hath conspired against thee in the midst of the

house of Israel; the land is not able to bear all his words. For thus
Amos saith:

> Jeroboam shall die by the sword,
> And Israel shall surely be led away captive out of his land.'

Also Amaziah said unto Amos: 'O thou seer, go, flee thee away into
the land of Judah, and there eat bread, and prophesy there; but
prophesy not again any more at Beth-el, for it is the king's sanctuary,
and it is a royal house.' Then answered Amos, and said to Amaziah:
'I was no prophet, neither was I a prophet's son; but I was a herd-
man, and a dresser of sycomore-trees; and the LORD took me from
following the flock, and the LORD said unto me: Go, prophesy unto
My people Israel. Now therefore hear thou the word of the LORD:

> Thou sayest: Prophesy not against Israel,
> And preach not against the house of Isaac;
> Therefore thus saith the LORD:
> Thy wife shall be a harlot in the city,
> And thy sons and thy daughters shall fall by the sword,
> And thy land shall be divided by line;
> And thou thyself shalt die in an unclean land,
> And Israel shall surely be led away captive out of his land.'

7: 10–17

THE BOOK OF HOSEA

*Little is known about Hosea save that he lived in the eighth cen-
tury, B.C., and followed in the wake of Amos as a religious exhorter.
He too inveighed against the profligacy of Israel, crying "there is no
truth, no mercy, no knowledge of God in the land," but only "swearing and lying and killing and stealing and committing adultery." But,
by contrast with Amos, he sees more chance of salvation, for to him
the Lord is a God of mercy, not merely justice.*

> Hear the word of the LORD, ye children of Israel!
> For the LORD hath a controversy with the inhabitants
>   of the land,
> Because there is no truth, nor mercy,

Nor knowledge of God in the land.
Swearing and lying, and killing, and stealing, and com-
    mitting adultery!
They break all bounds, and blood toucheth blood.
Therefore doth the land mourn,
And every one that dwelleth therein doth languish,
With the beasts of the field and the fowls of heaven;
Yea, the fishes of the sea also are taken away.

Yet let no man strive, neither let any man reprove;
For thy people are as they that strive with the priest.
Therefore shalt thou
    stumble in the
    day,
And the prophet also
    shall stumble with
    thee in the night;
And I will destroy thy
    mother.
My people are destroyed
    for lack of knowl-
    edge;
Because thou hast re-
    jected knowledge,
I will also reject thee,
    that thou shalt be
    no priest to Me;
Seeing thou hast forgotten the law of thy God,
I also will forget thy children.

The more they were increased, the more they sinned
    against Me;
I will change their glory into shame.
They feed on the sin of My people,
And set their heart on their iniquity.
And it is like people, like priest;
And I will punish him for his ways,
And will recompense him his doings.
And they shall eat, and not have enough,

They shall commit harlotry, and shall not increase;
Because they have left off to take heed to the LORD.

4: 1—10

And their women with child shall be ripped up,
Return, O Israel, unto the LORD thy God;
For thou hast stumbled in thine iniquity.
Take with you words,
And return unto the LORD;
Say unto Him: 'Forgive all iniquity,
And accept that which is good;
So will we render for bullocks the offering of our lips.
Asshur shall not save us;
We will not ride upon horses;
Neither will we call any more the work of our hands our
　　gods;
For in Thee the fatherless findeth mercy.'
I will heal their backsliding,
I will love them freely;
For Mine anger is turned away from him.
I will be as the dew unto Israel;
He shall blossom as the lily,
And cast forth his roots as Lebanon.
His branches shall spread,
And his beauty shall be as the olive-tree,
And his fragrance as Lebanon.
They that dwell under his shadow shall again
Make corn to grow,
And shall blossom as the vine;
The scent thereof shall be as the wine of Lebanon.
Ephraim [shall say]:
'What have I to do any more with idols?'
As for Me, I respond and look on him;
I am like a leafy cypress-tree;
From Me is thy fruit found.

Whoso is wise, let him understand these things,
Whoso is prudent, let him know them.
For the ways of the LORD are right,

And the just do walk in them;
But transgressors do stumble therein.

14: 1–10

THE BOOK OF ISAIAH

Not all the prophets were of lowly origin like Amos. Some came from the upper class, most notably Isaiah, who served as a sort of spiritual statesman in Judah throughout the last third of the eighth century B.C. *He too denounced the folly of a crudely sacerdotal religion, and the menace of a grossly unjust social order. He too was convinced that the God of Israel ruled over all the earth, and that righteousness alone could win His favor. For all these reasons he too was in the profoundest sense a revolutionist.*

Here are a few excerpts from the collection of Isaiah's sermons to be found in the first thirty-nine chapters of the book which bears his name:

The vision of Isaiah the son of Amoz, which he saw concerning Judah and Jerusalem, in the days of Uzziah, Jotham, Ahaz, and Hezekiah, kings of Judah.

Hear, O heavens, and give ear, O earth,
For the LORD hath spoken:
Children I have reared, and brought up,
And they have rebelled against Me.
The ox knoweth his owner,
And the ass his master's crib;
But Israel doth not know,
My people doth not consider.

Ah sinful nation,
A people laden with iniquity,
A seed of evil-doers,
Children that deal corruptly;
They have forsaken the LORD,
They have contemned the Holy One of Israel,
They are turned away backward. . . .

Hear the word of the LORD,
Ye rulers of Sodom;
Give ear unto the law of our God,
Ye people of Gomorrah.
To what purpose is the multitude of your sacrifices unto Me?
Saith the LORD;
I am full of the burnt-offerings of rams,
And the fat of fed beasts;
And I delight not in the blood
Of bullocks, or of lambs, or of he-goats.

When ye come to appear before Me,
Who hath required this at your hand,
To trample My courts?
Bring no more vain oblations;
It is an offering of abomination unto Me;
New moon and sabbath, the holding of convocations—
I cannot endure iniquity along with the solemn assembly.
Your new moons and your appointed seasons
My soul hateth;

They are a burden unto Me;
I am weary to bear them.
And when ye spread forth your hands,
I will hide Mine eyes from you;
Yea, when ye make many prayers,
I will not hear;
Your hands are full of blood.
Wash you, make you clean,
Put away the evil of your doings
From before Mine eyes,
Cease to do evil;
Learn to do well;
Seek justice, relieve the oppressed,
Judge the fatherless, plead for the widow.

Come now, and let us reason together,
Saith the LORD;
Though your sins be as scarlet,
They shall be as white as snow;
Though they be red like crimson,
They shall be as wool.
If ye be willing and obedient,
Ye shall eat the good of the land;
But if ye refuse and rebel,
Ye shall be devoured with the sword;
For the mouth of the LORD hath spoken.

1: 1—20

Woe unto them that join house to house,
That lay field to field,
Till there be no room, and ye be made to dwell
Alone in the midst of the land!
In mine ears said the LORD of hosts:
Of a truth many houses shall be desolate,
Even great and fair, without inhabitant.
For ten acres of vineyard shall yield one bath,
And the seed of a homer shall yield an ephah.

Woe unto them that rise up early in the morning
That they may follow strong drink;
That tarry late into the night,
Till wine inflame them!
And the harp and the psaltery, the tabret and the pipe,
And wine, are in their feasts;
But they regard not the work of the LORD,
Neither have they considered the operation of His
    hands.
Therefore My people are gone into captivity,
For want of knowledge;
And their honourable men are famished,
And their multitude are parched with thirst.
Therefore the nether-world hath enlarged her desire,
And opened her mouth without measure;
And down goeth their glory, and their tumult, and their
    uproar,

And he that rejoiceth among them.
And man is bowed down,
And man is humbled,
And the eyes of the lofty are humbled;
But the LORD of hosts is exalted through justice,
And God the Holy One is sanctified through righteous-
    ness.
Then shall the lambs feed as in their pasture,
And the waste places of the fat ones shall wanderers eat.

Woe unto them that draw iniquity with cords of vanity,
And sin as it were with a cart rope,
That say: 'Let Him make speed, let Him hasten His
    work,
That we may see it;
And let the counsel of the Holy One of Israel draw nigh
    and come,
That we may know it!'

Woe unto them that call evil good,
And good evil;
That change darkness into light,
And light into darkness;
That change bitter into sweet,
And sweet into bitter!

Woe unto them that are wise in their own eyes,
And prudent in their own sight!

Woe unto them that are mighty to drink wine,
And men of strength to mingle strong drink;
That justify the wicked for a reward,
And take away the righteousness of the righteous from
    him!
Therefore as the tongue of fire devoureth the stubble,
And as the chaff is consumed in the flame,
So their root shall be as rottenness,
And their blossom shall go up as dust;
Because they have rejected the law of the LORD of hosts.
And contemned the word of the Holy One of Israel.

Therefore is the anger of the LORD kindled against His
  people,
And He hath stretched forth His hand against them,
  and hath smitten them,
And the hills did tremble,
And their carcasses were as refuse in the midst of the
  the streets.
For all this His anger is not turned away,
But His hand is stretched out still.

5: 8–25

And there shall come forth a shoot out of the stock of
  Jesse,
And a twig shall grow forth out of his roots.
And the spirit of the LORD shall rest upon him,
The spirit of wisdom and understanding,
The spirit of counsel and might,
The spirit of knowledge and of the fear of the LORD.
And his delight shall be in the fear of the LORD;
And he shall not judge after the sight of his eyes,
Neither decide after the hearing of his ears;
But with righteousness shall he judge the poor,
And decide with equity for the meek of the land;
And he shall smite the land with the rod of his mouth,
And with the breath of his lips shall he slay the wicked.
And righteousness shall be the girdle of his loins,
And faithfulness the girdle of his reins.
And the wolf shall dwell with the lamb,
And the leopard shall lie down with the kid;
And the calf and the young lion and the fatling together;
And a little child shall lead them.
And the cow and the bear shall feed;
Their young ones shall lie down together;
And the lion shall eat straw like the ox.
And the sucking child shall play on the hole of the asp,
And the weaned child shall put his hand on the basilisk's
  den.
They shall not hurt nor destroy
In all My holy mountain;

For the earth shall be full of the knowledge of the
    Lord,
As the waters cover the sea.

And it shall come to pass in that day,
That the root of Jesse, that standeth for an ensign of
    the peoples,
Unto him shall the nations seek;
And his resting-place shall be glorious.

11: 1–10

THE BOOK OF MICAH

Micah was a contemporary of Isaiah, and perhaps a disciple. His aim, however, seems to have been to influence the people rather than their rulers, for he took pains to express himself in a language that the very simplest folk could understand. If he lacked originality in what he said, he more than made up for it by the brilliance with which he said it. For example:

Hear, ye peoples, all of you;
Hearken, O earth, and all that therein is;
And let the Lord God be witness against you,
The Lord from His holy temple.
For, behold, the Lord cometh forth out of His place,
And will come down, and tread upon the high places
    of the earth.
And the mountains shall be molten under Him,
And the valleys shall be cleft,
As wax before the fire,
As waters that are poured down a steep place.

1: 2–4

But in the end of days it shall come to pass,
That the mountain of the Lord's house shall be estab-
    lished as the top of the mountains,
And it shall be exalted above the hills;
And peoples shall flow unto it.
And many nations shall go and say:
'Come ye, and let us go up to the mountain of the Lord,

And to the house of the God of Jacob;
And He will teach us of His ways,
And we will walk in His paths';

For out of Zion shall go forth the law,
And the word of the LORD from Jerusalem.
And He shall judge between many peoples,
And shall decide concerning mighty nations afar off;
And they shall beat their swords into plowshares,
And their spears into pruning-hooks;
Nation shall not lift up
    sword against na-
    tion,
Neither shall they learn
    war any more.
But they shall sit every
    man under his vine
    and under his fig-
    tree;
And none shall make
    them afraid;
For the mouth of the
    LORD of hosts hath
    spoken.

For let all the peoples walk each one in the name of
    its god,
But we will walk in the name of the LORD our God for
    ever and ever.

In that day, saith the LORD, will I assemble her that
    halteth,
And I will gather her that is driven away,
And her that I have afflicted;
And I will make her that halted a remnant,
And her that was cast far off a mighty nation;
And the LORD shall reign over them in mount Zion from
    thenceforth even for ever.

4: 1–7

'Wherewith shall I come before the Lord,
And bow myself before God on high?
Shall I come before Him with burnt-offerings,
With calves of a year old?
Will the Lord be pleased with thousands of rams,
With ten thousands of rivers of oil?
Shall I give my first-born for my transgression,
The fruit of my body for the sin of my soul?'
It hath been told thee, O man, what is good,
And what the Lord doth require of thee:
Only to do justly, and to love mercy, and to walk humbly
　　with thy God.

6: 6–8

THE BOOK OF JEREMIAH

There is sufficient biographical material in this book to give us some notion of what hardships the prophets were made to suffer. Jeremiah himself, we read, was seized on at least one occasion, beaten, imprisoned, and left to die in a pit. When he escaped, it was only to continue agitating for the religious and moral reforms which he believed to be demanded by the Lord.

Jeremiah was born in 650 B.C., and preached during the most trying years in the history of Judah, years which saw it thrice invaded and finally subjugated by Babylonian armies. Throughout that period, one marked by the most intense nationalism, he kept insisting that Yahveh was the God of all nations, and that He would help the Judeans only if they repented their manifold sins. Said he:

Return, thou backsliding Israel,
Saith the Lord;
I will not frown upon you;
For I am merciful, saith the Lord,
I will not bear grudge for ever.
Only acknowledge thine iniquity,
That thou hast transgressed against the Lord thy God,
And hast scattered thy ways to the strangers

Under every leafy tree,
And ye have not hearkened to My voice,
Saith the LORD.

3: 12–13

If thou wilt return, O Israel,
Saith the LORD,
Yea, return unto Me;
And if thou wilt put away thy detestable things out of
      My sight,
And wilt not waver;
And wilt swear: 'As the LORD liveth,'
In truth, in justice, and in righteousness;
Then shall the nations bless themselves by Him,
And in Him shall they glory.

4: 1–2

The word that came to Jeremiah from the LORD, saying: Stand in the gate of the LORD's house, and proclaim there this word, and say: Hear the word of the LORD, all ye of Judah, that enter in at these gates to worship the LORD. Thus saith the LORD of hosts, the God of Israel:

Amend your ways and your doings, and I will cause you to dwell in this place. Trust ye not in lying words, saying: 'The Temple of the LORD, the temple of the LORD, the temple of the LORD, are these.' Nay, but if ye thoroughly amend your ways and your doings; if ye thoroughly execute justice between a man and his neighbour; if ye oppress not the stranger, the fatherless, and the widow, and shed not innocent blood in this place, neither walk after other gods to your hurt; then will I cause you to dwell in this place, in the land that I gave to your fathers, for ever and ever. Behold, ye trust in lying words, that cannot profit. Will ye steal, murder, and commit adultery, and swear falsely, and offer unto Baal, and walk after other gods whom ye have not known, and come and stand before Me in this house, whereupon My name is called, and say: 'We are delivered,' that ye may do all these abominations? Is this house, whereupon My name is called, become a den of robbers in your eyes? Behold, I, even I, have seen it, saith the LORD.

7: 1–10

THE SECOND ISAIAH

The temptation to lose themselves in Babylonia was very strong among the bedraggled exiles from Judah; but more prophets arose to carry on Jeremiah's work, and thanks to them the temptation was resisted. One of these was a supremely eloquent man whose name is unknown, but whose utterances are preserved in the latter part of the Book of Isaiah. For that reason modern scholars usually speak of him as the "Second Isaiah." The mission of this prophet was apparently threefold: first to keep his people from succumbing to the idolatry all around them; second, to remind them that righteousness, not ritualism, was what their God desired; third, to assure them that soon, very soon, they would be restored to their homeland, and that they would then be raised to a glory infinitely greater than any they had known before.

Comfort ye, comfort ye My people,
Saith your God.
Bid Jerusalem take heart,
And proclaim unto her,
That her time of service is accomplished,
That her guilt is paid off;
That she hath received of the LORD's hand
Double for all her sins.

Hark! one calleth:
'Clear ye in the wilderness the way of the LORD,
Make plain in the desert
A highway for our God.

Every valley shall be lifted up,
And every mountain and hill shall be made low;
And the rugged shall be made level,
And the rough places a plain;
And the glory of the LORD shall be revealed,
And all flesh shall see it together;
For the mouth of the LORD hath spoken it.'

40: 1–5

Break forth into joy, sing together,
Ye waste places of Jerusalem;
For the LORD hath comforted His people,
He hath redeemed Jerusalem.
The LORD hath made bare His holy arm
In the eyes of all the nations;
And all the ends of the earth shall see
The salvation of our God.

Depart ye, depart ye, go ye out from thence,
Touch no unclean thing;
Go ye out of the midst of her; be ye clean,
Ye that bear the vessels of the LORD.
For ye shall not go out in haste,
Neither shall ye go by flight;
For the LORD will go before you,
And the God of Israel will be your rearward.

53: 9–11

Thus saith the LORD:
Keep ye justice, and do righteousness;
For My salvation is near to come,
And my favour to be revealed.
Happy is the man that doeth this,
And the son of man that holdeth fast by it,
That keepeth the sabbath from profaning it,
And keepeth his hand from doing any evil.
Neither let the alien,
That hath joined himself to the LORD, speak, saying:
'The LORD will surely separate me from His people';
Neither let the eunuch say:

'Behold, I am a dry tree.'
For thus saith the LORD
Concerning the eunuchs that keep My sabbaths,
And choose the things that please Me,
And hold fast by My covenant:
Even unto them will I give in My house
And within My walls a monument and a memorial
Better than sons and daughters;
I will give them an everlasting memorial,
That shall not be cut off.
Also the aliens, that join themselves to the LORD,
        to minister unto Him,
And to love the name of the LORD,
To be His servants,
Every one that keepeth the sabbath from profaning it,
And holdeth fast by My covenant:
Even them will I bring to My holy mountain,
And make them joyful in My house of prayer;
Their burnt-offerings and their sacrifices
Shall be acceptable upon Mine altar;
For My house shall be called
A house of prayer for all peoples.
Saith the Lord GOD who gathereth the dispersed
        of Israel:
Yet will I gather others to him, beside those of him
        that are gathered.   56: 1–8

Behold, ye fast for strife and contention,
And to smite with the fist of wickedness;
Ye fast not this day
So as to make your voice to be heard on high.
Is such the fast that I have chosen?
The day for a man to afflict his soul?
Is it to bow down his head as a bulrush,
And to spread sackcloth and ashes under him?
Wilt thou call this a fast,
And an acceptable day to the LORD?
Is not *this* the fast that I have chosen?
To loose the fetters of wickedness,

To undo the bands of the yoke,
And to let the oppressed go free,
And that ye break every yoke?
Is it not to deal thy bread to the hungry,
And that thou bring the poor that are cast out to
thy house?
When thou seest the naked, that thou cover him,
And that thou hide not thyself from thine own flesh?
Then shall thy light break forth as the morning,
And thy healing shall spring forth speedily;
And thy righteousness shall go before thee,
The glory of the LORD shall be thy rearward.
Then shalt thou call, and the LORD will answer;
Thou shalt cry, and He will say: 'Here I am.'
If thou take away from the midst of thee the yoke,
The putting forth of the finger, and speaking wickedness;
And if thou draw out thy soul to the hungry,
And satisfy the afflicted soul;
Then shall thy light rise in darkness,
And thy gloom be as the noonday;
And the LORD will guide thee continually,
And satisfy thy soul in drought,
And make strong thy bones;
And thou shalt be like a watered garden,
And like a spring of water, whose waters fail not.
And they that shall be of thee shall build the old
waste places,
Thou shalt raise up the foundations of many generations;
And thou shalt be called The repairer of the breach,
The restorer of paths to dwell in.   58: 4–12

Arise, shine, for thy light is come,
And the glory of the LORD is risen upon thee.
For, behold, darkness shall cover the earth,
And gross darkness the peoples;
But upon thee the LORD will arise,
And His glory shall be seen upon thee.
And nations shall walk at thy light,
And kings at the brightness of thy rising.   60: 1–3

THE KETUBIM

The third main division of the Jewish Bible is called KETUBIM, "Writings," and it contains—among other documents—at least three that are in the classic sense Books of Wisdom. These are entitled PROVERBS, JOB, and ECCLESIASTES, and though traditionally ascribed to very ancient authors, all three are apparently of late origin. In their present form they belong to the period following 332 B.C., the year Alexander the Great overran Palestine.

Long before that date we find a new class of spiritual advisers emerging in Judea: the so-called hahamim, "sages." These are not the hereditary priests who laid down the "law," nor the inspired prophets who uttered the "word"; they are instead the deliberate men of learning who gave shrewd "counsel." They took their stand in the market place, or by the city gates, and proffered instruction to the people by means of parables. Or they collected disciples in their homes, and discoursed to them in strophes and proverbs. They thus resembled the early Greek philosophers, and once direct contact was established with the Greek-speaking world, this resemblance increased. That world had already amassed a great store of "wisdom literature," and it was only natural for the Jewish sages to covet a like store of their own. This led to more and more imitation of the Greek writings, and eventually considerable assimilation of the Greek ideas.

By the time that happened, however, the basic slant of the Jewish outlook on life had already become fixed; so Jewish wisdom was merely enriched, not unmade, by this new trend. The books that now began to be produced in Judea may have had a Greek coloring and texture, but the stuff inside them was still Hebraic through and through. Their abiding emphasis was still on God as the source of all things, and on morality as the way to all good. Wisdom, in them, was no vague mystical emanation, or recondite intellectual hypostasis. It was simply—Righteousness. First and last it was nothing but a sort of sanctified human decency.

THE BOOK OF PSALMS

The most renowned of the KETUBIM, *however, is a book of piety, not intellectualism. This is the collection of hymns called in Hebrew T'hillim ("Praises") and ascribed to various composers, among them King David.*

Other ancient peoples—for example, the Egyptians, Babylonians, and Hindus—produced great religious poetry; but none seems to have matched the Jews in this field. For loftiness of thought, intensity of emotion, simplicity of language, and grandeur of cadence, the Hebrew Psalms are quite without peer.

HAPPY ARE THE PIOUS

Psalm 1

Happy is the man that hath
    not walked in the coun-
    sel of the wicked,
Nor stood in the way of sin-
    ners,
Nor sat in the seat of the
    scornful.
But his delight is in the law
    of the LORD;
And in His law doth he medi-
    tate day and night.
And he shall be like a tree
    planted by streams of
    water,
That bringeth forth its fruit
    in its season,
And whose leaf doth not
    wither;
And in whatsoever he doeth
    he shall proper.

Not so the wicked;
But they are like the chaff which the wind driveth away.
Therefore the wicked shall not stand in the judgment,

Nor sinners in the congregation of the righteous.
For the LORD regardeth the way of the righteous;
But the way of the wicked shall perish.

THE FRIEND OF GOD

Psalm 15

LORD, who shall sojourn in Thy tabernacle?
Who shall dwell upon Thy holy mountain?
He that walketh uprightly, and worketh righteousness,
'Flee thou! to your mountain, ye birds'?
For lo, the wicked bend the bow,
They have made ready their arrow upon the string,
That they may shoot in darkness at the upright in heart.
When the foundations are destroyed,
What hath the righteous wrought?

The LORD is in His holy temple,
The LORD, His throne is in heaven;
His eyes behold, His eyelids try, the children of men.
The LORD trieth the righteous;
But the wicked and him that loveth violence His soul
        hateth.

THE GOOD SHEPHERD

Psalm 23

The LORD is my shepherd; I shall not want.
He maketh me to lie down in green pastures;
He leadeth me beside the still waters.
He restoreth my soul;
He guideth me in straight paths for His name's sake.
Yea, though I walk through the valley of the shadow
        of death,
I will fear no evil,
For Thou art with me;
Thy rod and Thy staff, they comfort me.
Thou preparest a table before me in the presence of mine
        enemies;

Thou hast anointed my head with oil; my cup runneth
  over.
Surely goodness and mercy shall follow me all the days
  of my life;
And I shall dwell in the house of the LORD for ever.

THE TRIUMPH OF THE PIOUS

Psalm 54

O God, save me by Thy name,
And right me by Thy might.
O God, hear my prayer;
Give ear to the words of my mouth.
For strangers are risen up against me,
And violent men have sought after my soul;
They have not set God before them.
                    Selah

Behold, God is my helper;
The Lord is for me as the upholder of my soul.
He will requite the evil unto them that lie in wait for me;
Destroy Thou them in Thy truth.
With a freewill-offering will I sacrifice unto Thee;
I will give thanks unto Thy name, O LORD, for it is good.
For He hath delivered me out of all trouble;
And mine eye hath gazed upon mine enemies.

THE ROYAL CODE

Psalm 101

I will sing of mercy and justice;
Unto Thee, O LORD, will I sing praises.
I will give heed unto the way of integrity;
Oh when wilt Thou come unto me?
I will walk within my house in the integrity of my heart.

I will set no base thing before mine eyes;
I hate the doing of things crooked;
It shall not cleave unto me.

A perverse heart shall depart from me;
I will know no evil thing.

Whoso slandereth his neighbour in secret, him will I destroy;
Whoso is haughty of eye and proud of heart, him will
    I not suffer.
Mine eyes are upon the faithful of the land, that they
    may dwell with me;
He that walketh in a way of integrity, he shall minister
    unto me.
He that worketh deceit shall not dwell within my house;
He that speaketh falsehood shall not be established
    before mine eyes.
Morning by morning will I destroy all the wicked of the
    land;
To cut off all the workers of iniquity from the city of
    the Lord.

IN PRAISE OF UNITY

Psalm 133

Behold, how good and how pleasant it is
For brethren to dwell together in unity!
It is like the precious oil upon the head,
Coming down upon the beard;
Even Aaron's beard,
That cometh down upon the collar of his garments;
Like the dew of Hermon,
That cometh down upon the mountains of Zion;
For there the Lord commanded the blessing,
Even life for ever.

THE BOOK OF PROVERBS

*Despite its opening line, this book clearly belongs to the period
when kings were no more than a romantic memory in Judea. Its earliest
sections date back perhaps to around the year 400, and its latest to*

around 200 B.C. This is made plain by the sort of problems that are discussed, and even more by those that are left unmentioned. No reference is made to the danger of idolatry which so exercised the prophets, nor the value of the temple ritual which the priests were so emphatic about. No time is spent discussing purely national matters— the name Israel does not occur even once in the proverbs themselves— and the counsel throughout is universalistic. There is a frank appreciation of the good things of this earth—its prizes, honors, riches, and pleasures—and much canny advice as to how these can best be attained. Monogamy is taken for granted, commerce is ranked above husbandry, and prudence, thrift, and enterprise—characteristically urban virtues—are praised without stint. All of which indicates a relatively advanced social life.

The underlying tone, however, is still the one to be found in the more ancient Hebrew books. Though salvation is almost equated with prosperity in this document, the way to attain it is still Righteousness.

THE WORDS OF THE WISE

The proverbs of Solomon the
son of David, king of
Israel;
To know wisdom and instruction;
To comprehend the words of
understanding;
To receive the discipline of
wisdom,
Justice, and right, and equity;
To give prudence to the simple,
To the young man knowledge
and discretion;
That the wise man may hear,
and increase in learning,
And the man of understanding may attain unto wise
counsels;
To understand a proverb, and a figure;
The words of the wise, and their dark sayings.

The fear of the LORD is the beginning of knowledge;
But the foolish despise wisdom and discipline.
Hear, my son, the instruction of thy father,
And forsake not the teaching of thy mother;
For they shall be a chaplet of grace unto thy head,
And chains about thy neck.

My son, if sinners entice thee,
Consent thou not.
If they say: 'Come with us,
Let us lie in wait for blood,
Let us lurk for the innocent without cause;
Let us swallow them up alive as the grave,
And whole, as those that go down into the pit;
We shall find all precious substance,
We shall fill our houses with spoil;
Cast in thy lot among us;
Let us all have one purse'—
My son, walk not thou in the way with them,
Restrain thy foot from their path;
For their feet run to evil,
And they make haste to shed blood.
For in vain the net is spread
In the eyes of any bird;
And these lie in wait for their own blood,
They lurk for their own lives.
So are the ways of every one that is greedy of gain;
It taketh away the life of the owners thereof.

1: 1—19

GO TO THE ANT

Go to the ant, thou sluggard;
Consider her ways, and be wise;
Which having no chief,
Overseer, or ruler,
Provideth her bread in the summer,
And gathereth her food in the harvest.
How long wilt thou sleep, O sluggard?

When wilt thou arise out of thy sleep?
'Yet a little sleep, a little slumber,
A little folding of the hands to sleep'—
So shall thy poverty come as a runner,
And thy want as an armed man.

THE WAY OF THE WICKED

A base person, a man of inquity,
Is he that walketh with a froward mouth;
That winketh with his eyes, that scrapeth with his feet,
That pointeth with his fingers;
Frowardness is in his heart, he deviseth evil continually;
He soweth discord.
Therefore shall his calamity come suddenly;
On a sudden shall he be broken, and that without remedy.

SIX EVILS

There are six things which the LORD hateth,
Yea, seven which are an abomination unto Him:
Haughty eyes, a lying tongue,
And hands that shed innocent blood;
A heart that deviseth wicked thoughts,
Feet that are swift in running to evil;
A false witness that breatheth out lies,
And he that soweth discord among brethren.

6: 6–19

APHORISMS

A wise son maketh a glad father;
But a foolish son is the grief of his mother.

Treasures of wickedness profit nothing;
But righteousness delivereth from death.

The Lord will not suffer the soul of the righteous to
    famish;
But He thrusteth away the desire of the wicked.

He becometh poor that dealeth with a slack hand;
But the hand of the diligent maketh rich.

A wise son gathereth in summer;
But a son that doeth shamefully sleepeth in harvest.

Blessings are upon the head of the righteous;
But the mouth of the wicked concealeth violence.

The memory of the righteous shall be for a blessing;
But the name of the wicked shall rot.

The wise in heart will receive commandments;
But a prating fool shall fall.

He that walketh uprightly walketh securely;
But he that perverteth his ways shall be found out.

He that winketh with the eye causeth sorrow;
And a prating fool shall fall.

The mouth of the righteous is a fountain of life;
But the mouth of the wicked concealeth violence.

Hatred stirreth up strifes;
But love covereth all transgressions.

In the lips of him that hath discernment wisdom is
    found;
But a rod is for the back of him that is void of under-
    standing.

Wise men lay up knowledge;
But the mouth of the foolish is an imminent ruin.

10: 1—14

THE WOMAN OF VALOUR

A woman of valour who can find?
For her price is far above rubies.
The heart of her husband doth safely trust in her,
And he hath no lack of gain.
She doeth him good and not evil
All the days of her life.
She seeketh wool and flax,
And worketh willingly with her hands.
She is like the merchant-ships;
She bringeth her food from afar.
She riseth also while it is yet night,
And giveth food to her household,
And a portion to her maidens.

She considereth a field, and buyeth it;
With the fruit of her hands she planteth a vineyard.
She girdeth her loins with strength,
And maketh strong her arms.
She perceiveth that her merchandise is good;
Her lamp goeth not out by night.
She layeth her hands to the distaff,
And her hands hold the spindle.
She stretcheth out her hand to the poor;
Yea, she reacheth forth her hands to the needy.
She is not afraid of the snow for her household;
For all her household are clothed with scarlet.
She maketh for herself coverlets;
Her clothing is fine linen and purple.
Her husband is known in the gates,
When he sitteth among the elders of the land.
She maketh linen garments and selleth them;
And delivereth girdles unto the merchant.
Strength and dignity are her clothing;
And she laugheth at the time to come.
She openeth her mouth with wisdom;
And the law of kindness is on her tongue.
She looketh well to the ways of her household,

And eateth not the bread of idleness.
Her children rise up, and call her blessed;
Her husband also, and he praiseth her:
'Many daughters have done valiantly,
But thou excellest them all.'
Grace is deceitful, and beauty is vain;
But a woman that feareth the LORD, she shall be praised.
Give her of the fruit of her hands;
And let her works praise her in the gates.

31: 10–31

THE BOOK OF JOB

The Book of Proverbs, despite its occasional flashes of cynicism, is essentially an orthodox document, for its whole philosophy is based on the conviction that the righteous and the wicked are rewarded or punished according to their just deserts. By contrast the Book of Job is essentially unorthodox, for it starts out by insisting that such a conviction is not borne out by the facts of life. Consequently critical scholars believe the document must have been composed at a relatively late date—perhaps the third or even second century B.C.—when their own bitter experience plus Greek influence combined to make the Jews less naive than in earlier times.

In form this book is a philosophical symposium built into the framework of what may have been an old folk tale. It deals with the most perplexing of human problems: Why do the innocent suffer? According to the story, Job was a virtuous old sheikh, a man "perfect and upright, who feared God and shunned wickedness." Nevertheless, of a sudden all manner of evils befell him: his seven sons and three daughters were killed, all his flocks were destroyed, all his slaves were slaughtered, and he himself was smitten with leprosy. His first reaction was to suffer in silence. When his wife, a less patient soul, urges him to "curse God and die," he answers:[2]

"You speak as one of the foolish women might speak. Should we, indeed, receive good from God, and should we not receive evil too?"

2: 10

[2] According to J. M. Powis Smith in *The Complete Bible: An American Translation* (University of Chicago Press, 1939).

Eventually three of his friends come to comfort him as he sits on an ash-heap and scrapes his sores, but when they seem unable to find words to express their sympathy, the strain proves too much for Job. He suspects that they, being conventional folk, probably imagine that God is punishing him for some sin he has committed. Whereupon he bursts forth bitterly:

"Why did I not die at birth,
Come forth from the womb
    and expire? . . .
For then I might have lain
    down and been quiet,
I would have slept and been at
    rest. . . .
Why is light given to the mis-
    erable,
And life to the embittered in
    spirit,
Who long for death, but it
    comes not. . . .
And who would be delighted
    if they could [but] find
    the grave?"

3: 11, 13, 21–22

This naturally shocks his friends, and they begin to argue with him. The first insists that God is probably disciplining Job for his own good. Says this friend:

"Happy, indeed, is the man whom God reproves;
So don't reject the instruction of the Almighty.
For he wounds, but he binds up;
He smites, but his hands heal.
He will rescue you from six troubles,
Yes, in seven no harm will touch you."

5: 17–19

Job, however, answers that he does not stand in need of any such disciplining. Addressing God, he cries:

"Have I sinned? What do I unto thee, O thou keeper of man?
Why dost thou make me a target for thyself?"

7: 20

Whereupon the second friend begins to upbraid Job, saying:

"How long will you utter such things? . . .
Does God pervert justice?
Or the Almighty pervert the right? . . .
If you were but pure and straight,
Then indeed he would bestir himself in your behalf."

8: 2, 6

To which Job replies:

"Nevertheless I will make complaint freely.
I will speak my own bitterness,
I will say unto God, 'Do not condemn me;
Tell me why thou dost quarrel with me. . . .
Why shouldst thou search for my sin,
Although thou knowest that I am not guilty?' "

10: 1, 6

Thereupon the third friend is so outraged that he cries:

"Shall your boastings put men to silence?
And when you scoff, is no one to rebuke you?
For you have said, 'My teaching is pure,
And I am clean in [God's] sight.'
But would that God might speak,
That He might open his lips against you,
And tell you the secrets of wisdom! . . .
For then you would know that God is exacting less of you than your
　　guilt deserves."

11: 3–6

*Thus the argument continues on and on. Job readily admits that
God is omniscient and omnipotent, but he insists that neither of these
attributes proves God to be just. Says he:*

"Lo, God destroys the blameless as well as the wicked,
If a scourge slays suddenly,
He mocks at the despair of the innocent!
The earth is given into the hand of the wicked. . . .
If it is not he [who does these things], then who is it?"

9: 22–24

God, it would seem, is deliberately seeking to put Job in the wrong:

"I know that . . . I am slated to be guilty. . . .
If I should wash myself in snow,
And clean my hands with lye,
Even then wouldst thou plunge me into the mire,
So that my own clothes would abhor me. . . .
O that there were an umpire between us,
Who would lay his hands on both of us. . . .
Then I might speak and not be afraid that God is dishonest toward
    me."

9:28–35

*In spite of all that his friends may say to the contrary, Job insists
that God deals most unfairly with human beings:*

"When I think of it, I am amazed,
And shuddering lays hold of my flesh.
Why do the wicked live,
Grow old, and amass wealth?
Their descendants are established with them in their sight,
And their offspring before their very eyes.

"Their houses are safe from terror,
And the rod of God is not upon them. . . .
Though they say to God, 'Get away! . . .
Who is the Almighty, that we should serve him?
And what good does it do to pray to him?' "

21: 6–15

*Thus does Job hold forth, challenging all that is taken for granted
by his orthodox friends, until finally God himself enters into the*

debate. He speaks out of a whirlwind, hurling one question after another at Job, and completely overwhelming him.

"Who is this that obscures counsel
By words without knowledge?
Gird up now your loins like a man,
That I may question you, and do you instruct me.

"Where were you when I laid the foundation of the earth?
Declare, if you have insight.
Who fixed its measurements? if you should know.
Or who stretched a line over it?
Upon what were its bases sunk,
Or who laid its cornerstone,
When the morning stars sang together,
And all the heavenly beings shouted for joy?

"Who enclosed the sea with doors,
When it burst forth, issuing from the womb,
When I made the cloud its covering. . . .
And said, 'Thus far shall you come and no farther,
And here shall your proud waves be stayed'?

"Have you ever in your life commanded the morning? . . .
Have you gone to the sources of the sea,
Or walked in the hollows of the deep?
Have the gates of death been revealed to you,
Or can you see the gates of darkness?
Have you considered the breadth of the earth?
Tell, if you know all this.

"Which is the way where light dwells,
And which is the place of darkness? . . .

"Gird up your loins now like a man;
I will ask you, and do you instruct me.
Will you, indeed, break down my right?
Will you make me guilty that you may be innocent?
Or have you an arm like God,

And can you thunder with a voice like his?
Deck yourself, now, with majesty and eminence,
Scatter abroad the rage of your wrath;
And look upon everyone that is proud and abase him.
Look upon everyone who is proud and bring him low;
And crush the wicked where they stand.
Bury them in the dust likewise;
Bind up their faces in the hidden place.
Then I indeed will praise you,
That your own right hand can deliver you."

38: 2-19; 41: 6-14

And thus Job is made to realize at last the arrogance of his complaints. He becomes aware that the entire problem of human suffering is infinitesimally small when seen in relation to the entire cosmic scheme. Whereupon he is forced to confess:

"Lo, I am of small account.
What shall I answer thee? . . .
I have uttered that which I did not understand,
Things too wonderful for me, which I did not know. . . .
I knew thee only by hearsay,
But now my eye has seen thee.
Therefore I retract and repent,
In dust and ashes."

40: 4; 42: 2-6

THE BOOK OF ECCLESIASTES

This extraordinary little book is said to have been written around 200 B.C. by some Jewish thinker who had evidently drunk deep of Greek worldliness and world-weariness. That it was ever allowed to become part of the Holy Writ can be explained only by the fact that the book was doctored by some pious editor, and attributed to King Solomon—who had lived fully seven centuries earlier! The original document was evidently a series of gently cynical jibes at those who saw any meaning in life. Ecclesiastes is the late Latin equivalent for the Hebrew Koheleth, meaning "preacher" or "cleric."

VANITY OF VANITIES

The words of Koheleth, the son of David, king in
    Jerusalem.

Vanity of vanities, saith Koheleth;
Vanity of vanities, all is vanity.

What profit hath man of all his labour
Wherein he laboureth under the sun?

One generation passeth away,
    and another generation
    cometh;
And the earth abideth for ever.
The sun also ariseth, and the
    sun goeth down,
And hasteth to his place where
    he ariseth.
The wind goeth toward the
    south,
And turneth about unto the
    north;
It turneth about continually in
    its circuit,
And the wind returneth again
    to its circuits.

All the rivers run into the sea,
Yet the sea is not full;
Unto the place whither the rivers go,
Thither they go again.
All things toil to weariness;
Man cannot utter it,
The eye is not satisfied with seeing,
Nor the ear filled with hearing.
That which hath been is that which shall be,
And that which hath been done is that which shall be
    done;
And there is nothing new under the sun.

Is there a thing whereof it is said: 'See, this is new'?—it hath been already, in the ages which were before us. There is no remembrance of them of former times; neither shall there be any remembrance of them of latter times that are to come, among those that shall come after.

I Koheleth have been king over Israel in Jerusalem. And I applied my heart to seek and to search out by wisdom concerning all things that are done under heaven; it is a sore task that God hath given to the sons of men to be exercised therewith. I have seen all the works that are done under the sun; and, behold, all is vanity and a striving after wind.

1: 1–13

EAT, DRINK AND BE MERRY

So I commended mirth, that a man hath no better thing under the sun, than to eat, and to drink, and to be merry, and that this should accompany him in his labour all the days of his life which God hath given him under the sun.

8: 15

> Go thy way, eat thy bread with joy,
> And drink thy wine with a merry heart;
> For God hath already accepted thy works.
> Let thy garments be always white;
> And let thy head lack no oil.

Enjoy life with the wife whom thou lovest all the days of the life of thy vanity, which He hath given thee under the sun, all the days of thy vanity; for that is thy portion in life, and in thy labour wherein thou labourest under the sun. Whatsoever thy hand attaineth to do by thy strength, that do; for there is no work, nor device, nor knowledge, nor wisdom, in the grave, whither thou goest.

9: 7–10

But . . .
[But the pious editor of this cynical little book has the last word, and very piously he concludes:]

The end of the matter, all having been heard: fear God, and keep His commandments; for this is the whole man. For God shall bring every work into the judgment concerning every hidden thing, whether it be good or whether it be evil.

12: 13–14

THE APOCRYPHA

It was once generally believed that the Old Testament was finished in the fifth century B.C., and that thereupon Israel's creative genius went into a coma until the first century B.C., when it abruptly and miraculously revived to bring forth the New Testament. Both those notions, however, have long since been exploded. Critical historians have proved (a) that the Old Testament was not actually completed until the second century B.C.; and (b) that the production of scriptures continued thereafter without any abatement whatsoever. If anything, the flow increased, for the ensuing centuries witnessed a prodigious widening of Israel's cultural horizons, and a tragic deepening of Israel's perplexities and woes. The New Testament, therefore, was in no sense a sudden and anomalous achievement. It was but one more product—and only in the Christian view the climacteric one—of that spiritual quest which Israel had been carrying on unflaggingly since the earliest times.

The literature belonging to the period between the Testaments was as rich in content as it was varied in form. It was written in three languages, thus giving the grossest proof of the extent to which the Jews had broadened their cultural contacts. Most of the documents were naturally couched in Hebrew, which was still Israel's holy tongue. Others, however, were set down in Aramaic, a Mesopotamian dialect which had belatedly become the vernacular throughout Palestine. Still others were written in Greek, the language most familiar to the millions of Jews who were now living all around the Mediterranean.

It is difficult to classify all that was produced in these three languages. The bulk of the literature was in a sense scriptural, since it was modelled on the writings which had already become sacred to the Jews. A number of the new documents came to be actually included in the Septuagint, the first Greek version of the Jewish Scriptures, and later in the Vulgate, the first Latin version. They formed what was eventually called the Apocrypha—a sort of semi-sacred appendix to the Old Testament.[3]

[3] The Apocrypha is still to be found in the Roman Catholic editions of the Bible, but almost all Protestant ones follow the example set in the Jewish versions. Fortunately, however, it is included in *The Complete Bible* published in "American" by the University of Chicago Press—thus making it possible for this anthology to quote again from that source.

We know almost nothing about the real authorship of the Apocryphal writings. Most of them are ascribed to very ancient and hallowed Hebrew worthies—for instance, Enoch, Abraham, Solomon, Daniel—but this, it seems, was done only in order to make those writings appear venerable and therefore deserving of devout study. This stratagem, as we have already seen, was by no means new; nor, it should be emphasized, was it consciously dishonest. Literary ethics in those days were unlike what they are now, especially in the field of religion. An author saw no wrong in attributing his book to someone more famous than himself. That, indeed, was the standard practice, and it was essentially innocent because the author usually believed his book was the sort that that more famous person might have written. In any case, whether innocent or no, the stratagem was certainly effective. Thanks to it, books which might otherwise have been ignored, or even proscribed, were often able to win wide and enduring veneration.

To be sure, the stratagem could no longer work to perfection. The canon of the Jewish Scriptures had already been effectually closed; so it was impossible for any new work to become absolutely sacred. But some could still become at least semi-sacred. And that actually happened to a considerable number of books written during this relatively late period. For example—

THE BOOK OF JESUS BEN SIRACH

This document, called in Latin Ecclesiasticus, closely resembles the Book of Proverbs. It is, however, the work of a single author, and—this is without parallel—it bears his own name. In addition, being a somewhat later product, it shows obvious traces of Hellenic influence. The customs described in it are typically Greek rather than Hebrew, and so are many of the attitudes. The author shares the taste of the Epicurean philosophers for bitter topics like the uncertainty of happiness, the unreliability of friends, and most of all the frailty of women. That, it seems, was the chief reason why the book, despite its strain of deep religiosity and stern moral tone, was never allowed into the Old Testament canon.

Nothing is known about the author except that he must have lived in Palestine early in the second century B.C., was a lay scholar, had evidently traveled, and wrote in Hebrew. (This last fact, curiously, was

*not established until after 1896, when fragments of the original
Hebrew text began to be discovered in a synagogue attic in Cairo.) His
maxims show him to have been adequately disillusioned about men,
completely distrustful of women, yet at the same time a warm advocate
of social justice and moral probity.*

APHORISMS ON FRIENDSHIP, ETC.

Do not forsake an old friend,
For a new one is not equal to him.
A new friend is new wine;
When it grows old, you will enjoy drinking it.
Do not envy the glory of a
    sinner;
For you do not know what dis-
    aster awaits him.

Do not indulge in too much
    luxury,
Do not be tied to its expense.
Do not be impoverished be-
    cause of feasting on bor-
    rowed money
When you have nothing in
    your purse.
A workman who is a drunkard
    will never get rich;
The man who despises little things will gradually fail;
Wine and women make men of understanding stand aloof;
And the man who is devoted to prostitutes is reckless. . . .

If you never repeat what you are told,
You will fare none the worse.
Before friend or foe do not recount it,
And unless it would be sinful of you, do not reveal it.
For someone has heard you and watched you,
And when the time comes he will hate you.
If you hear something said, let it die with you,
Have courage, it will not make you burst! . . .

Question a friend; perhaps he did not do it;
Or if he did, so that he will not do it again.

19: 5-13

One man keeps silence and is considered wise;
While another is hated for his loquacity.
One man keeps silence because he has nothing to say;
And another keeps silence because he knows it is the time for it.
A wise man will keep silence till his time comes,
But a boaster and a fool miss the fitting time.
The man who talks excessively is detested,
And he who takes it on himself to speak is hated.

20: 5-8

APHORISMS ON FOLLY AND WISDOM

A proverb on the lips of a fool will be refused.
For he will not utter it at the proper time.
One man is kept from sinning through poverty,
So his conscience does not prick him when he goes to rest.
Another loses his own life from sheer embarrassment,
And destroys it by his senseless expression.
Another out of embarrassment makes promises to his friend,
And so makes him his enemy for nothing.
A lie is a bad blot on a man;
It is continually found on the lips of the ignorant.
A thief is better than a habitual liar,
But they are both doomed to destruction.
Dishonor is habitual with a liar,
And his shame attends him continually.
A man who speaks wisely makes his way in the world,
And a man of good sense pleases the great.
The man who cultivates the soil makes his heap high,
And the man who pleases the great atones for wrongdoing.
Gifts and presents can blind the eyes of wise men,
And avert reproofs like a muzzle on the mouth.
Hidden wisdom and concealed treasure—
What is the use of either of them?
A man who conceals his folly is better
Than a man who conceals his wisdom.

20: 20-31

THE TESTAMENTS OF THE TWELVE
PATRIARCHS

One of the most illuminating books belonging to this twilit period is a work called THE TESTAMENT OF THE TWELVE PATRIARCHS. *It purports to record the last words and exhortations of the twelve sons of Jacob, and was probably written either in Hebrew or Aramaic toward the close of the second century* B.C. *The importance of the book lies in the striking likeness between certain of its ethical teachings and those attributed to Jesus several generations later.*[4]

For example, the Testament of Dan (5: 3) declares: "Love the Lord with all your life, and one another with a true heart." The Gospel of Matthew (22: 37–39) declares: "Love the Lord thy God with all thy heart and soul and mind . . . and thy neighbor as thyself." Again, the Testament of Gad (6: 3, 7) reads: "Love ye one another from the heart; and if a man sin against thee, speak peaceably to him . . . and if he repent and confess, forgive him. . . . But if he be shameless and persisteth in his wrongdoing, even so forgive him." The Gospel of Luke (17: 3–4) reads: "If thy brother sin against thee, correct him; and if he repent, forgive him. And if he sin against thee seven times in a day . . . thou shalt forgive him."

Such parallels are so common that this book eventually came to be mistaken for a Christian work, and was crudely interpolated with references to the Incarnation and the Crucifixion so as to give the appearance of truth to that error. Modern investigators, however, have had no difficulty in restoring the original text, and in recognizing it as definitely pre-Christian. And they have deduced from this—and much other evidence, of course—that Jesus's precepts were derived from ethical ideas which had been current in Israel for very many years.

SIMEON'S WARNING AGAINST ENVY

Now, my children, hearken unto me and beware of the spirit of deceit and of envy. For envy ruleth over the whole mind of a man, and suffereth him neither to eat nor to drink, nor to do any good

[4] Prof. R. H. Charles—from whose translation the excerpts below are taken—gives a long list of the parallels in the introduction (pp. lxxviii ff.) to his scholarly work entitled *The Testaments of the Twelve Patriarchs* (A. & C. Black, London, 1908).

thing. But it ever suggesteth [to him] to destroy him that envieth; and so long as he that is envied flourisheth, he that envieth fadeth away. . . .

For envy maketh savage the soul and destroyeth the body; it causes anger and war in the mind, and stirreth up unto deeds of blood, and leadeth the mind into frenzy, and causeth tumult to the soul and trembling to the body. For even in sleep some malicious jealousy, deluding him, gnaweth, and with wicked spirits disturbeth his soul, and causeth the body to be troubled, and waketh the mind from sleep in confusion; and as a wicked and poisonous spirit, so appeareth it to men. . . .

ZEBULON URGES COMPASSION

And now, my children, I bid you to keep the commands of the Lord, and to show mercy to your neighbors, and to have com-

passion towards all, not towards men only, but also towards beasts. . . . Have, therefore, compassion in your hearts, my children, because even as a man doeth to his neighbor, even so also will the Lord do to him. . . .

Hearken to my words, ye sons of Dan; and give heed to the words of your father. I have proved in my heart, and in my whole life, that truth with just dealing is good and well-pleasing to God, and that lying and anger are evil, because they teach man all wickedness. . . .

And now, my children, behold I am dying, and I tell you of a truth, that unless ye keep yourselves from the spirit of lying and of anger, and love truth and long-suffering, ye shall perish. For anger is blindness, and doth not suffer one to see the face of any man with truth. For though it be a father or a mother, he behaveth towards them as enemies; though it be a brother, he knoweth him not; though it be a prophet of the Lord, he disobeyeth him; though a righteous man, he regardeth him not; though a friend, he doth not acknowledge him. For the spirit of anger encompasseth him with the net of deceit, and blindeth his eyes, and through lying darkeneth his mind, and giveth him its own peculiar vision. And wherewith encompasseth it his eyes? With hatred of heart, so as to be envious of his brother. . . .

GOD URGES BROTHERLY LOVE

And now, my children, hearken to the words of truth to work righteousness, and all the law of the Most High, and go not astray through the spirit of hatred, for it is evil in all the doings of men. Whatsoever a man doeth the hater abominateth him: and though a man worketh the law of the Lord, he praiseth him not; though a man feareth the Lord, and taketh pleasure in that which is righteous, he loveth him not. He dispraiseth the truth, he envieth him that prospereth, he welcometh evil-speaking, he loveth arrogance, for hatred blindeth his soul. . . .

Love ye one another from the heart; and if a man sin against thee, speak peaceably to him, and in thy soul hold not guile; and if he repent and confess, forgive him. But if he deny it, do not get into a passion with him, lest catching the poison from thee he take to swearing and so thou sin doubly. Let not another man hear thy secrets when engaged in legal strife, lest he come to hate thee and become thy enemy, and commit a great sin against thee; for ofttimes he addresseth thee guilefully or burieth himself about thee with wicked intent. And though he deny it and yet have a sense of shame when reproved, give over reproving him. For he who denieth may repent so as not to wrong thee again; yea, he may also honor thee, and fear and be at peace with thee. But if he be shameless and persisteth in his wrong-doing, even so forgive him from the heart, and leave to God the avenging.

THE TALMUD

No anthology of the Scriptures of Judaism can be considered complete unless it includes selections from the TALMUD, for that work is in essence an extension of the Mosaic TORAH, and is still venerated as such by all Orthodox Jews.

The nature of the TALMUD is explained by its origin. The supreme crisis in the history of the Jews occurred in the year 70 A.D., when their holy city, Jerusalem, was razed by the Romans, and they were left without a home either for themselves or their God. Wrecked now both as a cult and a nation, it looked as though Israel would soon be destroyed even as a people. But then the Rabbis came to the fore, and the doom seemingly so inevitable was averted. They created the TALMUD—literally, the "Teaching"—and with it so walled in the Jews that they were able not merely to survive as a people, but even thrive.

In this the Rabbis were supplementing a feat already accomplished by the Prophets. The latter had furnished a final answer to the why of life for the Jew. They had told him he had been chosen for a holy mission, that he was the suffering servant of the Lord, and that he must survive despite all hardships because he alone could bring on the Reign of the Lord. And now the Rabbis came up with an answer to the how. They persuaded the Jew that, though landless now, he could still survive if he would but cling to the TORAH, the "Law." Ramparts of ritual, they insisted, could preserve him from the Gentiles more securely than any frontiers guarded by troops. And it was in the course of providing such ramparts that the Rabbis brought forth the TALMUD.

The project began with a number of fragmentary notebooks containing some of the countless new ordinances derived by "interpretation" from the original 613 set down in the ancient TORAH. (The earliest "interpreters" were called Pharisees, a term derived from the Hebrew verb pharash, meaning "to make clear.") Being uneven in their scope and authority, and also largely discrepant, those notebooks were finally supplanted—around 200 A.D.—by a master digest which came to be known as the MISHNA, the "Repetition." This consisted of six well-organized volumes, giving some 4,000 legal decisions regulating every phase of Jewish life.

438

No sooner, however, had the MISHNA *been compiled than this in turn became a subject for "interpretation"; whereupon further compilation became imperative, and thus a work called the* GEMARA, *the "Learning," emerged. The latter was far more than a mere law code. It was a vast anthology divided into sixty-three tractates which gave the gist of the endless discussions carried on in the rabbinical academies during all of three centuries. When the* GEMARA *was finally reduced to writing—around* 500 A.D.—*it was combined with the* MISHNA *and called the* TALMUD, *the "Teaching."*

I: FROM THE MISHNA

Tucked away in this law code there is a collection of ethical maxims which ranks as the most popular of all rabbinic writings, and certainly deserves inclusion in this Anthology. It is entitled PIRKE ABOTH *("Chapters of the Fathers") and its six chapters are still recited, one each Sabbath afternoon, as part of the traditional Jewish liturgy. The Fathers were the earliest Pharisaic teachers—the term* rabbi *("my master") did not become current until after the first century* A.D.—*and though primarily legalists, those men were not nearly so narrow and hidebound as is commonly assumed. Despite their rigid orthodoxy, they were capable of uttering the most liberal sentiments, and some—most notably the great Hillel, who taught shortly before the time of Jesus—were inclined to voice an altogether universal idealism. The proof is to be seen in the sayings which they left as memorials to the spirit in which they did their work of "interpreting" the holy* TORAH.[5]

Moses received the Law on Mount Sinai and handed it down to Joshua, who handed it down to the Judges, who handed it down to the Prophets, who handed it down to the Men of the Great Synod. These used to say three things: "Be deliberate in passing judgment, and raise up many disciples, and build a hedge [i.e. defenses] around the Law."

Simeon the Just [died around 270 B.C.] was one of the last members of the Great Synod. His favorite saying was: "The world is established on three things—on Law, on Worship, and on Generosity."

[5] Because of the archaic style of the current English translations of PIRKE ABOTH, the selections given here are in a version of my own made directly from the Hebrew. They constitute approximately four-fifths of the entire document.

Antigonos of Socho received the Torah from Simeon the Just. His favorite saying was: "Don't be like those servants who work solely for pay . . . and let the awe of Heaven be upon you."

[Next came] Jose ben Joezer and Jose ben Johanan. The former used to say: "Let your house be a gathering-place for the Wise, cover yourself with the dust of their feet, and drink in their words thirstily." The latter used to say: "Open your house wide, and let poor folk have a place in it, and don't talk too much to a woman." He meant [one should not talk too much] to one's own wife; therefore how much the more certainly not to a friend's wife. . . .

[Next came] Jehoshua ben Perakhjah and Nittai the Arbelite. The former used to say: "Get yourself a teacher, or find yourself a comrade, and judge every man according to his true merit." The latter used to say: "Stay away from an evil neighbor, steer clear of wicked companions, and never doubt that there is retribution."

[Next came] Shemaiah and Abtalion. The former used to say: "Love work, hate tyranny, and don't become [too well] known to the authorities." The latter used to say: "You wise men, watch what you say, lest you err and are exiled to a place of evil waters, and your disciples drink and die, and the name of Heaven be profaned."

[Next came] Hillel.[6] He used to say: "Be among the disciples of Aaron, loving peace, cherishing mankind, and bringing [people] ever closer to the Law." [Also] he would say: "He who advertises his name, loses it; he who does not increase [knowledge], diminishes it; he who

[6] Born about 50 B.C. in Babylonia—where a large Jewish community had maintained itself ever since the Exile in the sixth century B.C.—but migrated to Palestine as a youth. Despite poverty and other obstacles, Hillel succeeded in becoming the foremost of all the Pharisaic masters, and founded a relatively liberal type of rabbinism which dominated Jewish life for more than five centuries. He seems to have been a saint as well as a sage, and one can well understand why some historians suggest that he had a direct influence on the teachings of Jesus. Paul, we know, did actually study under Hillel's grandson, Gamaliel.

refuses to learn, merits extinction; and he who puts his talent to selfish use, commits spiritual suicide." [Also] he would say: "If I am not self-reliant, on whom shall I rely? But if I am selfish what [good] am I? And if [the time for action is] not now, when [is it]?"

Hillel [also] said: "Don't keep aloof from the people; and don't be [too] sure of yourself till the day you die; and don't condemn your comrade till you are in his place; and . . . don't say 'I shall study when I find the time,' because you may never find it."

He [also] said: "A boor does not fear sin, and a vulgar man cannot be a saint. A bashful man cannot learn, an ill-tempered man cannot teach, and one who preoccupies himself with worldly affairs cannot impart wisdom. Moreover, in a place where there are no men, show yourself a man."

On one occasion he saw a skull floating, and he said: "Because you drowned others, you were drowned, and in the end they that drowned you shall likewise be drowned."

He used to say:

"More flesh, more worms;
More wealth, more worry;
More women, more witchcraft;
More concubines, more lechery;
More slaves, more thievery.
(But) More Law, more life;
More study, more wisdom;
More counsel, more enlightenment;
More righteousness, more peace.

He who acquires a good name, acquires it for himself,
He who acquires knowledge of the Law, acquires life in the world
    to come.

Rabban Gamliel [7] used to say: "Get yourself a teacher, and keep away from doubtful matters, and never tithe by guesswork."

Simeon, his son, said: "All my life I have grown up among the

[7] Grandson of Hillel and the teacher of Saul (Paul) of Tarsus. He is referred to in the New Testament (*Acts* 5:34) as being "held in honor by all the people." The title "Rabban" indicates that he was President of the Sanhedrin.

wise, and I have found nothing better than silence. The chief thing is not to study but to do. And he who says too much, encourages sin."

Rabban Simeon ben Gamliel said: "The world rests on three things—Truth, Law, and Peace."

Rabban Gamliel, the son of Rabbi Jehudah the Prince, said: "It is good to follow a workaday occupation as well as to study the Torah, for between the two one forgets to sin.[8] . . . Beware of the [Roman] authorities, for they make no advances to a man except for their own purposes. They seem friendly when it is to their advantage, but desert a man when he is in trouble."

Rabban Jochanan ben Zakkai . . . used to say: "Don't feel self-righteous if you have learned much Torah, because that is what you were created for." He said to his disciples: "Go and discover what [best helps] a man to find the right way of life." Rabbi Eliezer answered: "A good eye." Rabbi Jehoshua answered: "A good comrade." Rabbi Jose answered: "A good neighbor." Rabbi Simeon answered: "Foresightedness." Rabbi Eleazar answered: "A good heart." Rabban Jochanan then said to them: "I prefer Rabbi Eleazar's answer, for his words include all of yours."

Rabbi Eliezer said: "Let your comrade's honor be as dear to you as your own; and do not be quick to get angry; also repent before it is too late. Warm yourself at the fire of the learned, but beware of their glowing coals, lest you get scorched. The bite of the learned is like the bite of a fox, their sting is like a scorpion's, their hiss like a serpent's, and all their words are like coals of fire."

Rabbi Jehoshua said: "The evil eye and the evil desire and hatred of humanity cut a man off from the world."

Rabbi Jose said: "Let the property of your comrade be as dear to you as your own. And set yourself to learn Torah, for you can never inherit it. And let all your actions be for the sake of Heaven."

Rabbi Simeon said: "Don't pray mechanically, but let your prayer be a [heartfelt] plea and entreaty before God."

Rabbi Elazar said: "Be avid to learn Torah, and know how to refute a disbeliever." . . .[9]

---

[8] The term "Torah" had many meanings to the Rabbis: the Pentateuch, the entire Bible, any learning based on the Bible, and sometimes all learning in general. It should be noted, incidentally, that the advice given in this maxim was widely accepted. As a rule the rabbinic sessions were conducted towards the close of the day, the majority of scholars being tradesmen or artisans.

[9] The Hebrew word is *Epikuros*—from the Greek, of course.

Akabya ben Mahalalel said: "Keep three things in mind, and you will escape the toils of wickedness—know whence you came, whither you are going, and before whom you will have to give a strict account of yourself. Whence did you come?—from a fetid drop [of sperm]. Whither are you going?—to a place of dust, worms, and maggots. Before whom will you have to give a strict account of yourself?—before the King of Kings, the Holy One, blessed be He."

Rabbi Hanina, deputy of the priests, said: "Pray for the stability of the government, because were it not for fear of the government, men would swallow each other alive."

Rabbi Hananyah ben Teradyon said: "When two sit together and fail to discuss Torah, lo, that is the 'seat of the scornful'! But when two sit together and do discuss Torah, the *Shekinah* ['Holy Spirit'] rests on them."

Rabbi Simeon said: "If three have eaten at one table and failed to speak words of Torah during the meal, it is as if they had eaten of the sacrifices to dead [spirits]."

Rabbi Hanina ben Hachinai said: "He who stays up all night, and he who keeps to himself, and he who devotes his mind to idle thoughts, lo, such a one ruins his own well-being!"

Rabbi Jacob said: "He who is walking along and studying, but then breaks off to remark, 'How lovely is that tree!' [or] 'How beautiful is that fallow field!'—Scripture regards such a one as having hurt his own well-being."

Rabbi Hanina ben Dosa used to say: "When one's deeds are even greater than one's knowledge, the knowledge is effective; but when one's knowledge is greater than one's deeds, the knowledge is futile." He would also say: "The spirit of God is pleased with one whom the spirit of man finds pleasing."

Rabbi Dosa ben Harchina said: "Sleep in the morning, wind during the day, childish talk, and association with boors; all these destroy a man's life."

Rabbi Elazar ha-Moddai said: "Whoever profanes sacred things, or despises the holy days, or shames his comrade in public, or voids the covenants of Father Abraham, or misinterprets the Torah, even though he have much learning and many virtuous deeds, he still has no place in the World to Come."

Rabbi Ishmail said: "Be obedient to a superior, affable to a petitioner, and friendly to all mankind."

Rabbi Akiba said: "Jesting and ribaldry lead a man to lewdness. Tradition protects the Torah, tithes protect wealth, vows protect virtue, and silence protects wisdom."

Rabbi Eleazar ben Azariah said: "Where there is no Torah there is no refinement, and where there is no refinement there can be no Torah. Where there is no wisdom there can be no reverence, and where there is no reverence there can be no wisdom. Where there is no knowledge there can be no insight, and where there is no insight there can be no knowledge. Where there is no food there can be no Torah, and where there is no Torah, there can be no food."

Ben Zoma said: "Who is wise? He who can learn from every man. Who is strong? He who can control his passions. Who is rich? He who can feel satisfied with his lot. Who is honored? He who honors mankind."

Ben Azai used to say: "Despise no man, and consider nothing impossible, for every man has his hour and everything its place."

Rabbi Levitas of Jabneh said: "Be extremely humble, for the destiny of mortal man is the worm."

Rabbi Johanan ben Berokah said: "He who profanes God in secret will be punished in the open, and this is true whether he commits the profanation out of ignorance or malice."

Rabbi Jose said: "He who honors the Torah is honored by mankind."

Rabbi Jonathan said: "He who fulfills the Torah amid poverty will in the end fulfill it amid wealth, and he who neglects the Torah amid wealth will in the end neglect it amid poverty."

Rabbi Meir said: "Be less busy with business and more busy with the Torah. . . . If you start neglecting the Torah, you will find more and more reasons to continue neglecting it."

Rabbi Elazar ben Shammua said: "Let the honor of your disciple be as dear to you as the honor of your colleague, the honor of your colleague as dear as your respect for your teacher, and your respect for your teacher as dear as your awe of God."

Rabbi Jehudah said: "Be cautious in teaching, for an error in teaching may lead to wilful sin."

Rabbi Simeon said: "There are three crowns—the crown of learning, the crown of priesthood, and the crown of royalty. But greater than any of these is the crown of a good name."

Rabbi Nehorai said: "Move to a place where there is learning, because you cannot expect learning to move to you."

Rabbi Jannai said: "It is beyond our power to explain either the prosperity of the wicked or the afflictions of the righteous."

Rabbi Mattithiah ben Harash said: "Be first in greeting all men, and be rather a tail to lions than a head to foxes."

Rabbi Jacob used to say: "This world is no more than the vestibule of the world to come, so get ready in the vestibule to enter the banquet hall. [However] one hour of repentance and good deeds in this world is better than a lifetime in the World to Come, and one hour of bliss in the World to Come is better than a lifetime in this world."

Rabbi Simeon ben Eleazar said: "Don't try to calm your comrade when he is in a rage, or console him when he is in despair, or question him when he is vowing; and don't try to see him in the hour of his disgrace."

Rabbi Samuel the Younger said: "Don't rejoice when your enemy falls, or be glad when he stumbles."

Elisha ben Abuya [10] said: "If one learns as a child, to what is it comparable? To writing on clean paper. And if one learns as an old man, to what is that comparable? To writing on blotted paper."

Rabbi Jose bar Jehudah of Khephar ha-Babli said: "He who learns from the immature, to what is he comparable? To one who eats unripe grapes and drinks wine fresh from the winepress. But he who learns from the aged? He is comparable to one who eats ripe grapes and drinks old wine."

Rabbi [11] said: "What is the proper path for a man to follow? Any that seems honorable in his own sight and that wins him honor from his fellowmen." [He also said:] "Don't look at the pitcher but at what it contains. Sometimes a new pitcher is full of old wine, and an old pitcher is empty even of new wine."

Rabbi Eleazar ha-Kappar said: "Envy, cupidity, and ambition drive a man from the world."

Jehudah ben Tama used to say: "At the age of five one is ready

[10] Although one of the most brilliant of the Talmudic sages, Elisha ben Abuya (born about 80 A.D.) was denied the title of Rabbi, perhaps because he eventually turned free-thinker.

[11] Judah the Holy One, or the Prince, is commonly referred to simply as "Rabbi" because of his distinction as final compiler of the *Mishna*. He is said to have been born in 135 A.D.

to study the Bible, at ten to study the *Mishna*, at thirteen to observe the Commandments, at fifteen to study the Talmud, at eighteen to get married, at twenty to start earning a livelihood, at thirty to enter into one's full strength, at forty to show discernment, at fifty to give counsel, at sixty to start feeling old, at seventy to turn white, at eighty for travail and trouble, at ninety for senility; and at one hundred . . . for death."

Ben Bag-Bag said: "Study it [the Torah] over and over again, for everything is in it. Grow gray and old studying it, and never forsake it, for there is no better path for a man to follow.

"This is the way of the studious life: eat a crust with salt, drink measured water, sleep on the floor, endure much hardship, and wrestle with the Torah. If you do all that, you will be happy and it will be well with you—that is, you will be happy in this world, and it will be well with you in the World to Come.

"Don't try to be a great one, and don't look for more honor than your learning merits. Don't crave to sit at the table of kings, for your own table is better than theirs, and your crown likewise."

Rabbi Jose ben Kisma said: "Once while on a walk, I met a man, and after we had exchanged greeting he said to me, 'Rabbi, whence do you hail?' I answered, 'From a great city where there are sages and scribes.' So then he said, 'If you agree to stay with us here, I'll give you a thousand thousand gold coins, as well as precious stones and pearls.' Whereupon I answered, 'If you were to offer me all the silver and gold and precious stones and pearls in creation, I'd still refuse to stay in any place where there is no study of the Torah!'"

There are seven traits in a wise man:
He does not speak in the presence of one wiser than himself;
He does not interrupt when a colleague speaks·
He does not rush out with a rejoinder;
He asks questions that are relevant, and gives answers that are logical;
He deals with first things first and last things last;
He readily admits when he does not know about a matter;
He acknowledges the truth.
The opposites of these traits mark the boorish man.

There are four types among men:
The ordinary one says: "What is mine is mine, and what is yours is
    yours."

The queer one says: "What is mine is yours, and what is yours is mine."

The saintly one says: "What is mine is yours, and what is yours is yours."

The wicked one says: "What is mine is mine, and what is yours is also mine."

II: FROM THE GEMARA

This voluminous work—of which there are two codifications, the smaller one originating in Palestine, and the larger in Babylonia—constitutes a whole literature in itself. Though devoted primarily to legal and ritualistic issues, it delves also into science, magic, folklore, history, philosophy, and every other subject discussed in the Rabbinic academies during more than five hundred years. The following miscellany can give at most a tiny peep into the GEMARA, *but one which the average reader may find illuminating. It will reveal something of the religious and ethical principles animating the sages who built the ramparts of Talmudic Judaism in order to preserve the Jewish people.*[12]

ON GOD

The Emperor said to Gamaliel: "You say that wheresoever ten men are assembled [for prayer] God comes to them. How many gods are there, then?" Gamaliel called his servant, and struck him lightly on the neck. The Emperor asked: "Why did you strike him?" "Because he let the sun shine into the house," answered Gamaliel. "But the sun is everywhere," said the Emperor. And Rabbi Gamaliel replied, "The sun is but one among the thousands of thousands and thousands of myriads which are before the Holy One, blessed be He: yet the sun is everywhere in the world. How much more so, then, is the Holy One everywhere." *Sanhedrin*

It happened that when Rabbi Samuel went to Rome, he chanced to find a bracelet belonging to the queen. A crier went about the kingdom and announced: "Whoever returns the bracelet within thirty days shall receive such and such a reward, but if it is found upon him after

[12] The selections have been culled from the admirable *Anthology of Rabbinic Literature* by Montefiore and Loewe (Macmillan and Co., London, 1938).

thirty days, his head will be cut off." Nevertheless Rabbi Samuel would not return it until after the thirty days had elapsed. When he finally did, the queen asked him: "Did you not hear the proclamation?" He answered, "Yes." So she said: "Then why did you not return it within the thirty days?" "In order," he answered, "that you should not say I feared you, for I returned it only because I feared God."

Whereupon the queen cried: "Blessed be the God of the Jews."   *T. J. Baba Mezia, 2: 5*

ON PRAYER

Rabbi Me'ir said: A man's words should always be few when addressing God.
Berakot, 61a

Rabbi Hiyya b. Abba said in the name of Rabbi Johanan: Whoever prolongs his prayer, and calculates on it (i.e., anticipates its fulfilment as a reward for its length), will eventually come to pain of heart.   *Ibid., 32b*

Rab said: He whose mind is not quieted should not pray. Rabbi Hanina was wont not to pray when he was irritated.   *Erubin, 65a*

Rabbi Johanan said: He who recounts the praise of God more than is fitting will be torn away from the world.   *Megillah, 18a*

Rab said: Whoever has it in his power to pray on behalf of his neighbor, and fails to do so, is called a sinner.   *Berakot, 12b*

ON EQUALITY AMONG MEN

One man alone was brought forth at the time of Creation in order that thereafter none should have the right to say to another, "My father was greater than your father."   *T. J. Sanhedrin, 4: 5*

Why was man created a solitary human being, without a companion? So that it might not be said that some races are better than others.   *Sanhedrin, 37*

The life of one man may not be sacrificed to save the life of another man.   *Ahalot, 7*

A man came to Raba and said, "The prefect of my town has ordered me to kill so and so, or he will kill me." Raba replied, "Let him kill you; do you commit no murder. Why should you think that your blood is redder than his? Perhaps his is redder than yours."

Pesachim, 25b

It was a favorite saying of the Rabbis of Jabneh: I am a creature [of God], and my neighbor is also His creature; my work is in the city, and his in the field; I rise early to my work, and he rises early to his. As he cannot excel in my work, so I cannot excel in his work. But perhaps you say, I do great things, and he does small things. We have learnt that [it matters not whether] a man does much or little, if only he direct his heart to Heaven.   *Berakot, 17a*

ON GENTILES

Blessed art thou, O Lord our God, King of the universe, who hast given of thy wisdom to *all* flesh and blood.   *Berakot, 58a*

Whoever renounces idol worship may be called a Jew.

Megillah, 13a

Even an idolator who studies Torah is like the High Priest.

Baba Kamma, 38

Rabbi Me'ir said: "A Gentile who lives a goodly life is like a High Priest."   *Abodah Zarah, 3a*

God says: "Both the Gentiles and the Israelites are my handiwork, therefore how can I let the former perish on account of the latter?"

Sanhedrin, 98b

Antoninus, the Emperor, once asked Rabbi Judah, the Patriarch: "Will I have a share in the World to Come?" Rabbi Judah replied:

"Yes." "But is it not prophesied," the heathen demanded, "that none shall be left of the house of Esau?" "Yes," came the quick reply of Rabbi Judah, "but that applies only to those who commit Esau's acts of violence!"   *Abodah Zarah, 10b*

The Jew is urged to resort to the aid of Gentiles in administering the affairs of his community.   *T. J. Gittin, 5, 9*

Said Rabbi Tanhuma: "If a non-Jew bless thee, respond Amen, as it is written: 'Thou shalt be blessed by all peoples.'"

T. J. Berakot, 8

In a city where there are both Jews and Gentiles, the collectors of alms collect both from Jews and Gentiles, and feed the poor of both, visit the sick of both, bury both, comfort the mourners whether they be Jews or Gentiles, and restore the lost goods of both.

T. J. Demai, 6: 6

To cheat a Gentile is even worse than cheating a Jew, for besides being a violation of the moral law, it brings Israel's religion into contempt, and desecrates the name of Israel's God.   *Baba Kama, 113b*

He who steals from a non-Jew is bound to make restitution to the non-Jew; it is worse to steal from a non-Jew than to steal from an Israelite because of the profanation of the Name.

T. J. Bab. K., 10: 15

ON KINDNESS

The highest wisdom is kindness.   *Berakot, 17a*

[In a time of drought] it was revealed to Abbahu in a dream that a certain Pentekaka [i.e., "man of five sins"] should pray for rain. Abbahu sent for him and asked what his occupation was. Pentekaka replied, "Five sins I commit daily; I make assignations for harlots; I deck their theatre; I take their garments to the baths; I clap and dance before them; and I beat the drum for their orgies."

Abbahu said to him, "Have you ever done one good deed?"

The man answered, "Once I was decking out the theatre when a woman came and wept behind one of the pillars. I asked her why she was weeping, and she told me that her husband was in prison, and that she was going to sell her body to obtain his ransom. So I pawned my bed and coverlet, and gave her the money, and said, 'Go, redeem thy husband, and sin not.'"

Abbahu said to him, "Worthy art thou to pray and to be answered." *T. J. Ta'anit, 1: 4*

"Thou shalt love thy neighbor as thyself." This is the great general rule in Torah. *T. J. Nedarim, 9: 4*

If two men claim thy help, and one is thy enemy, help him first.
Baba Metzia, 32b

Almsgiving and deeds of loving-kindness are equal to all the commandments of the Torah, but loving-kindness is greater. Almsgiving is exercised towards the living, but deeds of loving-kindness towards the living and the dead; almsgiving only to the poor, deeds of loving-kindness to the poor and to the rich. Also almsgiving is done with a man's money, deeds of loving-kindness with his money and in other ways. *Sukkah, 49b*

Better is he who shows a smiling countenance than he who offers milk to drink. *Ketubot, 111*

Whoever gives a small coin to a poor man has six blessings bestowed upon him, but he who speaks a kind word to him obtains eleven blessings. *Baba Batra, 9b*

He who has a claim for money upon his neighbor and knows that the latter is unable to pay, must not pass by him constantly.
Baba Metzia, 75

Rabbi Baruka of Huza frequented the market of Lapet. One day Elijah appeared to him there, and Rabbi Baruka asked him: "Is there among the people of this market any one that is destined to share in the World to Come?" Elijah replied, "There is none." But then two men appeared on the scene, and Elijah said to Rabbi Baruka, "No, here are two who will share in the World to Come."

Rabbi Baruka then asked them, "What is your occupation?" They said, "We are merry-makers. When we see a man who is downcast, we cheer him up; also when we see two people quarreling, we endeavor to make peace between them." *Ta'anit, 22a*

ON COMRADESHIP

People say: if two logs are dry and one is wet, the kindling of the two will kindle the wet log as well. *Sanhedrin, 93*

People say: either companionship or death. *Ta'anit, 23*

A torch in the hands of one who walks alone at night is like one companion; moonlight is like two companions. *Berakot, 43*

In choosing a friend, go up a step. *Yebamot, 63a*

He who entreats aid for his comrade, though he himself is in need, is answered first. *Baba Kamma, 92*

It is better for a man to cast himself into a flaming oven than to shame his comrade in public. *Berakot, 43*

Two dogs tending a flock were always quarreling. When the wolf attacked one, however, the other thought: "If I do not help my neighbor today, the wolf may attack me tomorrow." Thereupon the two dogs settled their differences, and together they killed the wolf. *Sanhedrin, 105a*

Rabbi Jeremiah said: He who occupies himself with the affairs of the community is as one who studies the Law. *T. J. Berakot, 5: 1*

If the community is in trouble, a man must not say, "I will go to my house, and eat and drink, and peace shall be with thee, O my soul." But a man must share in the trouble of the community, even as Moses did. He who shares in its troubles is worthy to see its consolation. *Ta'anit, 11a*

Honi ha-Ma'aggel once saw on his travels an old man planting a carob tree. He asked him when he thought the tree would bear fruit. "After seventy years," was the reply.

"Dost thou expect to live seventy years and eat the fruit of thy labor?"

"I did not find the world desolate when I entered it," said the old man, "and as my fathers planted for me before I was born, so do I plant for those who will come after me."   *Ibid., 23a*

The command to give charity weighs as much as all the other commandments put together. . . . He who gives alms in secret is greater than Moses.   *Baba Bathra, 9*

If a man sees that his means are straitened, let him give alms; and all the more if his means are large. He who cuts down his property, and gives alms, is preserved from the judgment of hell. It is like two sheep swimming over a stream. The one is shorn, the other not. The shorn sheep crosses in safety, the other is swept away.

Gittin, 7a

Let a man be generous in his charities, but let him beware of giving away all that he has.   *Arakin, 28a*

He who lends without interest is more worthy than he who gives charity, and he who invests money in the business of a poor man is the most worthy of all.   *Shabbat, 63*

Rabbi Jonah said: It is not written, "Happy is he who gives to the poor," but, "Happy is he who *considers* the poor" (Ps. 41: 1): i.e., he who ponders how to fulfil the command to help the poor. How did Rabbi Jonah act? If he met a man of good family, who had become impoverished, he would say, "I have heard that a legacy has been left to you in such a place; take this money in advance, and pay me back later." When the man accepted it, he then said to him, "It is a gift."

T. J. Pe'ah, 9: 21b

A Rabbi saw a man give a penny to a beggar publicly. He said to him: Better had you given him nothing than put him thus to shame.

Hagigah, 5a

No labor, however humble, is dishonoring.   *Nedarim, 49b*

Artisans are not required to stand up from their labor when a Sage passes by.   *Kiddushin, 33*

Rabbi Judah would enter the House of Study carrying a jug [which he himself had made], and Rabbi Simeon carrying a basket [which he himself had woven]. They said, "Great is handicraft, for it honors those who engage in it."   *Nedarim, 49b*

A man is obliged to teach his son a trade, and whoever does not teach his son a trade teaches him to become a robber. The person who has a trade in his hand is like a vineyard which is fenced in, so that cattle and beasts cannot get in, or passers-by eat of it.
Tosefta Kiddushin, 1:2

The Law declares that for stealing an ox one must repay fivefold, but for a lamb only fourfold *(Exod. 22:1)*. Rabbi Me'ir said, "See how God loves a worker! Why must the thief repay fivefold for an ox? Because the ox is a worker and his work was interrupted. But for the lamb, which is not a worker, the thief needs to repay only fourfold."
Tosefta Baba Kama, 7:10

Hire yourself out to a work which is beneath you rather than become dependent on others.   *T. J. Sanhedrin, 11 f. 30b*

Greater even than the pious man is he who eats that which is the fruit of his own toil; for Scripture declares him twice-blessed.
Berakot, 8a

ON THE WAGES OF LABOR

The right of the workingman always has precedence over that of his employer.   *Baba Metzia, 77*

Rabbi Johanan gave to his slave a portion of everything he himself ate. He said: "Did not He who made me also make him? Did not One fashion both of us in the womb?"   *T. J. Ketubot, 5*

The son of Rabbi Johanan ben Matthias hired several laborers and promised them their meals. His father said: "It would have been better had you given them their full hire in money, and let them buy their own meals . . . for a worker is entitled to eat what he himself prefers."   *Baba Metzia, 86*

Said Rabbi Huna: "The waiter should have his portion after the meal is over. But if fat meat or old wine is served, he must receive it immediately, that he may be spared the pain of longing for it."
Ketubot, 61

The gait of the ass is according to the amount of barley he receives.   *Sabbath, 51*

The chief merits are: at a wedding, to cause merriment; among mourners, to keep silent; at a lecture, to listen; at a seminar, to arrive early; at teaching, to concentrate; in time of fasting, to give charity.
Berakot, 6

God loves these three: the person who does not get angry; the one who does not get drunk; and the one who does not insist upon his privileges.

God hates these three: the person who says one thing with his mouth and thinks otherwise in his heart; the person who could give evidence in another's favor, but does not do so; and the person who, being alone, sees his neighbor sin, and gives unsupported testimony against him.

There are three types of men whose life is not worth living: he who is prone to rage; he who is too soft-hearted; and he who is too fastidious.   *Pesahim, 113*

There are three types of men whose life is not worth living: he who must eat at another's table; he whose wife rules over him, and he whose body is racked by pain.   *Betzah, 32*

Three things tranquillize a man's mind: a pleasant melody, a pleasant scene, and a fragrant odor. Three things broaden a man's mind: a fine house, a handsome wife, and beautiful furniture.
Berakot, 57b

Three things are good in a little measure and evil in large: yeast, salt, and hesitation.   *Ibid., 34*

Four classes of men will never see God's face: the scoffer, the liar, the slanderer, and the hypocrite.   *Sotah, 42a*

Of eight things a little is good and much is evil: travel, mating, wealth, work, wine, sleep, spiced drinks, and medicine.   *Gittin 70*

A single coin in a crock makes much noise, but if the crock is full of coins, it is silent.   *Baba Metzia, 85*

THE SCRIPTURES OF CHRISTIANITY

THE FOUR GOSPELS

THE BOOK OF ACTS

THE EPISTLES OF PAUL
I: *Romans*
II: *First Corinthians*
III: *Ephesians*
IV: *Second Thessalonians*
V: *First Timothy*

THE EPISTLE OF JAMES

INTRODUCTION

Christianity is the actual or nominal faith of nearly six hundred million people today—approximately thirty percent of the entire human race. Of these, more than a half are classed as Catholics, nearly a quarter as Protestants, and the rest as Orthodox. No other religion is as widespread and powerful as Christianity, nor as variegated and divided.

It began as a miniscule cult built around an obscure Jewish prophet and wonder-worker named Jesus (originally Jeshu) of Nazareth who was believed by his peasant followers to be the long-awaited Messiah. Convinced that he would live to usher in the Kingdom of Heaven, they were devastated when Jesus was condemned to death as a rebel against the empire of Rome. Their faith quickly revived, however, for they became persuaded that their Savior had risen from the grave, and would soon return to destroy this wicked world. Meanwhile they sought to practice the perfectionist doctrines he had advocated, setting up a utopian commune in which life could be lived as though the better world had already come.

Many such cults existed in Palestine during that period, for there was fierce hunger among the Jews for a way out of their miseries. Like most of the others, this was supported largely by poor and unlettered folk, and it too might soon have withered and died had it not providentially acquired a very gifted leader. He was a Jew born in Tarsus, a Greek settlement, a man of relatively wide culture and absolutely prodigious zeal. Once he became converted to the Nazarene cult, he saw in it a gospel of salvation for all men, not merely the Jews, and began preaching it as such throughout the Roman Empire. This entailed abandoning much that was traditionally Jewish—for example,

459

*circumcision and the dietary laws—and accepting even more that was
traditionally Gentile. Just as the apostle changed his own name from
the Hebrew Saul to the Latin Paulus, so he changed the Nazarene
cult from a vague heresy in Judaism to a new religion for all the world.*

*But Jesus had appeared on earth as a Jew, and the sole proof of his
Messiahship lay in the reputed conformity of his life to the predic-
tions given in the Jewish scriptures. Therefore those scriptures had to
be accepted in toto by this new religion; and so they were. Further
scriptures, however, were added as time went on: a set of* FOUR
GOSPELS *recounting the life and sayings of Jesus, a* BOOK OF ACTS *telling
how the belief in him became an organized movement, various*
EPISTLES *written by Paul and other of the early missionaries, and finally
a book of apocalyptic visions entitled* REVELATION. *These, grouped in a
canon named the New Testament, were bound together with the Old,
and called the Bible, meaning simply "The Book."*

THE FOUR GOSPELS

Apparently it was not until several decades after the death of Jesus, when the Christian cult had been carried far outside Palestine, that written records of his career first made their appearance. The earliest of which we have any knowledge is the GOSPEL ACCORDING TO MARK, *written probably in Rome around 70 A.D. It is based, it seems, on the tales recounted by Peter, who spent his last years as a missionary in Rome. Mark may have served as Peter's interpreter there, translating the old man's peasant Aramaic into the Greek still spoken by the immigrant population in Rome. After Peter was gone—he is said to have been killed during an anti-Christian riot in 64 A.D.—Mark evidently tried to set down what he remembered of the fisherman's reminiscences. These were largely confined to the deeds rather than the words of Jesus, to the devils he had exorcised and the miracles he had performed. Were Mark's our only Gospel, we would know nothing of the Beatitudes, the Lord's Prayer, the Golden Rule, and the great parables uttered by the Nazarene. (Nor, significantly, that he was believed to have been born of a virgin!)*

All that, and much else, got into two somewhat later Gospels which, though written independently, appear to have drawn on common source material. One was written, probably in Syria, by a Jewish apostle named MATTHEW, *and the other somewhere in the Aegean by a Gentile convert named* LUKE. *The differences between these two accounts are slight but illuminating. Matthew, the Jew, traces the descent of Jesus (through Joseph!) merely to Abraham; whereas Luke, the Gentile, traces it all the way back to Adam. Again, Matthew shows Jesus holding himself aloof from non-Jews (e.g., Matt. 15: 21–28), whereas Luke recounts episodes proving the precise opposite. (In Luke alone do we find the parable of the Good Samaritan.) Even more striking are the differences where both claim to quote Jesus' own words. For example:*

Luke 6: 20: *"Blessed are you poor."*
Matt. 5: 3: *"Blessed are the poor in spirit."*

461

Luke   6:21: *"Blessed are you that hunger now."*
Matt.   6:6: *"Blessed are those that hunger and thirst*
after righteousness."

Clearly Matthew recoils from making Jesus sound too radical, since even the rich can be poor "in spirit"—a point underscored by his failure to quote a verse that follows immediately in Luke: "But woe to you that are rich, for you already have your consolation."

Many more such discrepancies could be pointed out, and not alone between Matthew and Luke, but between both and Mark. Their importance, however, should not be exaggerated, for though each account has its distinctive character, reflecting the outlook of its author and the environment in which he wrote, all three tell very much the same tale. That is why these three are called the Synoptic Gospels—they see "eye to eye."

But there is also a fourth Gospel, JOHN, and this stands quite by itself. From all indications it is the product of a later generation and a completely alien soil, for in it Jesus is already divine rather than human, an avatar described in terms largely mystical and gnostic. All the following quotations from the King James Version—with a solitary exception—are therefore taken from the first three Gospels, since these are the most instructive ethically.

JOHN THE BAPTIST

The word of God came unto John the son of Zacharias in the wilderness. And he came into all the country about Jordan, preaching the baptism of repentance for the remission of sins; as it is written in the book of the words of Esais the prophet, saying, 'The voice of one crying in the wilderness. Prepare ye the way of the Lord, make his paths straight. Every valley shall be filled, and every mountain and hill shall be brought low; and the crooked shall be made straight, and the rough ways shall be made smooth; and all flesh shall see the salvation of God. Then said he to the multitude that came forth to be baptized of him, O generation of vipers, who hath warned you to flee from the wrath to come? Bring forth therefore fruits worthy of repentance, and begin not to say within yourselves, We have Abraham to our father: for I say unto you, that God is able of these stones to raise up children unto Abraham. And now also the axe is laid unto the root of the trees: every tree therefore which bringeth not forth good fruit is hewn down and cast into the fire. And the people asked him, saying What shall we do then? He answereth and saith unto them, He that hath two coats, let him impart to him that hath none; and he that hath meat, let him do likewise. Then came also publicans to be baptized, and said unto him, Master, what shall we do? And he said unto them, Exact no more than that which is appointed you. And the soldiers likewise de- manded of him, saying, And what shall we do? And he said unto them, Do violence to no man, neither accuse any falsely; and be content with your wages. And as the people were in expectation, and all men mused in their hearts of John, whether he were the Christ, or not; John answered, saying unto them all, I indeed bap- tize you with water; but one mightier than I cometh, the latchet of whose shoes I am not worthy to unloose: he shall baptize you with the Holy Ghost and with fire: whose fan is in his hand, and he will thoroughly purge his floor, and will gather the wheat into his garner; but the chaff he will burn with fire unquenchable. And many other things in his

exhortation preached he unto the people. But Herod the tetrach, being reproved by him for Herodias his brother Philip's wife, and for all the evils which Herod had done, added yet this above all, that he shut up John in prison. Now when all the people were baptized, it came to pass that Jesus also being baptized, and praying, the heaven was opened, and the Holy Ghost descended in a bodily shape like a dove upon him, and a voice came from heaven, which said, Thou art my beloved Son; in thee I am well pleased. And Jesus himself began to be about thirty years of age.

Luke 3: 2–23

JESUS AND THE TAX COLLECTOR

And after these things he went forth, and saw a publican, named Levi, sitting at the receipt of custom: and he said unto him, Follow me. And he left all, rose up, and followed him. And Levi made him a great feast in his own house: and there was a great company of publicans and of others that sat down with them. But their scribes and Pharisees murmured against his disciples, saying, Why do ye eat and drink with publicans and sinners? And Jesus answering said unto them, They that are whole need not a physician; but they that are sick. I came not to call the righteous, but sinners to repentance.

Luke 5: 27–32

ON SABBATH OBSERVANCE

At that time Jesus went on the sabbath day through the corn; and his disciples were an hungred, and began to pluck the ears of corn, and to eat. But when the Pharisees saw it, they said unto him, Behold, thy disciples do that which is not lawful to do upon the sabbath day. But he said unto them, Have ye not read what David did, when he was an hungred, and they that were with him; how he entered into the house of God, and did eat the shewbread, which was not lawful for him to eat, neither for them which were with him, but only for the priests? Or have ye not read in the law, how that on the sabbath days the priests in the temple profane the sabbath, and are blameless? But I say unto you, that in this place is one greater than the temple. But if ye had known what this meaneth, I will have mercy, and not sacrifice, ye would not have condemned the guiltless. For the Son of man is Lord even of the sabbath day.

Matthew 12: 1–8

And he was teaching in one of the synagogues on the sabbath. And, behold, there was a woman which had a spirit of infirmity eighteen years, and was bowed together, and could in no wise lift up herself. And when Jesus saw her, he called her to him, and said unto her, Woman, thou art loosed from thine infirmity. And he laid his hands on her: and immediately she was made straight, and glorified God. And the ruler of the synagogue answered with indignation, because that Jesus had healed on the sabbath day, and said unto the people, There are six days in which men ought to work: in them therefore come and be healed, and not on the sabbath day. The Lord then answered him, and said, Thou hypocrite, doth not each one of you on the sabbath loose his ox or his ass from the stall, and lead him away to watering? And ought not this woman, being a daughter of Abraham, whom Satan hath bound, lo, these eighteen years, be loosed from this bond on the sabbath day? And when he had said these things, all his adversaries were ashamed: and all the people rejoiced for all the glorious things that were done by him.

Luke 13: 10–17

SERMON ON THE MOUNT

And he lifted up his eyes on his disciples, and said, Blessed be ye poor: for yours is the kingdom of God. Blessed are ye that hunger now: for ye shall be filled. Blessed are ye that weep now: for ye shall laugh. Blessed are ye, when men shall hate you, and when they shall separate you from their company, and shall reproach you, and cast out your name as evil, for the Son of man's sake. Rejoice ye in that day, and leap for joy: for, behold, your reward is great in heaven: for in the like manner did their fathers unto the prophets. But woe unto you that are rich! for ye have received your consolation. Woe unto you that are full! for ye shall hunger. Woe unto you that laugh now! for ye shall mourn and weep. Woe unto you, when all men shall speak well of you! for so did their fathers to the false prophets.

But I say unto you which hear, Love your enemies, do good to them which hate you, bless them that curse you, and pray for them which despitefully use you. And unto him that smiteth thee on the one cheek offer also the other; and him that taketh away thy cloke forbid not to take thy coat also. Give to every man that asketh of thee; and of him that taketh away thy goods ask them not again. And as ye would that men should do to you, do ye also to them likewise.

Luke 6: 20–31

Ye are the salt of the earth: but if the salt have lost his savour, wherewith shall it be salted? it is thenceforth good for nothing, but to be cast out, and to be trodden under foot of men. Ye are the light of the world. A city that is set on an hill cannot be hid. Neither do men light a candle, and put it under a bushel, but on a candlestick;

and it giveth light unto all that are in the house. Let your light so shine before men, that they may see your good works, and glorify your Father which is in heaven.

Think not that I am come to destroy the law, or the prophets: I am not come to destroy, but to fulfil. For verily I say unto you, Till heaven and earth pass, one jot or one tittle shall in no wise pass from the law, till all be fulfilled. Whosoever therefore shall break one of these least commandments, and shall teach men so, he shall be called the least in the kingdom of heaven: but whosoever shall do and teach them, the same shall be called great in the kingdom of heaven. For I say unto you, that except your righteousness shall exceed the righteousness of the scribes and Pharisees, ye shall in no case enter into the kingdom of heaven.

Ye have heard that it was said by them of old time, Thou shalt not kill; and whosoever shall kill shall be in danger of the judgment: But I say unto you, that whosoever is angry with his brother without a cause shall be in danger of the judgment: and whosoever shall say to his brother, Raca, shall be in danger of the council: but whosoever shall say, Thou fool, shall be in danger of hell fire. Therefore if thou bring thy gift to the altar, and there rememberest that thy brother hath ought against thee; leave there thy gift before the altar, and go thy way; first be reconciled to thy brother, and then come and offer thy gift. Agree with thine adversary quickly, whiles thou art in the way with him; lest at any time the adversary deliver thee to the judge, and the judge deliver thee to the officer, and thou be cast into prison. Verily I say unto thee, Thou shalt by no means come out thence, till thou hast paid the uttermost farthing.

Ye have heard that it was said by them of old time, Thou shalt not commit adultery: but I say unto you, that whosoever looketh on a woman to lust after her hath committed adultery with her already in his heart. And if thy right eye offend thee, pluck it out, and cast it from thee: for it is profitable for thee that one of thy members should perish, and not that thy whole body should be cast into hell. And if thy right hand offend thee, cut it off, and cast it from thee: for it is profitable for thee that one of thy members should perish, and not that thy whole body should be cast into hell. It hath been said, Whosoever shall put away his wife, let him give her a writing of divorcement: but I say unto you, that whosoever shall put away his wife, saving for the cause of fornication, causeth her to commit adultery: and whosoever shall marry her that is divorced committeth adultery.

Again, ye have heard that it hath been said by them of old time, Thou shalt not forswear thyself, but shalt perform unto the Lord thine oaths: But I say unto you, Swear not at all; neither by heaven; for it is God's throne: nor by the earth; for it is his footstool: neither by Jerusalem; for it is the city of the great King. Neither shalt thou swear by thy head, because thou canst not make one hair white or black. But let your communication be, Yea, yea; Nay, nay: for whatsoever is more than these cometh of evil.

Ye have heard that it hath been said, An eye for an eye, and a tooth for a tooth: but I say unto you, that ye resist not evil: but whosoever shall smite thee on thy right cheek, turn to him the other also. And if any man will sue thee at the law, and take away thy coat, let him have thy cloke also. And whosoever shall compel thee to go a mile, go with him twain. Give to him that asketh thee, and from him that would borrow of thee turn not thou away.

Ye have heard that it hath been said, Thou shalt love thy neighbour, and hate thine enemy. But I say unto you, Love your enemies, bless them that curse you, do good to them that hate you, and pray for them which despitefully use you, and persecute you; that ye may be the children of your Father which is in heaven: for he maketh his sun to rise on the evil and on the good, and sendeth rain on the just and on the unjust. For if ye love them which love you, what reward have ye? do not even the publicans the same? And if ye salute your brethren only, what do ye more than others? do not even the publicans so? Be ye therefore perfect, even as your Father which is in heaven is perfect.

Take heed that ye do not your alms before men, to be seen of them: otherwise you have no reward of your Father which is in heaven. Therefore when thou doest thine alms, do not sound a trumpet before thee, as the hypocrites do in the synagogues and in the streets, that they may have glory of men. Verily I say unto you, They have their reward. But when thou doest alms, let not thy left hand know what thy right hand doeth: that thine alms may be in secret: and thy Father which seeth in secret himself shall reward thee openly. And when thou prayest, thou shalt not be as the hypocrites are: for they love to pray standing in the synagogues and in the corners of the streets, that they may be seen of men. Verily I say unto you,

They have their reward. But thou, when thou prayest, enter into thy closet, and when thou hast shut thy door, pray to thy Father which is in secret; and thy Father which seeth in secret shall reward thee openly. But when ye pray, use not vain repetitions, as the heathen do: for they think that they shall be heard for their much speaking. Be not ye therefore like unto them: for your Father knoweth what things ye have need of, before ye ask him. After this manner therefore pray ye: Our Father which art in heaven, hallowed be thy name. Thy kingdom come. Thy will be done in earth, as it is in heaven. Give us this day our daily bread. And forgive us our debts, as we forgive our debtors. And lead us not into temptation, but deliver us from evil: for thine is the kingdom, and the power, and the glory, for ever. Amen. For if ye forgive men their trespasses, your heavenly Father will also forgive you: but if ye forgive not men their trespasses, neither will your Father forgive your trespasses. Moreover when ye fast, be not, as the hypocrites, of a sad countenance: for they disfigure their faces, that they may appear unto men to fast. Verily I say unto you, They have their reward. But thou, when thou fastest, anoint thine head, and wash thy face; that thou appear not unto men to fast, but unto thy Father which is in secret: and thy Father, which seeth in secret, shall reward thee openly.

Lay not up for yourselves treasures upon earth, where moth and rust doth corrupt, and where thieves break through and steal: but lay up for yourselves treasures in heaven, where neither moth nor rust doth corrupt, and where thieves do not break through nor steal: for where your treasure is, there will your heart be also. The light of the body is the eye: if therefore thine eye be single, thy whole body shall be full of light. But if thine eye be evil, thy whole body shall be full of darkness. If therefore the light that is in thee be darkness, how great is that darkness!

No man can serve two masters: for either he will hate the one, and love the other; or else he will hold to the one, and despise the other. Ye cannot serve God and mammon. Therefore I say unto you, Take no thought for your life, what ye shall eat, or what ye shall drink; nor yet for your body, what ye shall put on. Is not the life more than meat, and the body than raiment? Behold the fowls of the air: for they sow not, neither do they reap, nor gather into barns; yet your heavenly Father feedeth them. Are you not much better than they? Which of you by taking thought can add one cubit unto his stature? And why take ye thought for raiment? Consider the lilies of the field, how they grow; they toil not, neither do they spin: And yet I say unto you, that even Solomon in all his glory was not arrayed like one of these. Wherefore, if God so clothe the grass of the field, which to-day is, and to-morrow is cast into the oven, shall he not much more clothe you, O ye of little faith? Therefore take no thought, saying, What shall we eat? or, What shall we drink? or, Wherewithal shall we be clothed? (For after all these things do the Gentiles seek:) for your heavenly Father knoweth that ye have need of all these things. But seek ye first the kingdom of God, and his righteousness; and all these things shall be added unto you. Take therefore no thought for the morrow: for the morrow shall take thought for the things of itself. Sufficient unto the day is the evil thereof.

Judge not, that ye be not judged. For with what judgment ye judge, ye shall be judged: and with what measure ye mete, it shall be measured to you again. And why beholdest thou the mote that is in thy brother's eye, but considerest not the beam that is in thine own eye? Or how wilt thou say to thy brother, Let me pull out the mote out of thine eye; and, behold, a beam is in thine own eye? Thou hypocrite, first cast out the beam out of thine own eye; and then shalt thou see clearly to cast out the mote out of thy brother's eye.

Give not that which is holy unto the dogs, neither cast ye your pearls before swine, lest they trample them under their feet, and turn again and rend you.

Ask, and it shall be given you; seek and ye shall find; knock, and it shall be opened unto you: for every one that asketh receiveth; and he that seeketh findeth; and to him that knocketh it shall be opened. Or what man is there of you, whom if his son ask bread, will he give him a stone? Or if he ask a fish, will he give him a serpent? If ye then, being evil, know how to give good gifts unto your children, how much more shall your Father which is in heaven give good things to them that ask him? Therefore all things whatsoever ye would that men should do to you, do ye even so to them: for this is the law and the prophets.

Enter ye in at the strait gate: for wide is the gate, and broad is the way, that leadeth to destruction, and many there be which go in thereat: because strait is the gate, and narrow is the way, which leadeth unto life, and few there be that find it.

Beware of false prophets, which come to you in sheep's clothing, but inwardly they are ravening wolves. Ye shall know them by their fruits. Do men gather grapes of thorns, or figs of thistles? Even so every good tree bringeth forth good fruit; but a corrupt tree bringeth forth evil fruit. A good tree cannot bring forth evil fruit, neither can a corrupt tree bring forth good fruit. Every tree that bringest not forth good fruit is hewn down, and cast into the fire. Wherefore by their fruits ye shall know them.

Not every one that saith unto me, Lord, Lord, shall enter into the kingdom of heaven; but he that doeth the will of my Father which is in heaven. Many will say to me in that day, Lord, Lord, have we not prophesied in thy name? and in thy name have cast out devils? and in thy name done many wonderful works? And then will I profess unto them, I never knew you: depart from me, ye that work iniquity.

Therefore whosoever heareth these sayings of mine, and doeth them, I will liken him unto a wise man, which built his house upon a rock: and the rain descended, and the floods came, and the winds blew, and beat upon that house; and it fell not: for it was founded upon a rock. And every one that heareth these sayings of mine, and doeth them not, shall be likened unto a foolish man, which built his house upon the sand: and the rain descended, and the floods came, and the winds blew, and beat upon that house; and it fell: and great was the fall of it. And it came to pass, when Jesus had ended these sayings, the people were astonished at his doctrine: for he taught them as one having authority, and not as scribes.

Matthew 5: 13–7: 29

THE SINFUL WOMAN

And one of the Pharisees desired him that he would eat with him. And he went into the Pharisee's house, and sat down to meat. And behold, a woman in the city, which was a sinner, when she knew that Jesus sat at meat in the Pharisee's house, brought an alabaster box of ointment. And stood at his feet behind him weeping, and began to wash his feet with tears, and did wipe them with the hairs of her head, and kissed his feet, and anointed them with the ointment. Now when the Pharisee which had bidden him saw it, he spake within himself, saying, This man, if he were a prophet, would have known who and what manner of woman this is that toucheth him: for she is a sinner. And Jesus answering said unto him, Simon, I have somewhat to say unto thee. And he saith, Master, say on. There was a certain creditor which had two debtors: the one owed five hundred pence, and the other fifty. And when they had nothing to pay, he frankly forgave them both. Tell me therefore, which of them will love him most? Simon answered and said, I suppose that he, to whom he forgave most. And he said unto him, Thou hast rightly judged. And he turned to the woman, and said unto Simon, Seest thou this woman? I entered into thine house, thou gavest me no water for my feet: but she hath washed my feet with tears, and wiped them with the hairs of her head. Thou gavest me no kiss: but this woman since the time I came in hath not ceased to kiss my feet. My head with oil thou didst not anoint: but this woman hath anointed my feet with ointment. Wherefore I say unto thee, Her sins, which are many, are forgiven; for she loved much: but to whom little is forgiven, the same loveth little. And he said unto her, Thy sins are forgiven. And they that sat at meat with him began to say within themselves, Who is this that forgiveth sins also? And he said to the woman, Thy faith hath saved thee; go in peace.

Luke 7: 36–50

PARABLES OF THE SOIL

The same day went Jesus out of the house, and sat by the sea side. And great multitudes were gathered together unto him, so that he went into a ship, and sat; and the whole multitude stood on the shore. And he spake many things unto them in parables, saying, Behold, a sower went forth to sow; and when he sowed, some seeds fell by the way side, and the fowls came and devoured them up: some fell upon stony places, where they had not much earth: and forthwith they sprung up, because they had no deepness of earth: and when the sun was up, they were scorched; and because they had no root, they withered away. And some fell among thorns; and the thorns sprung up, and choked them: but others fell into good ground, and brought forth fruit, some an hundredfold, some sixtyfold, some thirtyfold. Who hath ears to hear, let him hear.

Matthew 13: 1–9

Hear ye therefore the parable of the sower. When any one heareth the word of the kingdom, and understandeth it not, then cometh the wicked one, and catcheth away that which was sown in his heart. This is he which received seed by the way side. But he that received the seed into stony places, the same is he that heareth the word, and anon with joy receiveth it; yet hath he not root in himself, but dureth for a while; for when tribulation or persecution ariseth because of the word, by and by he is offended. He also that received seed among the thorns is he that heareth the word; and the care of this world, and the deceitfulness of riches, choke the word, and he becometh unfruitful. But he that received seed into the good ground is he that heareth the word, and understandeth it; which also beareth fruit, and bringeth forth, some an hundredfold, some sixty, some thirty.

Matthew 13: 18–23

THE KINGDOM OF HEAVEN

Again, the kingdom of heaven is like unto treasure hid in a field; the which when a man hath found, he hideth, and for joy thereof goeth and selleth all that he hath, and buyeth that field.

Again, the kingdom of heaven is like unto a merchant man, seeking goodly pearls: who, when he had found one pearl of great price, went and sold all that he had, and bought it.

Again, the kingdom of heaven is like unto a net, that was cast into the sea, and gathered of every kind: which, when it was full, they drew to shore, and sat down and gathered the good into vessels, but cast the bad away. So shall it be at the end of the world: the angels shall come forth, and sever the wicked from among the just. And shall cast them into the furnace of fire; there shall be wailing and gnashing of teeth. Jesus saith unto them, Have ye understood all these things? They say unto him, Yea, Lord. Then said he unto them, Therefore every scribe which is instructed into the kingdom of heaven is like unto a man that is an householder, which bringeth forth out of his treasure things new and old.

And it came to pass, that when Jesus had finished these parables, he departed thence. And when he was come into his own country, he taught them in their synagogue, insomuch that they were astonished, and said, Whence hath this man this wisdom, and these mighty works? Is not this the carpenter's son? is not his mother called Mary? and his brethren, James, and Joses and Simon, and Judas? And his sisters, are they not all with us? Whence then hath this man all these things? And they were offended in him. But Jesus said unto them,

A prophet is not without honour, save in his own country, and in his own house. And he did not many mighty works there because of their unbelief.

Matthew 13: 44–58

EATING WITH UNWASHED HANDS

Then came together unto him the Pharisees, and certain of the scribes, which came from Jerusalem. And when they saw some of his disciples eat bread with defiled, that is to say, with unwashen hands, they found fault. For the Pharisees, and all the Jews, except they wash their hands oft, eat not, holding the tradition of the elders. And when they come from the market, except they wash, they eat not. And many other things there be, which they have received to hold, as the washing of cups, and pots, brazen vessels, and of tables. Then the Pharisees and scribes asked him, Why walk not thy disciples according to the tradition of the elders, but eat bread with unwashen hands? He answered and said unto them, Well hath Esais prophesied of you hypocrites, as it is written, This people honoureth me with their lips, but their heart is far from me. Howbeit in vain do they worship me, teaching for doctrines the commandments of men. For laying aside the commandment of God, ye hold the tradition of men, as the washing of pots and cups: and many other such things ye do. And he said unto them, Full well ye reject the commandment of God, that ye may keep your own tradition. For Moses said, Honour thy father and thy mother; and whoso curseth father or mother, let him die the death: but ye say, If a man shall say to his father or mother, It is Corban, that is to say, a gift, by whatsoever thou mightest be profited by me; he shall be free. And ye suffer him no more to do ought for his father or his mother; making the word of God of none effect through your tradition, which ye have delivered: and many such like things do ye.

And when he had called all the people unto him, he said unto them, Hearken unto me every one of you, and understand: There is nothing from without a man, that entering into him can defile him: but the things which come out of him, those are they that defile the man. If any man have ears to hear, let him hear. And when he was entered into the house from the people, his disciples asked him concerning the parable. And he saith unto them, Are ye so without understanding also? Do ye not perceive, that whatsoever thing from without entereth into the man, it cannot defile him; because it entereth not into his heart, but into the belly, and goeth out into the draught, purging all meats? And he said, That which cometh out of the man, that defileth the man. For from within, out of the heart of men, proceed evil thoughts, adulteries, fornications, murders, thefts, covetousness, wickedness, deceit, lasciviousness, an evil eye, blasphemy, pride, foolishness: all these evil things come from within, and defile the man.

Mark 7: 1–23

INSTRUCTIONS TO THE DISCIPLES

These twelve Jesus sent forth, and commanded them, saying, Go not into the way of the Gentiles, and into any city of the Samaritans enter ye not: but go rather to the lost sheep of the house of Israel. And as ye go, preach, saying, The kingdom of heaven is at hand. Heal the sick, cleanse the lepers, raise the dead, cast out devils: freely ye have received, freely give. Provide neither gold, nor silver, nor brass in your purses, nor scrip for your journey, neither two coats, neither shoes, nor yet staves: for the workman is worthy of his meat. And into whatsoever city or town ye shall enter, inquire who in it is worthy; and there abide till ye go thence. And when ye come into an house, salute it. And if the house be worthy, let your peace come upon it: but if it be not worthy, let your peace return to you. And whosoever shall not receive you, nor hear your words, when ye depart out of that house or city, shake off the dust of your feet. Verily I say unto you, It shall be more tolerable for the land of Sodom and Gomorrha in the day of judgment, than for that city.

Behold, I send you forth as sheep in the midst of wolves: be ye therefore wise as serpents, and harmless as doves. But beware of men: for they will deliver you up to the councils, and they will scourge you in their synagogues; And ye shall be brought before governors and kings for my sake, for a testimony against them and the Gentiles. But when they deliver you up, take no thought how or what ye shall speak: for it shall be given you in that same hour what ye shall speak. For it is not ye that speak, but the Spirit of your Father which speaketh in you. And the brother shall deliver up the brother to death, and

the father the child: and the children shall rise up against their
parents, and cause them to be put to death. And ye shall be hated
of all men for my name's sake: but he that endureth to the end shall
be saved. But when they persecute you in this city, flee ye into another:
for verily I say unto you, Ye shall not have gone over the cities of
Israel, till the Son of man be come. The disciple is not above his
master, nor the servant above his lord. It is enough for the disciple
that he be as his master, and the servant as his lord. If they have
called the master of the house Beelzebub, how much more shall they
call them of his household? Fear them not therefore: for there is
nothing covered, that shall not be revealed; and hid, that shall not
be known. What I tell you in darkness, that speak ye in light: and
what ye hear in the ear, that preach ye upon the housetops. And fear
not them which kill the body, but are not able to kill the soul: but
rather fear him which is able to destroy both soul and body in hell.
Are not two sparrows sold for a farthing? and one of them shall not
fall on the ground without your Father. But the very hairs of your
head are all numbered. Fear ye not therefore, ye are of more value
than many sparrows. Whosoever therefore shall confess me before
men, him will I confess also before my Father which is in heaven.
But whosoever shall deny me before men, him will I also deny before
my Father which is in heaven. Think not that I am come to send
peace on earth: I came not to send peace, but a sword. For I am come
to set a man at variance against his father, and the daughter against
her mother, and the daughter in law against her mother in law. And
a man's foes shall be they of his own household. He that loveth father
or mother more than me is not worthy of me: and he that loveth
son or daughter more than me is not worthy of me. And he that
taketh not his cross, and followeth after me, is not worthy of me.
He that findeth his life shall lose it: and he that loseth his life for
my sake shall find it. He that receiveth you receiveth me, and he that
receiveth me receiveth him that sent me. He that receiveth a prophet
in the name of a prophet shall receive a prophet's reward; and he that
receiveth a righteous man in the name of a righteous man shall receive
a righteous man's reward. And whosoever shall give to drink unto one
of these little ones a cup of cold water only in the name of a disciple,
verily I say unto you, he shall in no wise lose his reward.

Matthew 10: 5–42

ON HUMILITY AND FORGIVENESS

At the same time came the disciples unto Jesus, saying, Who is the greatest in the kingdom of heaven? And Jesus called a little child unto him, and set him in the midst of them, And said, Verily I say unto you, except ye be converted, and become as little children, ye shall not enter into the kingdom of heaven. Whosoever therefore shall humble himself as this little child, the same is greatest in the kingdom of heaven. And whoso shall receive one such little child in my name receiveth me. But whoso shall offer one of these little ones which believe in me, it were better for him that a millstone were hanged about his neck, and that he were drowned in the depth of the sea.

Woe unto the world because of offences! for it must needs be that offences come; but woe to that man by whom the offence cometh! Wherefore if thy hand or thy foot offend thee, cut them off, and cast them from thee: it is better for thee to enter into life halt or maimed, rather than having two hands or two feet to be cast into everlasting fire. And if thine eye offend thee, pluck it out, and cast it from thee: it is better for thee to enter into life with one eye, rather than having two eyes to be cast into hell fire. Take heed that ye despise not one of these little ones; for I say unto you, that in heaven their angels do always behold the face of my Father which is in heaven. For the Son of man is come to save that which was lost. How think ye? if a man have an hundred sheep, and one of them be gone astray, doth he not leave the ninety and nine, and goeth into the mountains, and seeketh that which is gone astray? And if so be that he find it, verily I say unto you, he rejoiceth more of that sheep, than of the ninety and nine which went not astray. Even so it is not the will of your Father which is in heaven, that one of these little ones should perish.

Moreover if thy brother shall trespass against thee, go and tell him his fault between thee and him alone: if he shall hear thee, thou hast gained thy brother. But if he will not hear thee, then take with thee one or two more, that in the mouth of two or three witnesses every word may be established. And if he shall neglect to hear them, tell it unto the church: but if he neglect to hear the church, let him be unto thee as an heathen man and a publican. Verily I say unto you, Whatsoever ye shall bind on earth shall be bound in heaven: and whatsoever ye shall loose on earth shall be loosed in heaven. Again I say unto you, that if two of you shall agree on earth as touching any thing that they shall ask, it shall be done for them of my Father which is in heaven. For where two or three are gathered together in my name, there am I in the midst of them.

Then came Peter to him, and said, Lord, how oft shall my brother sin against me, and I forgive him? till seven times? Jesus saith unto him, I say not unto thee, Until seven times: but, Until seventy times seven. Therefore is the kingdom of heaven likened unto a certain king, which would take account of his servants. And when he had begun to reckon, one was brought unto him, which owed him ten thousand talents. But forasmuch as he had not to pay, his lord commanded him to be sold, and his wife, and children, and all that he had, and payment to be made. The servant therefore fell down, and worshipped him, saying, Lord, have patience with me, and I will pay thee all. Then the lord of that servant was moved with compassion, and loosed him, and forgave him the debt. But the same servant went out, and found one of his fellowservants, which owed him an hundred pence: and he laid hands on him, and took him by the throat, saying, Pay me that thou owest. And his fellowservant fell down at his feet, and besought him, saying, Have patience with me, and I will pay thee all. And he would not: but went and cast him into prison, till he should pay the debt. So when his fellowservants saw what was done, they were very sorry, and came and told unto their lord all that was done. Then his lord, after that he had called him, said unto him, O thou wicked servant, I forgave thee all that debt, because thou desiredst me: Shouldest not thou also have had compassion on thy fellowservant, even as I had pity on thee? And his lord was wroth, and delivered him to the tormentors, till he should pay all that was due unto him. So likewise shall my heavenly Father do also unto you, if ye from your hearts forgive not every one his brother their trespasses.

Matthew 18: 1–35

THE GOOD SAMARITAN

And, behold, a certain lawyer stood up, and tempted him, saying, Master, what shall do I do to inherit eternal life? He said unto him, What is written in the law? how readest thou? And he answering said, Thou shalt love the Lord thy God with all thy heart, and with all thy soul, and with all thy strength, and with all thy mind; and thy neighbour as thyself. And he said unto him, Thou hast answered right: this do, and thou shalt live. But he, willing to justify himself, said unto Jesus, And who is my neighbour? And Jesus answering said, A certain man went down from Jerusalem to Jericho, and fell among thieves, which stripped him of his raiment, and wounded him, and departed, leaving him half dead. And by chance there came down a certain priest that way: and when he saw him, he passed by on the other side. And likewise a Levite, when he was at the place, came and looked on him, and passed by on the other side. But a certain Samaritan, as he journeyed, came where he was: and when he saw him, he had compassion on him, and went to him, and bound up his wounds, pouring in oil and wine, and set him on his own beast, and brought him to an inn, and took care of him. And on the morrow when he departed, he took out two pence, and gave them to the host, and said unto him, Take care of him; and whatsoever thou spendest more, when I come again, I will repay thee. Which now of these three, thinkest thou, was neighbour unto him that fell among the thieves? And he said, He that shewed mercy on him. Then said Jesus unto him, Go, and do thou likewise.

Luke 10: 25–37

AGAINST THE HYPOCRITES

And as he spake, a certain Pharisee besought him to dine with him: and he went in, and sat down to meat. And when the Pharisee saw it, he marvelled that he had not first washed before dinner. And the Lord said unto him, Now do ye Pharisees make clean the outside of the cup and the platter; but your inward part is full of ravening and wickedness. Ye fools, did not he that made that which is without make that which is within also? But rather give alms of such things as ye have; and, behold, all things are clean unto you. But woe unto you, Pharisees! for ye tithe mint and rue and all manner of herbs, and pass over judgment and the love of God: these ought ye to have done, and not to leave the other undone. Woe unto you, Pharisees! for ye love the uppermost seats in the synagogues, and greetings in the markets. Woe unto you, scribes and Pharisees, hypocrites! for ye are as graves which appear not, and the men that walk over them are not aware of them.

Then answered one of the lawyers, and said unto him, Master, thus saying thou reproachest us also. And he said, Woe unto you also, ye lawyers! for ye lade men with burdens grievous to be borne, and ye yourselves touch not the burdens with one of your fingers. Woe unto you! for ye build the sepulchres of the prophets, and your fathers killed them. Truly ye bear witness that ye allow the deeds of your fathers: for they indeed killed them, and ye build their sepulchres. Therefore also said the wisdom of God, I will send them prophets and apostles, and some of them they shall slay and persecute: that the blood of all the prophets, which was shed from the foundation of the world, may be required of this generation; from the blood of Abel unto the blood of Zacharias, which perished between the altar and the temple: verily I say unto you, It shall be required of this generation. Woe unto you, lawyers! for ye have taken away the key of knowledge: ye entered not in yourselves, and them that were entering in ye hindered. And as he said these things unto them, the scribes and the Pharisees began to urge him vehemently, and to provoke him to speak of many things: laying wait for him, and seeking to catch something out of his mouth, that they might accuse him.

Luke 11: 37–54

CONCERNING COVETOUSNESS

And he spake a parable unto them, saying, The ground of a certain rich man brought forth plentifully: and he thought within himself, saying, What shall I do, because I have no room where to bestow my fruits? And he said, This will I do: I will pull down my barns, and build greater; and there will I bestow all my fruits and my goods. And I will say to my soul, Soul, thou hast much goods laid up for many years; take thine ease, eat, drink, and be merry. But God said unto him, Thou fool, this night thy soul shall be required of thee: then whose shall those things be, which thou hast provided? So is he that layeth up treasure for himself, and is not rich toward God.

And he said unto his disciples, Therefore I say unto you, Take no thought for your life, what ye shall eat; neither for the body, what ye shall put on. The life is more than meat, and the body is more than raiment. Consider the ravens: for they neither sow nor reap; which neither have storehouse nor barn; and God feedeth them: how much more are ye better than the fowls? And which of you with taking thought can add to his stature one cubit? If ye then be not able to do that thing which is least, why take ye thought for the rest? Consider the lilies how they grow: they toil not, they spin not; and yet I say unto you, that Solomon in all his glory was not arrayed like one of these. If then God so clothe the grass, which is to-day in the field, and to-morrow is cast into the oven; how much more will he clothe you, O ye of little faith? And seek not ye what ye shall eat, or what ye shall drink, neither be ye of doubtful mind. For all these things do the nations of the world seek after: and your Father knoweth that ye have need of these things.

But rather seek ye the kingdom of God; and all these things shall be added unto you. Fear not, little flock; for it is your Father's good pleasure to give you the kingdom. Sell that ye have, and give alms; provide yourselves bags which wax not old, a treasure in the heavens that faileth not, where no thief approacheth, neither moth corrupteth. For where your treasure is there will your heart be also.

Luke 12: 15–34

PARABLES OF GRACE

And the Pharisees and scribes murmured, saying, This man receiveth sinners, and eateth with them.

And he spake this parable unto them, saying, What man of you, having an hundred sheep, if he lose one of them, doth not leave the ninety and nine in the wilderness, and go after that which is lost, until he find it? And when he hath found it, he layeth it on his shoulders, rejoicing. And when he cometh home, he calleth together his friends and neighbours, saying unto them, Rejoice with me; for I have found my sheep which was lost. I say unto you, that likewise joy shall be in heaven over one sinner that repenteth, more than over ninety and nine just persons, which need no repentance.

Either what woman having ten pieces of silver, if she lose one piece, doth not light a candle, and sweep the house, and seek diligently till she find it? And when she hath found it, she calleth her friends and her neighbours together, saying, Rejoice with me; for I have found the piece which I had lost. Likewise, I say unto you, there is joy in the presence of the angels of God over one sinner that repenteth.

And he said, A certain man had two sons: and the younger of

them said to his father, Father, give me the portion of goods that falleth to me. And he divided unto them his living. And not many days after the younger son gathered all together, and took his journey into a far country, and there wasted his substance with riotous living. And when he had spent all, there arose a mighty famine in that land; and he began to be in want. And he went and joined himself to a citizen of that country; and he sent him into his fields to feed swine. And he would fain have filled his belly with the husks that the swine did eat: and no man gave unto him. And when he came to himself, he said, How many hired servants of my father's have bread enough and to spare, and I perish with hunger! I will arise and go to my father, and will say unto him, Father, I have sinned against heaven, and before thee, and am no more worthy to be called thy son: make me as one of thy hired servants. And he arose, and came to his father. But when he was yet a great way off, his father saw him, and had compassion, and ran and fell on his neck and kissed him. And the son said unto him, Father, I have sinned against heaven, and in thy sight, and am no more worthy to be called thy son. But the father said to his servants, Bring forth the best robe, and put it on him; and put a ring on his hand, and shoes on his feet: and bring hither the fatted calf, and kill it; and let us eat, and be merry: for this my son was dead, and is alive again; he was lost, and is found. And they began to be merry. Now his elder son was in the field: and as he came and drew nigh to the house, he heard musick and dancing. And he called one of the servants, and asked what these things meant. And he said unto him, Thy brother is come; and thy father hath killed the fatted calf, because he hath received him safe and sound. And he was angry, and would not go in: therefore came his father out, and intreated him. And he answering said to his father, Lo, these many years do I serve thee, neither transgressed I at any time thy commandment: and yet thou never gavest me a kid, that I might make merry with my friends: but as soon as this thy son was come, which hath devoured thy living with harlots, thou hast killed for him the fatted calf. And he said unto him, Son, thou art ever with me, and all that I have is thine. It was meet that we should make merry, and be glad: for this thy brother was dead, and is alive again; and was lost, and is found.

Luke 15: 2–32

PARABLE ON SELF-RIGHTEOUSNESS

And he spake this parable unto certain which trusted in themselves that they were righteous, and despised others: Two men went up into the temple to pray; the one a Pharisee, and the other a publican. The Pharisee stood and prayed thus with himself, God, I thank thee, that I am not as other men are, extortioners, unjust, adulterers, or even as this publican. I fast twice in the week, I give tithes of all that I possess. And the publican, standing afar off, would not lift up so much as his eyes unto heaven, but smote upon his breast, saying, God be merciful to me a sinner. I tell you, this man went down to his house justified rather than the other: for every one that exalteth himself shall be abased; and he that humbleth himself shall be exalted.

Luke 18: 9–14

CONCERNING DIVORCE

The Pharisees also came unto him, tempting him, and saying unto him, Is it lawful for a man to put away his wife for every cause? And he answered and said unto them, Have ye not read, that he which made them at the beginning made them male and female, and said, For this cause shall a man leave father and mother, and shall cleave to his wife: and they twain shall be one flesh? Wherefore they are no more twain, but one flesh. What therefore God hath joined together, let not man put asunder. They say unto him, Why did Moses then command to give a writing of divorcement, and to put her away? He saith unto them, Moses because of the hardness of your hearts suffered you to put away your wives: but from the beginning it was not so. And I say unto you, Whosoever shall put away his wife, except it be for fornication, and shall marry another, committeth adultery: and whoso marrieth her which is put away doth commit adultery.

Matthew 19: 3–9

THE RICH YOUNG MAN

And when he was gone forth into the way, there came one running, and kneeled to him, and asked him, Good Master, what shall I do that I may inherit eternal life? And Jesus said unto him, Why callest thou me good? there is none good but one, that is, God. Thou knowest the commandments, Do not commit adultery, Do not kill, Do not steal, Do not bear false witness, Defraud not, Honour thy father and mother. And he answered and said unto him, Master, all these have I observed from my youth. Then Jesus beholding him loved him, and said unto him, One thing thou lackest: go thy way, sell whatsoever thou hast, and give to the poor, and thou shalt have treasure in heaven: and come, take up the cross, and follow me. And he was sad at that saying, and went away grieved: for he had great possessions.

And Jesus looked round about, and saith unto his disciples, How hardly shall they that have riches enter into the kingdom of God! And the disciples were astonished at his words. But Jesus answereth again, and saith unto them, Children, how hard is it for them that trust in riches to enter into the kingdom of God! It is easier for a camel to go through the eye of a needle, than for a rich man to enter into the kingdom of God. And they were astonished out of measure, saying among themselves, Who then can be saved? And Jesus looking upon them saith, With men it is impossible, but not with God: for with God all things are possible.

Then Peter began to say unto him, Lo, we have left all, and have followed thee. And Jesus answered and said, Verily I say unto you, There is no man that hath left house, or brethren, or sisters, or father, or mother, or wife, or children, or lands, for my sake, and the gospel's, But he shall receive an hundredfold now in this time, houses, and brethren, and sisters, and mothers, and children, and lands, with persecutions; and in the world to come eternal life. But many that are first shall be last; and the last first.

Mark 10: 17–31

DRIVING OUT THE MONEYCHANGERS

And they come to Jerusalem: and Jesus went into the temple, and began to cast out them that sold and bought in the temple, and overthrew the tables of the moneychangers, and the seats of them that sold doves; And would not suffer that any man should carry any vessel through the temple. And he taught, saying unto them, Is it not written, My house shall be called of all nations the house of prayer? but ye have made it a den of thieves. And the scribes and chief priests heard it, and sought how they might destroy him: for they feared him, because all the people was astonished at his doctrine. And when even was come he went out of the city.

And in the morning, as they passed by, they saw the fig tree dried up from the roots. And Peter calling to remembrance saith unto him, Master, behold, the fig tree which thou cursedst is withered away. And Jesus answering saith unto them, Have faith in God. For verily I say unto you, That whosoever shall say unto this mountain, Be thou removed, and be thou cast into the sea; and shall not doubt in his heart, but shall believe that those things which he saith shall come to pass; he shall have whatsoever he saith. Therefore I say unto you, What things soever ye desire, when ye pray, believe that ye receive them, and ye shall have them. And when ye stand praying, forgive, if ye have ought against any: that your Father also which is in heaven may forgive you your trespasses. But if ye do not forgive, neither will your Father which is in heaven forgive your trespasses.

And they come again to Jerusalem: and as he was walking in the temple, there come to him the chief priests, and the scribes, and the elders, and say unto him, By what authority doest thou these things? and who gave thee this authority to do these things? And Jesus answered and said unto them, I will also ask of you one question, and answer me, and I will tell you by what authority I do these things. The baptism of John, was it from heaven, or of men? answer me. And they reasoned with themselves, saying, If we shall say, From heaven; he will say, Why then did ye not believe him? But if we shall say, Of men; they feared the people: for all men counted John, that he was a prophet indeed. And they answered and said unto Jesus, We cannot tell. And Jesus answering saith unto them, Neither do I tell you by what authority I do these things.

Mark 11:15–33

OF OSTENTATION AND OTHER SINS

Then spake Jesus to the multitude, and to his disciples, saying, The scribes and the Pharisees sit in Moses' seat: all therefore whatsoever they bid you observe, that observe and do; but do not ye after their works: for they say, and do not. For they bind heavy burdens and grievous to be borne, and lay them on men's shoulders; but they themselves will not move them with one of their fingers. But all their works they do for to be seen of men: they make broad their phylac-

teries, and enlarge the borders of their garments. And love the uppermost rooms at feasts, and the chief seats in the synagogues, and greetings in the markets, and to be called of men, Rabbi, Rabbi. But be
not ye called Rabbi: for one is your Master, even Christ; and all ye
are brethren. And call no man your father upon the earth: for one
is your Father, which is in heaven. Neither be ye called masters: for
one is your Master, even Christ. But he that is greatest among you
shall be your servant. And whosoever shall exalt himself shall be
abased; and he that shall humble himself shall be exalted.

But woe unto you, scribes and Pharisees, hypocrites! for ye shut up
the kingdom of heaven against men: for ye neither go in yourselves,
neither suffer ye them that are entering to go in. Woe unto you,
scribes and Pharisees, hypocrites! for ye devour widows' houses, and
for a pretence make long prayer: therefore ye shall receive the greater
damnation. Woe unto you, scribes and Pharisees, hypocrites! for ye
compass sea and land to make one proselyte, and when he is made,
ye make him twofold more the child of hell than yourselves. Woe
unto you, ye blind guides, which say, Whosoever shall swear by the
temple, it is nothing; but whosoever shall swear by the gold of the
temple, he is a debtor! Ye fools and blind: for whether is greater, the
gold or the temple that sanctifieth the gold? And, whosoever shall
swear by the altar, it is nothing; but whosoever sweareth by the gift
that is upon it, he is guilty. Ye fools and blind: for whether is greater,
the gift, or the altar that sanctifieth the gift? Whoso therefore shall
swear by the altar, sweareth by it, and by all things thereon. And
whoso shall swear by the temple, sweareth by it, and by him that
dwelleth therein. And he that shall swear by heaven sweareth by the
throne of God, and by him that sitteth thereon. Woe unto you,
scribes and Pharisees, hypocrites! for ye pay tithe of mint and anise
and cummin, and have omitted the weightier matters of the law,
judgment, mercy, and faith: these ought ye to have done, and not to
leave the other undone. Ye blind guides, which strain at a gnat, and
swallow a camel. Woe unto you, scribes and Pharisees, hypocrites!
for ye make clean the outside of the cup and of the platter, but within
they are full of extortion and excess. Thou blind Pharisee, cleanse first
that which is within the cup and platter, that the outside of them
may be clean also. Woe unto you, scribes and Pharisees, hypocrites!
for ye are like unto whited sepulchres, which indeed appear beautiful
outward, but are within full of dead men's bones, and of all unclean-

ness. Even so ye also outwardly appear righteous unto men, but within ye are full of hypocrisy and iniquity. Woe unto you, scribes and Pharisees, hypocrites! because ye build the tombs of the prophets, and garnish the sepulchres of the righteous, And say, If we had been in the days of our fathers, we would not have been partakers with them in the blood of the prophets. Wherefore ye be witnesses unto yourselves, that ye are the children of them which killed the prophets. Fill ye up then the measure of your fathers. Ye serpents, ye generation of vipers, how can ye escape the damnation of hell?

Matthew 23: 1–33

WHO IS WITHOUT SIN?[1]

Jesus went unto the mount of Olives. And early in the morning he came again into the temple and all the people came unto him; and he sat down, and taught them. And the scribes and Pharisees brought unto him a woman taken in adultery; and when they had set her in the midst, they say unto him, Master, this woman was taken in adultery in the very act. Now Moses in the law commanded us, that such should be stoned: but what sayest thou? This they said, tempting him, that they might have to accuse him. But Jesus stooped down, and with his finger wrote on the ground, as though he heard them not. So when they continued asking him, he lifted up himself, and said unto them, He that is without sin among you, let him first cast a stone at her. And again he stooped down, and wrote on the ground. And they which heard it, being convicted by their own conscience, went out one by one, beginning at the eldest, even unto the last: and Jesus was left alone, and the woman standing in the midst. When Jesus had lifted up himself, and saw none but the woman, he said unto her, Woman, where are those thine accusers? hath no man condemned thee?

John 8: 1–10

[1] There is some doubt as to the authenticity of this most dramatic passage. It reflects a latitudinarianism far more pagan than Hebraic, and many scholars suspect the story was told originally of some tolerant Greek philosopher, not Jesus. They point to the fact that the passage either does not appear at all in the most ancient manuscripts, or else crops up fugitively as a marginal note in Luke or an appended paragraph at the end of John. Finally some scribe must have inserted it—none too neatly, we can see—in the body of the Fourth Gospel, and there alone can it be found at present.

THE GREAT COMMANDMENT

And one of the scribes came, and having heard them reasoning together, and perceiving that he had answered them well, asked him, Which is the first commandment of all? And Jesus answered him, The first of all the commandments is, Hear, O Israel; The Lord our God is one Lord: And thou shalt love the Lord thy God with all thy heart, and with all thy soul, and with all thy mind, and with all thy strength: this is the first commandment. And the second is like, namely this, Thou shalt love thy neighbour as thyself. There is none other commandment greater than these. And the scribe said unto him, Well, Master, thou hast said the truth: for there is one God; and there is none other but he: and to love him with all the heart, and with all the understanding, and with all the soul, and with all the strength, and to love his neighbour as himself, is more than all whole burnt offerings and sacrifices. And when Jesus saw that he answered discreetly, he said unto him, Thou art not far from the kingdom of God. And no man after that durst ask him any question.

Mark 12: 28–34

THE BOOK OF ACTS

This document, according to its opening verse, is the "second part" of the Gospel written by Luke, and relates the history of the Nazarene movement after Jesus was crucified. The book begins with the Ascension, goes on to tell of the first gathering of the believers on Pentecost Day in Jerusalem, and then of the early missionary activities which carried the cult far and wide. Most of the book is concerned with the apostolic journeys of Paul, probably because the author participated in many of these journeys. The book closes abruptly with Paul's imprisonment at Rome.

THE NAZARENE COMMUNE

And the multitude of them that believed were of one heart and of one soul: neither said any of them that ought of the things which he possessed was his own; but they had all things common. And with great power gave the apostles witness of the resurrection of the Lord Jesus: and great grace was upon them all. Neither was there any among them that lacked: for as many as were possessors of lands or houses sold them, and brought the prices of the things that were sold, and laid them down at the apostles' feet: and distribution was made unto every man according as he had need. And Joses, who by the apostles was surnamed Barnabas, (which is, being interpreted, the son of consolation,) a Levite, and of the country of Cyprus, having land, sold it, and brought the money, and laid it at the apostles' feet.

But a certain man named Ananias, with Sapphira his wife, sold a possession, and kept back part of the price, his wife also being privy to it, and brought a certain part, and laid it at the apostles' feet. But Peter said, Ananias, why hath Satan filled thine heart to lie to the Holy Ghost, and to keep back part of the price of the land? Whiles it remained, was it not thine own? and after it was sold, was it not in thine own power? why hast thou conceived this thing in thine heart? thou hast not lied unto men, but unto God. And Ananias hearing these words fell down, and gave up the ghost: and great fear came on all them that heard these things. And the young men arose, wound him up, and carried him out, and buried him. And it was about the space of three hours after, when his wife, not knowing what was done, came in. And Peter answered unto her, Tell me whether ye sold the land for so much? And she said, Yea, for so much. Then Peter said unto her, How is it that ye have agreed together to tempt the Spirit of the Lord? behold, the feet of them which have buried thy husband are at the door, and shall carry thee out. Then

fell she down straightway at his feet, and yielded up the ghost: and the young men came in, and found her dead, and, carrying her forth, buried her by her husband. And great fear came upon all the church, and upon as many as heard these things.

Acts 4: 32–5: 11

THE GIFT BEYOND PRICE

Now when the apostles which were at Jerusalem heard that Samaria had received the word of God, they sent unto them Peter and John: who, when they were come down, prayed for them, that they might receive the Holy Ghost: (for as yet he was fallen upon none of them: only they were baptized in the name of the Lord Jesus.) Then laid they their hands on them, and they received the Holy Ghost. And when Simon saw that through laying on of the apostles' hands the Holy Ghost was given, he offered them money, saying, Give me also this power, that on whomsoever I lay hands, he may receive the Holy Ghost. But Peter said unto him, Thy money perish with thee, because thou hast thought that the gift of God may be purchased with money. Thou hast neither part nor lot in this matter:

for thy heart is not right in the sight of God. Repent therefore of this thy wickedness, and pray God, if perhaps the thought of thine heart may be forgiven thee. For I perceive that thou art in the gall of bitterness, and in the bond of iniquity. Then answered Simon, and said, Pray ye to the Lord for me, that none of these things which ye have spoken come upon me.

Acts 8: 14–24

PAUL AND THE ATHENIANS

Now while Paul waited for them at Athens, his spirit was stirred in him, when he saw the city wholly given to idolatry. Therefore disputed he in the synagogue with the Jews, and with the devout persons, and in the market daily with them that met with him. Then certain philosophers of the Epicureans, and of the Stoicks, encountered him. And some said, What will this babbler say? other some, He seemeth to be a setter forth of strange gods: because he preached unto them Jesus, and the resurrection. And they took him, and brought him unto Areopagus, saying, May we know what this new doctrine, whereof thou speakest, is? For thou bringest certain strange things to our ears: we would know therefore what these things mean. (For all the Athenians and strangers which were there spent their time in nothing else, but either to tell, or to hear some new thing.)

Then Paul stood in the midst of Mars' hill, and said, Ye men of Athens, I perceive that in all things ye are are too superstitious. For as I passed by, and beheld your devotions, I found an altar with this inscription, TO THE UNKNOWN GOD. Whom therefore ye ignorantly worship, him declare I unto you. God that made the world and all things therein, seeing that he is Lord of heaven and earth, dwelleth not in temples made with hands; neither is worshipped with men's hands, as though he needed any thing, seeing he giveth to all life, and breath and all things; and hath made of one blood all nations of men for to dwell on all the face of the earth, and hath determined the times before appointed, and the bounds of their habitation; that they should seek the Lord, if haply they might feel after him, and find him, though he be not far from every one of us: For in him we live, and move, and have our being; as certain also of your own poets have said, for we are also his offspring. Forasmuch then as we are the offspring of God, we ought not to think that the Godhead is like unto gold, or silver, or stone, graven by art and man's device. And the times of this ignorance God winked at; but now commandeth all men every where to repent: because he hath appointed a day, in the which he will judge the world in righteousness by that man whom he hath ordained; whereof he hath given assurance unto all men, in that he hath raised him from the dead.

And when they heard of the resurrection of the dead, some mocked: and others said, We will hear thee again of this matter.

Acts 17: 16–32

THE EPISTLES OF PAUL

The earliest written documents of the Christian religion appear to have been the letters which Paul circulated among his converts scattered all around the Mediterranean. Fourteen of these letters are to be found in the New Testament, all apparently products of the latter half of Paul's long ministry. They are exceedingly rich not alone in human interest and historical information, but also—and, from the point of view of this Anthology, most gratifyingly—in ethical teaching.

I

LETTER TO THE ROMANS

This was written from Corinth around 57 A.D., just before Paul went on his final visit to Jerusalem. He apparently intended to go on from there to Rome, and sent this letter to prepare the ground for his reception. In it he seeks to explain and justify the assimilationist doctrines which had made him the great "Apostle to the Gentiles," but had outraged the Nazarene believers who were still strict Jews.

JUDGE NOT

Therefore thou art inexcusable, O man, whosoever thou art that judgest: for wherein thou judgest another, thou condemnest thyself; for thou that judgest doest the same things. But we are sure that the judgment of God is according to truth against them which commit such things. And thinkest thou this, O man, that judgest them which do such things, and doest the same, that thou shalt escape the judgment of God? Or despisest thou the riches of his goodness and forbearance and longsuffering; not knowing that the goodness of God leadeth thee to repentance? But after thy hardness and impenitent

492

heart treasurest up unto thyself wrath against the day of wrath and revelation of the righteous judgment of God; who will render to every man according to his deeds: to them who by patient continuance in well doing seek for glory and honour and immortality, eternal life: but unto them that are contentious, and do not obey the truth, but obey unrighteousness, indignation and wrath. Tribulation and anguish, upon every soul of man that doeth evil, of the Jew first, and also of the Gentile; but glory, honour, and peace, to every man that worketh good, to the Jew first, and also to the Gentile: for there is no respect of persons with God. For as many as have sinned without law shall also perish without law: and as many as have sinned in the law shall be judged by the law; (for not the hearers of the law are just before God, but the doers of the law shall be justified. For when

the Gentiles, which have not the law, do by nature the things contained in the law, these, having not the law, are a law unto themselves: which shew the work of the law written in their hearts, their conscience also bearing witness, and their thoughts the meanwhile accusing or else excusing one another;) in the day when God shall judge the secrets of men by Jesus Christ according to my gospel. Behold, thou art called a Jew and restest in the law, and makest thy boast of God, and knowest his will, and approvest the things that are more excellent, being instructed out of the law; and art confident that thou thyself art a guide of the blind, a light of them which are in darkness. An instructor of the foolish, a teacher of babes, which hast the form of knowledge and of the truth in the law. Thou therefore which teachest another, teachest thou not thyself? thou that preachest a man should not steal, dost thou steal? thou that sayest a man should no commit adultery, dost thou commit adultery? thou that abhorrest idols, dost thou commit sacrilege? thou that makest thy boast of the law, through breaking the law dishonourest thou God?

Romans 2: 1–23

LET LOVE BE GENUINE

Let love be without dissimulation. Abhor that which is evil; cleave to that which is good. Be kindly affectioned one to another with brotherly love; in honour preferring one another; not slothful in business; fervent in spirit; serving the Lord; rejoicing in hope; patient in tribulation; continuing instant in prayer; distributing to the necessity of saints; given to hospitality. Bless them which persecute you: bless, and curse not. Rejoice with them that do rejoice, and weep with them that weep. Be of the same mind one toward another. Mind not high things, but condescend to men of low estate. Be not wise in your own conceits. Recompense to no man evil for evil. Provide things honest in the sight of all men. If it be possible, as much as lieth in you, live peaceably with all men. Dearly beloved, avenge not yourselves, but rather give place unto wrath: for it is written, Vengeance is mine; I will repay, saith the Lord. Therefore if thine enemy hunger, feed him; if he thirst, give him drink: for in so doing thou shalt heap coals of fire on his head. Be not overcome of evil, but overcome evil with good.

Romans 12: 9–21

II

FIRST LETTER TO THE CORINTHIANS

This epistle deals with a number of organizational and doctrinal problems which had arisen among the converts in Corinth (Greece), and concerning which Paul's advice had been solicited. One was the problem of insubordination, an evil threatening not alone the apostle's authority, but the very existence of the Corinthian church. Another was the problem of sex—whether the believers ought to practice celibacy, or be allowed to marry. Paul's comments on that issue are of at least historical interest. What they lead up to, however, the discourse on spiritual love, is immeasurably more important. This discourse, indeed, ranks as one of the noblest utterances in all of sacred literature.

ON MARRIAGE

Now concerning the things whereof ye wrote unto me: It is good for a man not to touch a woman. Nevertheless, to avoid fornication, let every man have his own wife, and let every woman have her own husband. Let the husband render unto the wife due benevolence: and likewise also the wife unto the husband. The wife hath not power of her own body, but the husband: and likewise also the husband hath not power of his own body, but the wife. Defraud ye not one the other, except it be with consent for a time, that ye may give yourselves to fasting and prayer; and come together again, that Satan tempt you not for your incontinency. But I speak this by permission, and not of commandment. For I would that all men were even as I myself. But every man hath his proper gift of God, one after this manner, and another after that. I say therefore to the unmarried and widows, It is good for them if they abide even as I. But if they cannot contain, let them marry: for it is better to marry than to burn. And unto the married I command, yet not I, but the Lord, Let not the wife depart from her husband: but and if she de-

part, let her remain unmarried, or be reconciled to her husband: and let not the husband put away his wife. But to the rest speak I, not the Lord: If any brother hath a wife that believeth not, and she be pleased to dwell with him, let him not put her away. And the woman which hath an husband that believeth not, and if he be pleased to dwell with her, let her not leave him. For the unbelieving husband is sanctified by the wife, and the unbelieving wife is sanctified by the husband: else were your children unclean; but now are they holy. But if the unbelieving depart, let him depart. A brother or a sister is not under bondage in such cases: but God hath called us to peace. For what knowest thou, O wife, whether thou shalt save thy husband? or how knowest thou, O man, whether thou shalt save thy wife?

But as God hath distributed to every man, as the Lord hath called every one, so let him walk. And so ordain I in all churches.

I Corinthians 7: 1–17

ON CELIBACY

Now concerning virgins I have no commandment of the Lord: yet I give my judgment, as one that hath obtained mercy of the Lord to be faithful. I suppose therefore that this is good for the present distress, I say, that it is good for a man so to be. Art thou bound unto a wife? seek not to be loosed. Art thou loosed from a wife? seek not a wife. But and if thou marry, thou hast not sinned; and if a virgin marry, she hath not sinned. Nevertheless such shall have trouble in the flesh: but I spare you. But this I say, brethren, the time is short: it remaineth, that both they that have wives be as though they had none; and they that weep, as though they wept not; and they that rejoice, as though they rejoiced not; and they that buy, as though they possessed not; and they that use this world, as not abusing it: for the fashion of this world passeth away. But I would have you without carefulness. He that is unmarried careth for the things that belong to the Lord, how he may please the Lord: but he that is married careth for the things that are of the world, how he may please his wife. There is difference also between a wife and a virgin. The unmarried woman careth for the things of the Lord, that she may be holy both in body and in spirit: but she that is married careth for the things of the world, how she may please her husband. And this I speak for your own profit; not that I may cast a snare upon you, but for that which is comely, and that ye may attend upon the Lord without distraction. But if any man think that he behaveth himself uncomely toward his virgin, if she pass the flower of her age, and need so require, let him do what he will, he sinneth not: let them marry. Nevertheless he that standeth stedfast in his heart, having no necessity, but hath power over his own will, and hath so decreed in his heart that he will keep his virgin, doeth well. So then he that giveth her in marriage doeth well; but he that giveth her not in marriage doeth better. The wife is bound by the law as long as her husband liveth; but if her husband be dead, she is at liberty to be married to whom she will; only in the Lord. But she is happier if she so abide, after my judgment: and I think also that I have the Spirit of God.

I Corinthians 7: 25–40

ON SPIRITUAL LOVE

Though I speak with the tongues of men and of angels, and have not charity, I am become as sounding brass, or a tinkling cymbal. And though I have the gift of prophecy, and understand all mysteries, and all knowledge; and though I have all faith, so that I could remove mountains, and have not charity, I am nothing. And though I bestow all my goods to feed the poor, and though I give my body to be burned, and have not charity, it profiteth me nothing. Charity suffereth long, and is kind; charity envieth not; charity vaunteth not itself, is not puffed up, doth not behave itself unseemly, seeketh not her own, is not easily provoked, thinketh no evil; rejoiceth not in iniquity, but rejoiceth in the truth; beareth all things, believeth all things, hopeth all things, endureth all things. Charity never faileth: but whether there be prophecies, they shall fail; whether there be tongues, they shall cease; whether there be knowledge, it shall vanish away. For we know in part, and we prophesy in part. But when that which is perfect is come, then that which is in part shall be done away. When I was a child, I spake as a child, I understood as a child, I thought as a child: but when I became a man, I put away childish things. For now we see through a glass, darkly; but then face to face: now I know in part; but then shall I know even as also I am known. And now abideth faith, hope, charity, these three; but the greatest of these is charity.

Follow after charity, and desire spiritual gifts, but rather that ye may prophesy. For he that speaketh in an unknown tongue speaketh not unto men, but unto God: for no man understandeth him; howbeit in the spirit he speaketh mysteries. But he that prophesieth speaketh unto men to edification, and exhortation, and comfort. He that speaketh in an unknown tongue edifieth himself; but he that prophesieth edifieth the church. I would that ye all spake with tongues, but rather that ye prophesied: for greater is he that prophesieth than he that speaketh with tongues, except he interpret, that the church may receive edifying.

I Corinthians 13: 1–13; 14: 1–5

III

LETTER TO THE EPHESIANS

This appears to have been a circular letter intended for all the churches in Asia Minor, not just the one at Ephesus. It was probably written around the year 62, and in its discussion of various doctrinal issues provides much light on Paul's ethical views.

PUT OFF YOUR OLD NATURE

This I say therefore, and testify in the Lord, that ye henceforth walk not as other Gentiles walk, in the vanity of their mind. Having the understanding darkened, being alienated from the life of God through the ignorance that is in them, because of the blindness of their heart: who being past feeling have given themselves over unto lasciviousness, to work all uncleanness with greediness. But ye have not so learned Christ; if so be that ye have heard him, and have been taught by him, as the truth is in Jesus: that ye put off concerning the former conversation the old man, which is corrupt according to the deceitful lusts; and be renewed in the spirit of your mind; and that ye put on the new man, which after God is created in righteousness and true holiness. Wherefore putting away lying, speak every man truth with his neighbour: for we are members one of another. Be ye angry, and sin not: let not the sun go down upon your wrath: neither give place to the devil. Let him that stole steal no more: but rather let him labour, working with his hands the thing which is good, that he may have to give to him that needeth. Let no corrupt communication proceed out of your mouth, but that which is good to the use of edifying, that it may minister grace unto the hearers. And grieve not the holy Spirit of God, whereby ye are sealed unto the day of redemption. Let all bitterness, and wrath, and anger, and clamour, and evil speaking, be put away from you, with all malice: and be ye kind one to another, tenderhearted, forgiving one another, even as God for Christ's sake hath forgiven you.

Ephesians 4: 17–32

BE IMITATORS OF GOD

Be ye therefore followers of God, as dear children; and walk in love, as Christ also hath loved us, and hath given himself for us an offering and a sacrifice to God for a sweetsmelling savour. But fornication, and all uncleanness, or covetousness, let it not be once named among you, as becometh saints; neither filthiness, nor foolish talking, nor jesting, which are not convenient: but rather giving of thanks. For this ye know, that no whoremonger, nor unclean person, nor covetous man, who is an idolater, hath any inheritance in the kingdom of Christ and of God. Let no man deceive you with vain words: for because of these things cometh the wrath of God upon the children of disobedience. Be not ye therefore partakers with them. For ye were sometimes darkness, but now are ye light in the Lord; walk as children of light: (for the fruit of the Spirit is in all goodness and righteousness and truth;) proving what is acceptable unto the Lord. And have no fellowship with the unfruitful works of darkness, but rather reprove them. For it is a shame even to speak of those things which are done of them in secret. But all things that are reproved are made manifest by the light: for whatsoever doth make manifest is light. Wherefore he saith, Awake thou that sleepest, and arise from the dead, and Christ shall give thee light. See then that ye walk circumspectly, not as fools, but as wise. Redeeming the time, because the days are evil. Wherefore be ye not unwise, but understanding what the will of the Lord is. And be not drunk with wine, wherein is excess; but be filled with the Spirit; speaking to yourselves in psalms and hymns and spiritual songs, singing and making melody in your heart to the Lord; giving thanks always for all things unto God and the Father in the name of our Lord Jesus Christ.

Ephesians 5: 1–20

BE SUBJECT TO ONE ANOTHER

Submitting yourselves one to another in the fear of God. Wives, submit yourselves unto your own husbands, as unto the Lord. For the husband is the head of the wife, even as Christ is the head of the church: and he is the saviour of the body. Therefore as the church is subject unto Christ, so let the wives be to their own husbands in every thing. Husbands, love your wives, even as Christ also loved the church, and gave himself for it; that he might sanctify and cleanse it with the washing of water by the word, that he might present it to himself a glorious church, not having spot, or wrinkle, or any such thing; but that it should be holy and without blemish. So ought men to love their wives as their own bodies. He that loveth his wife loveth himself. For no man ever yet hated his own flesh; but nourisheth and cherisheth it, even as the Lord the church: for we are members of his body, of his flesh, and of his bones. For this cause shall a man leave his father and mother, and shall be joined unto his wife, and they two shall be one flesh. This is a great mystery: but I speak concerning Christ and the church. Nevertheless let every one of you in particular so love his wife even as himself; and the wife see that she reverence her husband.

Children, obey your parents in the Lord: for this is right. Honour thy father and mother; (which is the first commandment with promise;) that it may be well with thee, and thou mayest live long on the earth. And, ye fathers, provoke not your children to wrath: but bring them up in the nurture and admonition of the Lord. Servants, be obedient to them that are your masters according to the flesh, with fear and trembling, in singleness of your heart, as unto Christ; not with eyeservice, as men-pleasers; but as the servants of Christ, doing the will of God from the heart; with good will doing service, as to the Lord, and not to men: knowing that whatsoever good thing any man doeth, the same shall he receive of the Lord, whether he be bond or free. And, ye masters, do the same things unto them, forbearing threatening: knowing that your Master also is in heaven; neither is there respect of persons with him. Finally, my brethren, be strong in the Lord, and in the power of his might. Put on the whole armour of God, that ye may be able to stand against the wiles of the devil.

Ephesians 5:21–6:11

IV

SECOND THESSALONIANS

SHUN THE IDLERS

Now we command you, brethren, in the name of our Lord Jesus Christ, that ye withdraw yourselves from every brother that walketh disorderly, and not after the tradition which he received of us. For yourselves know how ye ought to follow us: for we behaved not ourselves disorderly among you; neither did we eat any man's bread for nought; but wrought with labour and travail night and day, that we might not be chargeable to any of you: not because we have not power, but to make ourselves an ensample unto you to follow us. For even when we were with you, this we commanded you, that if any would not work, neither should he eat. For we hear that there are some which walk among you disorderly, working not at all, but are busybodies. Now them that are such we command and exhort by our Lord Jesus Christ, that with quietness they work, and eat their own bread. But ye, brethren, be not weary in well doing. And if any man obey not our word by this epistle, note that man, and have no company with him, that he may be ashamed. Yet count him not as an enemy, but admonish him as a brother. Now the Lord of peace himself give you peace always by all means. The Lord be with you all.

II Thessalonians 3: 6–16

V

FIRST LETTER TO TIMOTHY

This is said to have been written after Paul's first imprisonment in Rome (circa 66 A.D.), and is addressed to one of his younger co-workers, a half-Jew named Timothy. Paul had left him in charge at Ephesus, and here gives counsel on various organizational as well as ethical matters.

PRAY FOR ALL MEN

I exhort therefore, that, first of all, supplications, prayers, intercessions, and giving of thanks, be made for all men; for kings, and for all that are in authority; that we may lead a quiet and peaceable life in all godliness and honesty. For this is good and acceptable in the sight of God our Saviour; who will have all men to be saved, and to come unto the knowledge of the truth. For there is one God, and one media-

tor between God and men, the man Christ Jesus; who gave himself a ransom for all, to be testified in due time. Whereunto I am ordained a preacher, and an apostle. (I speak the truth in Christ, and lie not;) a teacher of the Gentiles in faith and verity. I will therefore that men pray every where, lifting up holy hands, without wrath and doubting. In like manner also, that women adorn themselves in modest apparel, with shamefacedness and sobriety; not with braided hair, or gold, or pearls, or costly array; but (which becometh women professing godliness) with good works. Let the woman learn in silence with all subjection. But I suffer not a woman to teach, nor to usurp authority over the man, but to be in silence. For Adam was first formed, then Eve. And Adam was not deceived, but the woman being deceived was in the transgression. Notwithstanding she shall be saved in childbearing, if they continue in faith and charity and holiness with sobriety.

I Timothy 2: 1–15

DUTIES OF A CHRISTIAN OFFICER

This is a true saying, If a man desire the office of a bishop, he desireth a good work. A bishop then must be blameless, the husband of one wife, vigilant, sober, of good behaviour, given to hospitality, apt to teach; not given to wine, no striker, not greedy of filthy lucre;

but patient, not a brawler, not covetous; one that ruleth well his own
house, having his children in subjection with all gravity; for if a man
know not how to rule his own house, how shall he take care of the
church of God? Not a novice, lest being lifted up with pride he fall
into the condemnation of the devil. Moreover he must have a good
report of them which are without; lest he fall into reproach and the
snare of the devil. Likewise must the deacons be grave, not double-
tongued, not given to much wine, not greedy of filthy lucre; holding
the mystery of the faith in a pure conscience. And let these also first
be proved; then let them use the office of a deacon, being found blameless. Even so must their wives be grave, not slanderers, sober, faithful
in all things. Let the deacons be the husbands of one wife, ruling their
children and their own houses well. For they that have used the office
of a deacon well purchase to themselves a good degree, and great
boldness in the faith which is in Christ Jesus.

I Timothy 3: 1–13

THE EPISTLE OF JAMES

The following excerpts are from a letter traditionally ascribed to one of Jesus' brothers, and therefore accorded first place in the "general epistles" of the New Testament. Its contents, however, are in the strictest sense Jewish, and the document may originally have had no connection whatsoever with the Christian movement. (The two solitary references to "Jesus Christ" are regarded by scholars as interpolations.) Though addressed to "the brethren," these may have been Essenes rather than Nazarenes, for their meeting-place is called a "synagogue," not a "church," and they are exhorted to emulate Job and Elijah, never Jesus. For these and other reasons even the earliest Church Fathers were inclined to doubt whether this epistle rightly belongs in the Christian canon. But none can question its inclusion in this Anthology.

BE MEEK

Wherefore, my beloved brethren, let every man be swift to hear, slow to speak, slow to wrath: for the wrath of man worketh not the righteousness of God. Wherefore lay apart all filthiness and superfluity of naughtiness, and receive with meekness the engrafted word, which is able to save your souls. But be ye doers of the word, and not hearers only, deceiving your own selves. For if any be a hearer of the word, and not a doer, he is like unto a man beholding his natural face in a glass: for he beholdeth himself, and goeth his way, and straightway forgetteth what manner of man he was. But whoso looketh into the perfect law of liberty, and continueth therein, he being not a forgetful hearer, but a doer of the work, this man shall be blessed in his deed. If any man among you seem to be religious, and bridleth not his tongue, but deceiveth his own heart, this man's religion is vain. Pure religion and undefiled before God and the Father is this, to visit the fatherless and widows in their affliction, and to keep himself unspotted from the world.

James 1: 19–27

LOVE ALL ALIKE

My brethren, have not the faith of our Lord Jesus Christ, the Lord of glory, with respect of persons. For if there come unto your assembly a man with a gold ring, in goodly apparel, and there come in also a poor man in vile raiment; and ye have respect to him that weareth the gay clothing, and say unto him, Sit thou here in a good place; and say to the poor, Stand thou there, or sit here under my footstool: are ye not then partial in yourselves, and are become judges of evil thoughts? Hearken, my beloved brethren, Hath not God chosen the poor of this world rich in faith, and heirs of the kingdom which he hath promised to them that love him? But ye have despised the poor. Do not rich men oppress you, and draw you before the judgment seats? Do not they blaspheme that worthy name by the which ye are called? If ye fulfil the royal law according to the scripture, Thou shalt love thy neighbour as thyself, ye do well: but if ye have respect to persons, ye commit sin, and are convinced of the law as transgressors. For whosoever shall keep the whole law, and yet offend in one point, he is guilty of all. For he that said, Do not commit adultery, said also, Do not kill. Now if thou commit no adultery, yet if thou kill, thou art become a transgressor of the law. So speak ye, and so do, as they that shall be judged by the law of liberty. For he shall have judgment without mercy, that hath shewed no mercy; and mercy rejoiceth against judgment. What doth it profit, my brethren, though a man say he hath faith, and have not works? can faith save him? If a brother or sister be naked, and destitute of daily food, and one of you say unto them, Depart in peace, be ye warmed and filled; notwithstanding ye give them not those things which are needful to the body; what doth it profit? Even so faith, if it hath not works, is dead, being alone. Yea, a man may say, Thou hast faith, and I have works: shew me thy faith without thy works, and I will shew thee my faith by my works. Thou believest that there is one God; thou doest well: the devils also believe, and tremble. But wilt thou know, O vain man, that faith without works is dead? Was not Abraham our father justified by works, when he had offered Isaac his son upon the altar? Seest thou how faith wrought with his works, and by works was faith made perfect? And the scripture was fulfilled which saith, Abraham believed God, and it was imputed unto him for righteousness: and he was called the Friend of God. Ye see then how that by works a man is justified, and not by faith only. Likewise also was not Rahab the harlot justified by works, when she had received the messengers, and had sent them out another way? For as the body without the spirit is dead, so faith without works is dead also.

James 2: 1–26

WARNING TO TEACHERS

My brethren, be not many masters, knowing that we shall receive the greater condemnation. For in many things we offend all. If any man offend not in word, the same is a perfect man, and able also to bridle the whole body. Behold, we put bits in the horses' mouths, that they may obey us; and we turn about their whole body. Behold also the ships, which though they be so great, and are driven of fierce winds, yet are they turned about with a very small helm, whithersoever the governor listeth. Even so the tongue is a little member, and boasteth great things. Behold, how great a matter a little fire kindleth! And the tongue is a fire, a world of iniquity: so is the tongue among our members, that it defileth the whole body, and setteth on fire the course of nature; and it is set on fire of hell. For every kind of beasts, and of birds, and of serpents, and of things in the sea, is tamed, and hath been tamed of mankind: but the tongue can no man tame; it is an unruly evil, full of deadly poison. Therewith bless we God, even the Father; and therewith curse we men, which are made after the similitude of God. Out of the same mouth proceedeth blessing and cursing. My brethren, these things ought not so to be. Doth a fountain send forth at the same place sweet water and bitter? Can the fig tree, my brethren, bear olive berries? either a vine, figs? so can no fountain both yield salt water and fresh. Who is a wise man and endued with knowledge among you? let him shew out of a good conversation his works with meekness of wisdom. But if ye have bitter envying and strife in your hearts, glory not, and lie not against the truth. This wisdom descendeth not from above, but is earthly, sensual, devilish. For where envying and strife is, there is confusion and every evil work. But the wisdom that is from above is first pure, then peaceable, gentle, and easy to be intreated, full of mercy and good fruits, without partiality, and without hypocrisy. And the fruit of righteousness is sown in peace of them that make peace.

James 3: 1–18

THE CAUSES OF WAR

From whence come wars and fightings among you? come they not hence, even of your lusts that war in your members? Ye lust, and have not: ye kill, and desire to have, and cannot obtain: ye fight and war, yet ye have not, because ye ask not. Ye ask, and receive not, because ye ask amiss, that ye may consume it upon your lusts. Ye adulterers and adulteresses, know ye not that the friendship of the world is enmity with God? whosoever therefore will be a friend of the world is the enemy of God. Do ye think that the scripture saith in vain, The spirit that dwelleth in us lusteth to envy? But he giveth more grace. Wherefore he saith, God resisteth the proud, but giveth grace unto the humble. Submit yourselves therefore to God. Resist the devil, and he will flee from you. Draw nigh to God, and he will draw nigh to you. Cleanse your hands, ye sinners; and purify your hearts, ye double minded. Be afflicted, and mourn, and weep: let your laughter be turned to mourning, and your joy to heaviness. Humble yourselves in the sight of the Lord, and he shall lift you up. Speak not evil one of another, brethren. He that speaketh evil of his brother, and judgeth his brother, speaketh evil of the law, and judgeth the law: but if thou judge the law, thou art not a doer of the law, but a judge. There is one lawgiver, who is able to save and to destroy: who art thou that judgest another?

James 4: 1–12

WOE TO THE RICH

Go to, now, ye rich men, weep and howl for your miseries that shall come upon you. Your riches are corrupted, and your garments are moth-eaten. Your gold and silver is cankered; and the rust of them shall be a witness against you, and shall eat your flesh as it were fire. Ye have heaped treasure together for the last days. Behold, the hire of the labourers who have reaped down your fields, which is of you kept back by fraud, crieth: and the cries of them which have reaped are entered into the ears of the Lord of sabaoth. Ye have lived in pleasure on the earth, and been wanton; ye have nourished your hearts, as in a day of slaughter. Ye have condemned and killed the just; and he doth not resist you.

James 5: 1–6

THE SCRIPTURES OF MOHAMMEDANISM

THE KORAN

INTRODUCTION

Mohammedanism, or more accurately Islam ("Surrender"—of self to Allah) is the youngest of the world religions, and nearly the most widespread. It commands the devotion of well over 200,000,000 people massed in a broad belt running from Morocco to the Philippines. Despite its decline politically, it is still expanding as a faith, carrying on missions in Africa and other regions which are said to be currently more successful than those of Christianity.

The religion was founded in Mecca by an Arab named Muhammed (570–632 A.D.), who believed himself to be the recipient of divine revelations. These were not too specific at first, merely condemning idolatry, commending charity, and offering lurid visions of apocalyptic Things to Come. Once he began to make them public, however, the local rulers became alarmed, for they considered such revelations politically subversive as well as theologically heretical. Finding his life menaced in Mecca, Muhammed migrated (622 A.D.) to the neighboring and rival city of Yathrib (later renamed Medina), where his revelations became both bolder and more detailed. Many Jews were living in Yathrib, and he adopted certain of their rites and all of their scriptures in the naive hope of persuading them to accept him as their Messiah. When they refused, he proceeded to get himself recognized as the Messiah of the Arabs. He announced a new revelation declaring Mecca rather than Jerusalem to be the Holy City, and waged a series of bloody campaigns which finally made him master of the ancient shrine. Thenceforth his authority became unchallenged throughout Arabia, and his religion was launched on a career of conquest destined to carry it very nearly around the world.

The core of Islam is the belief that there is no god but Allah, and no prophet like Muhammed. Though Allah is described as having hands and eyes and human attributes, He is altogether divine and beyond man's comprehension. His will is as unchallengeable as His might is despotic, and man's only hope of salvation lies in total submission to His commands. These were first imparted to Abraham, and then to a succession of prophets the last and greatest of whom was Muhammed. The commands include reciting Allah's praises five times each day, abstention from eating swine's flesh, observance of certain feasts and fasts, male circumcision (at puberty), female isolation, pilgrimage to Mecca, and various other ritual duties.

In addition, however, there are ethical obligations, and these are far higher than is commonly recognized. For one thing, Muhammed insisted that morality was a personal, not a tribal matter. "No burdened soul," said he, "shall bear the burden of another. . . . On the Day of Judgment everyone shall be answerable for himself alone." From this it followed that all believers were equal in the eyes of Allah, and Islam was a universal brotherhood in which justice and charity had to supersede all tribal laws.

Muhammed was quite definite about this justice and charity, naming specific virtues to be practiced as well as crimes to be avoided. Of the virtues, the highest was almsgiving—to the poor, the orphan, the stranger, the slave, and the prisoner. Equally high was hospitality, and also filial respect. The crimes included murder, infanticide, ignoring the rights of females, and a number of other acts which had carried no onus among the Arabs until he appeared. Whatever else Muhammed may have been, considering his background he was quite spectacularly a moral reformer.

He died leaving a body of teachings which were later compiled in a book called the KORAN, *and this has been revered ever since as the great holy book of Islam.*

THE KORAN

The one sacred scripture of Islam is the KORAN ("Reading"), and its daily recitation in all Moslem schools and mosques makes it the most widely-read book in existence. Approximately the size of the New Testament, it is made up entirely of the "revelations" vouchsafed to Muhammed during his career as the Prophet of Allah. These are all in rhymed prose, and for the most part highly rhetorical. Muhammed himself did not write them down—he may not have known how—but certain of his followers appear to have performed that task. They recorded his words on "flat stones, pieces of leather, ribs of palm-leaves," and the like. Not until some twenty years after his death were those fragmentary texts gathered up, collated, and compiled into a single book.

That book is divided into 114 chapters called surahs (literally "series"), each ostensibly complete in itself, like the Psalms in the Bible. Aside from the opening surah, which is an invocation comparable to the Christian Lord's Prayer or the Jewish Sh'ma, the arrangement is peculiar: the longer chapters come first, and the shorter ones last. This is unfortunate from a literary as well as chronological standpoint, for the longer chapters contain the later and least impressive revelations. To be most readily appreciated, therefore, the KORAN has to be read backwards.

But read either way, the non-believer usually finds it hard going. The magnificent ring of the Arabic is necessarily lost in translation, for the rhyme cannot be reproduced, and there is no rhythm to be copied. Deprived of its native eloquence, the KORAN sounds merely rhetorical. To the average "infidel" reader it seems little more than a collection of wild ravings, vicious invectives, tedious preachments, and barbarous taboos.

The fact remains, however, that few books in all of human history have warmed more hearts or exercised a more widespread cultural influence. Anyone who examines the following typical selections with sufficient care will almost certainly discern the reason.[1]

[1] All the selections and notes are reprinted from *The Koran*, by George Sale, eighth edition (Philadelphia, J. B. Lippincott Co., 1888).

FIRST SURAH

INTITLED, THE PREFACE, OR INTRODUCTION;[2]
REVEALED AT MECCA

In the Name of the Most Merciful God [3]

Praise be to God, the LORD of all creatures; the most merciful, the king of the day of judgment. Thee do we worship, and of thee do we beg assistance. Direct us in the right way, in the way of those to whom thou hast been gracious; not of those against whom thou art incensed, nor of those who go astray.

SECOND SURAH

INTITLED, THE COW; REVEALED PARTLY AT MECCA, AND
PARTLY AT MEDINA [4]

There is no doubt in this book; it is a direction to the pious, who believe in the mysteries of faith, who observe the appointed times of prayer, and distribute alms out of what we have bestowed on them, and who believe in that revelation, which hath been sent down unto thee, and that which hath been sent down unto the prophets before thee, and have firm assurance of the life to come: these are directed by their LORD, and they shall prosper. As for the unbelievers, it will be equal to them whether thou admonish them, or do not admonish them; they will not believe. GOD hath sealed up their hearts and their hearing; a dimness covereth their sight, and they shall suffer a grievous

[2] In Arabic *al Fâtihat*. This chapter is a prayer, and held in great veneration by the Mohammedans, who give it several other honourable titles; as the chapter of *prayer*, of *praise*, of *thanksgiving*, of *treasure*, &c. They esteem it as the quintessence of the whole Korân, and often repeat it in their devotions both public and private, as the Christians do the Lord's Prayer.

[3] This formula is prefixed to all the chapters (with the exception of one). It is expressly recommended in the Korân. The Mohammedans pronounce it whenever they slaughter an animal, and at the commencement of their reading, and of all important actions. It is with them that which the sign of the cross is with Christians.

[4] This surah has been described as "the Koran in little," for it mentions all the essential points in the Revelation.

punishment. There are some who say, We believe in GOD, and the last day; but are not really believers: they seek to deceive GOD, and those who do believe, but they deceive themselves only, and are not sensible thereof. There is an infirmity in their hearts, and GOD hath increased that infirmity, and they shall suffer a most painful punishment, because they have disbelieved. . . . When they meet those who believe, they say, We do believe: but when they retire privately to their devils, they say, We really hold with you, and only mock at those people: GOD shall mock at them, and continue them in their impiety; they shall wander in confusion. These are the men who have purchased error at the price of true direction: but their traffic hath not been gainful, neither have they been rightly directed. They are like unto one who kindleth a fire, and when it hath enlightened all around him, GOD taketh away their light and leaveth them in darkness, they shall not see; they are deaf, dumb, and blind, therefore will they not repent. Or like a stormy cloud from heaven, fraught with darkness, thunder, and lightning, they put their fingers in their ears because of the noise of the thunder, for fear of death; GOD encompasseth the infidels: the lightning  wanteth but little of taking away their sight; so often as it enlighteneth them, they walk therein, but when darkness cometh on them, they stand still; and if GOD so pleased, he would certainly deprive them of their hearing and their sight, for GOD is almighty. . . .

O children of Israel,[5] remember my favour wherewith I have favoured you; and perform your covenant with me, and I will perform my covenant with you; and revere me: and believe in the revelation which I have sent down, confirming that which is with you, and be

[5] The Jews are here called upon to receive the Korân, as verifying and confirming the Pentateuch, particularly with respect to the unity of God and the mission of Muhammed. And they are exhorted not to conceal the passages of their law, which bear witness to those truths, nor to corrupt them by publishing false copies of the Pentateuch, for which the writers were but poorly paid.

not the first who believe not therein, neither exchange my signs for a small price; and fear me. Clothe not the truth with vanity, neither conceal the truth against your own knowledge, observe the stated times of prayer, and pay your legal alms, and bow down yourselves with those who bow down. Will ye command men to do justice, and forget your own souls? yet ye read the book of the law: do ye not therefore understand? Ask help with perseverance and prayer; this indeed is grievous unless to the humble, who seriously think they shall meet their LORD, and that to him they shall return. O children of Israel, remember my favour wherewith I have favoured you, and that I have preferred you above all nations; dread the day wherein one soul shall not make satisfaction for another soul, neither shall any intercession be accepted from them, nor shall any compensation be received, neither shall they be helped. . . .

Surely those who believe, and those who Judaize, and Christians, and Sabians, whoever believeth in GOD, and the last day, and doth that which is right, they shall have their reward with their LORD; there shall come no fear on them, neither shall they be grieved.[6] Verily whoso doeth evil, and is encompassed by his iniquity, they shall be the companions of hell fire, they shall remain therein for ever: but they who believe and do good works, they shall be the companions of paradise, they shall continue therein for ever.[7]

Truth is from thy LORD, therefore thou shalt not doubt. Every sect hath a certain tract of heaven to which they turn themselves in prayer; but do ye strive to run after good things; wherever ye be, GOD

[6] From these words, which are repeated in the fifth chapter, several writers have wrongly concluded that the Mohammedans hold it to be the doctrine of their prophet, that every man may be saved in his own religion, provided he be sincere and lead a good life. It is true, some of their doctors do agree this to be the purport of the words; but then they say the latitude hereby granted was soon revoked, for that this passage is abrogated by several others in the Korân, which expressly declare that none can be saved who is not of the Mohammedan faith; and particularly by those words of the third chapter, *Whoever followeth any other religion than* Islâm (*i. e.* the Mohammedan), *it shall not be accepted of him, and at the last day he shall be of those who perish.* However, others are of opinion that this passage is not abrogated, but interpret it differently; taking the meaning of it to be, that no man, whether he be a Jew, a Christian, or a Sabian, shall be excluded from salvation, provided he quit his erroneous religion and became a Moslem, which they say is intended by the following words, *Whoever believeth in God and the last day, and doth that which is right.*

[7] By *evil* in this case the commentators generally understand polytheism or idolatry; which sin, the Mohammedans believe, unless repented of in this life, is unpardonable, and will be punished by eternal damnation; but all other sins they hold will at length be forgiven. This therefore is that irremissible impiety, in their opinion, which in the New Testament is called *the sin against the Holy Ghost.*

will bring you all back at the resurrection, for God is almighty. And from what place soever thou comest forth, turn thy face towards the holy temple, for this is truth from thy LORD; neither is God regardless of that which ye do. From what place soever thou comest forth, turn thy face towards the holy temple; and wherever ye be, thitherward turn your faces, lest men have matter of dispute against you; but as for those among them who are unjust doers, fear them not, but fear me, that I may accomplish my grace upon you, and that ye may be directed. As we have sent unto you an apostle from among you, to rehearse our signs unto you, and to purify you, and to teach you the book of the Korân and wisdom, and to teach you that which ye knew not: therefore remember me, and I will remember you, and give thanks unto me, and be not unbelievers. O true believers, beg assistance with patience and prayer, for God is with the patient. And say not of those who are slain in fight for the religion of God, that they are dead; yea, they are living: but ye do not understand. We will surely prove you by afflicting you in some measure with fear, and hunger, and decrease of wealth, and loss of lives, and scarcity of fruits: but bear good tidings unto the patient, who, when a misfortune befalleth them, say, We are God's, and unto him shall we surely return.[8] Upon them shall be blessings from their LORD and mercy, and they are the rightly directed. . . . Surely they who believe not, and die in their unbelief, upon them shall be the curse of God, and of the angels, and of all men; they shall remain under it forever, their punishment shall not be alleviated, neither shall they be regarded. . . . O true believers, eat of the good things which we have bestowed on you for food, and return thanks unto God, if ye serve him. Verily he hath forbidden you to eat that which dieth of itself, and blood and swine's flesh, and that on which any other name but God's hath been invocated.[9] But he who is forced by necessity, not lusting, nor returning to transgress, it shall be no crime in him if he eat of those things, for God is gracious and merciful. . . . It is not righteousness that ye turn your faces in prayer towards the east and the west, but righteousness is of him who believeth in God and the last day, and the angels, and the scriptures, and the prophets; who giveth money for God's sake unto his kindred,

[8] An expression frequently in the mouths of the Mohammedans, when under any great affliction, or in any imminent danger.

[9] For this reason, whenever the Mohammedans kill any animal for food they always say *Bismi'llah*, or *In the name of* God; which if it be neglected, they think it not lawful to eat of it.

and unto orphans, and the needy, and the stranger, and those who ask, and for redemption of captives; who is constant at prayer, and giveth alms; and of those who perform their covenant, when they have covenanted, and who behave themselves patiently in adversity, and hardships, and in time of violence; these are they who are true, and these are they who fear GOD. O true believers, the law of retaliation is ordained you for the slain: the free shall die for the free, and the servant for the servant, and a woman for a woman: but he whom his brother shall forgive may be prosecuted, and obliged to make satisfaction according to what is just, and a fine shall be set on him with humanity. This is indulgence from your LORD, and mercy. And he who shall transgress after this, by killing the murderer, shall suffer a grievous punishment. And in this law of retaliation ye have life, O ye of understanding, that peradventure ye may fear. . . .

O true believers, a fast is ordained you, as it was ordained unto those before you, that ye may fear GOD. A certain number of days shall ye fast: but he among you who shall be sick, or on a journey, shall fast an equal number of other days. And those who can keep it, and do not, must redeem their neglect by maintaining of a poor man. And he who voluntarily dealeth better with the poor man than he is obliged, this shall be better for him. But if ye fast it will be better for you, if ye knew it. The month of Ramadan shall ye fast, in which the Korân was sent down from heaven, a direction unto men, and declarations of direction, and the distinction between good and evil. Therefore, let him among you who shall be present in this month, fast the same month; but he who shall be sick, or on a journey, shall fast the like number of other days. GOD would make this an ease unto you, and would not make it a difficulty unto you; that ye may fulfil the number of days, and glorify GOD, for that he hath directed you, and that ye may give thanks.

When my servants ask thee concerning me, Verily I am near; I will hear the prayer of him that prayeth, when he prayeth unto me: but let them hearken unto me, and believe in me, that they may be rightly directed. It is lawful for you, on the night of the fast, to go in unto your wives; they are a garment unto you, and ye are a garment unto them. GOD knoweth that ye defraud yourselves therein, wherefore he turneth unto you, and forgiveth you. Now, therefore, go in unto them; and earnestly desire that which GOD ordaineth you, and eat and drink, until ye can plainly distinguish a white thread from a black thread by the day-break: then keep the fast until night, and go not in unto them, but be constantly present in the places of worship. These are the prescribed bounds of GOD, therefore draw not near them to transgress them. Thus GOD declareth his signs unto men, that ye may fear him.

Consume not your wealth among yourselves in vain; nor present it unto judges, that ye may devour part of men's substance unjustly, against your own consciences. . . .

And fight for the religion of GOD against those who fight against you; but transgress not by attacking them first, for GOD loveth not the transgressors. And kill them wherever ye find them, and turn them out of that whereof they have dispossessed you; for temptation to idolatry is more grievous than slaughter; yet fight not against them in the holy temple, until they attack you therein; but if they attack you, slay them there. This shall be the reward of infidels. But if they desist, GOD is gracious and merciful. Fight therefore against them, until there be no temptation to idolatry, and the religion be GOD's; but if they desist, then let there be no hostility, except against the ungodly. . . .

Contribute out of your substance toward the defence of the religion of GOD, and throw not yourselves with your own hands into perdition; and do good, for GOD loveth those who do good. Perform the pilgrimage of Mecca, and the visitation of GOD; and, if ye be besieged, send that offering which shall be the easiest; and shave not your heads,[10] until your offering reacheth the place of sacrifice. But, whoever among you is sick, or is troubled with any distemper of the head, must redeem the shaving his head, by fasting, or alms, or some offering. . . . But he who findeth not any thing to offer, shall fast three days in the pilgrimage, and seven when ye are returned: they shall be ten days complete. . . . And fear GOD, and know that GOD is severe in punishing. Make provision for your journey; but the best provision is piety: and fear me, O ye of understanding. It shall be no crime in you, if ye seek an increase from your LORD, by trading during the pilgrimage. . . .

People will ask thee what they shall bestow in alms: Answer, The good which ye bestow, let it be given to parents, and kindred, and orphans, and the poor and the stranger. Whatsoever good ye do, GOD knoweth it. . . .

[10] This was a sign they had completed their vow, and performed all the ceremonies of the pilgrimage.

They will ask thee concerning the sacred month, whether they may war therein: Answer, To war therein is grievous; but to obstruct the way of God, and infidelity towards him, and to keep men from the holy temple, and to drive out his people from thence, is more grievous in the sight of God, and the temptation to idolatry is more grievous than to kill in the sacred months. They will not cease to war against you, until they turn you from your religion, if they be able: but whoever among you shall turn back from his religion, and die an infidel, their works shall be vain in this world, and the next; they shall be the companions of hell fire, they shall remain therein for ever. But they who believe, and who fly for the sake of religion, and fight in God's cause, they shall hope for the mercy of God; for God is gracious and merciful.

They will ask thee concerning wine and lots: Answer, In both there is great sin, and also some things of use unto men; but their sinfulness is greater than their use. They will ask thee also what they shall bestow in alms: Answer, What ye have to spare. Thus God showeth his signs unto you, that peradventure ye might seriously think of this present world, and of the next. They will also ask thee concerning orphans: Answer, To deal righteously with them is best; and if ye intermeddle with the management of what belongs to them, do them no wrong; they are your brethren: God knoweth the corrupt dealer from the righteous; and if God please, he will surely distress you, for God is mighty and wise.

Marry not women who are idolaters, until they believe; verily a maid-servant who believeth, is better than an idolatress, although she please you more. And give not women who believe in marriage to the idolaters, until they believe: for verily a servant who is a true believer, is better than an idolater, though he please you more. They invite unto hell fire, but God inviteth unto paradise and pardon through his will, and declareth his signs unto men, that they may remember.

They will ask thee also concerning the courses of women: Answer, They are a pollution: therefore separate yourselves from women in their courses, and go not near them, until they be cleansed. But when they are cleansed, go in unto them as God hath commanded you, for God loveth those who repent, and loveth those who are clean. Your wives are your tillage; go in therefore unto your tillage in what manner soever ye will: and do first some act that may be profitable unto your souls; and fear GOD, and know that ye must meet him; and bear good tidings unto the faithful.

Make not GOD the object of your oaths, that ye will deal justly, and be devout, and make peace among men; for God is he who heareth and knoweth. GOD will not punish you for an inconsiderate word in your oaths; but he will punish you for that which your hearts have assented unto: GOD is merciful and gracious. They who vow to abstain from their wives, are allowed to wait four months: but if they go back from their vow, verily GOD is gracious and merciful; and if they resolve on a divorce, GOD is he who heareth and knoweth. . . .

A fair speech and to forgive, is better than alms followed by mischief. GOD is rich and merciful. O true believers, make not your alms of none effect by reproaching, or mischief, as he who layeth out what he hath to appear unto men to men to give alms, and believeth not in GOD and the last day. The likeness of such a one is as a flint covered with earth, on which a violent rain falleth, and leaveth it hard. They cannot prosper in any thing which they have gained, for GOD directeth not the unbelieving people. And the likeness of those who lay out their substance from a desire to please GOD, and for an establishment for their souls, is as a garden on a hill, on which a violent rain falleth, and it bringeth forth its fruits twofold; and if a violent rain falleth not on it, yet the dew falleth thereon: and GOD seeth that which ye do. Doth any of you desire to have a garden of palm trees and vines, through which rivers flow, wherein ye may have all kinds of fruits, and that he may attain to old age, and have a weak offspring? then a violent fiery wind shall strike it, so that it shall be burned. Thus GOD declareth his signs unto you, that ye may consider. O true believers, bestow alms of the good things which ye have gained, and of that which we have produced for you out of the earth, and choose not the bad thereof, to give it in alms, such as ye would not accept yourselves, otherwise than by connivance: and know that GOD is rich and worthy to be praised. The devil threateneth you with poverty, and commandeth you filthy covetousness; but GOD promiseth you pardon from himself and abundance: GOD is bounteous and wise. He giveth wisdom unto whom he pleaseth; and he unto whom wisdom is given hath received much good: but none will consider, except the wise of heart. And whatever alms ye shall give, or whatever vow ye shall vow, verily GOD knoweth it; but the ungodly shall have none to help them. If ye make your alms to appear, it is well; but if ye conceal them, and give them unto the poor, this will be better for you, and will atone for your sins: and GOD is well informed of that which ye do. The direction of them belongeth not unto thee; but GOD directeth whom he pleaseth. The good that ye shall give in alms shall redound unto yourselves; and ye shall not give unless out of desire of seeing the face of GOD. And what good thing ye shall give in alms, it shall be repaid you, and ye shall not be treated unjustly; unto the poor who are wholly employed in fighting for the religion of GOD, and cannot go to and fro on the earth; whom the ignorant man thinketh rich, because of their modesty: thou shalt know them by this mark, they ask not men with importunity; and what good ye shall give in alms, verily GOD knoweth it. They who distribute alms of their substance night and day, in private and in public, shall have their reward with the LORD; on them shall no fear come, neither shall they be grieved. . . .

Deal not unjustly with others, and ye shall not be dealt with unjustly. If there be any debtor under a difficulty of paying his debt, let his creditor wait till it be easy for him to do it; but if ye remit it as alms, it will be better for you, if ye knew it. And fear the day wherein ye shall return unto GOD; then shall every soul be paid what it hath gained, and they shall not be treated unjustly. O true believers, when ye bind yourselves one to the other in a debt for a certain time, write it down; and let a writer write between you according to justice, and let not the writer refuse writing according to what GOD hath taught him; but let him write, and let him who oweth the debt dictate, and let him fear God his Lord, and not diminish aught thereof. But if he who oweth the debt be foolish, or weak, or be not able to dictate himself, let his agent dictate according to equity; and call to witness two witnesses of your neighbouring men; but if there be not two men, let there be a man and two women of those whom ye shall choose for witnesses: if one of those women should mistake, the other of them will cause her to recollect. And the witnesses shall not refuse, whensoever they shall be called. And disdain not to write it down, be it a large debt, or be it a small one, until its time of payment: this will be more just in the sight of God, and more right for bearing witness, and more easy, that ye may not doubt. But if it be a present bargain which ye transact between yourselves, it shall be no crime in you, if ye write it not down. And take witnesses when ye sell one to the other, and let no harm be done to the writer, nor to the witness; which if ye do, it will surely be injustice in you: and fear God, and God will instruct you, for God knoweth all things. And if ye be on a journey, and find no writer, let pledges be taken: but if one of you trust the other, let him who is trusted return what he is trusted with, and fear God his Lord. And conceal not the testimony, for he who concealeth it hath surely a wicked heart: God knoweth that which ye do.

Whatever is in heaven and on earth is God's: and whether ye manifest that which is in your minds, or conceal it, God will call you to account for it, and will forgive whom he pleaseth, and will punish whom he pleaseth, for God is almighty. The apostle believeth in that which hath been sent down unto him from his Lord, and the faithful also. Every one of them believeth in God, and his angels, and his scriptures, and his apostles: we make no distinction at all between his apostles. And they say, We have heard, and do obey: we implore thy mercy, O Lord, for unto thee must we return. God will not force any one beyond its capacity: it shall have the good which it gaineth, and it shall suffer the evil which it gaineth. O Lord, punish us not, if we forget, or act sinfully: O Lord, lay not on us a burden like that which thou hast laid on those who have been before us; neither make us, O Lord, to bear what we have not strength to bear, but be favourable unto us, and spare us, and be merciful unto us. Thou art our patron, help us therefore against the unbelieving nations.

FOURTH SURAH

In the Name of the Most Merciful God

O men, fear your LORD, who hath created you out of one man, and out of him created his wife, and from them two hath multiplied many men, and women: and fear GOD by whom ye beseech one another; and respect women who have borne you, for GOD is watching over you. And give the orphans when they come to age their substance; and render them not in exchange bad for good: and devour not their substance, by adding it to your own substance; for this is a great sin. And if ye fear that ye shall not act with equity towards orphans of the female sex, take in marriage of such other women as please you, two, or three, or four, and not more. But if ye fear that ye cannot act equitably towards so many, marry one only, or the slaves which ye shall have acquired. This will be easier, that ye swerve not from righteousness. And give women their dowry freely; but if they voluntarily remit unto you any part of it, enjoy it with satisfaction and advantage. And give not unto those who are weak of understanding the substance which GOD hath appointed you to preserve for them; but maintain them thereout and clothe them, and speak kindly unto them. And examine the orphans[12] until they attain the age of marriage: but if ye perceive they are

[11] This title was given to this chapter, because it chiefly treats of matters relating to women; as marriages, divorces, dower, prohbited degrees, &c.

[12] *i. e.* Try whether they be well grounded in the principles of religion, and have sufficient prudence for the management of their affairs. Under this expression is also comprehended the duty of a curator's instructing his pupils in those respects.

able to manage their affairs well, deliver their substance unto them; and waste it not extravagantly, or hastily, because they grow up. Let him who is rich abstain entirely from the orphans' estates; and let him who is poor take thereof according to what shall be reasonable. . . .

These are the statutes of God. Whoso obeyeth God and his apostle, God shall lead him into gardens wherein rivers flow, they shall continue therein for ever; and this shall be great happiness. But whoso disobeyeth God, and his apostle, and transgresseth his statutes, God shall cast him into hell fire; he shall remain therein for ever, and he shall suffer a shameful punishment. If any of your women be guilty of whoredom, produce four witnesses from among you against them, and if they bear witness against them, imprison them in separate apartments until death release them, or God affordeth them a way to escape. And if two of you commit the like wickedness, punish them both: but if they repent and amend, let them both alone; for God is easy to be reconciled and merciful. Verily repentance will be accepted with God, from those who do evil ignorantly, and then repent speedily; unto them will God be turned: for God is knowing and wise. But no repentance shall be accepted from those who do evil until the time when death presenteth itself unto one of them, and he saith, Verily I repent now; nor unto those who die unbelievers; for them have we prepared a grievous punishment.

O true believers, it is not lawful for you to be heirs of women against their will, nor to hinder them from marrying others, that ye may take away part of what ye have given them in dowry; unless they have been guilty of a manifest crime: but converse kindly with them. And if ye hate them, it may happen that ye may hate a thing wherein God hath placed much good. If ye be desirous to exchange a wife for another wife, and ye have already given one of them a talent, take not away any thing therefrom: will ye take it by slandering her, and doing her manifest injustice? And how can ye take it, since the one of you hath gone in unto the other, and they have received from you a firm covenant?

Marry not women whom your fathers have had to wife; (except what is already past:) for this is uncleanness, and an abomination, and an evil way. Ye are forbidden to marry your mothers, and your daughters, and your sisters, and your aunts both on the father's and on the mother's side, and your brothers' daughters, and your sisters' daughters, and your mothers who have given you suck, and your foster-sisters, and your wives' mothers, and your daughters-in-law which are under your tuition, born of your wives unto whom ye have gone in, (but if ye have not gone in unto them, it shall be no sin in you to marry them,) and the wives of your sons who proceed out of your loins; and ye are also forbidden to take to wife two sisters, except what is already past: for GOD is gracious and merciful. Ye are also forbidden to take to wife free women who are married, except those women whom your right hands shall possess as slaves. This is ordained you from GOD. Whatever is beside this is allowed you; that ye may with your substance provide wives for yourselves, acting that which is right, and avoiding whoredom. And for the advantage which ye receive from them, give them their reward, according to what is ordained: but it shall be no crime in you to make any other agreement among yourselves, after the ordinance shall be complied with; for GOD is knowing and wise. Whoso among you hath not means sufficient that he may marry free women, who are believers, let him marry with such of your maid-servants whom your right hands possess, as are true believers; for GOD well knoweth your faith. Ye are the one from the other: therefore marry them with the consent of their masters; and give them their dower according to justice; such as are modest, not guilty of whoredom, nor entertaining lovers. And when they are married, if they be guilty of adultery, they shall suffer half the punishment which is appointed for the free women. This is allowed unto him among you, who feareth to sin by marrying free women; but if ye abstain from marrying slaves, it will be better for you; GOD is gracious and merciful. GOD is willing to declare these things unto you, and to direct you according to the ordinances of those who have gone before you, and to be merciful unto you. GOD is knowing and wise. GOD desireth to be gracious unto you; but they who follow their lusts, desire that ye should turn aside from the truth with great deviation. GOD is minded to make his religion light unto you, for man was created weak.

O true believers, consume not your wealth among yourselves in vanity; unless there be merchandizing among you by mutual consent: neither slay yourselves; for GOD is merciful towards you: and whoever doth this maliciously and wickedly, he will surely cast him to be broiled in hell fire; and this is easy with GOD. If ye turn aside from the grievous sins, of those which ye are forbidden to commit, we will cleanse you from your smaller faults; and will introduce you into paradise with an honourable entry. Covet not that which GOD hath bestowed on some of you preferably to others.

O true believers, come not to prayers when ye are drunk, until ye understand what ye say; nor when ye are polluted by emission of seed, unless ye be traveling on the road, until ye wash yourselves. But if ye be sick, or on a journey, or any of you come from easing nature, or have touched women, and find no water; take fine clean sand and rub your faces and your hands therewith; for GOD is merciful and inclined to forgive. . . .

He who intercedeth between men with a good intercession shall have a portion thereof; and he who intercedeth with an evil intercession shall have a portion thereof; for GOD overlooketh all things. When ye are saluted with a salutation, salute the person with a better salutation, or at least return the same; for GOD taketh an account of all things. GOD! there is no GOD but he; he will surely gather you together on the day of resurrection; there is no doubt of it: and who is more true than GOD in what he saith? . . .

It is not lawful for a believer to kill a believer, unless it happen by mistake; and whoso killeth a believer by mistake, the penalty shall be the freeing of a believer from slavery, and a fine to be paid to the family of the deceased, unless they remit it as alms: and if the slain person be of a people at enmity with you, and be a true believer, the penalty shall be the freeing of a believer; but if he be of a people in confederacy with you, a fine to be paid to his family, and the freeing of a believer. And he who findeth not wherewith to do this shall fast two months consecutively as a penance enjoined from GOD; and GOD is knowing and wise.

But whoso killeth a believer designedly, his reward shall be hell; he shall remain therein for ever; [13] and GOD shall be angry with him, and shall curse him, and shall prepare for him a great punishment.

O true believers, when ye are on a march in defence of the true religion, justly discern such as ye shall happen to meet, and say not unto him who saluteth you, thou art not a true believer; seeking the accidental goods of the present life; for with GOD is much spoil. Such

[13] That is, unless he repent. Others however understand not here an eternity of damnation (for it is the general doctrine of the Mohammedans that none who profess that faith shall continue in hell for ever), but only a long space of time.

have ye formerly been; but GOD hath been gracious unto you; therefore make a just discernment, for GOD is well acquainted with that which ye do.

Those believers who sit still at home, not having any hurt, and those who employ their fortunes and their persons for the religion of GOD, shall not be held equal. GOD hath preferred those who employ their fortunes and their persons in that cause to a degree of honour above those who sit at home; GOD hath indeed promised every one paradise, but GOD hath preferred those who fight for the faith before those who sit still, by adding unto them a great reward, by degrees of honour conferred on them from him, and by granting them forgiveness, and mercy; for GOD is indulgent and merciful. . . .

Whosoever flieth from his country for the sake of GOD's true religion, shall find in the earth many forced to do the same, and plenty of provisions. And whoever departeth from his house and flieth unto GOD and his apostle, if death overtake him in the way GOD will be obliged to reward him, for GOD is gracious and merciful.

When ye march to war in the earth, it shall be no crime in you if ye shorten your prayers, in case ye fear the infidels may attack you; for the infidels are your open enemy. . . . And when ye shall have ended your prayer, remember GOD, standing, and sitting, and lying on your sides. But when ye are secure from danger, complete your prayers: for prayer is commanded the faithful, and appointed to be said at the stated times. Be not negligent in seeking out the unbelieving people, though ye suffer some inconvenience; for they also shall suffer as ye suffer, and ye hope for a reward from GOD which they cannot hope for; and GOD is knowing and wise. . . .

He who doth evil, or injureth his own soul, and afterwards asketh pardon of God, shall find God gracious and merciful. Whoso committeth wickedness, committeth it against his own soul: GOD is knowing and wise. And whoso committeth a sin or iniquity, and afterwards layeth it on the innocent, he shall surely bear the guilt of calumny and manifest injustice. If the indulgence and mercy of GOD had not been upon thee, surely a part of them had studied to seduce thee; but they shall seduce themselves only, and shall not hurt thee at all. GOD hath sent down unto thee the book of the Korân and wisdom, and hath taught thee that which thou knewest not; for the favour of GOD hath been great towards thee.

There is no good in the multitude of their private discourses, unless in the discourse of him who recommendeth alms, or that which is right, or agreement amongst men: whoever doth this out of a desire to please GOD, we will surely give him a great reward. . . .

Whoso doth evil shall be rewarded for it; and shall not find any patron or helper, beside GOD; but whoso doth good works, whether he be male or female, and is a true believer; they shall be admitted into paradise, and shall not in the least be unjustly dealt with. Who is better in point of religion than he who resigneth himself unto GOD, and is a worker of righteousness, and followeth the law of Abraham the orthodox? since GOD took Abraham for his friend: and to GOD belongeth whatsoever is in heaven and on earth: GOD comprehendeth all things.

If a woman fear ill usage, or aversion from her husband, it shall be no crime in them if they agree the matter amicably between themselves; for a reconciliation is better than a separation. Men's souls are naturally inclined to covetousness: but if ye be kind towards women, and fear to wrong them, GOD is well acquainted with what ye do. Ye can by no means carry yourselves equally between women in all respects, although ye study to do it; therefore turn not from a wife with all manner of aversion, nor leave her like one in suspense: if ye agree, and fear to abuse your wives, GOD is gracious and merciful; but if they separate, GOD will satisfy them both of his abundance; for GOD is extensive and wise, and unto GOD belongeth whatsoever is in heaven and on earth.

We have already commanded those unto whom the scriptures were given before you, and we command you also, saying, Fear GOD; but if ye disbelieve, unto GOD belongeth whatsoever is in heaven and on earth; and GOD is self-sufficient, and to be praised; for unto GOD belongeth whatsoever is in heaven and on earth, and GOD is a sufficient protector. If he pleaseth he will take you away, O men, and will produce others in your stead; for GOD is able to do this. Whoso desireth the reward of this world, verily with GOD is the reward of this world, and also of that which is to come; GOD both heareth and seeth. O true believers, observe justice when ye bear witness before GOD, although it be against yourselves, or your parents, or relations; whether the party be rich, or whether he be poor; for GOD is more worthy than them both: therefore follow not your own lust in bearing testimony, so that ye swerve from justice. And whether ye wrest your evidence, or decline giv   acquainted with that which ye do. O true believers, believe in GOD and his apostle, and the book which he hath caused to descend unto his apostle, and the book which he hath formerly sent down. And whosoever believeth not in GOD, and his angels, and his scriptures, and his apostles, and the last day, he surely erreth in a wide mistake. . . .

The hypocrites act deceitfully with GOD, but he will deceive them; and when they stand up to pray, they stand carelessly, affecting to be seen of men, and remember not GOD, unless a little, wavering between faith and infidelity, and adhering neither unto these nor unto those: and for him whom GOD shall lead astray thou shalt find no true path. . . . The hypocrites shall be in the lowest bottom of hell fire, and thou shalt not find any to help them thence. But they who repent and amend, and adhere firmly unto GOD, and approve the sincerity of their religion to GOD, they shall be numbered with the faithful; and GOD will surely give the faithful a great reward. And how should GOD go about to punish you, if ye be thankful and believe? for GOD is grateful and wise. GOD loveth not the speaking ill of any one in public, unless he who is injured call for assistance; and GOD heareth and knoweth: whether ye publish a good action, or conceal it, or forgive evil, verily GOD is gracious and powerful. . . .

THIRTEENTH SURAH

INTITLED, THUNDER; REVEALED AT MECCA

In the Name of the Most Merciful God

These are the signs of the book of the Korân: and that which hath been sent down unto thee from thy LORD is the truth; but the greater part of men will not believe. It is GOD who hath raised the heavens without visible pillars; and then ascended his throne, and compelled the sun and the moon to perform their services; every of the heavenly bodies runneth an appointed course. He ordereth all things. He showeth his signs distinctly, that ye may be assured ye must meet your LORD at the last day. It is he who hath stretched forth the earth, and placed therein stedfast mountains, and rivers; and hath ordained therein of every fruit two different kinds. He causeth the night to cover the day. . . .

This is the description of paradise, which is promised to the pious. It is watered by rivers; its food is perpetual, and its shade also: this shall be the reward of those who fear God. But the reward of the infidels shall be hell fire. Those to whom we have given the scriptures, rejoice at what hath been revealed unto thee. Yet there are some of the confederates who deny thereof. Say unto them, Verily I am commanded to worship GOD alone; and to give him no companion: upon him do I call, and unto him shall I return. To this purpose have we sent down the Korân a rule of judgment, in the Arabic language. And verily, if thou follow their desires, after the knowledge which hath

been given thee, there shall be none to defend or protect thee against GOD. We have formerly sent apostles before thee, and bestowed on them wives and children; and no apostle had the power to come with a sign, unless by the permission of GOD.

Every age hath its book of revelation: GOD shall abolish and shall confirm what he pleaseth. With him is the original of the book. Moreover, whether we cause thee to see any part of that punishment wherewith we have threatened them, or whether we cause thee to die before it be inflicted on them, verily unto thee belongeth preaching only, but unto us inquisition. Do they not see that we come into their land, and straiten the borders thereof, by the conquests of the true believers. When GOD judgeth, there is none to reverse his judgment: and he will be swift in taking an account. Their predecessors formerly devised subtle plots against their prophets; but GOD is master of every subtle device. He knoweth that which every soul deserveth: and the infidels shall surely know, whose will be the reward of paradise. The unbelievers will say, Thou art not sent of God. Answer, GOD is a sufficient witness between me and you, and he who understandeth the scriptures.

SIXTEENTH SURAH

INTITLED, THE BEE; REVEALED AT MECCA

In the Name of the Most Merciful God

The sentence of GOD will surely come to be executed: wherefore do not hasten it. Praise be unto him! and far be that from him which they associate with him! He shall cause the angels to descend with a revelation by his command, unto such of his servants as he pleaseth, saying, Preach that there is no GOD, except myself; therefore fear me. He hath created the heavens and the earth, to manifest his justice: far be that from him which they associate with him! He hath created man of seed; and yet behold he is a professed disputer against the resurrection.[14] He hath likewise created the cattle for you; from them ye have wherewith to keep yourselves warm, and other advantages; and of them do ye also eat. And they are likewise a credit unto you, when ye drive them home in the evening, and when ye lead them forth to feed in the morning: and they carry your burdens to a distant country, at which ye could not otherwise arrive, unless with great difficulty to yourselves; for your LORD is compassionate and merciful. And he hath also created horses, and mules, and asses, that ye may ride thereon, and for an ornament unto you; and he likewise created other things which ye know not.

It appertaineth unto GOD to instruct men in the right way; and there is who turneth aside from the same: but if he had pleased, he would certainly have directed you all. It is he who sendeth down from heaven rain water, whereof ye have to drink, and from which plants,

[14] The person particularly intended in this place was Obba Ebn Khalf, who came to Mohammed with a rotten bone, and asked him whether it was possible for God to restore it to life.

whereon ye feed your cattle, receive their nourishment. And by means thereof he causeth corn, and olives, and palm-trees, and grapes, and all kinds of fruits, to spring forth for you. Surely herein is a sign of the divine power and wisdom unto people who consider. And he hath subjected the night and the day to your service; and the sun, and the moon, and the stars, which are compelled to serve by his command. Verily herein are signs unto people of understanding. And he hath also given you dominion over whatever he hath created for you in the earth, distinguished by its different colour. Surely herein is a sign unto people who reflect. It is he who hath subjected the sea unto you, that ye might eat fish thereout, and take from thence ornaments for you to wear; and thou seest the ships ploughing the waves thereof, that ye may seek to enrich yourselves of his abundance, by commerce; and that ye might give thanks. And he hath thrown upon the earth mountains firmly rooted, lest it should move with you, and also rivers, and paths, that ye might be directed: and he hath likewise ordained marks whereby men may know their way; and they are directed by the stars.

Shall God therefore, who createth, be as he who createth not? Do ye not therefore consider?

If ye attempt to reckon up the favours of GOD, ye shall not be able to compute their number; GOD is surely gracious and merciful; and GOD knoweth that which ye conceal, and that which ye publish. But the idols which ye invoke, besides GOD, create nothing, but are themselves created. They are dead, and not living; neither do they understand when they shall be raised.

Your GOD is one GOD! . . .

SEVENTEENTH SURAH

INTITLED THE NIGHT JOURNEY; REVEALED AT MECCA

In the Name of the Most Merciful God

. . . The fate of every man have we bound about his neck; and we will produce unto him, on the day of resurrection, a book wherein his actions shall be recorded: it shall be offered him open, and the angels shall say unto him, Read thy book; thine own soul will be a sufficient accountant against thee, this day. He who shall be rightly directed, shall be directed to the advantage only of his own soul; and he who shall err shall err only against the same: neither shall any laden soul be charged with the burden of another.

We did not punish any people, until we had first sent an apostle to warn them. And when we resolved to destroy a city, we commanded the inhabitants thereof, who lived in affluence, to obey our apostle; but they acted corruptly therein: wherefore the sentence was justly pronounced against that city; and we destroyed it with an utter destruction. And how many generations have we consumed since Noah? for thy LORD sufficiently knoweth and seeth the sins of his servants.

Whosoever chooseth this transitory life, we will bestow on him therein beforehand that which we please; on him, namely, whom we please: afterwards will we appoint him hell for his abode; he shall be thrown into the same to be scorched, covered with ignominy, and utterly rejected from mercy. But whosoever chooseth the life to come, and directeth his endeavour towards the same, being also a true believer; the endeavour of these shall be acceptable unto God. On all will we bestow the blessings of this life, both on these and on those, of the gift of thy LORD; for the gift of thy LORD shall not be denied unto any. Behold, how we have caused some of them to surpass others in wealth and dignity: but the next life shall be more considerable in degrees of honour, and greater in excellence.

Set not up another god with the true God, lest thou sit down in disgrace, and destitute. Thy LORD hath commanded that ye worship none besides him; and that ye show kindness unto your parents, whether the one of them, or both of them attain to old age with thee. Wherefore, say not unto them, Fie on you! neither reproach them, but speak respectfully unto them; and submit to behave humbly towards them, out of tender affection, and say, O LORD, have mercy on them both, as they nursed me when I was little.

Your LORD well knoweth that which is in your souls; whether ye be men of integrity: and he will be gracious unto those who sincerely return unto him. And give unto him who is of kin to you his due, and also unto the poor, and the traveller. And waste not thy substance profusely: for the profuse are brethren of the devils: and the devil was ungrateful unto his LORD. But if thou turn from them, in expectation of the mercy which thou hopest from thy LORD; at least, speak kindly unto them. And let not thy hand be tied up to thy neck; neither open it with an unbounded expansion,[15] lest thou become worthy of reprehension, and be reduced to poverty. Verily thy LORD will enlarge the store of whom he pleaseth, and will be sparing unto whom he pleaseth; for he knoweth and regardeth his servants.

Kill not your children for fear of being brought to want; we will provide for them and for you: verily the killing them is a great sin. Draw not near unto fornication; for it is wickedness, and an evil way. Neither slay the soul which GOD hath forbidden you to slay, unless for a just cause;[16] and whosoever shall be slain unjustly, we have given his heir power to demand satisfaction; but let him not exceed the bounds of moderation in putting to death the murderer in too cruel a manner, or by revenging his friend's blood on any other than the person who killed him; since he is assisted by this law. And meddle not with the substance of the orphan, unless it be to improve it, until he attain his age of strength: and perform your covenant; for the performance of your covenant shall be inquired into hereafter. And give full measure, when you measure aught; and weigh with a just balance. This will be better, and more easy for determining every man's due. And follow not that whereof thou hast no knowledge; for the hearing, and the sight, and the heart, every of these shall be examined at the last day. Walk not proudly in the land, for thou canst not cleave the earth, neither shalt thou equal the mountains in stature. All this is evil, and abominable in the sight of thy LORD. These precepts are a part of the wisdom which thy LORD hath revealed unto thee. . . . We have sent down the Korân with truth, and it hath descended with truth: and we have not sent thee otherwise than to be a bearer of good tidings, and a denouncer of threats. And we have divided the Korân, revealing it by parcels, that thou mightest read it unto men with deliberation: and we have sent it down, causing it to descend as occasion required. Say, Whether ye believe therein, or do not believe, verily those who have been favoured with the knowledge

[15] Prodigality, and squandering away one's substance in folly or luxury, being a very great sin. The Arabs were particularly guilty of extravagance in killing camels, and distributing them by lot, merely out of vanity and ostentation; which they are forbidden by this passage, and commanded to bestow what they could spare on their poor relations, and other indigent people.

[16] The crimes for which a man may justly be put to death are these; apostasy, adultery, and murder.

of the scriptures which were revealed before it, when the same is rehearsed unto them, fall down on their faces, worshipping, and say, Our LORD be praised, for that the promise of our LORD is surely fulfilled! and they fall down on their faces, weeping; and the hearing thereof increaseth their humility. Say, call upon GOD, or call on the Merciful: by whichsoever of the two names ye invoke him, it is equal; for he hath most excellent names. Pronounce not thy prayer aloud, neither pronounce it with too low a voice, but follow a middle way between these: and say, Praise be unto GOD, who hath not begotten any child; who hath no partner in the kingdom, nor hath any to protect him from contempt: and magnify him by proclaiming his greatness.

TWENTY-THIRD SURAH

INTITLED, THE TRUE BELIEVERS; REVEALED AT MECCA

In the Name of the Most Merciful God

Now are the true believers happy: who humble themselves in their prayer, and who eschew all vain discourse, and who are doers of almsdeeds; and who keep themselves from carnal knowledge of any women except their wives, or the captives which their right hands possess (for as to them they shall be blameless: but whosoever coveteth any woman beyond these, they are transgressors): and who acquit themselves faithfully of their trust, and justly perform their covenant; and who observe their appointed times of prayer: these shall be the heirs, who shall inherit paradise; they shall continue therein for ever.

We formerly created man in a finer sort of clay; afterwards we placed him in the form of seed in a sure receptacle: afterwards we made the seed coagulated blood; and we formed the coagulated blood into a piece of flesh: then we formed the piece of flesh into bones: and we clothed those bones with flesh: then we produced the same by another creation. Wherefore blessed be GOD, the most excellent Creator!

After this shall ye die: and afterwards shall ye be restored to life, on the day of resurrection. And we have created over you seven heavens: and we are not negligent of what we have created. And we send down rain from heaven, by measure; and we cause it to remain on the earth: we are also certainly able to deprive you of the same. And we cause gardens of palm-trees, and vineyards, to spring forth for you by means thereof; wherein ye have many fruits, and whereof ye eat. And we also raise for you a tree springing from Mount Sinai; which produceth oil, and a sauce for those who eat. Ye have likewise an instruction in the cattle; we give you to drink of the milk which is in their bellies, and ye receive many advantages from them; and of them do ye eat: and on them, and on ships, are ye carried. . . .

NINETEENTH SURAH

INTITLED, LIGHT; REVEALED AT MEDINA

In the Name of the Most Merciful God

This Surah have we sent down from heaven; and have ratified the same and we have revealed evident signs, that ye may be warned. The whore, and the whoremonger, shall ye scourge with a hundred stripes. And let not compassion towards them prevent you from executing the judgment of GOD; [17] if ye believe in GOD and the last day: and let some of the true believers be witnesses of their punishment. The whoremonger shall not marry any other than a harlot, or an idolatress. And a harlot shall no man take in marriage, except a whoremonger, or an idolater. And this kind of marriage is forbidden the true believers. But as to those who accuse women of reputation of whoredom, and produce not four witnesses of the fact, scourge them with fourscore stripes, and receive not their testimony for ever; for such are

---

[17] *i. e.* Be not moved by pity, either to forgive the offenders, or to mitigate their punishment. Mohammed was for so strict and impartial an execution of the laws, that he is reported to have said, *If* Fàtema *the daughter of* Mohammed *steal, let her hand be struck off.*

infamous prevaricators: excepting those who shall afterwards repent, and amend; for unto such will GOD be gracious and merciful. They who shall accuse their wives of adultery, and shall have no witnesses thereof, besides themselves; the testimony which shall be required of one of them shall be, that he swear four times by GOD that he speaketh the truth: and the fifth time that he imprecate the curse of GOD on him if he be a liar. And it shall avert the punishment from the wife, if she swear four times by GOD that he is a liar; and if the fifth time she imprecate the wrath of GOD on her, if he speaketh the truth. If it were not for the indulgence of GOD towards you, and his mercy, and that GOD is easy to be reconciled, and wise, he would immediately discover your crimes. . . .

O true believers, follow not the steps of the devil: for whosoever shall follow the steps of the devil, he will command them filthy crimes, and that which is unlawful. If it were not for the indulgence of GOD, and his mercy towards you, there had not been so much as one of you cleansed from his guilt for ever: but GOD cleanseth whom he pleaseth; for GOD both heareth and knoweth. Let not those among you, who possess abundance of wealth and have ability, swear that they will not give unto their kindred, and the poor, and those who have fled their country for the sake of GOD's true religion: but let them forgive, and act with benevolence towards them. Do ye not desire that GOD should pardon you? And GOD is gracious and merciful.

Moreover they who falsely accuse modest women, who behave in a negligent manner, and are true believers, shall be cursed in this world, and in the world to come; and they shall suffer a severe punishment. One day their own tongues shall bear witness against them, and their hands, and their feet, concerning that which they have done. On that day shall GOD render unto them their just due; and they shall know that GOD is the evident truth. The wicked women should be joined to the wicked men, and the wicked men to the wicked women; but the good women should be married to the good men, and the good men to the good women. These shall be cleared from the calumnies which slanderers speak of them; they shall obtain pardon, and an honourable provision.

O true believers, enter not any houses, besides your own houses, until ye have asked leave, and have saluted the family thereof: this is better for you; peradventure ye will be admonished. And if ye shall find no person in the houses, yet do not enter them, until leave be granted you: and if it be said unto you, Return back, do ye return back. This will be more decent for you: and GOD knoweth that which ye do. It shall be no crime in you, that ye enter uninhabited houses, wherein ye may meet with a convenience. GOD knoweth that which ye discover, and that which ye conceal.

Speak unto the true believers, that they restrain their eyes, and keep themselves from immodest action: this will be more pure for them; for GOD is well acquainted with that which they do. And speak unto the believing women, that they restrain their eyes, and preserve their modesty, and discover not their ornaments, except what necessarily appeareth thereof; and let them throw their veils over their bosoms, and not show their ornaments, unless to their husbands, or their fathers, or their husbands' fathers, or their sons, or their husbands' sons, or their brothers, or their brothers' sons, or their sisters' sons, or their women or the captives which their right hands shall possess, or unto such men as attend them, and have no need of women, or unto children, who distinguish not the nakedness of women. And let them not make a noise with their feet, that their ornaments which they hide may thereby be discovered. And be ye all turned unto GOD, O true believers, that ye may be happy. Marry those who are single among you, and such as are honest of your men-servants and your maid-servants: if they be poor, GOD will enrich them of his abundance; for GOD is bounteous and wise.

And let those who find not a match, keep themselves from fornication, until GOD shall enrich them of his abundance. And unto such of your slaves as desire a written instrument allowing them to redeem themselves on paying a certain sum, write one, if ye know good in them; and give them of the riches of GOD, which he hath given you. And compel not your maid-servants to prostitute themselves, if they be willing to live chastely; that ye may seek the casual advantage of this present life: but whoever shall compel them thereto, verily GOD will be gracious and merciful unto such women after their compulsion.

And now have we revealed unto you evident signs, and a history like unto some of the histories of those who have gone before you, and an admonition unto the pious. GOD is the light of heaven and earth: the similitude of his light is as a niche in a wall, wherein a lamp is placed, and the lamp inclosed in a case of glass; the glass appears as it were a shining star. It is lighted with the oil of a blessed tree, an olive neither of the east, nor of the west; it wanteth little but the oil thereof would give light, although no fire touched it. This is light added unto light. God will direct unto his light whom he pleaseth. God propoundeth parables unto men; for God knoweth all things. . . .

THIRTY-FIFTH SURAH

INTITLED, THE CREATOR; REVEALED AT MECCA

In the Name of the Most Merciful God

Praise be unto God, the creator of heaven and earth; who maketh the angels his messengers, furnished with two, and three, and four pair of wings: God maketh what addition he pleaseth unto his creatures; for God is almighty. The mercy which God shall freely bestow on mankind, there is none who can withhold; and what he shall withhold, there is none who can bestow, besides him: and he is the mighty, the wise. O men, remember the favour of God towards you: is there any creator besides God, who provideth food for you from heaven and earth? There is no God but he: how therefore are ye turned aside from acknowledging his unity? If they accuse thee of imposture, apostles before thee have also been accused of imposture: and unto God shall all things return. O men, verily the promise of God is true: let not therefore the present life deceive you, neither let the deceiver deceive you concerning God: for Satan is an enemy unto you; wherefore hold him for an enemy. . . .

This is God, your Lord: his is the kingdom. But the idols which ye invoke besides him have not the power even over the skin of a date-stone: if ye invoke them, they will not hear your calling; and although they should hear, yet they would not answer you. On the day of resurrection they shall disclaim your having associated them with God: and none shall declare unto thee the truth, like one who is well acquainted therewith. O men, ye have need of God; but God is self-sufficient, and to be praised. If he pleaseth, he can take you away, and produce a new creature in your stead: neither will this be difficult with God. A burdened soul shall not bear the burden of another: and if a heavy-burdened soul call on another to bear part of its burden, no part thereof shall be borne by the person who shall be called on, although he be ever so nearly related. Thou shalt admonish those who fear their Lord in secret and are constant at prayer: and whoever cleanseth himself from the guilt of disobedience, cleanseth himself to the advantage of his own soul; for all shall be assembled before God at the last day. The blind and the seeing shall not be held equal; neither darkness and light; nor the cool shade and the scorching wind: neither shall the living and the dead be held equal. God shall cause him to hear whom he pleaseth: but thou shalt not make those to hear who are in their graves.

Thou art no other than a preacher: verily we have sent thee with truth, a bearer of good tidings, and a denouncer of threats. There hath been no nation, but a preacher hath in past times been conversant among them: if they charge thee with imposture, they who were before them likewise charged their apostles with imposture. Their apostles came unto them with evident miracles, and with divine writings, and with the enlightening book: afterwards I chastised those who were unbelievers; and how severe was my vengeance!

FORTY-SEVENTH SURAH

INTITLED, MOHAMMED; REVEALED AT MEDINA [18]

In the Name of the Most Merciful God

God will render of none effect the works of those who believe not, and who turn away men from the way of God: but as to those who believe, and work righteousness, and believe the revelation which hath been sent down unto Mohammed (for it is the truth from their Lord), he will expiate their evil deeds from them, and will dispose their heart

---

[18] Some intitle this chapter *War;* which is therein commanded to be vigorously carried on against the enemies of the Mohammedan faith.

aright. This will he do, because those who believe not follow vanity, and because those who believe follow the truth from their LORD. Thus GOD propoundeth unto men their examples. When ye encounter the unbelievers, strike off their heads, until ye have made a great slaughter among them; and bind them in bonds; and either give them a free dismission afterwards, or exact a ransom; until the war shall have laid down its arms. This shall ye do. Verily if GOD pleased he could take vengeance on them, without your assistance; but he commandeth you to fight his battles, that he may prove the one of you by the other. And as to those who fight in defence of GOD's true religion, God will not suffer their works to perish: he will guide them, and will dispose their heart aright; and he will lead them into paradise, of which he hath told them.

O true believers, if ye assist GOD, by fighting for his religion, he will assist you against your enemies; and will set your feet fast: but as for the infidels, let them perish; and their works shall God render vain. This shall befall them, because they have rejected with abhorrence that which GOD hath revealed: wherefore their works shall become of no avail. Do they not travel through the earth, and see what hath been the end of those who were before them? GOD utterly destroyed them: and the like catastrophe awaiteth the unbelievers. This shall come to pass, for that GOD is the patron of the true believers, and for that the infidels have no protector.

Verily GOD will introduce those who believe, and do good works, into gardens beneath which rivers flow: but the unbelievers indulge themselves in pleasures, and eat as beasts eat; and their abode shall be hell fire. . . .

FORTY-NINTH SURAH

INTITLED, THE INNER APARTMENTS; REVEALED
AT MEDINA

In the Name of the Most Merciful God

. . . O true believers, if a wicked man come unto you with a tale, inquire strictly into the truth thereof; lest ye hurt people through ignorance, and afterwards repent of what ye have done; and know that the apostle of GOD is among you: if he should obey you in many things, ye would certainly be guilty of a crime, in leading him into a mistake. But GOD hath made the faith amiable unto you, and hath prepared the same in your hearts; and hath rendered infidelity, and iniquity, and disobedience hateful unto you. These are they who walk in the right way; through mercy from GOD, and grace: and GOD is knowing, and wise.

If two parties of the believers contend with one another, do ye endeavour to compose the matter between them: and if the one of them offer an insult unto the other, fight against that party which offered the insult, until they return unto the judgment of GOD; and if they do return, make peace between them with equity: and act with justice; for GOD loveth those who act justly. Verily the true believers are brethren; wherefore reconcile your brethren; and fear GOD, that ye may obtain mercy.

O true believers, let not men laugh other men to scorn; who per-adventure may be better than themselves: neither let women laugh other women to scorn; who may possibly be better than themselves. Neither defame one another; nor call one another by opprobrious appellations. An ill name it is to be charged with wickedness, after having embraced the faith: and whoso repenteth not, they will be the unjust doers. O true believers, carefully avoid entertaining a suspicion of another: for some suspicions are a crime. Inquire not too curiously into other men's failings: neither let the one of you speak ill of another in his absence. Would any of you desire to eat the flesh of his dead brother? Surely ye would abhor it. And fear GOD; for GOD is easy to be reconciled, and merciful.

O men, verily we have created you of a male and a female; and we have distributed you into nations and tribes, that ye might know one another. Verily the most honourable of you, in the sight of GOD, is the most pious of you: and GOD is wise and knowing. The Arabs of the desert say, We believe. Answer, Ye do by no means believe; but say, We have embraced Islâm: for the faith hath not yet entered into your hearts. If ye obey GOD and his apostle, he will not defraud you of any part of the merit of your works: for GOD is inclined to forgive, and merciful. Verily the true believers are those only who believe in GOD and his apostle, and afterwards doubt not; and who employ their substance and their persons in the defence of GOD's true religion: these are they who speak sincerely. Say, Will ye inform GOD concerning your religion? But GOD knoweth whatever is in heaven and in earth: for GOD is omniscient. They upbraid thee that they have embraced Islâm. Answer, Upbraid me not with your having embraced Islâm: rather GOD upbraideth you, that he hath directed you to the faith; if ye speak sincerely. Verily GOD knoweth the secrets of heaven and earth; and GOD beholdeth that which ye do.

FIFTY-SIXTH SURAH

INTITLED, THE INEVITABLE; REVEALED AT MECCA

In the Name of the Most Merciful God

When the inevitable day of judgment shall suddenly come, no soul shall charge the prediction of its coming with falsehood: it will abase some, and exalt others. When the earth shall be shaken with a violent shock; and the mountains shall be dashed in pieces, and shall become as dust scattered abroad; and ye shall be separated into three distinct classes: the companions of the right hand; (how happy shall the companions of the right hand be!) and the companions of the left hand: (how miserable shall the companions of the left hand be!) and those who have preceded others in the faith shall precede them to paradise. These are they who shall approach near unto God: they shall dwell in gardens of delight: (There shall be many of the former religions; and few of the last.) Reposing on couches adorned with gold and precious stones; sitting opposite to one another thereon. Youths which shall continue in their bloom for ever, shall go round about to attend them, with goblets, and beakers, and a cup of flowing wine: their heads shall not ache by drinking the same, neither shall their reason be disturbed: and with fruits of the sorts which they shall choose, and the flesh of birds of the kind which they shall desire. And there shall accompany them fair damsels having large black eyes; resembling pearls hidden in their shells: as a reward for that which they shall have wrought. They shall not hear therein any vain discourse, or any charge of sin; but only the salutation, Peace! Peace! And the companions of the right hand (how happy shall the companions of the right hand be!) shall have their abode among lote trees free from thorns, and trees of mauz loaded regularly with their produce from top to bottom; under an extended shade, near a flowing water, and amidst fruits in abundance, which shall not fail, nor shall be forbidden to be gathered: and they shall repose themselves on lofty beds. Verily we have created the damsels of paradise by a peculiar creation: and we have made them virgins, beloved by their husbands, of equal age with them; for the delight of the companions of the right hand. There shall be many of the former religions, and many of the latter.

And the companions of the left hand (how miserable shall the companions of the left hand be!) shall dwell amidst burning winds, and scalding water, under the shade of a black smoke, neither cool nor agreeable. For they enjoyed the pleasures of life before this, while on earth; and obstinately persisted in a heinous wickedness: and they said, After we shall have died, and become dust and bones, shall we surely be raised to life? Shall our forefathers also be raised with us? Say, Verily both the first and the last shall surely be gathered together to judgment, at the prefixed time of a known day. Then ye, O men, who have erred, and denied the resurrection as a falsehood, shall surely eat of the fruit of the tree of al Zakkum, and shall fill your bellies therewith: and ye shall drink thereon boiling water; and ye shall drink as a thirsty camel drinketh. This shall be their entertainment on the day of judgment.

We have created you: will ye not therefore believe that we can raise you from the dead? What think ye? The seed which ye emit, do ye create the same, or are we the creators thereof? We have decreed death unto you all: and we shall not be prevented. We are able to substitute others like unto you in your stead, and to produce you again in the condition or form which ye know not. Ye know the original production by creation; will ye not therefore consider that we are able to produce you by resuscitation? What think ye? The grain which ye sow, do ye cause the same to spring forth, or do we cause it to spring forth? If we pleased, verily we could render the same dry and fruitless, so that ye would not cease to wonder, saying, Verily we have contracted debts for seed and labour, but we are not permitted to reap the fruit thereof. What think ye? The water which ye drink, do ye send down the same from the clouds, or are we the senders thereof? If we pleased, we could render the same brackish: will ye not therefore give thanks? What think ye? The fire which ye strike, do ye produce the tree whence ye obtain the same, or are we the producers thereof? We have ordained the same for an admonition, and an advantage to those who travel through the deserts. Wherefore praise the name of thy LORD, the great GOD.

Moreover I swear by the setting of the stars; (and it is surely a great oath, if ye knew it;) that this is the excellent Korân, the original whereof is written in the preserved book: none shall touch the same, except those who are clean. It is a revelation from the LORD of all creatures. Will ye, therefore, despise this new revelation? . . .

SIXTY-FOURTH SURAH

INTITLED, MUTUAL DECEIT; REVEALED AT MECCA

In the Name of the Most Merciful God

Whatever is in heaven and earth celebrateth the praises of GOD: his is the kingdom, and unto him is the praise due; for he is almighty. It is he who hath created you; and one of you is predestined to be an unbeliever, and another of you is predestined to be a believer: and GOD beholdeth that which ye do. He hath created the heavens and the earth with truth; and he hath fashioned you, and given you beautiful forms: and unto him must ye all go. He knoweth whatever is in heaven and earth: and he knoweth that which ye conceal, and that which ye discover; for GOD knoweth the innermost part of men's breasts. Have ye not been acquainted with the story of those who disbelieved heretofore, and tasted the evil consequence of their behaviour? And for them is prepared in the life to come a tormenting punishment. This shall they suffer, because their apostles came unto them with evident proofs of their mission, and they said, Shall men direct us? Wherefore they believed not, and turned their backs. But

GOD standeth in need of no person: for GOD is self-sufficient, and worthy to be praised. . . O true believers, verily of your wives and your children ye have an enemy: wherefore beware of them. But if ye pass over their offences, and pardon, and forgive them; GOD is likewise inclined to forgive, and merciful. Your wealth and your children are only a temptation; but with GOD is a great reward. Wherefore fear GOD, as much as ye are able; and hear, and obey; and give alms, for the good of your souls; for whoso is preserved from the covetousness of his own soul, they shall prosper. If ye lend unto GOD an acceptable loan, he will double the same unto you, and will forgive you; for GOD is grateful, and long-suffering, knowing both what is hidden, and what is divulged; the Mighty, the Wise.

SIXTY-FIFTH SURAH

INTITLED, DIVORCE; REVEALED AT MEDINA

In the Name of the Most Merciful God

O Prophet, when ye divorce women, put them away at their appointed term; and compute the term exactly: and fear GOD, your LORD.[19] Oblige them not to go out of their apartments, neither let them go out, until the term be expired, unless they be guilty of manifest uncleanness. These are the statutes of GOD: and whoever transgresseth the statutes of GOD assuredly injureth his own soul. Thou knowest not whether GOD will bring something new to pass, which may reconcile them after this. And when they shall have fulfilled their term, either retain them with kindness, or part from them honourably: and take witnesses from among you, men of integrity; and give your testimony as in the presence of GOD. This admonition is given

---

[19] That is, when they shall have had their courses thrice, after the time of their divorce, if they prove not to be with child; or, if they prove with child, when they shall have been delivered. Al Beidâwi supposes husbands are hereby commanded to divorce their wives while they are clean; and says that the passage was revealed on account of Ebn Omar, who divorced his wife when she had her courses upon her, and was therefore obliged to take her again.—(When a Mohammedan has sworn that he will divorce his wife, he ceases to have intercourse with her. As soon as she hears of the oath, she covers herself with a veil, retires to her apartment, and ceases to let her husband see her. When the four months allowed for reconciliation are expired, all ties are dissolved, the wife recovers her liberty, and receives at her departure the dowry which was fixed by the marriage contract. The daughters go with the mother, the sons remain with the father.—Savary.)

unto him who believeth in God and the last day: and whoso feareth God, unto him will he grant a happy issue out of all his afflictions, and he will bestow on him an ample provision from whence he expecteth it not: and whoso trusteth in God, he will be his sufficient support; for God will surely attain his purpose. Now hath God appointed unto every thing a determined period.

As to such of your wives as shall despair having their courses, by reason of their age; if ye be in doubt thereof, let their term be three months: and let the same be the term of those who have not yet had their courses. But as to those who are pregnant, their term shall be, until they be delivered of their burden. And whoso feareth God, unto him will he make his command easy. This is the command of God, which he hath sent down unto you. And whoso feareth God, he will expiate his evil deeds from him, and will increase his reward.

Suffer the women whom ye divorce to dwell in some part of the houses wherein ye dwell; according to the room and conveniences of the habitations which ye possess: and make them not uneasy, that ye may reduce them to straits. And if they be with child, expend on them what shall be needful, until they be delivered of their burden. And if they suckle their children for you, give them their hire; and consult among yourselves, according to what shall be just and reasonable. And if ye be put to a difficulty herein, and another woman shall suckle the child for him, let him who hath plenty expend proportionably in the maintenance of the mother and the nurse, out of his plenty: and let him whose income is scanty expend in proportion out of that which God hath given him. God obligeth no man to more than he hath given him ability to perform: God will cause ease to succeed hardship. . . .

EIGHTY-FIRST SURAH

INTITLED, THE FOLDING UP; REVEALED AT MECCA

In the Name of the Most Merciful God

When the sun shall be folded up; and when the stars shall fall; and when the mountains shall be made to pass away; and when the camels ten months gone with young shall be neglected; and when the wild beasts shall be gathered together; and when the seas shall boil; and when the souls shall be joined again to their bodies; and when the girl who hath been buried alive shall be asked for what crime she was put to death; and when the books shall be laid open; and when the heaven shall be removed; and when hell shall burn fiercely; and when paradise shall be brought near; every soul shall know what it hath wrought. Verily I swear by the stars which are retrograde, which move swiftly and which hide themselves; and by the night, when it cometh on; and by the morning, when it appeareth; that these are the words of an honourable messenger, endued with strength, of established dignity in the sight of the possessor of the throne, obeyed by the angels under his authority, and faithful: and your companion Mohammed is not distracted. He had already seen him in the

clear horizon: and he suspected not the secrets revealed unto him. Neither are these the words of an accursed devil. Whither, therefore, are you going? This is no other than an admonition unto all creatures; unto him among you who shall be willing to walk uprightly: but ye shall not will, unless GOD willeth, the LORD of all creatures.

EIGHTY-THIRD SURAH

INTITLED, THOSE WHO GIVE SHORT MEASURE OR WEIGHT; REVEALED AT MECCA

In the Name of the Most Merciful God

Woe be unto those who give short measure or weight: who, when they receive by measure from other men, take the full; but when they measure unto them, or weigh unto them, defraud! Do not these think they shall be raised again, at the great day, the day whereon mankind shall stand before the LORD of all creatures? By no means. Verily the register of the actions of the wicked is surely in Sejjîn.[20] And what shall make thee to understand what Sejjîn is? It is a book distinctly written. Woe be on that day, unto those who accused the prophets of imposture; who denied the day of judgment as a falsehood! And none denieth the same as a falsehood, except every unjust and flagitious person: who, when our signs are rehearsed unto him, saith, They are fables of the ancients. By no means: but rather their lusts have cast a veil over their hearts. By no means. Verily they shall be shut out from their LORD on that day; and they shall be sent into hell to be burned: then shall it be said unto them by the infernal guards, This is what ye denied as a falsehood. Assuredly. But the register of the actions of the righteous is Illiyyun: and what shall cause thee to understand what Illiyyun is? It is a book distinctly written: those who approach near unto God are witnesses thereto. Verily the righteous shall dwell among delights: seated on couches they shall behold objects of pleasure; thou shalt see in their faces the brightness of joy. They shall be given to drink of pure wine, sealed; the seal whereof shall be musk: and to this let those aspire, who aspire to happiness: and the water mixed therewith shall be of Tasnim, a fountain whereof those shall drink who approach near unto the divine presence. They who act wickedly laugh the true believers to scorn: and when they pass by them, they wink at one another: and when they turn aside to their people, they turn aside making scurrilous jests; and when they see them, they say, Verily these are mistaken men. But they are not sent to be keepers over them. Wherefore one day the true believers, in their turn, shall laugh the infidels to scorn: lying on couches they shall look down upon them in hell. Shall not the infidels be rewarded for that which they have done?

NINETY-THIRD SURAH

INTITLED, THE BRIGHTNESS; REVEALED AT MECCA

In the Name of the Most Merciful God

By the brightness of the morning; and by the night, when it groweth dark: thy LORD hath not forsaken thee, neither doth he hate thee.

[20] *Sejjîn* is the name of the general register, wherein the actions of all the wicked, both men and genii, are distinctly entered. Sejn signifies a *prison;* and this book, as some think, derives its name from thence, because it will occasion those whose deeds are there recorded to be *imprisoned* in hell.

Verily the life to come shall be better for thee than this present life: and thy LORD shall give thee a reward wherewith thou shalt be well pleased. Did he not find thee an orphan, and hath he not taken care of thee? And did he not find thee wandering in error, and hath he not guided thee into the truth? And did he not find thee needy, and hath he not enriched thee? Wherefore oppress not the orphan: neither repulse the beggar: but declare the goodness of thy LORD.

HUNDREDTH SURAH

INTITLED, THE WAR-HORSES WHICH RUN SWIFTLY: WHERE IT WAS REVEALED IS DISPUTED

In the Name of the Most Merciful God

By the war-horses which run swiftly to the battle, with a panting noise: and by those which strike fire, by dashing their hoofs against the stones: and by those which make a sudden incursion on the enemy early in the morning, and therein raise the dust, and therein pass through the midst of the adverse troops: verily man is ungrateful unto his LORD; and he is witness thereof: and he is immoderate in the love of worldly good. Doth he not know, therefore, when that which is in the graves shall be taken forth, and that which is in men's breasts shall be brought to light, that their LORD will, on that day, be fully informed concerning them?

HUNDRED AND FIRST SURAH

INTITLED, THE STRIKING; REVEALED AT MECCA

In the Name of the Most Merciful God

The striking ! What is the striking? And what shall make thee to understand how terrible the striking will be? On that day men shall be like moths scattered abroad, and the mountains shall become like carded wool of various colours driven by the wind. Moreover he whose balance shall be heavy with good works, shall lead a pleasing life: but as to him whose balance shall be light, his dwelling shall be the pit of hell. What shall make thee to understand how frightful the pit of hell is? It is a burning fire.

HUNDRED AND SECOND SURAH

INTITLED, THE EMULOUS DESIRE OF MULTIPLYING; WHERE IT WAS REVEALED IS DISPUTED

In the Name of the Most Merciful God

The emulous desire of multiplying riches and children employeth you, until ye visit the graves. By no means should ye thus employ your time: hereafter shall ye know your folly. Again, By no means: hereafter shall ye know your folly. By no means: if ye knew the consequence hereof with certainty of knowledge, ye would not act thus. Verily ye shall see hell: again, ye shall surely see it with the eye of certainty. Then shall ye be examined, on that day, concerning the pleasures with which ye have amused yourselves in this life.

HUNDRED AND FOURTH SURAH

INTITLED, THE SLANDERER; REVEALED AT MECCA

In the Name of the Most Merciful God

Woe unto every slanderer, and backbiter: who heapeth up riches, and prepareth the same for the time to come! He thinketh that his riches will render him immortal. By no means. He shall surely be cast into al Hotama. And who shall cause thee to understand what al Hotama is? It is the kindled fire of GOD; which shall mount above the hearts of those who shall be cast therein. Verily it shall be as an arched vault above them on columns of vast extent.

HUNDRED AND SEVENTH SURAH

INTITLED, NECESSARIES; WHERE IT WAS REVEALED IS DISPUTED

In the Name of the Most Merciful God

What thinkest thou of him who denieth the future judgment as a falsehood? It is he who pusheth away the orphan; and stirreth not up others to feed the poor. Woe be unto those who pray, and who are negligent at their prayer: who play the hypocrites, and deny necessaries to the needy.

HUNDRED AND TWELFTH SURAH

INTITLED, THE DECLARATION OF GOD'S UNITY; WHERE IT WAS REVEALED IS DISPUTED[21]

In the Name of the Most Merciful God

Say, God is one God; the eternal GOD: he begetteth not, neither is he begotten: and there is not any one like unto him.

[21] This chapter is held in particular veneration by the Mohammedans, and declared, by a tradition of their prophet, to be equal in value to a third part of the whole Korân. It is said to have been revealed in answer to the Koreish, who asked Mohammed concerning the distinguishing attributes of the God he invited them to worship.

THE LAST SURAH

INTITLED, MEN; WHERE IT WAS REVEALED IS DISPUTED

In the Name of the Most Merciful God

Say, I fly for refuge unto the LORD of men, the king of men, the GOD of men, that he may deliver me from the mischief of the whisperer who slyly withdraweth, who whispereth evil suggestions into the breasts of men, from genii and men.

INDEX OF AUTHORS

INDEX OF TITLES

290.82
B88

Date Due

12-31-53			
MAY 29 59			
JUN 11			
MAY 23 '61			
JUN 2 '61			
JUN 2 '61			
FEB 28 '62			
APR 12 '66			
MAY 23 '66			
MAY 22 '68			
DEC 10 70			
DEC 15 '70			

LINCOLN BIBLE INSTITUTE